D1478611

The Altar at Home

THE ALTAR AT HOME

SENTIMENTAL LITERATURE
AND NINETEENTH-CENTURY
AMERICAN RELIGION

CLAUDIA STOKES

PENN

UNIVERSITY OF PENNSYLVANIA PRESS

PHILADELPHIA

Published by
University of Pennsylvania Press
Philadelphia, Pennsylvania 19104-4112
www.upenn.edu/pennpress

Printed in the United States of America
on acid-free paper
10 9 8 7 6 5 4 3 2 1

Library of Congress Cataloging-in-Publication Data

Stokes, Claudia.
  The altar at home : sentimental literature and nineteenth-century American religion /
Claudia Stokes. — 1st ed.
      p. cm.
  Includes bibliographical references and index.
  ISBN 978-0-8122-4637-7 (hardcover : alk. paper)
  1. Religion and literature—United States—History—19th century. 2. Sentimentalism
in literature. 3. Christianity in literature. 4. American literature—Women authors—
History and criticism. 5. American literature—19th century—History and criticism. I.
Title.
  PS374.R47S76 2014
  810.9′3823—dc23
                                                                              2014003710

For my mother, Sophie Aron Stokes

CONTENTS

Introduction   1

Chapter 1. Revivals of Sentiment: Sentimentalism
and the Second Great Awakening   21

Chapter 2. My Kingdom: Sentimentalism and the Refinement
of Hymnody   67

Chapter 3. The Christian Plot: Stowe, Millennialism,
and Narrative Form   103

Chapter 4. Derelict Daughters and Polygamous Wives: Mormonism
and the Uses of Sentiment   142

Chapter 5. The Mother Church: Mary Baker Eddy
and the Practice of Sentimentalism   181

Notes   217

Bibliography   255

Index   273

Acknowledgments   279

INTRODUCTION

IT HARDLY seems to bear remarking that sentimental literature of the American nineteenth century is steeped in Christian piety. As anyone acquainted with this female-centered literary aesthetic well knows, sentimental novels and poems routinely depict religious faith as a balm to the restless spirit and a beneficent influence on unruly behavior. Countless sentimental texts contain scenes of devout prayer, ardent hymn singing, and religious instruction. Heart-rending deathbed scenes and leave-takings are softened by promises of reunion in the afterlife, and Bibles and hymnals serve as the premier tokens of affection or goodwill.

To readers today, sentimental piety may seem colorless or indistinct. Prayer, Bible reading, and the pursuit of self-betterment are the principal requirements of Christian observance in sentimental literature; in contrast with the teachings of Calvinism or Catholicism, salvation in sentimental literature seems to be available to anyone with faith, with neither ritual nor conversion required. Without the delimiting contours of these conventional features of Christian observance, sentimental piety appears to be denominationally impartial and untouched by doctrinal specifics. Early scholarship registered this perception, as with Ann Douglas's foundational study of sentimental literature, *The Feminization of American Culture* (1977). In that work, Douglas interpreted the absence of Calvinist rigor in sentimentalism as evidence of a general lack of theological substance, and she characterized sentimental piety as "peculiarly unassertive and retiring."[1] David S. Reynolds similarly described the religious life portrayed in sentimental literature as "determinedly nonintellectual and plain."[2] In response to the perception of sentimentalism as theologically vacant, Jane Tompkins offered a spirited defense of sentimental piety in *Sensational Designs* (1985), in which she documented the influence of religious typologies of sacrifice and renewal on sentimental narratives, as with her analysis of the death of Eva St. Clare in Harriet Beecher

Stowe's *Uncle Tom's Cabin* (1852). Tompkins argued that sentimentalism was not devoid of content, and she showed instead how the sentimental constitution of Christianity was poised to effect social change and impart authority to those on the social periphery, such as children, slaves, and widows.[3]

This book seeks to build on this foundational work by analyzing both the religious beliefs inherent in sentimental literature and the social implications of these religious allegiances. Such scholars as Nina Baym, Dawn Coleman, Tracy Fessenden, Sharon Kim, and Abram Van Engen have continued the work begun by Jane Tompkins by cataloging the religious contents of sentimental piety, and this project likewise aspires to unearth and historicize some of the beliefs intrinsic to sentimental literature that are often imperceptible to modern eyes, either by deliberate authorial calculation or by the historical erasures that inevitably occur with the passage of time.[4] To that end, this book takes as its starting point the constraints of Tompkins's own terminology in describing sentimental piety, which she broadly categorized as "Christian," a general term the precise definition of which was very much in dispute in the nineteenth century. This study seeks to provide greater denominational specificity to our understanding of the religious contents of sentimental literature to show that the seemingly general, broad Christianity at the center of these texts was in fact a highly sectarian, partisan configuration born out of contemporary religious developments.

Concentrated analysis of the doctrinal, sectarian specifics of sentimental literature reveals the insufficiency of the binary nature of the "Douglas-Tompkins debate," as Laura Wexler termed it, which alternately characterized sentimental piety as repressive or emancipatory.[5] As this study aims to show, the richly textured and complex nature of sentimental piety renders it resistant to such clear-cut classifications. In some instances, sentimental writers promoted doctrines that afforded new religious authority to select constituencies, but, in so doing, they contributed to the further marginalization of already vulnerable social groups. In other instances, sentimental writers endorsed populist religious movements, but their approbation worked above all else to fortify their own burgeoning religious authority. Moreover, in the dense and contentious religious climate of the mid-nineteenth century, all public avowals of religious belief functioned both as sectarian affirmations and as renunciations, implicitly set in opposition to other competing religious groups, and so sentimental piety, with its varied and complex array of constituent features, was inevitably enmeshed in numerous religious alliances and rivalries. While this positioning was sometimes inadvertent, in innumerable cases sentimental writers placed their own religious beliefs in direct opposition to others they depicted as questionable or heretical. Even sentimental religious antipathy was multifaceted, and, as this study will show, in some instances sentimentalism proved to be a generative and influential wellspring for several marginal, contested religious movements, which appropriated sentimental rhetoric and tropes in their pursuit of public acceptance.

Complex, pliable, and instrumental, sentimentality piety was hardly the diffident, conformist fount of convention that it may at first appear. Some of the sectarian allegiances of sentimental literature deviate sharply from what we might expect, for many of the doctrines and practices endorsed in sentimental texts were new, topical products of recent religious movements that diverged from established custom and found widespread disfavor among mainline Protestant denominations. In particular, the theological contents of sentimental piety derive primarily from Methodism and the vibrant culture of revivalism it sparked. Though Methodism today is respectable and mainstream, its status in the first half of the nineteenth century was more tenuous, and it was denounced by critics as a heretical, vulgar menace that threatened to topple orthodoxy and dissolve the staid propriety expected of religious worship. Methodism was controversial in part because of its public, populist character, for it moved worship outside the sanctified confines of the church or meetinghouse and into public spaces where anyone might attend and even preach. With its unruly revival and camp meetings, unordained circuit riders, and willingness to permit common people, women included, to assume ministerial duties, Methodism was the antithesis of the decorum, conventionalism, and deferential obedience that have so often been attributed to literary sentimentalism.[6] Despite this seeming incompatibility, sentimental literary texts absorbed and propounded some of the signature beliefs and practices associated with this controversial new movement, such as its egalitarian efforts to authorize laypeople, its creation of a congregationally-centered form of worship, and its heterodox belief that salvation was available to anyone seeking it.

This sectarian alliance has a number of implications and consequences. To be sure, it highlights the discontinuity between the polite domestic seclusion of religious observance in sentimental literature and the contemporary climate of religious discourse that framed many of the doctrines inherent in sentimental literature. Where sentimental piety was private, domestic, and refined, Methodist revivalism was public, collective, and highly contentious. One could read hundreds of sentimental texts and seldom catch a glimpse of the contemporary religious climate that surrounded both Methodism and sentimentalism, an environment riven by alarmist diatribes, violent assaults, and public riots deriving from disagreement about the nature, substance, and practice of religious belief. Sentimental texts appear to withdraw altogether from this environment and fashion an alternate world in which religious discourse is grounded in loving intimacy and religious observance restricted to the warm enclosures of private domesticity. But while sentimental writers were portraying tranquil scenes of private bedtime prayer, the contemporary public sphere was suffused with belligerent religious factionalism, which was staged in the pulpit, the street brawl, and the polling place. For participants in this public discourse, the stakes of these religious debates were very high: in addition to the insuperable question of the route by which one could achieve salvation and divine favor, the very future of the United States, and indeed of humanity itself, seemed to hang in the balance. In an era in which the number of religious sects seemed to increase by the day, religious denominations vied for supremacy by attacking the doctrines and practices of their rivals. Mainline Protestant denominations, such as Presbyterianism and Congregationalism, lost their preeminence to Methodism in spite of the exhortations of orthodox clergy that Methodism was heretical, unlearned, and hazardous to the salvation of worshippers. New religious movements such as Campbellism, Millerism, Mormonism, and Oneida Perfectionism produced yet more alternative religious possibilities and consequently received widespread public denunciation and, on some occasions, encountered violence at the hands of angry mobs. The Irish famine and successive revolutions in Europe led to increasing numbers of Catholic immigrants, and critics insisted that the mass immigration of Catholics derived from a clandestine European plot to overturn American democracy.[7] Rival Protestant denominations found common cause in a far-reaching anti-Catholic campaign that produced such influential missionary organizations as the American Bible Society, the American Home Missionary Society, and the American Tract Society as well as such periodicals as the *American Protestant,* the *Protestant Advocate,* and the *Christian Alliance.* Anti-Catholic fervor was widespread and virulent: in 1834, an angry mob in Charlestown, Massachusetts, burned an Ursuline convent to the ground, and, a decade later, a mob of thousands attacked a Catholic church in Philadelphia in a cannon battle that lasted a week and resulted in twenty deaths and dozens of injuries.[8] In 1849, the Know-Nothing Party was founded specifically to prevent Catholics from holding elected office, and, in the 1850s, it sparked anti-Catholic riots in cities across the North Atlantic region and as far west as Cincinnati, Louisville, and St. Louis.[9]

In classifying the specific religious contents of sentimental piety, this book examines the complex engagement of sentimental literature in this divisive religious period. Sentimental literary texts occupied a complicated place in this era, for, although they embraced many of the popular new religious beliefs produced in this climate, they rejected the incendiary nature of contemporary religious debate as well as the earthy public character of revivalism. Sentimental literary writers deftly played several sides at once. They absorbed new populist beliefs and sectarian antipathy but moved them indoors, into the private domestic sphere and into a polite, conventional social setting more in keeping with established social custom than the carnivalesque world of revivalism. The relocation of contemporary religious practice into the parlor may account for the seeming ordinariness and even invisibility of these beliefs, which seldom announce their partisan character but evoke instead undisputed traditionalism. Domestication effectively denuded these religious teachings of any vestiges of public controversy and imparted benevolent domestic warmth to highly contested positions. Sentimental domesticity also implicitly vouched for the morality and legitimacy of these new beliefs, for, in affirming their compliance with established familial and household custom, it corroborated their virtuous outcomes and moral bona fides. Domestication thereby contributed to their appeal among readers, who are implicitly invited to assimilate these tendentious new beliefs regardless of their own denominational affiliation. In this way, the domestic register allowed sentimental literary texts to exert influence on and contribute to public religious discourse while seeming to withdraw from it. Domesticity, this study aims to show, provides both a cover and a forum for the promotion of some contentious, topical religious beliefs.

Domestication falsely presents sentimentalism as a refuge from the bitter public factionalism of contemporary religious discourse, but this literary elision of contemporary partisanship comes at a cost. To be sure, it contributed to the ahistoricity of nineteenth-century American Protestantism. In depositing these beliefs in tidy New England drawing rooms, sentimental texts effectively uprooted them from their local, contextual moorings and omitted acknowledgment of the specific social and denominational contexts that gave rise to these doctrines. For instance, some of the beliefs and practices promulgated in sentimental literature emerged among outlying geographical regions and humble social spheres, such as among western frontiersmen and rural communities in Tennessee and Kentucky. In deracinating and appropriating these beliefs, sentimental literature contributed to the public perception of these sectarian beliefs as broadly nondenominational when they were nothing of the sort. Sentimental literary texts thus present the sectarian as ecumenical and the partisan as disinterested. In tracking this enterprise on numerous fronts, this study extends Tracy Fessenden's argument that sentimentalism contributed to the perception of "particular forms of Protestantism" as "an 'unmarked category' in American religious and literary history."[10]

The seeming withdrawal of sentimental literature from contemporary sectarian acrimony was a fiction that not only camouflaged its marked religious agenda but also eradicated any dissent or objection to the religious views proffered in these texts. Rarely in sentimentalism do we directly encounter the contentious public discourse surrounding these beliefs, nor do we see portraits of the bitter factionalism that characterized the era. In its stead, sentimental texts typically present the religious world as unitary and harmonious, these tendentious beliefs passed seamlessly and without dispute from one believer to another. While this vision of a unified, harmonious Christianity gestures toward a desire to quell the era's virulent sectarianism, it also functions as a decisive, definitive salvo within those disputes. In expunging the religious world of rancorous disputation and violence, sentimental literary texts in effect conclude and resolve these conflicts by eliminating and even silencing all objections to these beliefs. Sentimental texts thus offer a triumphalist portrait of a religious world in which a particular religious belief set has successfully vanquished its critics and found absorption into the mainstream, its sectarian specifics replaced by intimations of ecumenical unity.

Having effectively silenced all opposition or debate, the sentimental text and its author emerge as the primary authoritative voices on religious matters. This assumption of religious authority is consistent with the larger theological interests of sentimental literary texts, for among the many diverse new religious beliefs incorporated into sentimentalism, the common feature that unites them is their shared promotion of religious autonomy in general and female religious authority in particular. This characteristic may be surprising because religious piety so often appears to provide the moral fetters that justify submission in sentimental literature, as Marianne Noble has shown.[11] However, sentimental literary texts repeatedly promoted new beliefs that derive from a foundational commitment to religious independence and self-reliance freed from the strictures of authoritarian intervention. Deriving from such diverse sources as Campbellite primitivism and Methodist perfectionism, the new religious beliefs promoted in sentimental literary texts repeatedly inveigh against the intrusive mediation of ecclesiastical power and assert instead that individuals are authorized for themselves to make sound interpretations of scripture, to supervise their own salvation, and to assume duties traditionally allotted to clergy. The theological contents of sentimental piety therefore comport with the larger engagement of sentimental literature in the philosophical discourse of liberty and self-determination, as analyzed by such critics as Nancy Bentley, Bruce Burgett, Elizabeth Maddock Dillon, and Julia Stern.[12] Analysis of sentimental literature within this context demonstrates that religious doctrine was just as significant as moral-sense philosophy and liberal political theory in supplying rhetoric and ideological support for the sentimental pursuit of liberty. Indeed, these religious beliefs may help account for the receptivity of sentimental writers to secular social philosophies that theorize the place of the subject in relation to structures of power.

However, as depicted in sentimental literary texts, the chief beneficiary of this new discourse of religious liberty is most often the white, middle-class, Protestant, North Atlantic woman, for whom these doctrines enable unprecedented religious authority, both personal and administrative. Against the grain of sentimentalism's own seeming retreat from sectarian struggles for preeminence and despite the avowals of pious female submission that fill the pages of sentimental literature, sentimental writers often vied specifically for the public standing of their own demographic cohort. This book aims to show that the redistribution of gendered religious authority underlies sentimental literature at every turn. At the level of theological allegiance, sentimental literary texts repeatedly sponsor new doctrines and practices that enabled women to evade biblical interdiction and acquire religious influence, whether in their assumption of clerical duties or the public recognition of their vital contribution to the national religious climate. This advocacy is evident, for instance, in the alignment of sentimentalism with Methodism, a denomination that permitted women to violate Pauline edict and preach publicly; it likewise underlies the sentimental promotion of hymns, a genre that provided a new forum for female religious self-expression. Sentimental texts frequently challenged the traditional gendering of religious authority to suggest that, in defiance of biblical prohibition, women are well qualified to interpret the nature of the divine will, to elucidate religious scripture, and to offer ministerial counsel, and it supported these doctrines with narratives that corroborated the salubrious consequences of female religious leadership.

Furthermore, sentimental writers used their literary writings to acquire this religious authority for themselves. In telling readers what they should believe, feel, and do, sentimental writers assumed ministerial duties and positioned themselves as important cultural arbiters of religious opinion. The seeming domestic withdrawal from public religious debate contributed to this endeavor, for it tacitly presented these women writers, albeit falsely, as nonpartisan and untouched by sectarian biases, as able to transcend factional conflict and forge religious unity and peace out of a climate of bitter religious enmity. The very ability to domesticate and refine beliefs associated with uncouth revivalism confirms the suitability of middle-class, Protestant white women to assume leadership roles, for, unlike rabble-rousing preachers or unworldly clergy, these women implicitly assert that they are able to establish compromise and find a middle ground that capitulates to numerous warring parties. While domestic retreat and putative traditionalism may appear to neutralize the insurgent, activist energies of the new climate of revivalism whose teachings sentimentalism gleaned, it becomes clear that sentimental women writers instead commandeered these powers for themselves; in relocating these contentious religious innovations within the home, they channeled the attendant new religious authority solely to women whose taste, judgment, and domestic abilities demonstrated their fitness for religious leadership. Sentimental domestication may have enabled these new religious movements and beliefs to acquire the patina of social respectability and to circulate more broadly, but it did so by reallocating the religious authority associated with revivalism from a subaltern lower-class populace to the middle-class, Protestant white woman.

This book charts the evolution of sentimentalism from a rhetoric of female moral and religious authority into a rhetoric employed by women in official positions of religious authority, one used to moderate and temper their unseemly eminence. While sentimental literature discursively assumed ministerial duties, in some instances sentimental writers went further by claiming even higher authority for their works, characterizing their texts as a kind of modern scripture and portraying themselves as prophets able to voice the divine will. The most famous instance of this suggestion is Harriet Beecher Stowe's renowned assertion that "God wrote" *Uncle Tom's Cabin*, a statement that implicitly styled her as a vessel of divine communication and her novel as a sacred text. As this study will illustrate, Stowe was by no means the sole sentimental writer credited with divinatory powers, nor was *Uncle Tom's Cabin* the only sentimental text vested with visionary, scriptural authority. The contributions of sentimentalism to the constitution of female religious authority, however, reveal that there was nonetheless a distinct line that could not be crossed by women seeking mainstream recognition as legitimate sources of moral, religious authority. Such critics as Elizabeth Maddock Dillon, Amy Schrager Lang, and Helen Papashvily have traced the enduring specter of the seventeenth-century firebrand Anne Hutchinson within nineteenth-century conceptions of female propriety.[13] Hutchinson's aggressive public criticism of clergy and assumption of ministerial duty caused her to be exiled as a heretic and to become a watchword for unacceptable female audacity, and she provided a continuing example of the dire consequences of female religious impudence. This study considers how sentimentality, with its discourse of domestic modesty, helped simultaneously camouflage and legitimize women's claims to public religious authority. Following the work of Elizabeth Maddock Dillon on the public literary constitution of female privacy, this study analyzes how professions of domesticity in sentimental literature served as evidence attesting to a woman's suitability for public religious leadership. In several instances that this book will consider in detail, the writing of domestic literature functioned as the starting point for women who would become official religious leaders, such as Eliza R. Snow and Mary Baker Eddy. But in breaking from religious convention and advocating for insurgent new doctrines, such sentimental writers as Catharine Sedgwick and Harriet Beecher Stowe were following Hutchinson's example of female religious leadership while simultaneously covering their tracks with assurances of domestic traditionalism.

There is one particularly vexed means by which sentimental women writers both executed and confirmed their religious authority. The sentimental promotion of religious liberty was not content merely to advocate and depict female religious independence, but it also participated in the public condemnation of religious movements that were understood to violate that independence: sentimental engagement in contemporary religious developments took the form not only of inclusion and promotion but also of denunciation, by publicly disparaging other competing religious movements for beliefs and practices deemed oppressive and inordinately hierarchical. It is for this reason that sentimental literature often criticized, either directly or implicitly, denominations that were believed to restrict the autonomy of the female believer and render her either passive or submissive. Religious movements that advocated female religious autonomy are often rendered in these texts as denominationally neutral and ecumenical, while those that did not were characterized as partisan and narrowly dogmatic. In her study of sentimentalism, Gillian Brown observed that "to think of the domestic as reformist or revolutionary, therefore, is to register only one of its operations," and the textured nature of sentimental piety evidences one particularly suggestive instance in which sentimental literature advocated in favor of some new religious ideas while simultaneously campaigning against others.[14] Correspondingly, sentimental writers advocated for the authority of their own social demographic while appropriating the nascent religious authority of other marginal constituencies. Following the work of Lora Romero, this study considers how sentimental piety frequently adopts a "progressive stance in one arena" to enable or camouflage the adoption of a reactionary one elsewhere.[15]

In some instances, this condemnation was explicit. In *Agnes of Sorrento* (1862), Stowe drew on widespread stereotypes in her portrayal of Catholic clergy as tyrannical and sexually licentious, thereby concurring with such sensationalistic anti-Catholic works as Maria Monk's fictitious memoir *Awful Disclosures of the Hotel Dieu Nunnery* (1836), in which she depicted nuns as sexual slaves subject to the abuses of lascivious priests. In *Little Women* (1868), Louisa May Alcott likewise channeled Protestant anxiety about the proselytizing ambitions of Catholic immigrants with her portrait of Esther, a French housemaid who encourages Amy March to practice Catholic ritual. And as a later chapter in this book will show, numerous novels in the sentimental vein took aim at Mormonism, portraying it as analogous to both Catholicism and slavery and thus a dire threat to the American home and family.

Otherwise, however, sentimental literary texts more commonly promoted religious beliefs that were colored by sectarian suspicion and found purchase in American culture because of their usefulness in opposition to a perceived national foe. These religious teachings were not abstractly theological and thus divorced from contemporary social context (if such a thing can be said to exist), but they instead constitute acutely social responses to contemporary religious antagonism. In the period's crowded, reactive religious climate, every new religious belief or practice emerged in opposition to innumerable other possible options, and so many of the beliefs and practices advocated in sentimental literary texts were freighted with a wealth of partisan associations and uses that, through their literary adoption and promotion, were implicitly transferred to these texts. By reading sentimental literature and presumably absorbing many of the beliefs inherent in it, readers might be outfitted with a number of beliefs, such as an insistence on the primacy of Bible reading and a belief in the purposeful nature of providential history, which not only promulgated a foundational belief in religious autonomy but might also render them skeptical of alternate belief systems characterized as hostile to this autonomy. In thus educating the reader about potential religious dangers and advancing innumerable beliefs inflected by sectarian antipathy, sentimental women writers worked as vital foot soldiers in campaigns against these contested religious movements. The end result of this participation in sectarian antipathy is the confirmation of their stature as venerable matriarchs on a national stage, supervising the moral well-being of young people nationwide.

It bears remarking, however, that sentimental literature operated in ways that were strikingly similar to those demonized religious movements. In the first place, the sentimental sanctification of domestic maternity often verges on Catholic Mariolatry, as Laura Wexler has shown.[16] Though Catholicism was widely denounced because of the putative excesses of its clerical authority, this one Catholic authority figure, the Virgin Mary, is exempt from sentimental censure, for she provided necessary scriptural precedent and justification for female religious leadership. Her Catholic trappings often expunged, she reappears throughout this study, appropriated and reconfigured in numerous guises, as the apotheosis of womanly holiness that sentimental literature often attributes to its own social demographic. Though Catholicism functions as a metonym in sentimental literature for the repressive excesses of clerical authority, it nonetheless supplied the exemplar of the hallowed white matron whom sentimental texts position as incontrovertible religious authority.

Second, sentimental literary texts evince the same proselytizing ambitions imputed to Catholicism and Mormonism and that incited public outrage against them. Public discourse of the mid-century alleged that both these denominations actively sought to convert the American multitude through covert missionaries who ensnared unsuspecting victims with warm assurances of familiarity, only to transplant them into a tenacious, alien belief system that forbade escape.[17] While sentimental literature promoted a set of beliefs designed to render the reader resistant to the suasions of such missionaries, sentimental literature itself used some of the techniques associated with missionary work. It proffered a series of controversial religious positions, but it seldom broadcast them as such. Instead, it promoted these beliefs surreptitiously, without announcement or explanation, and it encouraged readers to adopt beliefs and practices that may have been in explicit opposition to their own denominational affiliations. Sentimental domestication thus functioned like a Trojan horse for some heterodox beliefs, serving as a protective shield camouflaging the infiltration of some contested new beliefs. Just as nineteenth-century Protestant alarmists warned that the proselytizing of Catholics would gradually transform the United States into a papal state, the clandestine sectarianism of sentimental literature also portrayed a religious world that had already absorbed and been transformed by these new teachings. Sentimentalism thus contributed to the widespread circulation and normalization of once-dubious religious beliefs, many of which were depicted as already conventional. In this way, sentimentalism evidences "the process by which the unimaginable becomes, finally, the obvious," to use Philip Fisher's formulation, as sentimentalism contributed to the domestication of marginal, suspect doctrines by constituting them as such.[18]

In glossing the religious contents, contexts, and consequences of sentimentalism, this study seeks to show, above all else, that the sentimental literary archive is more capacious and tensile than we have perhaps recognized. This literary discourse of female piety was not limited to such standard forms as the novel, the poem, the genteel ladies' periodical, or the gift book, but, as the works studied here show, it also manifested in such devotional genres as the hymn, the spiritual autobiography, and the religious revelation. In these forms, sentimentalism was able to acquire wide circulation beyond the conventional channels of literary distribution, and it was thereby able to exert profound influence on the religious lives of countless readers, whether in shaping their personal beliefs or their devotional practices. Furthermore, analysis of the specific sectarian expressions of sentimental piety demonstrates the insufficiency of the current sentimental canon, the corpus of nineteenth-century texts currently studied and taught.

By focusing our attention on the national literary mainstream, we have perhaps overlooked the ways in which sentimentality found receptive readerships, new cohorts of authors, and distinctive sectarian manifestations in various religious settings. Some of the most influential sentimental women writers of the nineteenth century have never been recognized as such because their work both circulated within confined sectarian circles and openly promoted a sectarian belief set. Though they saw themselves as peers of such famous sentimentalists as Stowe and achieved comparable influence, their explicit sectarianism placed them on the national religious periphery, just as these writers have remained outside the sentimental canon. There are doubtless innumerable other writers of significance as well as other sectarian manifestations of sentimentalism that we have overlooked, and our understanding of sentimentality's full scope and reach will likely remain partial until we are able to consider its local expressions in individual religious communities and settings.

Some of the claims offered here about the religious influence of sentimentalism merit justification. It is commonplace for scholars to make broad statements asserting the wide cultural influence of sentimentalism. Jennifer Brady has recently drawn attention to the "fuzzy" process by which sentimentalism is so often credited with exerting influence on the public sphere.[19] The transfer from the printed page to the wider national culture, Brady suggests, is often implied and presumed rather than elucidated specifically. In the case of sentimental piety, this transmission from literary text to cultural practice was enabled by the centrality of reading and literature to nineteenth-century religious faith, observance, and education. Reading was, and remains, an activity believed to effect self-improvement and moral reform, and, since the Protestant Reformation, the reading of scripture has reigned as the primary means by which one may gain access to the divine will. Moreover, through the cogitation, imagination, and reflection requisite to reading, it was believed that the reader might literally internalize the words of the divine by absorbing them into consciousness.[20] The success of religious literature hinged on the reader's ability to ingest and implement the contents of the printed page, to allow the text to exert influence on belief and conduct. Religious periodicals and volumes often expressly schooled readers in techniques designed to enable texts to take hold and influence behavior. For instance, an 1839 issue of the Methodist *Sunday School Magazine* instructed readers to read devotional literature carefully, prayerfully, and habitually, with the explicit intention of committing the texts to memory and allowing the text to guide behavior and belief.[21]

Christians of innumerable denominations and time periods have long been encouraged to perceive the New Testament as a kind of conduct manual and to imitate the literary example of Christ. Candy Gunther Brown has shown that religious texts in the Protestant transatlantic often explicitly invited reader emulation with narrative biographies of devout worthies whose lives were constituted as deserving of imitation, such as Sarah Pierpont Edwards, the pious wife of Jonathan Edwards, or eighteenth-century missionary David Brainerd.[22] The foundational English-language exemplar of religious reader emulation was doubtless John Bunyan's *The Pilgrim's Progress* (1678), which recounts the trials and triumph of the Christian journey toward heavenly salvation. Bunyan explicitly encouraged the reader to identify with and imitate the narrative in his prefatory question to the reader:

Wouldest thou loose thy self, and catch no harm?
And find thy self again without a charm?
Would'st read thy self, and read thou know'st not what

And yet know whether thou art blest or not,
By reading the same lines? O then come hither,
And lay my Book, thy Head and Heart together.[23]

To read *The Pilgrim's Progress*, Bunyan suggests, is to see oneself and one's own life playing out in the narrative, a suggestion that presents the journey of the pilgrim, Christian, as analogous to that of the reader. The opening paragraph of *The Pilgrim's Progress* contains a scene of intensive reader emulation, as Christian falls to weeping and trembling upon reading the Bible's prediction of Judgment Day. Christian shortly thereafter meets the Evangelist, who gives him a scroll that reads, "Fly from the wrath to come," a direction that inspires him to begin his journey (9). The text thus commences by demonstrating the virtues of imitative religious reading, thereby instructing the reader in the proper mode by which Bunyan's own text should be read.

Suzanne Ashworth has shown that sentimental texts often functioned like conduct literature by teaching readers how to deport themselves, and this function is explicit in their encouragement of readers to emulate the religious diligence depicted in these works.[24] And just as *The Pilgrim's Progress* contained scenes of emulative reading to prompt such a response in the reader, so sentimental texts often depicted the benefits of imitating devotional literature; unsurprisingly, the religious text most often read and imitated in such works as Susan Warner's *The Wide, Wide World* (1850) and Martha Finley's *Elsie Dinsmore* (1867) is none other than Bunyan's religious romance, which provides a model of conduct and devotion that the sentimental characters actively seek to replicate in their own behavior.[25] This readerly imitation is quite literal in Alcott's *Little Women,* in which the March sisters reenact and dramatize scenes from *The Pilgrim's Progress* in addition to other texts, such as Dickens's *Pickwick Papers* (1836–37), a depiction of copycat reading that implicitly invites the reader to do likewise. And if readers followed the conventions of devotional reading and heeded the cues contained within these sentimental texts, they likely absorbed new heterodox doctrines and emulated practices deriving from populist revivalism, all the while trusting the religious authority and guidance of these women writers.

The carry-over from the printed page to religious practice was also enabled by the fertile climate of religious publishing in the nineteenth century. The evangelical press flourished during the first half of the nineteenth century, with the proliferation of countless religious periodicals, tracts, and sectarian publications.[26] As Candy Gunther Brown and David Paul Nord have shown, in the second quarter of the nineteenth century the workings of the American Tract Society and the American Bible Society solidified the widespread cultural understanding that the reading of devotional literature—whether theology, tracts, sermons, or narratives—was a vital component of religious practice.[27] Numerous contemporary observers noted that the printed page was poised to outpace or even replace the pulpit as the nation's primary organ of religious instruction. Horace Bushnell, for instance, wryly remarked in 1844 that American evangelicals regarded the press "as if God would offer man a mechanical engine for converting the world, . . . or as if types of lead and sheets of paper may be the light of the world."[28] Literary critic Henry Tuckerman similarly noted in 1866 that the "press has, indeed, in a measure, superseded the pulpit. No intelligent observer of the signs of the times can fail to perceive that as a means of influence, the two are at least equal. In the pages of journals, in the verses of poets, in the favorite books of the hour, we have homilies that teach charity and faith more eloquently than the conventional Sunday discourse; they come nearer to experience; they are more the off-spring of earnest conviction, and therefore enlist popular sympathy."[29] By the time sentimentalism reached its apotheosis in the 1850s, readers had already come to regard devotional reading as an important source of spiritual instruction, and they had already been primed to absorb and emulate the religious teachings contained therein.

This book begins with a discussion of the wider religious context that occasioned the meteoric rise of the religious press and that by extension fostered literary sentimentalism. To that end, the first chapter situates sentimentalism within the context of the Second Great Awakening (1790–1840), a period of extraordinary religious innovation that shaped the religious values, ideas, and practices documented in sentimental texts. A ferment of religious populism, the Second Great Awakening produced a cultural climate hospitable to the production of female-authored religious texts and molded the religious views of the major contributors to literary sentimentalism. Many of the signature features of sentimental literature—such as its ecumenism, emotionalism, and encouragement of private Bible study—were recent products of the Second Great Awakening and its populist climate of revivalism. As this chapter will show, many of the new beliefs promoted by sentimental texts were ones that imputed religious authority to women and provided new avenues and justifications for the religious stewardship of female believers. They were able to effect this end, too, by actively participating within contemporary sectarian conflict, propounding doctrines that, by the mid-nineteenth century, had acquired particular currency because of their opposition to a perceived Catholic menace. For instance, while the sentimental advocacy of private Bible reading may seem unremarkable to modern readers, it nonetheless constituted a direct response to contemporary suspicion that Catholicism sought to curtail Bible reading.[30] Similarly, sentimental texts often depict clergy as unnecessary and even obstructive to religious observance, a belief that spread in the Second Great Awakening and that, by the 1850s, became associated with Protestant denunciation of the sovereignty of Catholic priests. As these instances show, sentimental literature advocated beliefs of the Second Great Awakening that not only imparted authority to white, middle-class women but also did so through the public denunciation of competing religious movements.

This discussion is followed by a chapter that examines the hymn, a genre popularized in the Second Great Awakening. Hymns interlard the pages of sentimental fiction with such frequency that they altogether eclipse the fact that hymns had long been a marginal religious form, prohibited from congregational worship because of their indeterminate provenance and uncertain theological contents. It was through the endorsement of mid-century sentimental women writers that hymns finally found widespread acceptance in public worship, and this chapter outlines how sentimental women writers assumed the authority provided by the hymn form both by allaying conservative trepidation and by appropriating its activist energies. As a populist genre that literally gave common people a public voice in religious worship, it attracted the attention of scores of women, who used this form to express their religious views and circumvent traditional biblical prohibitions barring them from the pulpit. Well before such female hymnists as Fanny J. Crosby and Frances Willard became beloved public figures, sentimental writers helped make the hymn a distinctively female-centered devotional genre: Louisa May Alcott, Phoebe Cary, Julia Ward Howe, Lydia Sigourney, Harriet Beecher Stowe, Anna Warner, and Susan Warner all wrote religious lyrics that were set to music and included within hymnals. By examining how these hymns evidence the explicit religious engagement, aspirations, and influence of sentimental writers, this chapter seeks both to restore this devotional form to its rightful place in the sentimental canon and to show how it enabled sentimental women writers to assume public religious authority. The development of this new literary platform came at a cost, however, for, in claiming hymns for themselves, sentimental women writers attempted to appropriate a religious genre that had long provided a forum for the self-expression of people on the social margins. Though sentimental writers helped establish the respectability of this suspect religious genre to effect their own social ascent, they did so by working to neutralize and usurp the form's insurrectionary associations.

The third chapter examines sentimentalism in the context of mid-century millennialism, the growing eschatological conviction that Jesus's return was imminent and that human history would soon draw to a close. Scholars have long recognized the influence of millennialism on Stowe's *Uncle Tom's Cabin*, and this chapter seeks to demonstrate the broader, more pervasive influence of millennialism on the sentimental philosophy of human history. To that end, this chapter investigates the influence of millennialism on sentimental narrative form. This consideration focuses on the domestic novels of Harriet Beecher Stowe, which march ineluctably toward a providential conclusion in which families are reunited and wrongs set to right. In showing the engagement of sentimentalism in this pervasive theology of the period, this chapter illustrates that this theology contributed to the sentimental promotion of female religious authority, for Stowe's millennialist domestic fiction repeatedly suggests that the fulfillment of Christian prophecy hinges upon the active contributions of women. In such works as *The Minister's Wooing* (1859), *The Pearl of Orr's Island* (1862), and *Oldtown Folks* (1869), Stowe suggests that the millennium will be instigated not by clergy but by housewives and housekeepers, whose daily labors do considerable work in healing and perfecting the world. In this way, Stowe's domestic fiction constitutes a feminist alternative to the traditional jeremiad form: she envisioned the reversal of conventional religious hierarchies and the official consecration of the traditional female role, ideas that such religious innovators as Ellen Gould White and Elizabeth Cady Stanton would adapt in their respective writings.

The sectarian character of sentimentalism comprised not only the promotion of numerous new religious beliefs but also the denunciation of others, and the fourth and fifth chapters respectively examine two controversial new sects that were on the receiving end of such condemnation. Sentimentalism figured prominently in the vicious public attacks suffered by these two sects, and both pursued public acceptance by the active enlistment of sentimental rhetoric and forms. These final two chapters also demonstrate the effectiveness of literary sentimentalism in enabling female religious authority, for both chapters consider the career of an important female religious leader whose fitness for governance was demonstrated through the writing of sentimental poetic lyric. In addition, these two chapters demonstrate that the relation between sentimentalism and religious belief was reciprocal and mutual: where the first three chapters show that sentimental texts incorporated and promoted numerous contemporary religious beliefs, these final two chapters illustrate that sentimentality proved immensely influential in the constitution and contents of several nascent sects of the nineteenth century. Sentimentalism provided important source material for these new American religious movements, supplying rhetoric, tropes, and scenarios that became concretized and officially sanctioned in the form of doctrine and typology. As these instances confirm, sentimentality was not simply a literary register for the presentation or narration of religious experience, but it instead became a constituent, integral feature of several important new religious movements.

These implications are at the center of the fourth chapter, which investigates the complex status of sentimentalism among nineteenth-century Mormons, for whom sentimentalism was both an overt impediment to and an instrument of public approval. In the aftermath of *Uncle Tom's Cabin*, innumerable writers sought to capitalize on the new popularity of sentimental sensationalism with the publication of novels modeled after Stowe's blockbuster that offered a similar literary exposé of the sufferings of women under Mormon polygamy. As with such works as Maria Ward's *Female Life Among the Mormons* (1855) and Metta Fuller's *Mormon Wives* (1856), sentimentalism in the mid-century became a source of public mortification for Mormons, and they responded by coopting sentimentalism in an effort to defend themselves from public attack and demonstrate their compliance with normative domestic values. As with the Mormon women's magazine *Woman's Exponent* and numerous published defenses of polygamy, Mormons actively enlisted sentimentalism in their efforts to protect themselves from it. But sentimentalism was more than merely a useful public rhetoric for the Mormons, and this chapter also glosses the profound influence of sentimentalism on Mormon theology. In particular, this chapter considers the influential poetry of Eliza R. Snow, the nineteenth-century Mormon poet laureate whose sentimental poems are central to the Mormon poetic canon. Recognized as a prophetess and seer, Snow transcribed her religious visions in sentimental poetic forms, and her poem "O My Father" is perhaps the single most influential sentimental poem of the nineteenth century. In that poem, Snow revealed and introduced the Mormon belief in Heavenly Mother, the divine consort who births all human souls in heaven. Snow's poem thus enabled the sentimental consecration of domesticity and maternity to become literal theological belief. For the Mormons, homebound motherhood is literally divine, a theological attribution of supreme authority to women made possible by a mid-century sentimental poem.

The final chapter examines the controversial efforts of Mary Baker Eddy, the founder of Christian Science, to use sentimentalism to shape her public persona. Eddy grew up reading and writing sentimental poetry, throughout her life using it to shape her public image. In her role as the leader of Christian Science, Eddy softened her authority by patterning it after the idealized sentimental mother; in support of this goal, she issued a wealth of sentimental poetry and narrative that affirmed her compliance with sentimental feminine convention. While sentimentalism indisputably paved the way for Eddy to become a formal religious leader of unprecedented authority, it also posed a grave liability to her public credibility. By the time she rose to power in the late century, this aesthetic had already become outmoded, and her sentimental writings elicited the scorn of turn-of-the-century critics and writers such as Willa Cather and Mark Twain, whose realist aesthetic sensibilities made her invocations of antebellum sentimentalism seem ludicrous. For Eddy, sentimentalism had outlived its usefulness, but her sentimentalized religious authority enabled later generations of women to assume religious leadership roles without apology or the public conformity to literary prototypes.

In his foundational essay "The Recovery of American Religious History," Henry F. May noted that "the history of American Protestantism" is characterized by "long efforts to institutionalize successive religious impulses," and this book attempts to show the significant contributions of nineteenth-century literary sentimentalism to the institutionalization of numerous new religious beliefs and practices, among them the heterodox belief that women should be permitted to hold positions of religious authority. It likewise seeks to "[restore] a knowledge of the mode, even the language, in which most Americans, during most of American history, did their thinking about human nature and destiny," modes that would have been recognizable to contemporary readers of sentimental literature but that, because of the genre's successes in concealing and institutionalizing those modes, have been invisible to successive generations of readers.[31] However controversial the advocacy of sentimental literature for female religious authority may seem, especially in light of its many protestations of modesty, it bears remarking that sentimentalism coincided with numerous contemporary religious and social movements that also reconsidered the status of women in domestic, civil, and religious structures of authority. Scholars have observed the coincidence of sentimentalism with the feminist movement consolidated in the 1848 Seneca Falls convention, but we less frequently observe its coincidence with the religious feminism of such contemporary religious movements as the Shakers and the Oneida Perfectionists.[32] The widening sense that women should, and would soon, play a central role in religious affairs is evident in the closing paragraphs of Nathaniel Hawthorne's *The Scarlet Letter* (1850). Despite his oft-quoted 1855 denunciation of the "damned mob of scribbling women" that flooded the mid-century literary market with sentimental novels and poems, Hawthorne concluded *The Scarlet Letter* with a prophecy that an era characterized by female religious authority was imminent:

> Women . . . came to Hester's cottage, demanding why they were so wretched, and what the remedy! Hester comforted and counselled them, as best she might. She assured them, too, of her firm belief, that, as some brighter period, when the world should have grown ripe for it, in Heaven's own time, a new truth would be revealed, in order to establish the whole relation between man and woman on a surer ground of mutual happiness. Earlier in life, Hester had vainly imagined that she herself might be the destined prophetess. . . . The angel and apostle of the coming revelation must be a woman, indeed, but lofty, pure, and beautiful; and wise, moreover, not through dusky grief, but the ethereal medium of joy; and showing how sacred love should make us happy, by the truest test of a life successful to such an end![33]

Hawthorne was prescient in his anticipation of an impending religious era heralded by female religious leadership and characterized by the female elevation of love, for Susan Warner would soon publish *The Wide, Wide World* and a year Stowe later would begin serializing *Uncle Tom's Cabin*; with those two best-selling works, the golden age of sentimentalism began, and with it came the advocacy of female religious leadership. However, as this study will show, that leadership was constituted at the public expense of numerous vulnerable constituencies, among them Catholics, Mormons, the evangelical lower class, and Calvinists, all of whom were denounced or disempowered so that white, middle-class Protestant North Atlantic women might evince and execute authority. A few of the sentimental women writers considered here imagined that they themselves might be that female prophet anticipated by Hawthorne. But it was chiefly through their writing of female-centered devotional literature that this prophecy would be fulfilled, with the exertion of religious influence and the spread of new religious ideals that would permanently change the American religious landscape.

CHAPTER 1

Revivals of Sentiment

Sentimentalism and the Second Great Awakening

O UR UNDERSTANDING of the sectarian contours of sentimental literature
derives primarily from Ann Douglas's foundational study, *The Feminization of American Culture* (1977), in which she analyzed sentimentalism
within the context of Calvinism, a focus that left sentimentalism by contrast
seeming lax and doctrinally vague. According to Douglas, Calvinism was both
destroyed and succeeded by sentimentalism, which institutionalized a loose,
"anti-intellectual" lay religion that replaced theology and scholarly rigor with
feeling and domesticity, a transition exemplified by her claim that the minister
was replaced by the housewife as the national arbiter of morality.[1] Douglas's
conception of the religious character of sentimental literature found a bracing
response from Jane Tompkins, who in *Sensational Designs* (1985) sought to
rehabilitate sentimental piety by arguing that sentimentalism boldly aspired
to "remak[e] the social and political order."[2] Though Tompkins's critique permanently dimmed the academic luster of Douglas's study, Douglas's analysis
of sentimentalism within the context of Calvinism has proved highly durable.
While recent scholars such as Sharon Kim, Marianne Noble, and Abram Van
Engen have disagreed with Douglas's assessment of the precise relationship
between sentimentalism and Calvinism, they have nonetheless preserved this
pairing by tracing the enduring vestiges of Calvinist theology in sentimental
literature.[3]

This chapter seeks to integrate an additional variable into our understanding of the sectarian character of sentimental piety: the Second Great
Awakening (1790–1840). A sprawling, grassroots movement that toppled
numerous established conventions and hierarchies in American Protestant-

ism, the Second Great Awakening has long evaded the notice of scholars of
the era's most popular literature, but, I argue, the Awakening contributed far
more to the growth of sentimentalism than did Calvinism. In essence, Ann
Douglas was correct to link the relative fortunes of sentimentalism and Calvinism, but she mischaracterized this relationship as causal rather than as
correlative, for the respective rise and fall of both movements were enabled
by the Second Great Awakening. This period of religious ferment provided
the backdrop for the larger cultural transition she describes, with new sects
springing up practically overnight and with a multitude of new religious
leaders—among them Alexander Campbell, William Miller, John Humphrey
Noyes, and Barton Stone—attracting sizable followings with new interpretations of scripture and new ideas about salvation. Despite Douglas's narrative
of a declining clergy, the American pastorate grew exponentially during the
Second Great Awakening, rising from 1,800 ministers in the late eighteenth
century to about 40,000 by 1845.[4] While the orthodoxy of New England may
have been on the wane, religion thrived outside the North Atlantic and in
rural territories of upstate New York, Ohio, Pennsylvania, Kentucky, and Tennessee, fueled by the Methodist circuit riders and itinerant preachers roam-
ing the land, organizing revivalist camp meetings, and inciting their listeners
to emotionally anguished conversions in often boisterous public meetings.
And despite the sounded death knells of organized religion, church membership rose in this era; even taking into account the nation's growing population during this period, the Methodists alone doubled in size to number half
a million members in the 1820s and became the nation's biggest Protestant
denomination by 1850.[5] Calvinism thus had bigger problems to contend with
than simply the rise of sentimentalism, and by the time sentimental literature
reached its apogee in the 1850s, Calvinism was already a shadow of its former
self, reduced by the upstart religious movements of the Second Great Awakening to a vestigial, regional relic of an earlier time.

The Second Great Awakening permanently changed the American religious landscape, both by breaking the tenacious hold of Calvinism on the
North Atlantic and by ushering in a religious climate characterized by populism and mounting democratic inclusiveness, which relaxed ecclesiastical
hierarchy and enabled figures on the religious periphery to move closer to
the center. This milieu provided the new social opportunities and religious
doctrines that enabled the development of nineteenth-century literary sentimentalism; without it, sentimentalism would never have evolved beyond

its eighteenth-century expression in the seduction novel, for this religious epoch provided the particular religious tenets, tropes, and narrative forms that are distinctive of this later iteration. All of the major figures of sentimentalism grew up in this vital period of American religious transformation, and their personal religious histories register its influence: for instance, Catharine Sedgwick, Harriet Beecher Stowe, and Susan Warner all rejected the Calvinism in which they were raised and embraced instead many of the new teachings and practices developed in this period. The Second Great Awakening was not merely an adjoining historical context that framed sentimental literature. Instead, the Second Great Awakening provides an important etiology for sentimental literature, for many of the period's distinctive qualities became, through their textual assimilation, signature features of this literature: the female-centeredness, emotionalism, and anti-clericalism characteristic of the Second Great Awakening became distinguishing generic traits of sentimental literature. Sentimentalism's hallmark attributes bear witness to the influence of this cultural progenitor.

The context of the Second Great Awakening reveals that sentimental piety was significantly more topical and tendentious than it may at first appear, and its constituent features comprised not weak responses to Calvinism but strong endorsements of the contemporary movements that precipitated Calvinism's decline. The contents of sentimental literature therefore evidence the active participation of sentimental writers and texts in contemporary religious debate, although this participation is often inconspicuous because of its extraction from the immediate sectarian moorings in the public spheres of the pulpit and the broadside, and its relocation to the private spheres of the home and the affections. However, sentimental ratification of the Second Great Awakening was not absolute, and there were in fact many new doctrines and practices that sentimental literary texts did not absorb or promote. For instance, the reinvention of marriage by such groups as the Mormons, the Oneida Perfectionists, and the Shakers did not find support in sentimental writings. Nor did the revival meeting, the era's trademark event, receive a benison in sentimental texts, which tended to favor the private and the domestic over the public and declamatory. However, as will become clear, the new beliefs that did permeate and circulate within sentimental texts tended to share a particular trait: the promotion of religious liberty. This quality may be surprising, as religion often seems to provide discursive justification for submission in sentimental literature, as Marianne Noble has shown, but these texts repeatedly absorbed and sponsored beliefs that promote religious auton-omy, liberated from clerical supervision or the mediation of established reli-gious custom.[6] These beliefs are supported by countless narratives and poems that question the necessity of religious hierarchy in arbitrating religious expe-rience, and they instead vest common people with religious authority on the basis of sincerity and sentiment rather than education and stature.

However, lest the sentimental endorsement of these teachings seem wholly egalitarian, it bears remarking that in sentimental texts these doc-trines enable not the wide democratic dispersal of religious authority, as was the case amid the Second Great Awakening, but the reassignment of that leadership along gendered, classed, raced, and regional lines—specifically, to white, middle-class North Atlantic Protestant women. Though the popu-list climate of the Second Great Awakening enabled and informed the work of sentimental writers, they were chiefly preoccupied with the advancement of their own social demographic. As applied in sentimental texts, the new populist teachings of the Second Great Awakening work above all else to enable and justify the empowerment of this constituency alone, and their fitness for this standing is often evidenced by their effective participation in the ugly sectarian conflicts that characterized the Second Great Awaken-ing and from which sentimentalism putatively withdrew through domestic enclosure.

Though the Second Great Awakening and its doctrines may seem emanci-patory because of their promotion of religious liberty, that liberty was consti-tuted along sectarian lines, for it was used to justify the public condemnation of religious groups deemed repressive and at odds with religious autonomy. Indeed, Calvinism itself was often the subject of sentimental denunciation because its doctrines and clericalism were presumed to stand in violation of the religious liberty at the heart of sentimental piety. However, the principal target in the era's promotion of religious liberty was without question Ca-tholicism, and, by promulgating teachings that announced their commitment to religious autonomy, sentimental literary texts actively contributed to an-ti-Catholic discourse and suspicion. Participation in sectarian divisiveness was not an accidental consequence of the sentimental foundation in the Sec-ond Great Awakening. Rather, it was strategic and opportunistic, for it was at the expense of these maligned denominations that sentimental women writers and texts were able to execute and justify the authority they pursued. In simultaneously championing emancipatory new doctrines and dissuading readers from these authoritarian sects, sentimental writers appointed themselves the protectors of the reader's own religious authority, a task that by extension allowed them to claim that authority for themselves.

Contexts of the Awakening

Though the Second Great Awakening may seem an unlikely ally of sentimentalism, this period of a half century, from roughly 1790 to 1840, produced the cultural climate necessary for the development of this literary movement. Where the first Great Awakening of the 1740s was firmly rooted in New England orthodoxy, the Second Great Awakening was diffuse, denominationally heterogeneous, and geographically expansive, encompassing both East Coast cities and rural frontier regions alike. The Second Great Awakening was a period of immense theological innovation and creativity, giving rise to a dramatic spike in religious fervor and the formation of innumerable new denominations and sects, such as the Campbellites, the Church of Jesus Christ of Latter-day Saints, the Millerite Adventists, and the Oneida Perfectionists. According to William McLoughlin, the Second Great Awakening can be understood as the religious extension of the new political sovereignty afforded by the American Revolution, for the period was characterized both by the active pursuit of personal religious independence and an overt antipathy for governing clerical authority.[7] The changing denominational landscape of the period offers ample evidence of this shift, as with the declining fortunes of Calvinist orthodoxy. In the aftermath of the American Revolution, the orthodox belief in predestination became irreconcilable with the era's preoccupation with liberty and self-determination, and the inexplicable salvation of the elect disconcertingly evoked an aristocratic caste whose superior status was the product of the felicitous accidents of birth rather than merit. The rolls of orthodox Calvinist denominations consequently plummeted, the membership of the Congregationalists alone falling from 20 percent of American church members in 1776 to 4 percent in 1850.[8] Public attitudes toward Catholicism in this era also register the influence of post-revolutionary anxieties about the incompatibility of older religious movements with new American independence and the suspicion that such sects might reinstate authoritarian rule. Amid escalating immigration of European Catholics as well as growing numbers of conversions to Catholicism, Protestant critics across denominations denounced Catholicism as inherently incompatible with American democracy, for it demanded unquestioning submission to unelected clergy as well as to the European regime of the pope himself. Critics publicly decried Catholic immigrants to the United States as the pawns of a conspiratorial plot between European monarchies and the papacy to overturn American democracy, and much of the evangelical fervor of the Second Great Awakening derived from a pan-Protestant campaign to arrest the spread of Catholic influence by inciting widespread Protestant conversion, as with the anti-Catholic mission of such vital evangelical organizations as the American Home Missionary Society and American Tract Society.[9]

While the public image of Calvinism and Catholicism suffered grievously amid this preoccupation with religious independence, Methodism by contrast grew exponentially in this climate, for Methodism was distinguished by an anti-aristocratic belief in religious self-determination and a populist reconstitution of religious authority. Methodism, for instance, rejected the orthodox belief that one's salvation had already been predetermined, and it championed instead the heretical doctrine of Arminianism, which insisted that conversion and redemption were available to anyone willing to experience such phenomena. The Methodist emphasis on self-determination also resulted in the loosening of conventional hierarchical strictures that elevated clergy over the laity, and it consequently permitted common people to preach and assume ministerial duties without attending seminary or undergoing ordination. To become an itinerant Methodist preacher or circuit rider, one merely had to possess dedication to evangelical ministry and ardent religious faith. Methodism thus enabled anyone—women, children, slaves—to assume moral and religious authority that had heretofore been available only to an educated male (and presumably white) elite.[10] In revival meetings, for instance, it was by no means unusual for diffident white men to find themselves publicly exhorted to repent by people on the social periphery, whether women or African Americans.[11] Populism also underlay the Methodist practice of conducting public worship in open spaces accessible to anyone, regardless of religious affiliation, class, or race, an innovation that gave rise to the camp or tent meeting, the signature religious event of that era. The openness of these meetings enabled the intermingling of people across the social spectrum in the common endeavor of religious worship, and the breakdown of social stratification was likewise accompanied by the erosion of traditional church decorum, which was replaced by lively, energetic worship services in which the attendees played an active role: where conventional services usually rendered the worshipper passive and silent, with the occasional opportunity for scripted participation in the recitation of psalms and prayer, the Methodist tent meeting was famous for the raucous participation of worshippers, who openly wept, publicly testified about sins and trials, and replied to preachers. In all these ways, traditional practices and hierarchies gave way to a genuinely populist religious culture, characterized by congregation-centered worship in which clergy were now mere facilitators to the central focus of the event, which was the participants' own experience.[12] Nathan Hatch has argued that Methodist populism enabled the "democratization" of American Protestantism, and it consequently became the nation's fastest-growing denomination, rising from about 3 percent of American church members in 1776 to 34 percent of affiliated church members by the mid-nineteenth century. By 1850, the year typically dated as the inauguration of the golden age of sentimentalism, Methodism was the nation's largest denomination, amounting to nearly three million members.[13]

Methodism's influence spread well beyond its own sectarian borders, for, in elevating the religious authority of common people, it created a populist religious environment amenable to the emergence and acceptance of self-styled religious prophets, who sprang up in remarkable numbers and claimed to possess revealed religious truth on the authority only of their own testimony and conviction.[14] A nation already familiar with the rough, untrained oratory of Methodist circuit riders and revivalists proved receptive to such self-anointed religious leaders as William Miller and Joseph Smith, who respectively founded two major sects in the makeshift religious environment of the Second Great Awakening. The Methodist acknowledgment of the social exclusivity of traditional church worship also gave rise to sundry Free Church movements, such as the one that took place in New York in the 1830s, which revolted against the elitism that enabled only affluent families to attend church and agitated that church attendance ought to be free and open to the public, regardless of class or status.[15] The spread of religious populism did not go unchallenged, for the clergy of more traditional denominations, such as Presbyterian Lyman Beecher, balked at what they perceived as the vulgarity and dangerous ignorance of these developments.[16] However, Methodism proved so popular that the Presbyterians, in their struggle to retain parishioners and public authority, fragmented in the 1830s owing to internal discord about how best to respond to the incursion of Methodism, and the New School Presbyterians seceded because of their willingness to incorporate some of the revivalist methods popularized by Methodists.

Commentators have long observed that the religious populism of the Second Great Awakening was fortified by larger social trends, such as the disestablishment of churches from formal government affiliation, a change that formally confirmed the lesser status of clergy and, Ann Douglas has argued, refashioned clergy from independent leaders into service providers whose sheer financial survival depended upon obliging their congregants.[17] The Second Great Awakening likewise coincided with the Jacksonian era, a period dubbed by historians "the era of the common man" because of its ardent populism and attendant skepticism about the inherent merit of social and economic elites whose superior education and resources transformed in this era from objects of veneration among their social subordinates to markers of inherited privilege deemed incompatible with American democracy.[18] Though Ann Douglas blamed sentimentalism for the decline in the status of American clergy, that change derived from the period's larger climate of populist skepticism, which rendered suspect the conventional trappings of clerical authority: the educational requirements of ordination, the inaccessible cogitations of theology, and the oratorical formality of the pulpit all became suspect because of their requirement of education and resources unavailable to anyone other than a leisured, economic elite.[19] Nor was erudition required of worshippers during the Second Great Awakening, for revivalism caused widespread rejection of the creedal affirmations and the formal clerical examination required by both orthodoxy and Catholicism, as scores of worshippers experienced sudden conversion and professed faith without much knowledge of the Bible or the finer points of doctrine.[20]

The boisterous revival meetings and lower-class character of the Second Great Awakening would seem to be a far cry from the well-appointed parlors and decorous civility central to much of sentimental literature. However, this literary movement owes a considerable debt to this religious epoch since its populist opposition to religious hierarchy extended also to a willingness to reconsider the marginal place of women within religious observance.[21] It was because of the innovations of the Second Great Awakening that the United States would be amenable to the public religious appeals and teachings of American women, whether in the genre of sentimental literature or any other setting. Mary P. Ryan has shown that "the Second Great Awakening indicates that the history of class and religion was hopelessly entangled with questions of family and gender," and these religious debates overturned millennia of long-standing doctrine delimiting the institutional roles of women in organized religion and fostered an environment newly receptive to female religious leadership.[22] In particular, this era saw the breakdown of the interdiction against women preachers. Though individual women might be regarded as paragons of virtue worthy of emulation, women had long been barred from preaching and public religious instruction.[23] In his epistles to early Christian communities, Paul specifically forbade women from assuming responsibilities of public religious instruction, commanding that women remain "silent in the churches, for they are not permitted to speak, but should be subordinate, as the law also says. If there is anything they desire to know, let them ask their husbands at home. For it is shameful for a woman to speak in church" (1 Cor. 14:34–35). The first letter to Timothy similarly asserts, "Let a woman learn in silence with full submission. I permit no woman to teach or to have authority over a man; she is to keep silent" (1 Tim. 2:11–12).[24]

This injunction forbidding women from public religious expression became increasingly tenuous during the Second Great Awakening. The Methodist spirit of religious autonomy considerably undermined this restriction by permitting women to speak at revival meetings, and those many thousands of worshippers who attended revivals were accustomed to the sight of women publicly offering religious testimony and instruction.[25] Nor was it unusual for revivals to commence because of the public urgings of prominent community women seeking to incite conversion among their families and peers.[26] Outside the particularly carnivalesque setting of the revival, women gradually assumed some of the roles that had been restricted to clergy. Just as the secular Jackson era has been termed the age of the common man, so may its religious corollary in the Second Great Awakening be understood by the complementary designation as the age of the churchwoman, with the widespread appointment of women to roles as church organizers and lay leaders. Disestablishment forced clergy to focus on raising and managing funds, a reapportionment of clerical attention that caused clergy of all denominations to delegate some ministerial tasks to female parishioners.[27] The day-to-day administration of the church was increasingly delegated to able female leadership, who formed a wealth of female-centered organizations—among them the Cent Society, Dorcas Society, Female Charitable Society, Female Domestic Missionary Society, and Female Praying Society—that enabled them to distribute resources to the needy, evangelize to the unchurched, and become the public face of church compassion.[28] In offering religious instruction to children and people on the social periphery, these leadership positions required women to violate the long-standing injunctions against preaching, albeit in limited settings outside the main worship service, and, with women assuming these ministerial duties, the prohibitions against preaching became progressively precarious and obsolete.[29] Though conservatives such as Lyman Beecher remonstrated that public preaching was unfeminine and indecorous, dozens of women in the Second Great Awakening were unwilling to be consigned to preaching on the margins and instead assumed the pulpit itself, urging listeners to examine their consciences, repent, and convert.[30] Charles Finney, Beecher's longtime gadfly and the era's most mainstream popularizer of revivalist innovations, openly supported female preachers, endorsed women-only prayer meetings, and authorized his wife, Lydia Andrews Finney, to lead and organize such meetings.[31]

The contribution of Methodism to the dissolution of this biblical prohibition was at the center of an 1841 essay by Lydia Maria Child in the *National Anti-Slavery Standard*. It describes her conversation with a Calvinist minister in anticipation of an impending antislavery address by Angelina Grimké several years before, in 1837. After realizing that the local schoolhouse would be unable to accommodate the anticipated throngs, the orthodox minister balked at the prospect of Grimké's speaking in the meetinghouse, quoting 1 Timothy in justification. Child proposed instead that Grimké speak in the Methodist meetinghouse, explaining that "it is common for women to speak in the Methodist church." Moreover, she acknowledges that "the sects called evangelical, were the first agitators of the woman question. . . . In modern times, the evangelical sects have highly approved of female prayer meetings. In the cause of missions and the dissemination of tracts, they have eloquently urged upon women their prodigious influence."[32] Child's essay takes particular aim at Calvinism for its conservative opposition to female religious leadership, but it bears remarking that the rise of female authority in this era was also spurred by anxieties about growing Catholic influence. Ray Billington has observed that women were disproportionately motivated by anti-Catholic fears to undertake evangelical work, and many of the organizations that gave Protestant women their start in evangelical ministry were avowedly anti-Catholic, such as the American Tract Society and the American Home Mission Society.[33] In this way, the rising authority of Protestant women derived from their effectiveness at directing potential converts toward religious beliefs compatible with American independence and away from those deemed suspiciously authoritarian.

The Second Great Awakening thus created a climate in which female religious leadership was openly debated and increasingly practiced. It consequently laid the cultural and religious groundwork for sentimental authors to engage in public efforts of evangelism by way of narratives about the benefits of conversion and Christian piety. The controversial public exhortations of such female preachers as Antoinette Brown Blackwell, Harriet Livermore, and Nancy Towle helped cushion the public's reception of sentimental literature, which, by contrast, seems a more appropriate setting for female evangelizing than the pulpit or the revival meeting. The medium of literature moderated the public, declamatory, and oral character of the pulpit, and it conveyed religious lessons in a more discreet and conventionally feminine manner: sentimental literature was merely suggestive in its proposals for reader conduct, its silence on the printed page likewise expressing a fidelity to Pauline edict. In sharp contrast with the public authority of the pulpit, literature might be composed and consumed within the private confines of the home, a setting that allowed women to maintain their womanly modesty while engaging in the public world of moral reform.[34]

Subsequent chapters will consider several instances in which the writing of sentimental literature served as a starting place for women who would later become formal religious leaders, but, at this juncture in the mid-century, literature enabled women to abide by scriptural prohibition while extending the practice of female ministry that began amid the populism of the Second Great Awakening. Despite its attestations of feminine modesty, there is no discounting the specific, overt interest of much of sentimental literature in working to spark conversion in the reader and to incite personal reform and repentance. In some instances, women's fiction explicitly aspired to perform clerical duties that had long been forbidden to women. Catharine Sedgwick, for example, was intent on using her writings to influence readers' religious views. Amid the Second Great Awakening, Sedgwick admitted to having ministerial, even prophetic ambitions for her prose, confessing in her journal in the 1830s that "when I feel that my writings have made any one happier or better, I feel an emotion of gratitude to Him who has made me the medium of blessings to my fellow-creatures. And I do feel that I am but the instrument."[35] Though raised a Calvinist, she became a Unitarian as a young adult, and her writing career began out of a desire to minister to other disenchanted Calvinists: in the 1820s she began writing a tract detailing the ills of Calvinism, only to find that the text's illustrative narrative example overtook the piece altogether, and she ended up publishing this enlarged narrative exposé as her first novel, *A New-England Tale*, in 1822. Her 1835 novel, *Home*, started similarly, at the behest of a minister who approached her with the idea of "a series of narratives, between a formal tale and a common tract, so as to present to view an image, a portrait of the Christian religion . . . and at once enlighten readers by a familiar exposition of principles, and improve them by a display of their modes of operation."[36] To that end, Sedgwick crafted a romance about a devout, loving Christian family, the Barclays, to depict Christianity as a beneficent influence on day-to-day life and as a means of effective childrearing rather than as a private belief or as an activity reserved solely for the Sabbath. And in the spirit of the Second Great Awakening, *Home* endorsed the era's democratization of religious authority, as with a scene in which the youngest Barclay, little Willie, offers the shortest sermon in a family exercise in sermon writing: "'My peoples, if you are good, you'll go to heaven; and if you an't, you won't.'" Praised by the senior Barclay as "'a *very* good sermon,'" it inspires a skeptical nonbeliever to observe the Sabbath with greater care and feeling, thereby modeling the renewed piety intended for the reader and implicitly corroborating the widespread populist belief that even the lowliest person can preach effectively.[37]

Anna Warner, a renowned hymnist and prolific sentimental novelist in her own right, used similar clerical language in describing the literary efforts of her sister, Susan Warner, author of *The Wide, Wide World* (1850). In her memoir, Anna asserts that Susan wrote "in closest reliance upon God: for thoughts, for power, and for words. Not the mere vague wish to write a book that should do service to her Master: but a vivid, constant, looking to him for guidance and help: the worker and her work both laid humbly at the Lord's feet. In that sense, the book was written upon her knees: and the Lord's blessing has followed it. . . . How many of whom even have I heard, trace their heart conversion straight to that blessing on the pages of the 'Wide, Wide World.'"[38] As she saw it, her sister was a vessel for divine communication, and the novel was a kind of sacred text, just as capable of effecting conversion as the Bible itself. Susan Warner received a wealth of letters from clergy that corroborated this perception of the novel. For example, Rev. Thomas Skinner, a prominent Presbyterian minister who oversaw the Warner sisters' conversion and who helped found the Union Theological Seminary, described *The Wide, Wide World* as a sermon of the highest order. He wrote, "The spirit in your book is the spirit of the Gospel. The teaching of it, [*sic*] is the teaching of the Evangelical Pulpit. In a legitimate way, you are preaching to the unreachable reader of Christ, and I would that you might become a preacher thereof to every creature under heaven."[39] Her novel, Skinner suggests, is more effective at preaching the gospel than is the traditional pulpit because the novel is not confined to a circumscribed physical space but, like an itinerant preacher, it can circulate and minister widely, moving into spheres otherwise inaccessible to pastoral reach.[40] In this respect, Skinner suggests that the effectiveness of Warner's novel derived from its resemblance to Methodist, revivalist clergy, who moved preaching out of the church and into the spaces of daily life.

As Dawn Coleman has shown, Harriet Beecher Stowe also actively enlisted ministerial style in *Uncle Tom's Cabin* (1852), as she thunderously urged her readers to a religious awakening.[41] An 1859 letter to Stowe from James Russell Lowell suggests that her writings continued to be perceived in a clerical vein, even after she began writing domestic fiction. Lowell wrote, "I am only honestly anxious that what I consider a very remarkable genius should have faith in itself. Let your moral take care of itself, and remember that an author's writing-desk is something infinitely higher than a pulpit." By way of example, he described a passage in a recent installment of *The Minister's Wooing* (1859) as "grand preaching and in the right way."[42] Stowe's 1871 novel, *My Wife and I*, acknowledged the novelistic assumption of clerical duties, with one character noting that the novel form has "very great power" for it "has access to us at all hours and gets itself heard as a preacher cannot."[43]

Augusta Evans's *St. Elmo* (1866) contains a scene in which the novel's heroine, the writer Edna Earl, argues with a minister about the religious appropriateness of her public writing career. In reply to the minister's assertion that she should cease writing and direct her efforts to more conventional womanly pursuits such as "the wash-tub," she replies by defending literature as a legitimate female vocation on a par with his own calling as minister: the deity, she asserts, "'will strengthen and guide me and bless my writing, even as he blesses your preaching.'"[44] Her writing, she maintains, is no less inspired by divine influence than are his own ministerial labors. As all of these instances suggest, sentimental literature seems to have been a recognized route for the execution of the female pastoral ambitions activated in the Second Great Awakening, but it did so by tempering the pulpit's unfeminine publicity by operating within a form that was both composed and consumed in silence and privacy. In this way, sentimental forms enabled women to strike an acceptable, modest balance between the uncouth publicity of Methodism and the passive silence of Calvinism

In addition to paving the way for women to offer public religious instruction, the Second Great Awakening also helped create a readership receptive to such literary works. One of the great mysteries of nineteenth-century American literary history is the unexpected spike in readership for novels about female piety in the 1850s, when such works had already been in circulation for some time. This sudden popularity is all the more puzzling because, by numerous cultural indicators, Warner's blockbuster novel, *The Wide, Wide World,* hardly seemed to have had its finger on the pulse of the zeitgeist at the time of its publication. Evangelical zeal declined after the failure of William Miller's millennialist predictions in 1843–44: the public's religious interest was diverted elsewhere, toward spiritualism, animal magnetism, phrenology, and Swedenborgian ideas, while numerous separatist communities formed in fulfillment of the communitarian teachings of the New Testament (specifically Acts 2:44–47) but did so by withdrawing into seclusion.[45] Two of the era's biggest revivalists receded from view: Lyman Beecher retired, and Charles Finney decamped to Oberlin, Ohio, for life as a seminary professor. Ralph Waldo Emerson packed lecture halls with addresses that preached the intertwined divinity of all life, regardless of denomination, and expressed skepticism about the mediations of organized religion; for instance, at Amory Hall in 1844, Emerson itemized many of these quasi-religious fads, remarking that this diffusion was "directly in the spirit and genius of the age," but he took these developments as sure signs that "the Church . . . is falling from the church nominal."[46] Amid the dissolution of evangelical fervor, Warner's manuscript was repeatedly rejected by publishers, who failed to discern a marketable project in it. The Harper brothers, for example, rejected the manuscript with the explanation of a single word, "Fudge," which succinctly conveys their skepticism about the narrative's value.[47]

But what the Harper brothers and other publishers failed to recognize is that the Second Great Awakening, which had concluded a decade before, created a huge market of evangelical women. In contrast with the first Great Awakening, in which the majority of converts had been men, the Second Great Awakening had been particularly successful at converting women, who vastly outnumbered men at revival meetings and who were twice as likely as men to be church members; observers have noted that men typically participated in revivals of the Second Great Awakening only when brought there by their wives and sisters.[48] The Second Great Awakening accordingly had numerous immediate implications for the literary history of sentimentalism. In the first place, it reconstituted Christianity as hospitable to and welcoming of women, even going so far as allowing women to assume the pulpit and preach. It created a legitimate, expansive, and intensive culture of female piety that was a necessary precondition for the production and embrace of sentimental literature on that very subject. It thus laid the cultural table, as it were, for the golden age of sentimentalism in the 1850s. At the same time, the dissolution of the Second Great Awakening left in its wake a fallow, untapped market of devout women indifferent to the various secular fads of the 1840s. The decline of the Second Great Awakening thus created an extraordinary market opportunity that Stowe, Warner, and others took advantage of, with Warner's novel alone reprinted sixty-seven times.[49] It was due primarily to the influence of a devout female reader that *The Wide, Wide World* saw print at all: upon receiving the manuscript, George Putnam deemed it unremarkable, and he gave it to his mother to read as mere "amusement"; after reading it, she replied decisively, "If you never publish another book, publish this," and her son complied, to great success.[50] As this example attests, the success of *The Wide, Wide World* is directly traceable to the sympathies, both literary and religious, of an older female generation shaped by an earlier era and less attuned to the current era's skepticism.[51]

In addition, the Second Great Awakening helped create a readership for sentimentalism by directly changing public reading tastes and judgments. In particular, it enabled a significant change in public attitudes toward the religious propriety of novelistic, melodramatic narrative. To be sure, narrative had long been used for Christian religious instruction, as with the parables attributed to Jesus in the New Testament and the allegorical travels in John Bunyan's *The Pilgrim's Progress* (1678). Despite the widespread use of narrative in Christian instruction, however, novels had tenuous status among conservative evangelicals who often denounced them as an inducement to sin, whether in fostering habits of indulgent idleness or in endearing readers to sin and immorality.[52] Lyman Beecher, for instance, forbade his children from reading fiction, although his daughter Harriet would later become one of the most influential religious novelists of the nineteenth century. Widespread campaigns of public evangelism in the Second Great Awakening led to growing recognition that absorbing narratives could prove useful in reaching the unconverted, who were disinclined to read theological works enjoining them to repent. For instance, a pamphlet circulated in 1814 extolled the particular power of narrative to engage the unconverted reader: "A plain didactic essay on a religious subject may be read by a Christian with much pleasure; but the persons for whom these Tracts are chiefly designed, will fall asleep over it. This will not do; it is throwing labour and money away. There must be something to allure the listless to read, and this can only be done by blending entertainment with instruction. Where *narrative* can be made the medium of conveying truth, it is eagerly to be embraced, as it not only engages the attention, but also assists the memory, and makes a deeper impression on the heart. *Dialogue* is another way of rendering a Tract entertaining."[53] Narrative, the author suggests, may activate the sympathies and offer gentle instruction for the secular reader more effectively than traditional religious oratory. One outcropping of this recognition was the proliferation of popular biographies narrating the pious lives and heartbreaking early deaths of devout young people, such as the *Memoirs of Miss Huldah Ann Baldwin* (1814), a form that provided the narrative kernel of premature, pious death that would prove central to so many sentimental novels and poems.[54] Religious tracts, which were widely distributed amid the anti-Catholic zeal of the Second Great Awakening, likewise relied heavily on gripping, even salacious narratives relating the dire consequences of sin and the redemptive powers of piety.[55] Although, as David Paul Nord has shown, the American Tract Society always claimed that the tales included in these tracts were true stories, these documents posited the reading of riveting narratives about the trials of believers as instrumental to conversion and piety.[56] Jane Tompkins has traced the narrative roots of sentimentalism in tract literature, observing that some of the central tropes of sentimental literature, such as the deaths of pious children, can be genetically traced to the tracts in circulation in the Second Great Awakening.[57] To be sure, the derivation of sentimentalism in tract literature suggests that, from the very outset, it was freighted with pointedly sectarian associations and ambitions; while tract literature aims specifically for the Protestant conversion of the reader, it also served as a textual gateway to the reading of pious narrative generally and sentimental literature in particular, a form that, Jane Tompkins has suggested, often offered full-length narrative amplifications of the stock tropes of tract literature. This generic debt is visible, for instance, in the commencement of Sedgwick's first novel, *A New-England Tale*, as an anti-Calvinist tract whose narrative exposition outgrew its confined length as well as the suggestion from a minister in the 1830s that she write "a series of narratives, between a formal tale and a common tract" to demonstrate the benefits of Christian piety. It is likewise apparent in the subtitle, "A Tract," given to Hannah Lee's 1837 novel, *Three Experiments of Living*, about the trials of a married couple living in poverty. The relationship between sentimentalism and tract literature seems to have been a reciprocal one, for the popularity of sentimentalism after the Second Great Awakening spurred a resurgence of tract publication by publishers hoping to capitalize on renewed public interest in such narratives of piety.[58]

The transfer of readers from one form to the next may have also been enabled by the similarity in delivery structure between the two forms. Within the circuit of female lay ministry of the era, middle-class female volunteers played a vital role in the circulation of tract literature engineered to combat Catholicism, their status affording them the time and the resources to canvas neighborhoods door-to-door and to help fill in the considerable regional gaps left by colporteurs.[59] In turn, their daytime house calls were usually received by housewives, as is evident in Susan Warner's diary entry in 1843, in which she recounts conversing only with several such women in her rounds distributing tracts.[60] Tract narratives of pious suffering therefore were often distributed from female purveyor to female consumer, a mode of transmission that implicitly carried with it the authorizing imprimatur of the larger religious organization, whether the American Tract Society or another such body. Though sentimental literature carried no such official sanction, the explicit gendering of its circulation, from female author to female reader, suggestively mirrors and evokes that of tract literature, a similarity that may have implicitly enabled the extension of authority from the tract genre to the sentimental one.[61] In addition, the authorizing penumbra of tract literature may have helped legitimize sentimental literature as an agent of Protestant evangelism and enable it to evade the long-standing censure against fiction, novels in particular. In telling factual stories of drunken license and fatally ill children, tract literature occasionally bordered on impropriety by exposing to public view the unfortunate and often shameful sufferings of others. Its exhibitionism and sensationalistic content positioned the tract at the perimeter of acceptable taste, a conflict between evangelistic zeal and etiquette that sentimentalism, its narrative descendant, neatly resolves. Though fiction had been denounced as an inducement to sin, the context of tract literature presents sentimental fictionality as an honorable concession to taste and discretion by preserving the privacy of anguished sinners and troubled households. Fiction, that is, drops the veil of respectability over the outré contents of tract narrative, mediating between evangelism and wholesomeness.

There is yet another feature of the Second Great Awakening that may have contributed to the readership of sentimental literature: the biographical allure of sentimental stock narrative for readers who themselves experienced the Awakening. It is a truism that sentimental fiction habitually narrates the travails of itinerant young people separated from their families and who develop devout religious faith in their efforts to reconstitute community. Narratives in this vein pervade the genre, including Warner's *The Wide, Wide, World*, Maria Susanna Cummins's *The Lamplighter* (1854), Martha Finley's *Elsie Dinsmore* (1867), Augusta Evan's *St. Elmo*, and Stowe's *Poganuc People* (1878).

Even significant narrative departures or parodies of the genre, such as E. D. E. N. Southworth's *The Hidden Hand* (1859) and Caroline Chesebro's *Isa* (1852), likewise build on this narrative trope. In the 1993 introduction to the second edition of her 1978 foundational study, *Woman's Fiction*, Nina Baym reiterated the centrality of this narrative to the form, distilling the entire genre of "woman's fiction" of the mid-century as narratives "about a young woman who has lost the emotional and financial support of her legal guardians—indeed who is often subject to their abuse and neglect—but who nevertheless goes on to win her own way in the world."[62] As Baym affirms, this narrative has provided the central structure on which so much sentimental fiction is scaffolded.

Despite what one critic has termed the "dehistoricizing logic" of sentimental literature, the context of the Second Great Awakening allows us to recognize this stock narrative as an evocative depiction of the social and economic circumstances that precipitated widespread female participation in this era of unprecedented religious activity.[63] In her reconstruction of early American women's history, Nancy Cott has argued that the preponderance of women in the Second Great Awakening derived in part from the widespread displacement of young women from their customary station in the traditional household economy. With the mechanization of textile manufacture in the second quarter of the nineteenth century, she argues, young women lost their traditional domestic responsibilities of carding, spinning, and weaving; without any means of contributing to the household economy, young women left their homes in large numbers in the hopes of finding work elsewhere, whether at these new mills or in domestic labor. Thus dislocated from their homes and without the stewardship of parents, young women, Cott notes, were particularly receptive to the pervasive religious activity of the era in an effort to replace the communities and moral guidance they left behind at home.[64] This scenario strikingly echoes the plots of countless sentimental novels, which recount the susceptibility of nomadic young women, often separated from their families for economic reasons, to the religious instruction of those whom they encounter on their journeys and whose new faiths allow them to create a surrogate community of coreligionists.[65] In depicting the dislocation of so many young women in that era, sentimental literature thus recounted the social circumstances that enabled the religious faith of innumerable female readers during their youths. This narrative accordingly enabled sentimentalism to describe the historical conditions that enabled its own production and readership. That is, this narrative evocation of female experience during the Second Great Awakening provides an etiology of sentimentalism itself: it describes the conditions that created its own readership of devout women. It is thus little wonder that so many women would embrace a genre that documented their own life experiences and beliefs.

The Doctrinal Foundations of Sentimentality

With their depiction of domestic orisons and substitution of private counsel for public exhortation, sentimental literary texts may seem like a repudiation of the public, histrionic character of the Second Great Awakening.[66] Some of the central women writers of the sentimental movement did express distaste for revival meetings and the tenacious evangelizing of the era. Catharine Sedgwick, for example, admitted feeling annoyance with the efforts of missionaries who, she intimates, make nuisances of themselves while trying to incite conversion.[67] Harriet Beecher Stowe was equally ambivalent. Though her father, Lyman Beecher, was a renowned revivalist, she portrayed camp meetings in her 1856 novel *Dred: A Tale of the Great Dismal Swamp* as vulgar public spectacles unsupported by sincere belief or ethics. Susan Warner seems to have been equally wary of this phenomenon. Though she and her sister were for decades close friends with Methodist circuit rider and minister Benjamin Adams, they rebuffed his strenuous efforts to get them to attend a revival meeting, preferring instead their own private domestic devotions.[68]

Despite this aversion, the signature attribute for which sentimentalism was best known—namely, its explicit emotionalism—was the direct product of revivalism, which provided the constituent features of the sentimental constitution of emotion and without which sentimentalism's depictions and solicitations of powerful emotion might never have found a hospitable reception among contemporary readers. Though sentimental literature moved these expressions of emotion out of the public setting of the revival meeting and depicted them firmly ensconced instead within the private domain, they nonetheless adopted these new religious ideas of the moral significance of emotion. From Elsie Dinsmore's uncontrollable bouts of weeping to the abject despair of Alice Cary's poem "Life," no feature of literary sentimentalism has received fuller scholarly attention than its overt affective designs, with its many heartrending scenes of suffering and its designs to elicit a mimetic emotional response from the reader. Its very name betokening its apparent avowal of extravagant emotionalism, sentimental literature was derided for these

profusions of feeling, as with, for example, Fred Louis Pattee's characteriza-
tion of sentimentalism as "a tearful flood of poems and novels."[69] In one of the
earliest studies of sentimentalism, Herbert Ross Brown in 1940 asserted that
readers of sentimentalism were "exquisite devotees of the cult of the 'hanky'
and the tear."[70] Helen Papashvily in 1956 likewise marveled at the "conta-
gious, almost epidemic, melancholia" of Warner's *The Wide, Wide World.*[71]
More recently, such scholars as Elizabeth Barnes, Glenn Hendler, June Howard, Mary Louise Kete, Dana Luciano, and Marianne Noble have sought to
recover sentimentalism from the invective or, even worse, total disregard of
realist-modernist critics inclined to discount the genre for its expressions of
feeling, a critical posture Philip Fisher attributes to the "struggle against sentimentality [that] is so closely identified with the modern period."[72] Joanne
Dobson has suggested that the sentimental preoccupation with emotion registers a "primary vision of human connection in a dehumanized world," and
Karen Sánchez-Eppler has likewise affirmed that "reading sentimental fiction
is . . . a bodily act, and the success of a story is gauged, in part, by its ability
to translate words into heartbeats and sobs."[73] Lauren Berlant has recently
argued that the sentimental regard for "the authority of true feeling" nonetheless extends well into the twentieth century, evident in cinematic melodrama
of the twentieth century.[74]

   In recent years, the study of the intellectual origins of sentimentality has
focused on its derivation in eighteenth-century moral philosophy; more recently, Abram Van Engen has sought to trace its origins even further back,
into seventeenth-century theology.[75] A thorough account of the intellectual foundations of sentiment necessitates the addition of contemporary
nineteenth-century religious practice and belief into this enterprise of historical genealogy. To read sentimentality within the context of revivalism is
to see how closely these texts adhere both to the period's designation of affect
as the seat of the religious life and to the protocols instituted by revivalists to
elicit such feeling within worshippers. Revivalists of the Second Great Awakening fashioned a "set of emotional scripts," to use June Howard's phrase, that
altered public understandings of the religious significance of emotions and
that governed the patterns of sentimentality in these texts.[76]

   The sentimental adoption of revivalist attitudes toward emotion has a
number of implications. As I will show, the revivalist celebration of emotion
figured prominently in the era's climate of anti-clerical religious populism,
and it thus contributed directly to the era's campaigns against authoritarian
denominations. And just as this campaign enabled Protestant women to as-

sume new duties and authority, so revivalist understandings of emotion also provided a particularly gendered justification for women and girls alike to assume such roles, for it was believed that no one was more adept at feeling strong emotion than they. Consequently, the adoption of revivalist emotion in sentimental texts constitutes another means by which these texts both participated in sectarian factionalism and imputed religious authority to women. In particular, sentimental literary texts themselves often employed the very techniques favored by revivalist preachers to incite feeling in worshippers and spark conversion; sentimental texts not only narrate the allocation of religious authority to girls and women but also assume this paramount clerical duty by working to stimulate emotion and conversion in the reader.

First, however, this religious context merits some explanation. Amid early nineteenth-century populism and skepticism about religious authority, the Second Great Awakening overturned long-standing Calvinist skepticism about emotion. Because of the interlocking beliefs that emotions are vulnerable to influence and that the intellect is a more exacting judge of theological merit, Calvinist ministers traditionally reserved the emotional or behavioral "applications" of their sermons to the very end, after elaborate argument and scriptural interpretation established the intellectual credentials for these latter assertions. Religious convictions in the orthodox tradition required prolonged study and deliberation, and, by the same token, sudden surges or changes in religious feeling were taken as evidence of enthusiasm rather than sincere conversion.[77] This attitude fell precipitously out of favor in the Second Great Awakening, which interpreted intellectuality not only as elitist and thus inherently undemocratic but also as inimical to the genuine religious feeling Calvinists believed would emerge from intellectual persuasion. In contrast with the Calvinist belief that the intellect was the gateway to conversion, revivalists maintained instead that conversion could be triggered solely through emotion, and, because it could be activated without any previous intellectual knowledge of scripture or denominational affiliation, conversion could be available to literally anyone, without the approval of clerical sanction. While this new tactic overturned long-standing Calvinist safeguards, it also implicitly constituted a critique of Catholicism, which required potential converts to undergo instruction, participate in rites, and provide supporting documentation. For revivalists, one need only feel genuine religious emotion in order to convert and become a Christian, a requirement that stood as a silent rebuke to denominations ruled by the exacting supervision of clergy.

The new emphasis on emotionalism originated in Methodist evangelicalism but found its most influential public advocate in Charles Finney, the leading revivalist of the 1820s and 1830s, who openly questioned the value of the intellect in fostering sincere faith. The catechizing and study that had for so long been required for orthodox church membership, he claimed, were authoritarian impediments to faith rather than instruments of it; the church should be composed, he argued, of the most emotionally earnest, and not the most knowledgeable, in their professions of faith, a criterion that made church membership more readily available to the populace than did the orthodox insistence on both knowledge and conversion. He summarized this distinction in an 1827 sermon: "We have reason to believe," he averred, "that holy angels and devils apprehend and embrace *intellectually* the same truths, and yet how differently are they affected by them. . . . The difference in the effect consists [in] the heart or affections . . . truths to which the experience of every man will testify."[78] According to Finney, theological knowledge on its own merits by no means implied sincere Christian conviction, and one could pass the traditional theological examination without a shred of actual belief. He continued this argument in his *Lectures on Revivals of Religion* (1835), claiming that the "devil is an intellectual believer, and that is what makes him tremble."[79] To know something intellectually, he maintained, was not necessarily to accept or to live by it, whereas feelings register a level of conviction and commitment that mere knowledge or understanding alone could never transmit.[80] Rather, for Finney and the era's legion of uneducated, self-taught preachers, one had only to have strong feelings to be converted to Christianity, and the sudden, overwrought feelings once disputed by Calvinist clergy now came to evidence sincerity and repentance.

Susan Warner experienced this transition firsthand. In 1841, she and her sister, Anna, decided to become members of the Mercer Street Presbyterian Church in New York. As was customary in the orthodox tradition, they were questioned by the minister about their beliefs and knowledge, and they responded to each question with either silence or an admission of ignorance.[81] Under normal circumstances, they probably would have been refused membership, but the minister, the previously mentioned Rev. Thomas Skinner, had already distinguished himself as a pioneer of the Presbyterian New School and thus was open to many of the revivalistic "new measures," as they were called. Where other ministers might have seen ignorance and rashness, Skinner instead saw intense religious feeling, and the sisters were accepted as church members. As Anna Warner described it over sixty years later, Skinner "kept [his] search very close to the personal side of religion; what it was to us, what we were willing it should be": that is, he cared more about how they felt than about what they knew.[82]

Revivalism aimed above all else to kindle the strong torrents of emotion that provided an essential precondition of conversion, and such popular preachers as Francis Asbury and Lorenzo Dow did so by banishing theology from their sermons and relying instead on explicit emotionalism, publicly weeping in front of hundreds of people to model the affective personal reaction they aimed to spark in their listeners.[83] This technique was openly populist, as it eliminated theological cerebrations that might be accessible solely to an educated minority and appealed instead to the common denominator of emotion. To stimulate a conversion-inducing emotional state, revivalist preachers often resorted to publicly censuring individual audience members, condemning their life decisions, and commenting with some specificity on their sins. Audiences responded in kind with candid expressions of feeling, whether by publicly exclaiming with grief or joy, praying aloud, or weeping openly for their souls. It was in this milieu that evangelicalism came to be known as the "religion of the heart," a faith born not from the intellect but from emotional experience.[84] Critics have speculated that this evangelical emotionalism contributed to the strong presence of women in the Second Great Awakening, hypothesizing that, in emphasizing an already-gendered sphere of experience, this new practice both rendered the church appealing to women and ascribed new religious authority to women, who were presumably better able than men to fulfill these new affective expectations.[85]

Sentimental texts categorically broke with orthodox tradition by incorporating nineteenth-century evangelical attitudes toward emotions. The theological examination that traditionally preceded church membership is totally expunged from sentimental literature, and it is replaced instead with scenes of weeping, prayer, and resolution.[86] As was increasingly the case in the Second Great Awakening, the only criterion of conversion in sentimental literature was sincere, deep feeling.[87] In this religious setting, tears are a potent signifier, expressing externally the inward turmoil, repentance, and humility obligatory to conversion but invisible because of their seclusion within the confines of the human heart. Whereas mere words or verbal professions of faith can be easily counterfeited, it was believed that tears, as outward excretions of the unseen workings of the heart, metonymically affirmed the sincerity of these private convictions.[88] Tears in sentimental literature often function in just this way, outwardly expressing the internal, and thus imperceptible, conviction of the devout believer: for example, in Susan Warner's novel *Queechy* (1852), the best-selling follow-up to *The Wide, Wide World*, the heroine Fleda Ringgan weeps while evangelizing to her unbelieving aunt: "The mixture of feelings was too much for Fleda . . . and she wept aloud . . . with her very heart gushing out at these words, '*dear* aunty,' " she implores, " 'Christ came for such sinners—for just such as you and I.' "[89] Fleda's irrepressible tears here serve as evidence of her private feelings, and, in sparking sympathy in her aunt, they presumably inspire religious sentiment in her audience and enable her to assume the work of the revivalist, whose own public tears are designed to trigger feeling and conversion in the audience.

The use of emotion to assume ministerial authority is also evident in the concluding remarks of Harriet Beecher Stowe's *Uncle Tom's Cabin*, in which she famously enjoined her readers to "*feel right*," urging them to examine their feelings: "See, then, to your sympathies in this matter! Are they in harmony with the sympathies of Christ?"[90] Dawn Coleman has observed that Stowe in *Uncle Tom's Cabin* uses the exhortatory language of the evangelical preacher intent on rousing an audience, and this register is nowhere more visible than in her imperative command that her reader "feel right." The reader, she claims, should evaluate and adjust her feelings to ensure that she is righteous and fully converted; only then may she hope to enact the divine will. In inciting her readers to an emotional self-examination, Stowe replicates the evangelical convention of "baptism through tears": through feelings, we are reformed, renewed, and inducted into a new community of fellow believers.

Sentimental literary texts undertook ministerial duties by employing yet another common revivalist technique. While tears both incite and corroborate conversion, they were also believed to serve as tangible, empirical evidence of the emotional imbalance and frustration believed to be characteristic of unbelievers in need of such conviction. William James has observed that religious conversion is often preceded by a period of grave discontent characterized by feeling "inwardly vile and wrong" or "a sense of incompleteness."[91] These feelings of despondency, it was believed, confirm the individual's utter helplessness and consequent need for divine help and mercy.[92] In the revivalist setting, preachers primed their listeners for conversion by instilling such feelings of unhappiness and did so by several different techniques: reminding them of their sins and moral failings, recounting poignant stories of loss and grief, or describing their own conversion, detailing their own experiences with unhappiness and the relief afforded by surrendering their cares to a loving redeemer. In all these cases, the public expression of grief signaled a borderline state of emotional readiness for conversion. Sentimental texts adopted this revivalist belief in their frequent depiction of the profusion of grief typically endured by the sentimental heroine before her conversion, her sorrow signaling both her disbelief in the consoling promise of an eternal life and her egocentric defiance of divine providence.

This dynamic is visible in Augusta Evans's *Beulah* (1859) when the novel's heroine, the orphan Beulah, is rebuked by her guardian, Dr. Hartwell, for her uncontrollable weeping over the uncertain future of her beloved friend Eugene, an emotional state that he, in accord with contemporary religious contexts, interprets as an indication of the insufficiency of her religious faith. He instructs her to stop crying and deport herself in ways that express her trust in the divine: "'Get up and be satisfied, and eat your breakfast,'" he commands. "'You have asked [the deity] to save and protect Eugene, and, according to the Bible, He will certainly do it; so no more tears. If you believe in your God, what are you so wretched about?'"[93] In the course of the novel, Beulah's emotional continence increases in direct proportion to her growing religious faith. In Madeline Leslie's *The Household Angel in Disguise* (1857), the kindly Mrs. Stanley attributes her own former unrestrained anguish to "an unsubmissive spirit" and her "rebelling against the afflictions God, in his wisdom, saw to be needed by me." Her emotional excesses, she understands retrospectively, signaled her need for the equanimity and poise that can only be achieved through obedience to the divine will.[94] Warner's *The Wide, Wide World* provides another illustrative case in point. Ellen Montgomery is emotionally volatile before her conversion to Christianity, weeping at the slightest provocation, whether for her lost mother, her inability to attend school, or her regular conflicts with her irascible aunt. Within the emotional idiom of revivalism, her weeping communicates her need for conversion, and Warner complies with this expectation with the insertion of numerous scenes in which Ellen's grief invites the ministrations of several pious strangers, who interpret her emotional instability as an invitation to evangelize and consequently offer her spiritual counsel. And in further compliance with the conventions of evangelicalism, Ellen's conversion renders her more stable and better able to endure daily trials with greater equanimity.

In addition to depicting the uses of emotion in effecting conversion, sentimental texts themselves employed these techniques in attempting to incite a similar response in the reader. According to Joycelyn Moody, "The purpose of sentimentality is to induce a *process* by which the reader's desire for psychic union with characters and tropes is aroused, particularly as these objects function as embodiments . . . of some moral virtue, Christian concept . . . that readers want to manifest or affirm in themselves."[95] The process that Moody describes was made possible by emotional mimesis and readerly identification. Sympathy with the travails of the heroine was a potent method of manufacturing grief in the reader, for scenes of loss and heartbreaking separation worked to instill in the reader the liminal feelings of grief that typically border conversion. If the reader is able to forge a compassionate identification with the heroine, she is also implicitly invited to take a similar moral inventory of her character and to recognize her own sinfulness and need for divine help. In inviting the reader to feel sympathetic sorrow, sentimental writers replicate the dynamics of sympathetic spectatorship employed by revivalist preachers to engender an emotional state ripe for conversion. In both settings, the observer—whether the revivalist audience or the reader—witnesses a public display of suffering and encounters a narration of conversion, whether that of the heroine or the preacher. Both media, the revival meeting and the sentimental narrative, strive for conversion by propelling the audience toward a state of compassionate self-recognition.

The sentimental provocation of conversion also relied heavily on another contemporary practice popularized in revival meetings. This practice, known as witnessing, derives from the conversion narratives that were requisite to Calvinist orthodoxy and that Sandra Gustafson has discerned as a generic source for sentimental fiction.[96] In the act of witnessing, believers publicly recount their conversion and testify to the transformative powers of Christianity in their lives. But whereas the conversion narrative was designed chiefly to affirm its own legitimacy, the Methodist practice of witnessing had explicit designs on the audience: the aim of this public act of testimony is not only to attest to divine might and compassion but also to convert unbelieving listeners. In hearing the speaker recount his or her worldly ordeals and the relief engendered by conversion, the listener is encouraged to identify with the speaker's story to a degree that he or she undergoes the same emotional transition from sorrow to joy at the sudden consciousness of divine love and mercy.[97] In her study of contemporary practices of witnessing, Susan Harding argues that the narrative of conversion "is not just a monologue that constitutes its speakers. . . . [Rather,] it is a dialogue that reconstitutes its listeners." "At the moment of salvation," she continues, the listener undergoes her own conversion experience and in so doing "becomes a speaker" of her own analogous tale, which she will at a later date transmit in the hopes of sparking a similar change of heart in her audience.[98] Sympathetic identification here may not only reform the audience's character and communal commitments, as numerous scholars have suggested, but it may also enable soteriological salvation: through narrative sympathy, that is, one may be converted and redeemed.

Sentimental narrative contains innumerable examples of witnessing, as characters recount their own conversion experiences to listeners who then reenact these stories through their own corresponding emotional awakenings. For example, in Maria Susanna Cummins's *The Lamplighter*, Emily Graham relays the story of her conversion to Gertrude Flint, who immediately feels "her heart penetrated with that deep love and trust" of the Lord, a scene that depicts the transmission of faith from speaker to audience through the very act of narration.[99] Likewise, in Alcott's *Little Women*, Mrs. March describes the contributions of religious belief to her lifelong struggle to achieve self-control, a lesson she hopes her listener, her unruly daughter Jo, will emulate. These interpolated episodes of narration function as meta-textual references to the larger function and object of the novels themselves, which likewise aim to use narratives of conversion to effect change in the reader. Having read and been transformed by these texts, the reader, it is presumed, will have her own conversion narrative to tell, and in this way the sentimental novel transforms the reader into an author, an infinite circuit of narrative generation and evangelical circulation. As Paul Griffiths has asserted, "To be religious is to give an account . . . to tell a story about it," and sentimental literature is constructed so as to transform the reader into an author.[100]

The Doctrinal Contents of Sentimentalism

The indebtedness of sentimentalism to the Second Great Awakening is extensive, and virtually every constituent feature of sentimental piety—with its scenes of private prayer, solitary Bible reading, and quiet counsel—is the direct product of that era. The common feature among the new tenets embraced by sentimentalism is their shared promotion of religious autonomy freed from the intrusion of ecclesiastical rule. This quality is particularly evident in the sentimental embrace of the signature tenet of the Second Great Awakening and of Methodism itself, which is the theology of Arminianism. For centuries, North American Protestantism had been dominated by the Calvinist conviction that human beings are entirely depraved and deserving of eternal punishment; salvation is wholly dependent upon divine grace, and the deity alone determines who will be saved from damnation and cannot be swayed by one's conduct or repentance. Within this worldview, neither faith nor works yield any direct reward from the divine, and the Christian is entirely powerless in effecting his or her own salvation. Arminianism runs counter to this belief and is thus heretical in the Reformed tradition. Developed by sixteenth-century Dutch theologian Jacobus Arminius, Arminianism enjoyed a revival in the eighteenth century through the advocacy of John Wesley, who concurred that salvation need not be entirely contingent upon divine grace; rather, he maintained that human agency, will, and commitment may instigate conversion and reform. The rapid spread of Methodism in the late eighteenth and early nineteenth centuries widely circulated the Arminian belief in religious self-determination, what Jean Miller Schmidt has termed "radical spiritual egalitarianism."[101] While Arminianism overtly rejected Calvinist orthodoxy, its new popularity in the first half of the nineteenth century was also facilitated by widespread Protestant antipathy for Catholicism. In an era preoccupied with the seeming despotism of Catholicism, Arminianism functioned as a popular Protestant foil for Catholicism because of its advocacy of personal religious sovereignty.

This heretical doctrine found a potent advocate in Charles Finney, who, as a Presbyterian, had been indoctrinated in orthodoxy but gradually came to preach Arminianism and sever his ties with Presbyterianism.[102] According to Finney, Calvinism ran at cross-purposes with evangelical revivalism because it promoted bovine passivity, since one could only wait, hope, and look for external signs of one's election. In the place of this learned helplessness, Finney promoted an active, inclusive Christianity born out of the Arminian belief that salvation is available to anyone willing to pray, repent, and accept Christ.[103] While he conceded that these human capacities are due entirely to divine grace, he nonetheless maintained that "*religion is the work of man*" and that an overemphasis on Calvinist teachings will result only in "Antinomianism in the church, and sinners [hiding] themselves behind the delusion that they can do nothing."[104] Perry Miller summarized the populist flavor of Finneyite Arminianism by dubbing it "wholly American: everybody *can* help it."[105] As Finney himself put it, " 'Don't wait for feeling, DO IT.' "[106]

Though Sedgwick, Stowe, and Warner were all raised in the orthodox tradition, all three would come to abandon its core teachings and publish works that depict human will, agency, and action as contributing directly to Christian faith and salvation.[107] Marianne Noble has indexed the residual traces of Calvinist conceptions of matrimony in sentimental literature, but it bears stressing that the doctrines of predestination and election are nowhere taken seriously in the sentimentalist worldview, although they are the subject of some mockery in texts like Sedgwick's *New-England Tale*, Stowe's *The Minister's Wooing* and *My Wife and I*, and Warner's *The Old Helmet* (1863).[108] Otherwise, the resurgent Arminian belief in religious self-determination everywhere pervades sentimental piety: Christian faith, salvation, and regeneracy are available to everyone in sentimental literature, regardless of character or personal history, and sentimental texts typically depict salvation as the result not of a sudden conversion experience but of a resolute determination to become a Christian. For example, Nina Gordon, the heroine of Stowe's *Dred*, becomes a Christian after protracted efforts: doctrinal inquiries, Bible reading, and conversation with a devout believer. In addition, her conversion is ratified by the change in her character from flighty belle to selfless altruist, intent on abolishing slavery and helping the victims of a cholera epidemic. Similarly, Ellen Montgomery in Warner's *The Wide, Wide World* embarks on an active campaign of Christian self-improvement: she sets aside time to pray and read the Bible, learns with difficulty to hold her tongue, and resolves to behave kindly when she would prefer to rebel, although on occasion she backslides into her former misconduct. The Christian life, both Stowe and Warner suggest, is a systematic process executed through diligence and strenuous effort.

On occasion, sentimental texts explicitly announced their sympathies with Arminianism. For instance, Caroline Chesebro's novel about seventeenth-century Puritan settlers, *Victoria* (1856), early on establishes its investment in Arminian self-reliance. While en route to the New World, the pious schoolteacher Margaret Gladstone offers religious encouragement to a fellow traveler skeptical of the Calvinist doctrine of election. In response to his observation that, according to orthodoxy, "none can follow Him except those whom He permits," Margaret invites him to "be sure that you elect yourself"; he should not wait passively for divine confirmation but should assume responsibility for his own salvation.[109] In *Woman in America* (1850), Maria McIntosh affirmed a belief in Arminianism, declaiming, "Thou art free; free to develop thyself as thy will shall prompt, and thy powers permit. This world is God's world, and He hath given thee so much of it as thou, with thy best faculties, canst conquer."[110] Similarly, in *Queechy*, Susan Warner clearly outlined her belief in an activist, participatory Christianity through a conversation between the heroine, Fleda, and the unbelieving Mr. Carleton:

"But if that be so, Elfie, God can make them all good without our help?"

"Yes, but I suppose he chooses to do it with our help, Mr. Carleton . . ."

"But is not this what you speak of," said he, half smiling,—"rather the business of clergymen? you have nothing to do with it?"

"No," said Fleda,—"everybody has something to do with it, the Bible says so; ministers must do it in their way and other people in other ways; everybody has his own work."[111]

The salvific, reforming powers of Christianity cannot take place without the determined participation of the believer. In her many novels about the devout Christian life, Warner repeatedly stresses that the Christian life is the result of effortful habits, will power, and self-control, and not the effortless divine gift of election. In *Say and Seal* (1860), a novel she coauthored with her sister Anna, Warner defines a Christian as "one who, trusting in Christ as his only Saviour, thenceforth obeys Him as his only King."[112] That is, a Christian is defined by his or her freely chosen actions. Though characters in sentimental narrative may be powerless over some of their life circumstances, their religious life is something they can and should have total control over, a belief that can also be understood as signaling a decisive repudiation of both Calvinism and Catholicism.

At the same time, the sentimental advocacy of Arminianism provided theological justification for the dramatic redistribution of religious authority that recurs throughout sentimental literature. Though clergy frequently appear in sentimental texts as husbands, fathers, and potential suitors, they are rarely depicted as capable religious stewards deserving of obedience.[113] On occasion, sentimental texts engaged directly with contemporary populist skepticism about the overweening power of clergy, as with Maria McIntosh's *Charms and Counter-Charms* (1848), in which the character Euston Hastings aggressively challenges the authority of clergy, asking, "Do you think . . . that the promise made to a man who has been decorated by a certain dress and called a priest, will be more binding on us than those which we have made to each other, when all else on earth was forgotten,—or that I shall love you better for having stood beside you in a building, which they call a church, and told others than you were dear to me?"[114] Stowe, too, portrayed Calvinist clergy, in both *The Minister's Wooing* and *Sam Lawson's Oldtown Fireside Stories* (1871), as so absorbed in rarefied intellectual questions that they are unable to counsel their parishioners, and in *Agnes of Sorrento* (1862), she rendered Catholic priests as lascivious, deceitful rakes. Generally, however, contemporary anti-clericalism surfaces in the recurring suggestion in sentimentalism that clergy are altogether peripheral to religious observance, and sentimental texts depict a world in which clergy have already been demoted from their supernal religious authority and are, for the most part, irrelevant to the religious lives of girls and women. Alcott's *Little Women* is an instructive example: though the March family patriarch is a minister, neither his wife nor children attend church or practice religion in any formal way other than reading and attempting to apply the lessons of *The Pilgrim's Progress* and the Bible. Nor are the duties of clergy in administering sacraments or rites in any way necessary in sentimental literature to a faithful Christian life: new converts need not undergo any rites of initiation such as baptism, nor are they required to attend church to be devout Christians. In fact, church attendance repeatedly appears in sentimental literature as a formality of questionable motive or even as an actual impediment to true piety. For example, the irreligious Lindsays in *The Wide, Wide World* attend church as a public performance of virtue but frown on all sincere private devotions, such as domestic hymn singing and prayer.

This is not to suggest, however, that sentimental literature propounded a laissez-faire attitude toward piety, in which worshippers are left to devise their own beliefs and practices. On the contrary, the implicit anti-clericalism of sentimental texts often functions as a convenient opportunity for the reallocation of that authority elsewhere. In conformity with the contemporary dispersal of clerical roles to common citizens, sentimental texts repeatedly attribute religious authority to girls and women whose chief qualification is not specialized training or ordination but experience with trials and sympathetic identification with the sufferings of others.[115] Examples of this phenomenon abound in sentimental literature. For instance, in *The Wide, Wide World*, it is Alice Humphreys—and not her minister father, who throughout the novel remains secluded in his study—who chiefly provides religious instruction to Ellen Montgomery, a role that Emily Graham also plays for Gerty Flint in Maria Cummins's *The Lamplighter*. Elizabeth Stuart Phelps's *The Gates Ajar* (1868) follows a similar trajectory: the Calvinist minister's orthodox severity causes Mary Cabot to despair after the Civil War death of her brother, a condition rectified only by the attentive, sympathetic ministry offered by her aunt Winifred. This attribution of religious authority to women is more common in sentimental novels situated within a Protestant

context. In texts that criticize Catholic clergy, women do not typically function as kindly alternatives to faulty clergy: because women in Catholicism
may assume formal religious authority as nuns and abbesses, they are often
as equally flawed as priests. Their faults provide compounding evidence in
these texts of the failings of clergy and of Catholicism in particular for effecting the corruption of pious women.

The use of contemporary theology to validate female religious authority
also underlay the sentimental adoption of another emergent religious tenet,
which, unlike Arminianism, failed to take root in American Protestant culture, although for several decades in the nineteenth century it was popular
and influential. Sentimental literary texts often depict an "angel in the home,"
to use the nineteenth-century term: a devout female believer whose unwav-
ering piety and altruism render her faultless and even incapable of sin. Such
figures include Mrs. Vawse in Warner's *The Wide, Wide World* and Emily
Graham in Cummins's *The Lamplighter*, and these women constitute the apotheosis of female piety in sentimental literature, whose example serves as a
source of inspiration for the novels' heroines and presumably for the reader as
well. This stock figure of sentimentalism has been the subject of some scholarly scrutiny, as with Barbara Welter's analysis of its centrality to "the cult
of true womanhood," the nineteenth-century idealization of femininity that
found its fullest expression in sentimental literature, and with the consid-
erations of Marianne Noble and Laura Wexler into the power dynamics of
female self-sacrifice and disembodiment.[116] This signature feature of sentimental piety constitutes a literary elaboration of a contemporary theological
idea in wide circulation in the first half of the nineteenth century and which,
in the hands of sentimental writers, provided a route by which women could
acquire supernal, even divine authority unrivaled even by clergy.

This belief, which was termed Christian perfectionism, acquired ample
circulation through the spread of Methodism. In the 1740s John Wesley came
to believe that the Christian must dedicate him- or herself so fully as to effect a complete transformation of character: as he described it, "'Love has
purified [the genuine Christian's] heart from envy, malice, wrath, and every
unkind temper. It has cleansed him from pride, whereof 'only cometh contention;' . . . His one intention at all times and in all places is, not to please
himself, but Him whom his soul loveth. . . . There is not a motion in his heart
but is according to His will. Every thought that arises points to Him, and is
in 'obedience to the law of Christ.'"[117] Perfectionism broke with the Calvinist
belief in the total depravity of human beings to claim instead that human

beings might perfect themselves by giving themselves over completely to the divine.[118] Perfectionist theologians of the Second Great Awakening such as Charles Finney, John Fletcher, Asa Mahan, and George Peck asserted that the believer should commune so fully with the divine that he or she becomes a kind of mystic filled with boundless love who intuitively knows the divine will and automatically performs the work of the deity.[119] As a logical extension of Arminian belief, this state was thought to be achievable through the dedicated exertions of the believer, who would be rendered saintly through sheer force of will and diligence, an assumption that revealed the less saintly, by default, to be insufficiently devoted. Perfectionism was both anti-hierarchical and populist, for it provided a route, albeit a demanding one, by which any believer, regardless of social rank, might develop saintliness and become an agent of the divine will in possession of supreme religious authority. And in contrast with Calvinism and Catholicism, perfectionism could be cultivated privately and without the permission or intervention of clergy. Charles Finney summarized the expectation bluntly when he pronounced that Christians "*should aim at being perfect.* . . . It is one thing to *profess to be perfect*, and another thing to profess and feel that you *ought to be perfect.* . . . But it is the duty of all to *aim* at being perfect."[120] Harriet Beecher Stowe endorsed perfectionism in an essay published in the *Christian Diadem* in which she urged Christians to attain "a state in which the mind is so bent and absorbed by the love of Christ, that all inducements to worldliness lose their power, and the mind becomes as indifferent to them as a dead body to physical allurements." Moreover, this condition, she maintained, should become "the common experience of all Christians."[121]

The doctrine in its original formulation by John Wesley was not explicitly gendered or understood as having particular uses for women, but it was nonetheless embraced in sentimental texts to defend both the demotion of ordained clergy and the attribution of religious authority to American lay women, despite their lack of credentialing qualification. Though it was rarely acknowledged explicitly, the new doctrine of perfectionism underlay the transformative powers of faith in sentimental literature, in which Christian belief transforms sinners into idealized models of piety. In sentimental texts, it is concentrated belief, and not ritual performance or the benison of clergy, that enables girls and women to become models of religious wisdom capable of providing effective ministry to those around them.

Cummins's best-selling *Lamplighter* registers the influence of perfectionism on sentimental depictions of female religious authority. At the center of the novel is the transformation of Gertrude Flint, who over the course of the narrative changes from an unruly, homeless waif into an elegant Christian woman who acts with reflexive kindness and selflessness. Though she does not aspire to religious leadership, her example of Christian virtue inspires other characters in the novel to imitate her by seeking greater religious devotion, a chain of transmission that appoints the saintly, unassuming Christian woman as a compelling source of religious influence. Cummins repeatedly describes Gerty as "perfect," a term whose theological connotations contemporary readers likely recognized. One character describes Gertrude as a "perfect lady"; another remarks that her companionship affords "perfect rest" and her home a model of "perfect neatness and order," and so on.[122] Gerty's status as a paragon of Christian perfectionism is made plain in the epigraph prefacing the novel's twentieth chapter, when Cummins picks up the thread of Gerty's story after a lapse of several years, during which time Gerty has undergone steady Christian instruction. Cummins frames this transformation within a religious context by preceding it with an epigraph from William Wordsworth's poem "She Was a Phantom of Delight":

> A perfect woman, nobly planned,
> To warn, to comfort, and command,
> And yet a spirit still, and bright,
> With something of an angel light.[123]

This excerpt visibly invokes the nineteenth-century trope of the woman as the "angel in the home," selfless and devoted to the care of others, but this excerpt, too, suggests that the angelic, saintly woman who personifies Christian perfection occupies a position of authority, for she may both "warn" and "command."

Though it was optimistic in its hopes for the potential and power of human beings, perfectionism caused great anxiety for adherents worried about their capacity to reach these high standards, and, in positing perfectionism as an ideal state worthy of emulation, sentimental texts likely contributed to readers' anguish at their inability to achieve such heights of holiness. Idealistic and oppressive in equal parts, perfectionism imposed insuperable moral and behavioral standards on believers, who were expected not only to behave with total correctness but also to root out any antisocial thoughts or emotions. Catharine Sedgwick in 1828 confessed her feelings of inadequacy in failing to reach perfection, writing in her journal, "All is not right with me,

I know. I still build on sandy foundations; I still hope for perfection, where perfection is not given."[124] Though it supplied the doctrinal verification for female religious authority, the sentimental advocacy of perfectionism may have backfired by presenting impossibly high standards for Christian piety. Perfectionism was too high a challenge even for George Beecher, himself a minister and a member of the august Beecher clan (and a brother of Harriet Beecher Stowe), who despaired under the weight of perfectionism and committed suicide in 1843.[125] Though sentimentalism promoted perfectionism as a vehicle by which modest, pious women could achieve authority and even become Christ-like emissaries of the divine will, these texts doubtless caused despair and apostasy in readers who attempted, and failed, to emulate this mystical state.

Biblical Authority and Sectarianism

Amid the sentimental demotion of clergy and the pressures of perfectionism, there remains one source of religious authority in sentimental literature that is beyond dispute: the Bible. In sentimental literature, Bible reading is a recurrent and productive religious act that effects immediate personal reform and provides the final word in religious dispute. For instance, in Maria McIntosh's *Charms and Counter-Charms*, the reading of the Bible sparks conversion and personal reform in Euston Hastings, the troubled husband whose Bible reading causes him to devote himself to his marriage; it likewise effects a total transformation of the rake St. Elmo Murray, who becomes an ordained minister at the close of Augusta Evans's *St. Elmo*. While this bibliocentricism may today seem unremarkable, Bible reading was the subject of heated, even ferocious sectarian debate in the Second Great Awakening, and it was strongly advocated by Protestants across denominations out of the belief that access to scripture was an inherent, inalienable right. Within the Anglo-American Protestant tradition, Bible reading figures as the premier expression of religious autonomy, for it enables individuals to access and determine for themselves the nature of the divine will. This tenet acquired a new urgency amid mounting anxiety about the cultural influence of Catholics, who were widely believed to be not only opposed to Bible reading but also forbidden it by repressive priests intent on keeping worshippers ignorant and obedient. The American Bible Society was founded in 1816 specifically to combat Catholicism, and it did so by widely distributing the King James

Version of the Bible, which, as a Protestant translation, became the era's prin-cipal instrument of anti-Catholic activity.[126] Catholic clergy responded with outrage at the distribution of a Protestant translation, but this response was widely interpreted as evidence of Catholic hostility to the Bible itself.[127] This presumption was fortified in 1842 when a Catholic priest burned copies of the King James Bible that had been circulated by Bible societies, an act that met with widespread national outrage.[128]

The perception of Catholicism as hostile to scripture pervades Protestant writings of the mid-nineteenth century, and it surfaced to dramatic effect in several sensationalist publications claiming to be personal memoirs of the abuses perpetrated by Catholic clergy. For instance, in *Six Months in a Convent* (1835), Rebecca Theresa Reed claims to have been denied access to the Bible: she writes, "While in the Convent I asked once or twice for a Bible, but never received any, and never saw one while there. The Bishop often said that the laity were not qualified to expound the Scriptures, and that the *successors* of the apostles [that is, Catholic priests] alone were authorized to interpret them, *&c.*"[129] Maria Monk made a similar claim in *Awful Disclosures of the Hotel Dieu Nunnery* (1836), her scandalous fictitious memoir of the sexual slavery she claims to have endured in a convent, claiming, "I often heard the Protestant Bible spoken of, in bitter terms, as a most dangerous book, and one which never ought to be in the hands of common people."[130] Protestant clergy used this belief to incite widespread Protestant outrage toward Catholics. For instance, Harriet Beecher Stowe's brother Edward Beecher railed against Catholic opposition to the Bible in his 1855 manifesto, *The Papal Conspiracy Exposed*, in which he marveled at the Catholic antipathy for scripture: "Five bulls against Bible societies have been issued in the last 30 years—the last in 1844. It chills the blood to hear in what manner they speak of the Bible and of the 'crafty device' of circulating the revealed word of God. The devil, it would seem, in his rage against Rome, has become the great patron of Bible societies. It is hard to tell whether this is most blasphemous or ludicrous. And what is the flimsy pretext of all this?"[131] There are innumerable instances of heated sectarian conflict about the promotion of Bible reading, but this battle often focused on the Bible-reading habits of school children as a way of embedding Protestant sympathies within Catholic children and thereby arresting that denomination's growth. For instance, the American Bible Society in 1839 focused its anti-Catholic energies with a campaign to require the reading of the King James Version in American classrooms. In the years that followed, Catholics and Protestants fought bitterly over the presence of this

Protestant translation in public schools, with Catholics demanding that this sectarian translation be removed from schools.[132]

The centrality of Bible reading in sentimental literature constitutes an explicit contribution to this bitter public debate. Sentimental texts repeatedly appoint the Bible as a central fixture of religious observance without which one cannot legitimately claim to be a Christian and which serves as the sole infallible religious authority. While this bibliocentrism today may seem benign, in the mid-century it constituted a decisive foray in contemporary sectarian conflict, for it offered explicit public support to a controversial Protestant position and participated in these anti-Catholic efforts by encouraging readers, regardless of denomination, to cultivate a habit of private Bible reading. The particular attention in sentimental literature to the Bible reading of children illustrates its indebtedness to the activist efforts of Protestant anti-Catholicism. The sectarian character of sentimental bibliocentrism is particularly perceptible in the repeated citation of the King James Version, which figures as the default translation quoted in sentimental texts. For instance, in Stowe's *Uncle Tom's Cabin*, Eva St. Clare persistently reads and recites verses from the King James Version even though she is a Catholic, a detail that reveals the novel's participation within the Protestant campaign to promote Bible reading among Catholic children. Similarly, in Warner's *The Wide, Wide World*, Ellen Montgomery meets a kindly stranger on a ferry, who offers her solace by quoting liberally from the King James Version. He asks, "Were there ever sweeter words of kindness than these?—'Suffer the little children to come unto me, and forbid them not; for of such is the kingdom of heaven.' 'I am the good shepherd; the good shepherd giveth his life for the sheep.' 'I have loved thee with an everlasting love; therefore with loving kindness have I drawn thee.'"[133] The distinctive style of the King James Version quoted here would have been readily recognizable to nineteenth-century readers, and this scene both depicts and participates in the contemporary anti-Catholic campaign to encourage Bible reading among children, implicitly urging the reader to recognize that there are no "sweeter words" than those of the King James Version and to undertake a similar practice of Bible reading.

The treatment of the Bible in sentimental literature as the only irrefutable source of religious opinion also constitutes an implicit critique of the primacy of clergy, whose authority in these texts is secondary, even tertiary, to that of the Bible. In *The Wide, Wide World*, seminary student John Humphreys consoles Ellen Montgomery during a lapse of faith by urging her simply to "carry your heart and life to the Bible and see how they agree. . . . If you find your own feelings and manner or life at one with these Bible words, you may hope that that the Holy Spirit has changed you and set his mark upon you."[134] That is to say, one's rectitude and salvation can be assessed by the unfaltering heuristic of the Bible, an argument that concisely reduces Christian stewardship to a simple matter of collating oneself with the Bible. And in Susan Warner's novel *Queechy*, the only act necessary to convert an unbeliever is the gift of a Bible, the reading of which causes Mr. Carleton, the novel's male lead, to better his ways and commit himself fully to a devout Christian life. Furthermore, sentimental literary texts repeatedly suggest that through the Bible everyone, regardless of rank or station, may personally ascertain the divine will, without the mediating intervention of clerical opinion. For instance, in *Queechy*, when Mr. Carleton expresses doubts about the redemptive powers of Christ, Fleda counters by showing him a verse in the Gospel according to Matthew in which Jesus indirectly affirms his own divinity, and Carleton replies as if summarizing a logical syllogism: " 'You are right. . . . I do not see how those who honour the authority of the Bible and the character of Jesus Christ can deny the truth of His own declaration [in that Bible verse]."[135] This scene shows Warner's belief in the clarion evidentiary authority of the Bible, which is to be accepted on its terms in every respect. Though she is a child, Fleda's intimate knowledge of the Bible enables her both to understand the divine will and exert spiritual influence over an older man, teaching him religious truths and sparking his own nascent piety; in this way, Fleda's knowledge of the Bible allows her to function in a ministerial capacity by offering religious instruction and encouragement to an unbeliever.

The use of the Bible in support of anti-Catholic activism also contributed to the resurgence of primal Protestantism, which encouraged ordinary people to take their religious cues directly from scripture, without the mediation of clerical interpretation or religious convention.[136] Numerous back-to-basics movements emerged out of this enthusiasm for scriptural originalism, such as the self-termed Christians, the Church of Christ, the Church of Jesus Christ of Latter-day Saints, and the Disciples of Christ. While these movements did not emerge in direct response to Catholicism, they nonetheless developed in a cultural climate in which the Bible was heralded as the *sine qua non* of Christian observance, and the religious movements that developed in this milieu are consequently characterized by their respective rejection of secondary clerical authority and return to primordial source material, both of which were already inflected with anti-Catholic connotations. Any aspect of Christian observance that did not have an immediate scriptural antecedent became suspect in this climate of Protestant bibliocentrism; for example, the followers of Alexander Campbell rejected all religious rites not explicitly recommended in the Bible.[137]

This biblically based Christian Primitivism, as it was called, was also distinguished by the rejection of sectarian factionalism on the grounds that denominationalism postdated foundational Christian writings, and adherents instead aspired to a broadly non-denominational Christianity that replicated the early apostolic Christianity documented in the New Testament.[138] This broad ecumenism, however, did not include Catholicism, but it was instead a coalition of Protestant denominations united both in their shared investment in the Bible as the infallible wellspring of Christianity and in their staunch opposition to the spread of Catholicism, which was understood as decidedly anti-scriptural in its alleged opposition to private Bible reading and its insistence on rites lacking in scriptural justification. The revival of 1831 was heralded as the epitome of this anti-denominational mood, with the unspoken agreement that all preachers would refrain from publicly identifying their sectarian affiliation, but all the speakers at this event were Protestants who suppressed their denominational association in the spirit of pan-Protestant unity. Ecumenical organizations such as the Protestant Union, the American Protestant Society, the Society for the Diffusion of Christian Knowledge, and the Know-Nothing political party harnessed the period's enthusiasm for trans-denominational Protestant fellowship but did so with the express purpose of combating Catholicism. What presented itself as a spirit of ecumenism in the Second Great Awakening was in fact a Protestant coalition that elevated biblical precedent in order to legitimize its sectarian agenda and undermine Catholicism.

The conflation of bibliocentrism and ecumenism in support of a thinly veiled Protestantism abounds in sentimental literature. For instance, in Catharine Sedgwick's *Hope Leslie* (1827), the novel's title character is distinguished by her embrace of "variant religious sentiments" and her skepticism about the constraints of Calvinism: Sedgwick writes, "She enjoyed the capacities of her nature, and permitted her mind to expand beyond the contracted boundaries of sectarian faith. Her religion was pure and disinterested . . . [and] had not been coined into a particular form, or received the current impress."[139] Strict denominationalism, Sedgwick suggests, conveys an excessive attachment to worldly, human-made structures of ecclesiastical rule in lieu of genuine faith. In Sedgwick's *New-England Tale,* scripturally based ecumenism similarly stands in sharp contrast with the severe and questionable sectarianism of Calvinism, as practiced by the selfish Mrs. Wilson, who justifies her sinful behavior with the uncritical espousal of the Calvinist doctrine of predestination. Where the Calvinist sectarianism in *A New-England Tale* is reflexive, parochial, and ignorant, the ecumenical piety of the novel's heroine, Jane, is rooted solely in the Bible, thanks to the urging of her Methodist servant that she "'make the Bible [her] counselor.'" Though reared in the Calvinist church, Jane quotes freely from John Wesley, and her theological open-mindedness leads her Methodist servant to describe her appreciatively as inclined to "pick fruit from every good tree, no matter whose vineyard it grows in." The novel's designation of the Bible as the foremost source of religious knowledge and the concomitant distaste for denominational creeds are also evident in the hostile remarks of the novel's antagonist, Edward Wilson, about Quakerism, the religion practiced by Mr. Lloyd, his rival for Jane's affections and the novel's hero. Wilson questions the absence of a Quaker creed, commenting, "If they are an upright, frank people, why is the world kept in ignorance of their belief? The Quakers have no creed; and though I have no great faith in the professors of any sect, yet they ought to let you know what they do think; it is fair and above board." Jane replies, "There is a book . . . that contains the creed of the Quakers: a creed to which they have never presumed to add any thing, nor have they taken any thing from it; the only creed to which they think it right to require the assent of man, and from which no rational man can dissent—that book is *the Bible!*"[140] In accord with contemporary Protestant ecumenism, Sedgwick looks with skepticism upon human-made sectarian creeds and suggests instead that to be a true Christian, one must obey nothing but the Bible itself; by extension, any religion that does otherwise cannot legitimately claim to be Christian.

Just as Sedgwick's *New-England Tale* uses ecumenism to assail Calvinism, so Warner's *Wide, Wide World* takes particular aim at Catholicism. The minister Humphreys is summoned to the deathbed of an Irish Catholic boy who requests him in place of a Catholic priest. Unable to administer the rite of supreme unction, Humphreys instead converses with the boy, John Dolan, about Jesus's redemptive powers; in response to Humphreys's inquiry whether Jesus "has washed away" his sins, John replies assuredly with a Bible verse, "'Suffer the little children to come unto me" (Matt. 19:14).[141] While this scene posits scripture and belief in Christ as sources of ecumenical confederation between the Protestant minister and the Catholic child, there are numerous indications in this scene of the triumph of Protestantism over its most contested rival. In the first place, John Dolan's preference for Mr. Humphreys signals the victory of Protestantism over Catholicism in their respective pursuit of the allegiance of the Catholic child. Moreover, the substitution of scripture for Catholic ritual implicitly suggests that proper ministerial practice should derive solely from biblical precedent and not from institutional precedent or denominational convention. The use of the King James Version to console the child also suggests the irrefutable primacy not just of scripture, Protestantism's textual metonym in this period, but of the Protestant translation in particular. That the dying child finds solace in this snippet of Protestant scripture serves as the final word decisively evidencing the superiority of Protestant belief over that of Catholicism, which is able to offer no such comfort because of its putative prohibition of scripture.

More typically, however, bibliocentric ecumenism is the province of girls and women, who, because of the prohibition against the ordination of women, usually hold denominationalism lightly precisely because they have no authoritative investment in it. And, as with the aforementioned scene in *Queechy* in which Fleda quotes scripture to the ignorant Mr. Carleton, girls and women are also usually the premier authorities of scripture in sentimental texts. The combination of these two qualities in sentimental texts affords girls and women the ability to evaluate which aspects of religious observance derive from scripture (and thus merit practice) and which derive from clerical or denominational interpretation (and thus merit dismissal). In denouncing human-made religious creeds as unscriptural and in propounding instead an unaffiliated piety rooted in scriptural engagement, sentimental writers at once undermined worldly religious authority while establishing their own. That is to say, sentimental women writers mobilized the sectarian rhetoric of ecumenical scripturalism to appoint themselves reliable sources of religious authority; sentimental women writers thus benefited from sectarianism while presenting it as ungodly. This implication is evident, for instance, in Alice Cary's poem "My Creed," which registers contemporary distaste for denominational creeds, the poem's very title expressing the prevailing populist sensibility that infused religious discourse of the era. In the logic of the poem, ardent faith alone distinguishes the sincere Christian, not the man-made ritual observances of "the wide phylactery,/Nor stubborn fast, nor stated prayers."[142] Not only may the poem's speaker develop with impunity her own confessional standards, but the will to break from these denominational creeds also stands as a marker of the genuine Christian. In this respect, ecumenism renders the pious believer her own theologian and her own minister.

The professions of Protestant ecumenism inherent in Augusta Evans's novel *Beulah* are matched only by its antipathy for ordained clergy. The novel's heroine, Beulah Benton, is an orphan in the sentimental prototype, who wanders from home to home in her search for kinship and religious conviction, her spiritual struggles leading her to experiment with numerous belief systems, such as metaphysics and science. In a heated conversation about religion, her friend Cornelia launches into a tirade against denominationalism and clericalism, which she deems mutually dependent: "'The clergy, as a class, I found strangely unlike what I had expected,'" she admits. "'Instead of earnest zeal for the promotion of Christianity, I saw that the majority were bent only on the aggrandizement of their particular denomination. Verily, I thought in my heart, Is all this bickering the result of their religion? How these churches do hate each other! According to each, salvation could only be found in their special tenets—within the pale of their peculiar organization; and yet, all professed to draw their doctrines from the same book; and, Beulah, the end of my search was, that I scorned all creeds and churches, and began to find a faith outside of a revelation which gave rise to so much narrow-minded bigotry.'"[143] In her own spiritual searches, Beulah directly encounters this "narrow-minded bigotry" in her dealings with Mr. Mortimor, a forbidding minister whose sectarian sternness renders him cold and quarrelsome, and Beulah comes to concur with Cornelia's position and reject all existing denominations, developing instead her own form of ecumenical, Bible-centered piety independent of clerical supervision. She thus becomes her own spiritual steward and follows the spirit of religious autonomy of the Second Great Awakening by fashioning her own brand of religious observance, which the reader is implicitly invited to follow. The sectarian disposition of Beulah's pursuit of religious sovereignty is evident in the influence of the characters of Dr. and Mrs. Asbury, a loving older couple who provide succor to Beulah in her pained wanderings; their last name references both Francis Asbury, the famed bishop who helped spread Methodism in North America in the eighteenth century, and the larger influence of Methodism, Evans's own denominational affiliation, in fostering a climate that enabled women to assume clerical authority.

This confluence of beliefs is also evident in the papers of Susan and Anna Warner. Though as Presbyterians they were members of a denomination with a long list of confessional creeds, they repeatedly denounced the integrity of such human-made doctrinal inventories and pointed toward the Bible as the only dependable source of religious knowledge, a belief that was decidedly and pointedly Protestant. Susan Warner made this position clear in a letter to a friend: "Anything that [you] find clearly in the Bible hold fast, as for life & death. But anything—no matter by whom put forward—that you cannot clearly find there [in the Bible],—well, let it wait. Do not make it an article of your creed. *Nothing* is to be absolutely trusted save the word of the Lord alone."[144] Anna Warner expressed similar views years later in her correspondence with a former student who had begun teaching Sunday school: she wrote, "There is no need to say a word about sects or creeds. All *you* have to do, and all the church can require is that you teach glad tidings of salvation. If you must needs also make the children learn the catechism, there is no need to spend more time than just to hear the words said over." She continued this line of reasoning with an affirmation of the primacy of the Bible: "My objection to teaching [the catechism] anywhere is that the human colouring in such uninspired formulas, tends to confuse and mislead. Bible truths are often there set forth in such a style, that the poor teacher could not make her class understand, if she gave the whole time to explanations. Better teach the sweet Bible words, which they can remember and take home. . . . I *know* that Bible words are simpler and safer."[145] In *Queechy*, Susan Warner characterized sectarianism as deriving from faulty biblical interpretations. In response to one character's observation that "everyone runs to the Bible . . . it is the general armoury, and all parties draw from it to fight each other," Mr. Carleton replies that these rifts occur "only while they draw partially [from the Bible]. No man can fight the battle of truth but in the whole panoply; and no man so armed can fight any other."[146] The thorough reading and embrace of the Bible will cause all sectarianism to vanish because the propagation of such a practice would cause the spread of Protestantism and, thus, the decisive eradication of all other sects.

It is not insignificant that Warner herself urges this widespread Bible reading, the occasion of bibliocentrism enabling her to assume the responsibility of telling her many readers how best to practice Christianity. Both Susan and Anna Warner undertook this responsibility throughout their lives by offering Bible-study classes for both children and adults of innumerable denominations, and the many published testimonies of former students repeatedly stress that neither woman ever propounded a recognizably sectarian agenda but instead affirmed the unifying centrality of biblical texts to all believers.[147] In this instance, the disavowal of sectarian denominationalism in the name of Protestant bibliocentrism worked directly toward their own assumption of religious authority, their expressions of denominational skepticism working to bolster their status and legitimacy as both teachers and shapers of their students' religious opinions. Susan's belief in the primacy of the Bible is apparent in her scripted remarks to her students, urging them to "show that you believe God's least word; and do all you can by your steady living, loving, & rejoicing, to prove to others that religion is a joy, & the Bible a great reality."[148] Moreover, Susan's Bible-study lesson plans evidence a particular interest in the story of Babel in Genesis, an episode she returned to repeatedly in her classes. A biblical etiology of division and fragmentation, the story allowed her to characterize sectarianism as a sign of the fallen state of human beings and to enjoin her students to reject the impulse to disparage other believers on denominational grounds, thereby perpetuating the perception of biblically based ecumenism.

The culmination of this insistence on the primacy of the Bible was *The Law and the Testimony*, Susan's voluminous companion to Bible study, published in 1853 at the peak of her popularity and market viability. That she would publish this volume at all speaks to the impact of *The Wide, Wide World* in providing her with the forum and authority to offer biblical exegesis, a role heretofore unavailable to women, especially those in the orthodox tradition from which Warner hailed. In her introductory remarks, she clarifies that the book is "a gathering of facts for the purposes of induction. It is a setting together of the mass of Scripture testimony on each of the grand points of Scripture teaching; in the hope that when the whole light of the scattered rays is flung on the matter, the truth may be made manifest. . . . [The writer] had but little knowledge of the theological world."[149] She here expresses her populist belief that neither theology nor accrued denominational doctrine is necessary for genuine piety or knowledge of biblical "truth," thereby undermining the interpretive authority of trained clergy. More immediately, this democratization of scriptural understanding provides the justification and opportunity for Warner to take it upon herself to provide biblical interpretation to a receptive readership and thereby to assume the task of scriptural exegesis typically reserved for trained, ordained clergy.

Though sentimental texts were grounded in the contemporary religious culture of anti-authoritarian populism, that culture provided the means and justification for sentimental texts and writers to coopt for themselves the very religious authority that the era sought to disperse. While it may appear that sentimental writers narratively disperse religious authority to women in general, they more specifically impute that authority largely to themselves, for these sympathetic female lay leaders function as metonymic substitutes for sentimental women writers, who, although they lack formal credentials for religious leadership, dispense religious counsel to the reader through the auspices of the texts. While inviting readers to regard ordained clergy as irrelevant and even obstructive to religious enlightenment, sentimental texts urge readers to trust instead the narratively substantiated religious guidance and inspiration provided within those texts, positing sentimental literature as a superior substitute for clerical supervision.

They thereby instate new religious leadership that, in execution, is just as potentially problematic as the clerical structures of authority that it replaces, for neither sentimental novels nor the female sources of religious instruction in them openly declare their ministerial, missionary ambitions, but they instead present themselves as kindly and sympathetic rather than superintendent. Shirley Samuels has observed that sentimentalism often runs the risk of being emotionally coercive, which is never more evident than in the strategic use of revivalist techniques on the reader.[150] Nancy Bentley has likewise analyzed the primacy of consent in sentimental narratives of submission, and yet the reader is not afforded a similar opportunity to consent willingly to conversion since these techniques work covertly to incite conversion by manipulating the conventional readerly experience of sympathy and identification: sentimental texts dramatize the importance of consent while potentially overriding that of the reader.[151] While the religious contents of sentimentalism rendered the novel newly respectable in conservative religious opinion, its designs on the reader end up confirming long-standing anxieties about the capacity of the novel to exert influence on the unwitting reader, an opinion summarized in Henry James's quip that "there is danger of [a novel's] hurting you before you know."[152]

A number of new positions adopted by sentimentalism took root in American culture, such as the belief in the primacy of the Bible in Christian observance and the suspicion of denominationalism as an unnecessary appurtenance, as evidenced by the exponential growth of non-denominational Protestantism over the last century. Furthermore, sentimentalism was wholly successful in positing the literary text as a worthy surrogate for clergy. In 1871, Mark Twain declared that most Americans received religious instruction "through the despised novel . . . and NOT from the drowsy pulpit."[153] That same year, Harriet Beecher Stowe also observed that the novel had overtaken the pulpit as the nation's foremost seat of religious authority and instruction. In the preface to her novel *My Wife and I*, she wryly commented,

> It is now understood that whoever wishes to gain the public ear, and
> to propound a new theory, must do it in a serial story. . . . Soon it will
> be necessary that every leading clergyman should embody in his the-
> ology a serial story, to be delivered from the pulpit Sunday after Sun-
> day. We look forward to announcements in our city papers such as
> these: The Rev. Dr. Ignatius, of the Church of St. Mary the Virgin, will
> begin a serial romance, to be entitled "St. Sebastian and the Arrows,"
> in which he will embody the duties, the trials, and the temptations of
> the young Christians of our day. The Rev. Dr. Boanerges, of Plymouth
> Rock Church, will begin a serial story, entitled "Calvin's Daughter," in
> which he will discuss the distinctive features of Protestant theology.[154]

Stowe's prediction proved correct, for by the 1870s male clergy attempted to
restore their status as paramount religious authority by coopting the literary forms that imputed authority to women a generation before. Some of the
best-selling writers of the last quarter of the nineteenth century were male
clergy such as Edward Eggleston, E. P. Roe, and Charles Sheldon who used
the novel form as a literary expansion of the pulpit.[155] Sheldon's blockbuster
novel, *In His Steps: What Would Jesus Do?* (1897), began in precisely the way
Stowe envisioned, as a serialized narrative delivered in weekly installments in
order to lure his parishioners to return for the second Sunday service at his
Congregationalist church. These late-century male religious novelists would
define their work against the template of sentimentalism, as with the assertion of James Lane Allen, author of such religious novels as *The Choir Invisible*
(1897), that sentimentalism is a "literature of the overcivilized, the hyper-
fastidious . . . the fragile, the trivial, the rarified, the bloodless."[156] Despite this
denunciation, many of these male novelists continued the sentimental tradition by using fiction as a forum for the circulation of new religious doctrines,
such as the Social Gospel and the Gospel of Wealth, as with Washington
Gladden's *The Christian League of Connecticut* (1884) and George Hepworth's
Hiram Golf's Religion; or, The Shoemaker by the Grace of God (1893), respectively. Their novels, too, communicate a recognition that narrative dramatiza-
tion, reader identification, and emotion were more effective means of inciting
conversion than theology, assumptions that continue to underwrite modern
religious fiction and modern preaching technique. Though succeeded by male
clerical novelists, sentimentalism provided the enduring generic blueprint.

CHAPTER 2

My Kingdom

Sentimentalism and the Refinement of Hymnody

F EW FEATURES of nineteenth-century women's literature seem as foreign and outdated today as the omnipresence of hymns. In countless literary works, hymns are quoted, sung, and contemplated. Hymns in these texts are rivaled in influence only by the Bible and are potent catalysts of religious experience, sparking conversion in the unbeliever and offering reassurance to the faithful during times of trouble. In the literary world of the American mid-century, the singing of a hymn could bring tears to the eyes of even the most hardened unbeliever. During Ellen Montgomery's cheerless trip to live with her Aunt Fortune in Susan Warner's *The Wide, Wide World*, a kindly stranger ministers to her by inviting her to read a hymn and then gives her a hymnal. In *Uncle Tom's Cabin*, Harriet Beecher Stowe excerpts the revival hymns favored by slaves and depicts Tom as such an avid singer of hymns that he can be revived on his deathbed only by the recitation of a few lines from a hymn by Isaac Watts. In Louisa May Alcott's *Little Women*, the March sisters sing their "father's favorite hymn" after learning of his grave illness, and, at the height of her own illness, Beth March plays and sings John Bunyan's hymn "He That Is Down Need Fear No Fall."[1]

For modern readers, these scenes of popular hymnody may seem quaintly old-fashioned and evoke a religious life steeped in homely, wholesome piety. While hymns today may seem respectable and genteel, it would be a mistake to impose these modern assumptions on the nineteenth-century literary texts that so celebrate their significance to the Christian life. Rather, to read these novels in the complex history of hymnody in the English-speaking world is to see this fond, warm portrayal of hymnody as a deft literary construction so convincing as to eclipse the genre's long association with controversial religious radicalism, anti-authoritarianism, and populism. Though hymns were deemed acceptable material for private reading and contemplation, they were, until the mid-nineteenth century, widely prohibited from congregational worship on the grounds that they might circulate dubious doctrine and prompt unseemly behavior in worshippers. In the eyes of conservatives, hymns were associated with heterodoxy, vulgar public displays, and lax doctrinal supervision, and it was only in the Second Great Awakening that hymns were thrust into the religious mainstream, popularized at revival meetings and strongly promoted by Methodists; as a religious genre both composed and sung by common citizens, without the sanction or supervision of clergy, the hymn encapsulated the era's populist, anti-clerical spirit. In accord with their promotion of some of the new teachings of the Second Great Awakening, sentimental women writers contributed significantly to the mainstream acceptance of hymnody, constituting hymns as upright, even requisite implements of piety and providing public assurances that hymns might facilitate, and not jeopardize, refinement and convention. In countless sentimental novels about the growth and self-control afforded by Christian faith, hymns are fully compatible with middle-class feminine sensibility, decorum, and modesty, a rendering that radically revised the public presentation of this long-marginal devotional form.

But these literary endorsements did not altogether expunge the genre of its complex history. As avid hymn enthusiasts, these women writers were familiar with the vexed history and considerable baggage accompanying hymnody. The Warner family library, for instance, contained dozens of different hymnals and hymn collections from a wide range of denominations, and Anna Warner, Susan Warner's younger sister, edited numerous hymn collections, such as *Hymns of the Church Militant* (1858) and *Wayfaring Hymns* (1869). Harriet Beecher Stowe also knew the genre's history, and her 1862 novel *Agnes of Sorrento* included a brief summary of English-language hymn history as well as excerpts from numerous medieval hymns. To be sure, sentimental portrayals of hymnody at once refined the genre's public reputation while retaining some of its populist features. The genre's demotic energies discernibly pulsate in sentimental novels about the trials of lowly, powerless people seeking relief from the abuses of worldly authority, for in these texts hymns repeatedly enable the dissolution of social hierarchies. However, these depictions often stop short of fully embracing the lively contemporary culture of populist hymnody and manufacture an image of hymnody that is denuded of its unsavory associations and brought in line with conventional notions of propriety and modesty. What emerges in these engagements— both in fictional depictions of hymn culture and in actual forays in hymn writing—is a syncretic compromise that tempered the form's inherent populism with an insistence on decorum and gentility.

Whereas hymns in revival meetings were renowned for their ability to endow common people with clerical authority and to upend traditional power hierarchies, the primary social change effected by hymns in sentimental texts is in inspiring personal reform and in bringing worshippers in line with normative standards of genteel conduct. While the sentimentalization of hymns enabled the genre's acceptance in the religious mainstream, it also collaborated with the efforts of mainline denominations to defuse hymns' potential for religious and social insurgency. Though sentimental women writers were ultimately unsuccessful in neutralizing a genre known for its subversive powers, they did succeed in using the hymn as a medium by which they could transmute their own literary influence into formal religious authority: the hymn medium enabled their writings to be included in worship services, their interpretations of scripture to find widespread circulation and acceptance, and their role as sources of religious instruction made official. Just as sentimental women writers took advantage of some of the developments of the Second Great Awakening to advocate for greater religious authority, so the advent of hymnody in this era also proffered women a similar opportunity, and women writers strategically played both sides of the debate: women writers were able to work within the hymn form because of its long tradition of egalitarian, populist inclusivity, but they were able to do so without attracting criticism because their literary depictions of hymnody cooperated with conservative efforts to refine the form. In thus restricting the powers of the hymn form to effect social change, mid-century literary women attempted to reserve these subversive powers for themselves and become formal, sanctioned sources of religious instruction.[2]

The Radical Populism of Devotional Song

While hymn singing today may seem wholly conventional, hymns are actually a fairly new addition to Anglo-American Christian worship, despite their considerable biblical precedent. The Hebrew Bible amply endorses the singing of religious lyric, as with Psalm 33:3,

> Sing to [the Lord] a new song,
> play skillfully on the strings, with
> loud shouts.

Paul's letters also urged his readers to do so, as with his recommendation that the Colossians "sing psalms and hymns and spiritual songs with thankfulness in your hearts to God" (Col. 3:16). These explicit endorsements notwithstanding, hymns were often regarded with suspicion because of the idiosyncrasies of their content and composition. Unlike psalms, hymns diverged from the biblical script, and, as the products of authors lacking the august pedigree and divine sanction of the psalmist, hymns were deemed acceptable for private devotional use but inappropriate for congregational worship, for it was feared that they might broadcast ideas of faulty theology.

The Protestant Reformation invigorated interest in hymnody because it provided a vernacular forum for common people to recount and celebrate religious experience without the intercession of clerical authority. Martin Luther himself was a prolific hymnist, and the German-language Protestant world enjoyed a vibrant culture of hymnody that would not flourish in Anglo-America until the nineteenth century.[3] Though Elizabeth I formally sanctioned hymns in 1559 and even composed hymns herself, the genre failed to find widespread favor among both conservatives and reformers. John Calvin insisted that scripture alone provide content for devotional song, a position shared by Anglican conservatives, who would shun hymns and advocate instead psalmody, the singing of metrical translations of the psalms.[4]

In practice, psalmody did not typically foster the joy and gladness described in the Bible as characteristic of devotional song. Clergy habitually complained about the poor quality of their congregants' singing, as with John Wesley's instructions that congregants should "sing modestly. Do not bawl . . . that you may not destroy the harmony; but strive to unite your voices together, so as to make one clear melodious sound."[5] In some instances, clergy limited congregational participation altogether and consigned recitation to an individual chorister, a choir, or a precentor, a clergyman charged with supervising service music. In addition, psalms were traditionally recited in successive order throughout the ecclesiastical year, regardless of the text's relevance to feast days or the sermon. *The Bay Psalm Book* (1640), the first

English-language book printed in North America, was issued to satisfy the Calvinist belief in the "necessity of the heavenly Ordinance of singing Scripture Psalmes in the Churches of God," although the translators of this Psalter openly acknowledged that their versions were aesthetically wanting and were not "always so smooth and elegant as some may desire or expect."[6] In all of these ways, psalmody typically reified the clerical authoritarianism and ceremonial formalism that the Protestant Reformation had so vehemently combated, and the transition from psalmody to hymnody was associated with heterodox criticism of clerical mediation and rote, somber religious custom. Where psalmody rendered congregants passive and routinized worship, hymnody aimed to activate worshippers, both by eliciting their participation in devotional song and by accepting lay-authored religious lyric as suitable content for worship service. The remoteness and alienation fostered by psalmody were succeeded by a new form that sought to engender engagement, emotion, and intimacy.

From the very outset, English-language hymnody was advocated by religious dissenters and innovators, and its history thus parallels that of the Second Great Awakening because of its association with anti-clerical populism and the social periphery. Hymnody was so problematic that even Nonconformists deemed it objectionable, although it found some advocates, among them Baptist minister Benjamin Keach (1640–1704), who originated the idea of including hymns in worship service, and writer and theologian Philip Doddridge (1702–1751), whose colleague and friend Isaac Watts (1674–1748) would become the first major contributor to English-language hymnody.[7] A dissenter and evangelical Nonconformist who suffered discrimination for his refusal to vow allegiance to the Church of England, Watts was a dedicated educational reformer who authored numerous textbooks and pedagogical guides that exerted influence in North America and England well into the nineteenth century. His collections of devotional song—*Horae Lyricae* (1706–1709), *Hymns and Spiritual Songs* (1707), *Divine and Moral Songs for the Use of Children* (1715), and *The Psalms of David Imitated in the Language of the New Testament* (1719)—would become the foundation of the Protestant English-language hymn tradition. His influence on the genre cannot be overstated, for he not only legitimized and energized this new devotional form but also produced a vast literary corpus that would become the universal standard of craftsmanship against which all later hymnists would be measured. Though Watts was a Congregationalist, he diverged from Calvinist doctrine by recommending a departure from psalmody, a decision he would explain in the preface to *Hymns and Spiritual Songs*: "In these last Days of the Gospel we are almost within sight of the Kingdom of our Lord; yet we are very much unacquainted with the Songs of the New Jerusalem, and unpractised in the Work of Praise. To see the dull Indifference, the negligent and the thoughtless Air, that sits upon the Faces of a whole Assembly, while the Psalm is on their Lips, might tempt even a charitable Observer to suspect the Fervency of Inward Religion; and it is much to be feared, that the Minds of most of the Worshippers are absent or unconcerned." He continued, "That very Action, which should elevate us to the most delightful and divine Sensations, doth not only flatten our Devotion but too often awakens our Regret, and touches all the Springs of Uneasiness within us." The central problem, according to Watts, is that the psalms are not actually Christian: though they may express joy in the divine and forecast the advent and sacrifice of Christ, the psalm as a form "hath something in it so extremely Jewish and cloudy, that it darkens our Sight of God the Saviour."[8] As a genre originating in the religious antecedent of Christianity but not directly emanating from it, the psalm is too much at a remove from, and even detrimental to, the emotional immediacy and intimacy that Watts believed ought to result from devotional song, and its recitation too much privileges historical convention and precedent to be emotionally potent in the present. For Watts, circumstances demanded the formation of a new devotional genre.

The radicalism of this endeavor was furthered by Watts's hope that modern congregational song could contribute in a meaningful way to the dissolution of the divisions—denominational, social, and economic—that separate Christians from each other. The simple act of joining in song and affirming common beliefs, Watts averred, could dissolve worldly differences in denomination or class. For example, in the preface to *Hymns and Spiritual Songs*, he explains that his hymns "have avoided the more obscure and controverted Points of Christianity, that we might all obey the Direction of the Word of God, and sing his Praises with Understanding. . . . The Contentions and distinguishing Words of Sects and Parties, are secluded, that whole Assemblies might assist at the Harmony, and different Churches join in the same Worship without Offence."[9] In joining voices in song, hymns may encourage this unity by avoiding divisive matters and inviting worshippers simply to "sing [God's] Praises with Understanding." Likewise, in *Divine and Moral Songs for Children*, Watts expressed his hopes that "children of high and low degree, of the Church of England and Dissenters, baptized in infancy or not, may all join together in these songs." Hymns, for Watts, ought to "be of the more universal use and service," and the task of the hymn is to spark direct, unmediated feelings of love for the divine and to unite fellow believers in shared belief, regardless of provenance or sect.[10]

To these ends, Watts deliberately crafted his hymns in accessible language apprehensible even to what he called "the Vulgar Capacities." As he explained in *Hymns and Spiritual Songs*, he omitted from his hymns "lines that were too sonorous, and [has] given an Allay to the Verse, lest a more exalted Turn of Thought or Language should darken or disturb the Devotion of the weakest Souls."[11] More elevated language, he feared, might confuse or alienate less educated worshippers and thereby reinstate the divisions of class and education he hoped his hymns might diminish. This egalitarianism underlay his excision of theological cerebrations from his hymns and the liberal inclusion of forthright emotional prompts: in the evangelical climate in which Watts lived and wrote, it is affective sincerity—not scholarship—that distinguishes the genuine Christian, and intensity of feeling is available to everyone, regardless of rank. He thus filled his hymns with emotional appeals to emphasize common sentiments amid differing social classes and widen the reach of Christianity among the less privileged.

These qualities of Watts's work—his insistence on the emotional potency of hymns and their broad ecumenicity—would become universal standards by which subsequent works in this genre would be judged, and they would profoundly influence the ways in which mid-century women writers would portray hymns.[12] In the 1850s Henry Ward Beecher, the nation's most prominent celebrity minister and a leading advocate of congregational song, would flatly assert that a "hymn is a lyrical discourse to the feelings. It should either excite or express feelings."[13] In the preface to their well-regarded collection *Sabbath Hymn and Tune Book* (1859), Lowell Mason, Edwards Park, and Austin Phelps affirmed a belief that congregational song is implicitly egalitarian, for it "is adapted alike to the voices of the young and the old, of the uncultivated and of the cultivated. . . . As individual voices are lost in the chorus of the many, one is naturally led to feel his own insignificance."[14] Subsequent generations of hymnists and hymnal editors would likewise acclaim the power of the hymn to forge fellowship out of worldly differences, and they selected hymns on the basis of their broad inclusiveness, making the sectarian hymn a veritable rarity in hymnody, doomed to obscurity outside parochial confines. For example, in the preface to her collection *Hymns of the Church Militant*, hymnist and novelist Anna Warner would assert that hymns "tell that the Church is one," although "one denomination will war with another."[15]

In 1892, hymnologist Emma Pittman concurred in her assertion that "we verily believe that there is more true Christian unity to be found in hymns than in anywhere else."[16] More recently, S. Paul Schilling, a professor at Boston University School of Theology and a commentator on church music, placed ecumenicity foremost among his criteria for hymn selection, urging readers to "inquire whether what a hymn asserts is in harmony with the experience of the Christian community as a whole." An effective hymn, he maintains, must be "inclusive and universal in nature."[17]

The association of hymnody with the heterodox rejection of hierarchy and sectarian divisiveness would be confirmed with the growth of the Moravian church, a pietistic Protestant denomination that exerted great influence on English-language hymnody. Formally called the Unitas Fratrum, which means "the united brotherhood," the Moravians were led by Count Nicolaus Ludwig von Zinzendorf (1700–1760), a German aristocrat who, like his acquaintance Isaac Watts, was a strong advocate of ecumenism (Zinzendorf is even credited with coining the word *ecumenism*) and believed strongly in the power of hymnody to foster such broad Christian fellowship. In his pursuit of Christian concord, Zinzendorf believed that the act of collective singing could unite disparate people, and in the course of his life he composed over two thousand hymns and fostered a religious culture in which hymn singing pervaded virtually every aspect of Moravian worship.[18] Moravians, for example, celebrated the *Singstunde*, a form of worship organized around the singing of thematically linked hymns, and they likewise composed hymns tailored expressly for the special needs of individual trades and occupations, such as watchmen, farmers, missionaries, and travelers.[19] Zinzendorf's belief in the power of hymnody to effect ecumenism informed his work as a hymnist, for his hymns explicitly avoided engaging doctrinal debates so as to appeal to a broad swath of Christians. He likewise edited numerous hymnals distinguished by the diversity of their provenance, incorporating hymns from a broad range of denominations and affiliations. For example, his English-language *Collection of Hymns of the Children of God in All Ages* (1754) has been hailed as the first truly ecumenical, interdenominational hymnal that reprinted texts from Eastern Orthodox, Catholic, and various Protestant sources.[20]

Although in the English-speaking world hymns had long been opposed for public worship because their origins and content were potentially problematic and insufficiently deferential to church authority and scripture, Zinzendorf celebrated the extra-biblical nature of hymns, remarking that the "hymnal is a kind of response to the Bible, an echo and an extension thereof. In the Bible one perceives how the Lord communicates with mankind; and in the hymnal how mankind communicates with the Lord."[21] Armed with the belief that hymns and the Bible allowed human beings to engage in dialogue with the divine, Zinzendorf embraced the capacity of hymns to offer instruction without the sanction of clergy. He proudly wrote, "There is more dogma in our canticles than in our prose," and in 1733 he admitted, "Our little children we instruct chiefly by hymns."[22]

Though Zinzendorf has been largely forgotten in the popular memory of Anglo-American religious history, his influence on that tradition and its hymnody is considerable. Zinzendorf resided in England until 1755, was an active force in English evangelical circles, and was admired by such dissenting hymnists as Watts and Doddridge.[23] Though some of their beliefs were unorthodox and even heretical, the Moravians were accepted by the Protestant mainstream, and they were officially recognized by the Anglican church until the late nineteenth century.[24] Zinzendorf's hymns were widely translated and included in later English hymnals, and in 1742 Zinzendorf issued an English-language Moravian hymnbook that was among the first such works published in England.[25] Extending the generic tradition forged by Watts, Zinzendorf's use of hymnody to dissolve distinctions between disparate peoples—Catholics and Protestants, the elite and the masses, men and women—would remain part of the tradition and legacy of hymnody, one that nineteenth-century women writers would take up fully and that would extend even into the twentieth century, as with the use of spirituals by activists in the Civil Rights movement.

English-language hymnody might never have flourished without Zinzendorf, for it was through exposure to the Moravians that John Wesley, the founder of Methodism, would come to embrace this form. As an Anglican trained to favor psalmody, Wesley first encountered hymnody during his missionary travels to North America in the 1730s. On his journey to the colonies, he observed the joyous hymn singing of some traveling Moravians, and Wesley came to believe that singing could both generate and express sincere, powerful religious feeling. In an effort to spark such a response, Wesley in 1737 published in Charleston, South Carolina, *A Collection of Psalms and Hymns*, the first hymnal designed for Anglican congregational worship and the first hymn collection published in North America.[26] In thus deviating from Anglican canon and practice, Wesley faced criticism and even formal censure; according to complaints made against him to a Grand Jury in

Georgia, Wesley was accused of including "into the church and service at the altar, compositions of Psalms and Hymns not inspected or authorized by any proper judicature."[27] This reception amply illustrates what was at stake in the rise of hymnody. As a bottom-up, populist genre that enabled common people to have an active voice in church, whether by singing or by writing such works themselves, hymns threatened to circumvent, compromise, and even erode clerical authority.

As founder and leader of Methodism with his brother Charles (1707–88), John Wesley became the foremost champion of English-language hymnody. Though the Wesley brothers always remained ordained Anglican clergy, they diverged from the Established Church in their ardent advocacy of hymnody. In continuation of the tradition forged by Watts and Zinzendorf, Wesley asserted that hymn singing could inspire strong religious feeling and reach worshippers outside the confines of the church. Where Anglican psalmody was formal and stubbornly obscure to Christian worshippers, Moravian hymnody was adaptable, emotional, and acutely personal, and the Methodists made sure to retain these qualities in their own hymn tradition. Wesley was particularly struck by Moravian ecumenism, observing that "they have all one Lord and one faith, so they are all partakers of one Spirit, the Spirit of meekness and love, which uniformly and continually animates all their conversation."[28] Wesley translated and included several of Zinzendorf's hymns in the Methodist hymnal; he also mined Zinzendorf's own hymn collections for material, and Wesley's hymn "Now I Have Found the Ground" is translated from Johann Andreas Rothe's hymn "Ich habe nun den Grund gefunden," which was published in Zinzendorf's *Christ-Catholisches Singe- und Bet-Büchlein* (1727), his hymnal composed for Catholics. Wesley also adopted Zinzendorf's belief that hymns could provide valuable religious instruction, famously describing the Methodist hymnal as a "little body of experimental and practical divinity," a phrase that noticeably echoes Isaac Watts's own description of his songs as a "Piece of Experimental Divinity" as well as Zinzendorf's heterodox embrace of hymnody as an official primer of theology.[29]

According to Wesley, the task of the hymn was to spark religious feeling and to make the worshipper feel a close, personal love for the divine without the mediation of clergy or ritual. In his introduction to the Methodist hymnal, he clarified that the hymn is "a means of raising or quickening the spirit of devotion, of confirming [one's] faith, of enlivening [one's] hope; and of kindling or increasing [one's] love to God and Man. When Poetry thus keeps its place, as the handmaid of Piety, it shall attain . . . a Crown that fadeth not away."[30] Emotion was not prized for its own sake, but, in the Wesleyan tradition of focused diligence, Wesley insisted that worshippers aim for strictly pious emotion and should avoid getting carried away by the music or the sheer pleasure of congregational singing. He made this stipulation clear in his 1761 tract "Directions for Singing," in which he urged worshippers to "see that your *heart* is not carried away with the sound, but offered to God continually" and to "attend strictly to the sense of what you sing."[31]

These formal developments were complemented by Methodism's considerable association with egalitarianism and populism, as discussed in the preceding chapter.[32] The Wesleys were unrelenting in their evangelical fervor and developed an array of unorthodox pastoral techniques—such as open-air preaching, peripatetic clergy, and lay ministry—designed to extend Christian ministry beyond the confines of the pulpit and reach the multitudes in their own environment. Methodism quickly developed a reputation for an indecorous populism because of its efforts to recruit the lower classes and willingness to allow common citizens untrained in theology or oratory to preach and perform ministerial duties.[33] Methodists were permitted and even expected to confess their sins to each other rather than to clergy, enjoin each other to greater holiness, and offer prayer for their brethren. The Methodist democratization of worship saw the creation of prayer meetings and so-called love feasts in which attendees were required to offer public testimony of their religious conversions, confirming that, for the Methodists, personal religious conviction alone provided sufficient qualification for clerical standing. And, as mentioned earlier, the Methodists were known to allow women to preach, despite the Pauline edict forbidding women from speaking in church in any capacity.[34] The Methodist dispersal of clerical authority was accompanied by the erosion of traditional church decorum; the conventional solemnity of worship services gave way to famously raucous, unruly revival meetings, in which worshippers writhed, groaned, wept, shouted for joy, or unashamedly replied to preachers.[35] This breakdown of authority extended even into Methodist theology, which rejected the predestinarian belief that God attributed salvation only to the elect, regardless of their apparent merit. For the Methodists, salvation is within reach of everyone and can be attained through simple faith and application.

Hymnody figured prominently in the Methodist democratization of Christian piety. The common language of song enabled the Methodists to reach the lower classes, whose inability to pay pew fees kept them away from church but who nonetheless encountered potent ministry through memorable tunes and repetitive lyrical phrasings. According to Gareth Lloyd, Methodist hymns could be heard "not just in chapels, but in the workplace, the home, and the street," and thereby carried out the Methodist plan of extending the church beyond the delimited confines of sanctified houses of worship and permeating daily life with Christian piety. Though Wesley implicitly advocated the private reading of hymns, their popularity in North America derived from their promotion at revival meetings, in which singing was boisterous, passionate, and infamous. In spite of Wesley's stipulation that hymn singing remain mindful, Methodist devotional song developed a reputation for being uninhibited and extravagant, on a par with the public displays of emotion typical of revival meetings. Singing quickly became part of the attraction, spectacle, and expectation of revival meetings, and hymns enabled huge numbers of people— across class, gender, age, and race—to join together, if only in song.[36] As Watts had hoped and as conservatives feared, hymns became the voice of the people, and as such they threatened to overshadow and even silence the authority of clergy.

The resonant echo of hymns in day-to-day life afforded the Methodists a wider cultural presence and influence than they might have had otherwise, considering their questionable reputation. At the same time, this strong denominational affiliation ultimately hampered the spread of hymnody among other Protestant denominations, which were reluctant to align themselves with a form of public worship that was not only perceived as unruly and improper but was also associated with people on the social periphery. After famed Methodist preacher George Whitefield popularized the hymns of Isaac Watts in North America, revivalism was able to overcome the long-standing resistance of the more orthodox denominations, with the Congregationalists finally embracing the hymns of Isaac Watts in the late eighteenth century and the Presbyterians in the early nineteenth.[37] By the 1820s, it became clear that congregational hymnody was no passing fad but a permanent addition to Anglo-American Christianity.[38] The immense popularity of Methodism left more conservative denominations feeling endangered, and, as discussed in the preceding chapter, in 1837 the liberal wing of Presbyterians, the so-called New School, voted to adopt some of the untraditional evangelical practices, the so-called New Measures, employed in revivals.[39] The competitive adaptation to Methodism included a broad denominational willingness to incorporate hymnody into worship services, which yielded a more dynamic, passionate form of worship that temporarily shifted the focus from the clergy to the congregation by enabling active public participation.

By the second quarter of the nineteenth century, various Protestant denominations began to compile and issue their own sectarian hymnals, a genre that, by its very nature, undermined the integrationist ambitions of early hymnists by fortifying sectarian divisions.[40] Denominational hymnals sought to oversee this populist form and reinforce the primacy of hierarchical authority.[41] The hymnal editor, typically a member of the clergy, scrutinized hymns for content and quality before allowing them admission to their collections.[42] Texts were appraised for their literary caliber, broad appeal, and theological regularity, and, because the hymn had long been associated with egalitarianism and populism, the hymnals of more conservative denominations sought to reinstate criteria tethered to exclusivity and privilege. For example, conservative denominations declined to include in hymnals the songs favored in revivals and camp meetings. These populist hymns were typically characterized by features that enabled them to be accessible to a wide span of the public, such as simple vernacular lyrics, repeated refrains, and reliance on popular tunes. These songs were both improvised spontaneously and composed expressly for revivals, as with Joshua Leavitt's collection, *The Christian Lyre* (1831), which functioned as a musical companion to Charles Finney's revival meetings and went through twenty-six editions within fifteen years.[43] While hymns of this genre would find a receptive home among Methodists and Baptists, mainline denominations typically regarded them as unsuitable for formal worship and selected instead hymns whose more sophisticated poetic lyricism and musical arrangements exhibited discernment and polish. For example, in contrast to the wide use of popular tunes in camp-meeting hymns, hymn editors and arrangers from these latter denominations frequently enlisted themes by classical composers such as J.S. Bach, Beethoven, Haydn, and Mendelssohn as accompaniment to hymn lyrics, a decision that raised the taste and pedigree of this form.

Asahel Nettleton's *Village Hymns for Social Worship* (1824) is an illustrative case in point. In 1820, the General Association of Connecticut determined that "the prosperity of religion within their limits" warranted the creation of a hymnbook, especially in light of "the prevalence of revivals," and Nettleton, a Congregationalist clergyman and an itinerant revivalist, collected material for this new collection by researching popular songs and soliciting material from amateur writers. Though never intended for use in congregational worship, *Village Hymns* is a landmark work that sought to diversify hymnody beyond the opus of Isaac Watts, sparked the growth of missionary hymnody, and tried to promote the careers of home-grown American hymnists.[44]

Nettleton's distillation of contemporary hymnody found a receptive audience, and in three years it was reissued seven times.[45] At the same time, his collection is motivated by a desire to reinstate literary standards and expunge earthy revival hymns from the canon. In his preface, Nettleton writes that he "had hoped to find, in the style of genuine poetry, a greater number of hymns adapted to the various exigencies of revival. Laborious research has, however, led me to conclude that not many such compositions are in existence." Though he concedes that revival hymns "have been sung with much pleasure and profit," he deems such songs "ephemeral" because they are "entirely destitute of poetic merit." Revival hymns, according to Nettleton, are "utterly unfit for the ordinary purposes of devotion," and thus "the safest course is to leave them generally out."[46] For Nettleton, literary caliber and taste justified the exercise of clerical interdiction, the restoration of exclusionary standards, and the omission of populist revival hymns from an embryonic canon.

Reading Hymnody in Nineteenth-Century Fiction

While hymns in the revivalist style would continue to be perceived as déclassé among more conservative denominations, hymns would eventually overcome long-standing prohibitions and be widely included in congregational worship. Two landmark publications in the 1850s are generally regarded by hymnologists as heralding the mainstream acceptance of hymns: the 1855 *Plymouth Collection* edited by Henry Ward Beecher and the 1859 *Sabbath Hymn and Tune Book* edited by Andover Seminary professor Edwards A. Park, Austin Phelps, and hymnist Lowell Mason. However, in the complex history of English-language hymnody, sentimental women writers of the mid-century played a vital, if overlooked, role in mollifying concern about the genre's lingering associations with social unrest and in imparting the respectability necessary for its mainstream acceptance. Well before the publication of these two renowned hymn collections, women writers did considerable work in refining the public image of and attitude toward hymns. With the inclusion of countless scenes of hymn singing and reading in women's and children's literature, such writers as Stowe and Warner implicitly refashioned and domesticated the hymn, tempering its associations with the controversial public demonstrations of revivalism and bringing it in line with the private, modest pieties of normative mid-century femininity that these women were so instrumental in codifying and circulating.[47] In this way, sentimental literary texts continued to carry out the work of such mainline clergy-men as Asa Nettleton in reinstating genteel criteria of taste and respectability. Their depictions are often characterized by a distinct effort to raise the form's stature, as with their decision to omit revival or camp-meeting hymns and their inclusion instead of hymns marked by poetic craft and aesthetic sensibility. While the status of hymns might still be vexed in the churchgoing lives of nineteenth-century readers, in the universe of sentimental fiction hymns have been disarmed of their potential to effect destabilizing social change, and they are instead depicted as capable of preserving the very social order that they were originally charged with upending. As depicted in innumerable novels, hymns remain the rightful property of lowly people, who turn to these songs for help when worldly authority fails to offer assistance in times of trouble. However, whereas hymns in the context of Methodist revivalism were poised to level hierarchy altogether, hymns in sentimental novels instead reify social stratification by inspiring people on the margins to raise their standing in the world, whether morally or materially. In this respect, these writers somewhat sanction the laity-centered, populist hymnody that commenced with Watts and animated the Moravians, the Wesleys, and their revivalist successors, but in these novels hymns are less the vehicle of populist rabble-rousing and faulty theology, as conservatives feared, than the means by which marginal, struggling people can improve themselves and adapt to normative standards of respectability and decorum. Hymns, that is, enable the betterment of the lowly, not the spread of lower-class popular culture or a worrisome insistence on the leveling of class.

For example, in Warner's *The Wide, Wide World,* hymns function like an underground ministry, exchanged casually among believers and offering impromptu religious instruction and inspiration in remote places far from the pulpit: on a ferry, in a rural farm, in the household of apostates. Hymns figure prominently in the moral and religious education of orphan Ellen Montgomery, and throughout the novel she persistently turns to the hymnal given to her by a benevolent stranger, finding comfort and consolation there in times of trouble. Key moments in Ellen's maturation are usually signaled by the reprint of hymn lyrics: for instance, John Newton's hymn "Poor, Weak, and Worthless Though I Am" inspires Ellen to take responsibility for her role in a squabble with her brusque aunt, Miss Fortune, and shortly thereafter Charles Wesley's hymn "A Charge to Keep I Have" prompts Ellen to adopt "untiring gentleness, obedience, and meekness" in her future dealings with Miss Fortune.[48] While Warner leaves little doubt about the morally and spiritually transformative powers of hymns, the novel repeatedly suggests that hymns may effect moderate change in social hierarchies as well. In a particularly suggestive scene, Ellen ministers to clergyman Mr. Humphreys after the death of his daughter, Alice, by singing hymn after hymn. In a pared-down depiction of the capacity of hymns to authorize the worshipper and disempower clergy, this episode reveals how hymnody may challenge traditional hierarchy, allowing orphan girls the wisdom and poise to offer counsel to religious authority figures, but the power reversals here are mild and merely temporary in comparison with the unfettered social disorder of Methodism. The diminished power of hymns to effect transformation is likewise visible late in the novel after Ellen moves to Scotland to live with her mother's family, who consider her piety distasteful and demand that she renounce her attachments to the Humphreys family. In one scene, her private hymn singing causes her domineering uncle, Mr. Lindsay, to inquire, "Is all your heart in America, Ellen, or have you any left to bestow on us?" (545). In this instance, Lindsay detects in her hymn singing a threat to his primacy and questions whether other emotional loyalties may be undermining his rule, an assumption that signals the lingering associations of hymnody with anti-authoritarianism and populist self-governance.

At the same time, the novel cleaves to a distinctly genteel model of hymnody. Though in her 1864 novel, *The Old Helmet*, Warner would portray both congregational hymnody and camp-meeting song as legitimate expressions and incitements of faith, *The Wide, Wide World* envelops hymnody within the mantle of conventional propriety and politesse. In the first place, the novel gives decided preference to the class of hymns associated with more conservative denominations, reprinting only the stately, poetically sophisticated lyrics of such hymnists as Philip Doddridge, John Newton, Augustus Toplady, and Charles Wesley, and omitting revivalist and camp-meeting hymns altogether. Though Warner in this work declines to offer an outright opinion on the propriety of public song, the novel secretes hymnody behind closed doors, presenting it as material appropriate for private reflection and intimate conversation rather than public performance.[49] In thus avoiding any scenes of genuinely public hymn singing, the novel domesticates hymnody and brings it into alignment with contemporary feminine, middle-class mores, which privilege the private over the public, the written over the oral, and the refined over the spontaneous.[50] Directly countering anxiety that hymns might incite the frenzied emotional climate of revivalism, Warner presents hymns as enabling instead an antipodal affect characterized by self-control and the dutiful suspension of private feelings: for example, the reading of hymns inspires Ellen to hold her tongue and behave with perfect composure. Hymns enable restraint and self-censorship, not unseemly public emotional intemperance.[51]

While hymns play a central role in Ellen's religious and moral instruction, they no less participate in her social and intellectual refinement, allowing her to receive, albeit in an abbreviated and adapted way, the education expected of young ladies of privilege. Whereas the public singing of camp-meeting songs might signal Ellen's precipitous social and economic decline into a milieu often denounced as vulgar by the social elite, the private reading and singing of canonical, time-honored hymns indicate instead a commitment to the predilections for discernment and self-mastery associated with respectability and even social ascent. In a household with little appreciation for education, literary matters, or piety, hymns provide Ellen with carefully curated reading material and contribute to her development into a sensitive, appreciative reader, a skill expected of a young woman of respectable birth but one that she would otherwise struggle to cultivate living with Miss Fortune. The habitual reading of hymns fosters the perception of reading not as idle entertainment—an attitude that her future husband, seminarian John Humphreys, will warn her against—but instead as a means of self-improvement and moral development. And although her circumstances prevent her from having the musical education expected of accomplished young ladies, hymns serve as a pious substitute for a secular pastime in allowing her to practice her singing skills and to conduct the private domestic recitals common among affluent households. In all of these ways, Warner affirms that, however much hymns may enable the contestation and reversal of social authority, they may preserve middle-class ideals of taste and decorum, effectively improving and refining those with whom they come into contact. In this respect, she suggests that hymns may level authority by enabling social mobility. Thus, for Warner, Christian egalitarianism need not be implemented through the radical erasure of class but instead may be effected by the refinement and education of the lowly, with hymns serving a vital role in that effort.

Harriet Beecher Stowe offered a similar position on hymnody, using narrative and exposition to extol the virtues and respectability of hymns while also explicitly allaying lingering concerns about the form's aesthetics and pedigree. For instance, in *Agnes of Sorrento* Stowe attempted to rehabilitate the public standing of the Moravians and Methodists in an effort to endear the reader to the hymnody championed by both denominations. In tacit acknowledgment that a more conservative reader might reject out of hand these heterodox sects and the devotional song they celebrated, Stowe reframes these denominations' ardor as evidencing not vulgarity but an admirably artless religious piety. In the modern-day hymn, Stowe affirms, "the Moravian quaintness and energy [intermingled] with the Wesleyan purity and tenderness," a statement that presents Moravian unorthodoxy as mere aesthetic charm and repackages Methodist exhibitionism as simple emotional sincerity. What in conventional opinion might seem to be a worrisome public display of unrestrained feeling she here cannily presents as deriving from the same religious feelings shared by her ostensibly respectable reader. Lest her Protestant readers balk at the many Catholic hymns interleaved throughout the novel, she clarifies that "in its English dress, [one of these hymns] has thrilled many a Methodist class-meeting and many a Puritan conscience, telling, in the welcome they meet in each Christian soul, that there is a unity in Christ's Church which is not outward,—a secret, invisible bond, by which, under warring names and badges of opposition, His true followers have yet been one in Him, even though they discerned it not."[52] Using orthodoxy as a benchmark of Protestant respectability, Stowe avers that hymns still possess the power to foster ecumenicity and dissolve worldly differences, and she models the pan-Christian open-mindedness that she—as well as Isaac Watts and others—attributes to hymns themselves. In her 1876 story "The First Christmas of New England," she describes the devotional singing of early American settlers, reminding her readers that "the treasures of sacred song which are the liturgy of modern Christians had not arisen in the church. There was no Watts, and no Wesley, in the days of the Pilgrims," but only Psalters.[53] *Oldtown Folks* (1869) likewise documents the lingering suspicion of hymnody's extra-biblical character, as with the withering remark of the minister Dr. Lothrop upon hearing a congregant recite a hymn verse: "That, madam, is not the New Testament, but Dr. Isaacs Watts, allow me to remind you."[54]

In *Uncle Tom's Cabin*, Stowe suggests that she concurs with evangelical opinion that psalmody is too aloof and formal to incite genuine religious feeling.[55] In the novel's first chapter, when Mr. Shelby coaxes little Harry Harris to entertain the slaver trader Haley, he prompts the child to "show us how old Elder Robbins leads the psalm," and the boy "drew his chubby face down to a formidable length, and commenced toning a psalm tune through his nose, with imperturbable gravity."[56] The transformation here of a gleeful, energetic child into a dour church elder implicitly speaks volumes about the joyless formality and emotional impassivity of psalmody. But especially suggestive is its practice among white self-interested slave owners for whom Christianity seems to be little more than a torpid weekly ritual devoid of feeling or conviction. Stowe commits the rest of the novel to defending her ardent contention that sincere Christian faith renders slavery abhorrent and intolerable, but she begins her novel with a parodic portrait of the sterile psalmody practiced among slave-holders to suggest that, in failing to spark powerful emotion, such apathetic religious routine is indirectly responsible for the national sin of slavery.

In accord with the long-standing associations of hymnody with the struggles of the social periphery, Stowe dwells in some detail on the lively evangelical hymnody of slave congregations, which, unlike psalmody, proceeds "to the evident delight of all present." Like Warner, Stowe also moderates the subversive potential of hymns, suggesting that it affects social change by sparking not insurrection but personal betterment. In an early scene of a slave meeting at Tom's cabin, one elderly slave participant is visibly transformed by the experience of hymn singing. She remarks, "I'm mighty glad to hear ye all and see ye all once more, 'cause I don't know when I'll be gone to glory; but I've done got ready, chil'en; 'pears like I'd got my little bundle all tied up, and my bonnet on, jest a waitin' for the stage to come along and take me home."[57] Hymns cause her to see her worldly travails as temporary circumstances on her larger life journey to salvation, and thus afford her comfort and relief.[58] As Stowe describes it, the singing of hymns allows the slaves to resist the despotic rule of their captors not by inspiring mutinous rebellion but by inspiring piety, peace, and compliance with authoritarian rule. Hymnody thus enables capitulation with a socially stratified status quo.

This formulation is also evident in Tom's dealings with the brutal slave owner Simon Legree. In one pivotal scene, Legree tempts Tom to "join my church" by abandoning his faith and becoming one of Legree's willing slave minions. To that end, Legree mocks Christianity as a "mess of lying trumpery" and undermines Tom's hope for redemption by reasserting the finality of his own authority. 'The Lord an't going to help you," Legree taunts; "if he had been, he wouldn't have let me get you!" According to Legree, even divine authority cannot be relied upon for support or comfort, and so Tom would be well advised to grasp whatever worldly help he can find: "Ye'd better hold to me," Legree says; "I'm somebody, and can do something."[59] Tom feels momentary despair, his "dejected soul" sinking "to the lowest ebb," and he responds by singing "Amazing Grace," which John Newton famously composed after conversion caused him to renounce his work as a slave trader. Stowe excerpts several lesser-known verses that, in showcasing divine might, implicitly undermine the power of worldly authority:

The earth shall be dissolved like snow,
     The sun shall cease to shine;
But God, who called me here below,
     Shall be forever mine.

And when this mortal life shall fail,
     And flesh and sense shall cease,
I shall possess within the veil
     A life of joy and peace.

And when we've been there ten thousand years,
     Bright shining like the sun,
We've no less days to sing God's praise
     Than when we first begun.[60]

This depiction of divine sublimity restores Tom's equanimity and, in implicitly constituting enslavement as a temporary trial to be endured, consequently diminishes Legree's authority. Tom feels "an inviolable sphere of peace," and "so short now seemed the remaining voyage of life,—so near, to vivid, seemed eternal blessedness,—that life's uttermost woes fell from him unharming."[61] The hymn renders him impervious to "insult or injury," and it consequently equips him with the poise and self-control to continue to endure Legree's torment. Legree soon thereafter becomes enraged upon overhearing Tom sing Isaac Watts's hymn "When I Can Read My Title Clear," which defiantly asserts that,

Should earth against my soul engage,
And hellish darts be hurled,
Then I can smile at Satan's rage,
And face a frowning world.[62]

In forecasting a time when Tom "can read [his] title clear," the hymn substantiates Tom's hope that he will eventually own himself, and the hymn thereby confirms that Simon Legree's authority is merely temporary. While the hymn somewhat enables the lowly, powerless slave to delimit the authority of those in power over him, it also indefinitely defers that reversal to the afterlife. Until then, Tom remains compliant and respectful, and his resistance is confined solely to the domain of piety.

In sharp contrast with the associations of hymnody with social insurrection, Stowe by no means suggests that hymns incite slave uprisings or violent rebellion. Rather, in enabling slaves to direct their hopes for freedom to the afterlife, hymns restrict slave insubordination to the affections and aspirations. In a novel about a culture that most Northern readers would never know directly, hymns also function as a distinctly normalizing, familiarizing force that combats reader estrangement and cultivates sympathy and identification. Similar to the way a photographer might include in an image a commonplace object such as a coin to indicate scale, Stowe uses hymnody to present slaves as recognizably upright Christian brethren who, in reciting and reflecting on hymns in times of trouble, presumably replicate the worship practices and hymn preferences of readers. For example, she takes care to clarify that slaves do habitually sing "the well-known and common hymns" by such eminent hymnists as Newton and Watts, suggesting that slaves share a hymn canon with readers and thus possess a developed literary sensibility sufficient to appreciate such refined poetic lyric. In this respect, Stowe somewhat extends the tradition, established by Watts and Wesley, of using hymns to dissolve worldly differences in class, station, denomination, or race and to forge fellowship among Christians across these differences. At the same time, Stowe acknowledges that the "wild and spirited" practices and styles of slave hymnody may not comport with the reader's notions of propriety. Lest the reader dismiss such songs out of hand, she clarifies that the emotional vibrancy of slave hymnody, however uncouth a conservative reader may find it, actually enables self-control, patience, and forbearance among slaves, allowing them to release their unruly, rebellious feelings and thus bear their burdens with pious resignation. As with the fortitude of the old slave woman at the meeting and Tom's renewed courage after singing a hymn by Newton, hymns foster a self-command and restraint among slaves similar to that of Ellen Montgomery. And in conformity with conservative opinion, Stowe depicts slaves' hymnody as a largely domestic practice, as with Tom's private recitation of "Amazing Grace" and the gathering held in Tom's cabin shortly before his departure. Though some slave hymns may seem "wilder" than what readers are used to, hymns in *Uncle Tom's Cabin* both affirm and produce the religious respectability of slaves.[63]

Stowe openly allayed concerns about the taste and propriety of such populist hymnody in *Dred: A Tale of the Great Dismal Swamp* (1856), her follow-up to *Uncle Tom's Cabin*. Midway through the novel, a group of slave-owning Southerners ventures to a camp meeting in search of amusement and spectacle. After a member of their party succumbs to the altar call the night before, they fall into a discussion about the propriety of such emotional public declarations of faith, hymns and song among them. At the heart of the discussion is the perceived incongruity of gentility with such open avowals of feeling. Anne Clayton, a mannerly and reserved young woman, contends that such declarations are "an invasion of that privacy and reserve which belong to our most sacred feelings."[64] In her insistence that " 'there is a reserve about these things which belong to the best Christians," Anne voices skepticism about the public expression of religious feeling, adding that as an extension of this belief, she "always had a prejudice against that class of hymns and tunes" favored at camp meetings (16). Her brother, the antislavery lawyer Edward Clayton, replies by defending the congregational song of camp meetings, remarking that such songs are habitually "misjudge[d]" by "refined, cultivated women . . . who are brought up in the kid-slipper and carpet view of human life" (16). According to Clayton, a sensibility defined by both financial privilege and domesticity makes well-to-do women particularly disinclined to appreciate songs associated with the public devotions of the masses, and he urges greater open-mindedness toward religious expressions unhindered by such constraints. He urges Anne to overlook the informality or commonness of such works and to attend instead to the genuineness of their feeling. " 'What faith is there!' " he exclaims. " 'What confidence in immortality! How could a man feel it, and not be ennobled?' " (17). Regardless of a hymn's content or origin, its sincere sentiments may improve and enrich one's character; such works, he argues, may perfect the religious life of even the most cultivated gentlewoman. In this way, Stowe assuages anxieties about populist hymnody by asserting that they may effect the same civilizing ends as more elite hymns; despite the coarseness of their packaging, they need not be feared by religious traditionalists bound by class constraints.

Louisa May Alcott's 1877 novel, *Under the Lilacs*, similarly depicts hymns as a means of uplift for vulnerable, marginal people and endorses a hymnody rooted in conventional ideals of propriety. *Under the Lilacs* depicts the friendship of the middle-class Moss children with Ben Brown, a homeless boy who has run away from the circus in search of his lost father. In their efforts to socialize and reform Ben of his rough-and-tumble ways, the Moss children introduce him to the pious domestic rituals of the Sabbath, which include privately studying and memorizing a hymn, but Ben's limited education causes him to recoil from the formal, elevated language of the hymns he finds. In response, the children encourage him to read a hymn written by Miss Celia, their kindly neighbor. The hymn reads as follows:

A little kingdom I possess,
    Where thoughts and feelings dwell;
And very hard I find the task
    Of governing it well.
For passion tempts and troubles me,
    A wayward will misleads,
And selfishness its shadow casts
    On all my words and deeds.

How can I learn to rule myself,
    To be the child I should,—
Honest and brave,—nor ever tire
    Of trying to be good?
How can I keep a sunny soul
    To shine along life's way?
How can I tune my little heart
    To sweetly sing all day?

Dear Father, help me with the love
    That casteth out my fear!
Teach me to lean on thee, and feel
    That thou art very near;
That no temptation is unseen,
    No childish grief too small,
Since Thou, with patience infinite,
    Doth soothe and comfort all.

I do not ask for any crown,
    But that which all may win;
Nor seek to conquer any world
    Except the one within.
Be Thou my guide until I find,
    Let by a tender hand,
Thy happy kingdom in *myself*,
    And dare to take command.[65]

Ben warms to the hymn's informal, direct language, and he declares, "'I like that! . . . I understand it, and I'll learn it right away.'" He soon memorizes the hymn and repeats it at bedtime for his evening prayers, in this way sanctioning the use of hymns in private devotion and efforts of self-improvement. Just as the study of hymns signals Ellen Montgomery's growing maturation, so this hymn marks a turning point in Ben's development, providing him with simple, comprehensible language—in the vein of Watts, Zinzendorf, and Wesley—to confess his failings and resolve to do better. This scene confirms hymnody's affinity for people on the lower echelons of society—who in this case include children, orphans, and the uneducated poor—and narratively affirms the usefulness of hymns in their efforts to raise themselves up, both materially and morally. This episode offers an implicit defense of populist hymns composed for less educated people on the grounds that this constituency may not be able to understand loftier texts, a concern that occupied Isaac Watts centuries before. The favorable results of Ben's hymn study suggest that the lowliness of a text's register or style need not mitigate the text's ability to inspire uplift and improvement. And in accordance with the egalitarian heritage of hymnody, this hymn suggests that the ultimate "crown" of salvation is one "which all may win," although the hymn clarifies that the speaker aims not to topple or overturn established authority but instead to "conquer" the "world . . . within" through self-discipline and betterment. The hymn concedes that this struggle for self-mastery has wider social and political implications. To rule oneself is, in effect, to assume the authority of the ruler and to become a member of that elite class. That is precisely what happens in the novel: through a religious and moral education activated by the reading of a hymn, a homeless waif on the very bottom of society ascends into uprightness and respectability.

The Literary Persona of the Female Hymnist

Hymnody nonetheless evaded these efforts to impose supervision and refinement. Public appetites for ecumenical hymnbooks only expanded, and the populist hymns that failed to meet these standards grew exponentially in number and popularity. The revival of 1857–58 and the revivals led after the American Civil War by preacher Dwight Moody and his musical collaborator, Methodist composer Ira D. Sankey, sparked enthusiasm for hymns in the populist revival style, which Sankey termed "gospel hymns." The great success of Sankey's collection *Gospel Hymns and Sacred Songs* (1875) confirmed the growing popularity of devotional song geared to less elite sensibilities, despite the efforts of genteel editors and arrangers to elevate the literary and musical standards of hymnody. Gospel hymns were so popular that by the century's end, approximately 1,500 gospel songbooks alone had been published.[66] Nor did hymnody submit to denominational and clerical supervision, but it seeped outside those bounds, pervading American public and private life well beyond the reach of clergy and hymn editors. As published texts, hymns made their way into scrapbooks, journals, and letters of the period, and were integrated into the daily lexicon of evangelical Christians. Hymnals were upheld as the only text other than the Bible necessary for Christian observance; hymn lyrics and tunes were an essential source of poetry and music for Americans in the nineteenth century, and the singing and recitation of hymns were common leisure pastimes in American homes. In addition to providing inspiration or consolation to readers, hymns became a popular literary form in private writing, used by ordinary people seeking to transcribe, document, and order their religious feelings and experiences. Henry Ward Beecher affirmed the pervasiveness of devotional song in daily life and its particular favor among people of humble status: "We carry [hymns] with us upon our journey. We sing them in the forest. The workman follows the plow with sacred songs. Children catch them, and [sing] only for the joy it gives them."[67]

While the efforts to refine hymns ultimately failed, the involvement of sentimental women writers in this endeavor proved beneficial to their own pursuit of religious authority. Though sentimental novels presented hymns as capable of instilling obedience and compliance in potentially fractious worshippers, hymns enabled sentimental writers themselves to traverse any number of conventional religious restrictions, for, in working to quell the subversive powers of hymns, sentimental women writers in essence reserved that power for themselves. In some cases, their novels bear witness to these mutually dependent objectives. While Susan Warner's *Wide, Wide World* affirms that hymns may enable refinement and compliance with gendered norms, the novel tacitly oversteps traditional gender limits by assuming the clerical duty of hymn compilation. *The Wide, Wide World* reprinted the lyrics of nearly a dozen separate hymns, and in this respect it functioned like a well-curated miniature hymn collection, which attested to Warner's editorial taste and judgment in selecting hymns she deemed worthy of attention and inclusion. Indeed, the novel was so replete with hymn lyrics that it would provide the inspiration for a song cycle, W. H. Bellamy and C. W. Glover's

Lyrics from "The Wide, Wide World" (1853), which adapted some of its pivotal scenes into dramatic songs. Poet Phoebe Cary openly undertook this work in editing the 1869 collection *Hymns for All Christians*, but in collaborating with her pastor, Rev. Charles Deems, she acknowledged that this was a traditionally clerical task, although one she did not shirk from assuming. While Susan Warner declined to undertake this endeavor, her younger sister Anna became a successful and prolific hymn editor, single-handedly compiling several hymn collections, *Hymns of the Church Militant* and *Wayfaring Hymns*. Furthermore, as a sentimental novelist in her own right, Anna Warner used her novels as a venue by which she circulated her own hymn lyrics. For instance, the novel *Say and Seal* (1860), coauthored with Susan, included lyrics to Anna's hymn "Jesus Loves Me," which, after its initial publication in *Say and Seal*, rapidly became the single most popular children's hymn in history.

As the example of Anna Warner attests, women writers did not limit their ambitions solely to the task of supervising and editing hymns, but they instead directed their attention to the hymn form itself, writing countless hymns in which they channeled sentimental characterizations of femininity, domesticity, and piety. Lydia Sigourney, Harriet Beecher Stowe, and Susan Warner all wrote numerous hymns that were set to music, included in hymnals and hymnbooks, and sung by congregations. Julia Ward Howe is best remembered for her "Battle Hymn of the Republic," and Margaret Fuller is credited with the hymn "Jesus, a Child His Course Begun." Until their recent rediscovery by scholars of women's literature, Alice and Phoebe Cary were best remembered as the authors of such hymns as "Nearer Home" and "Dying Hymn."[68] Popular women writers celebrated in their own time but overlooked by literary history were also important contributors to the hymn form, such as Elizabeth Prentiss, author of the best-selling novel *Stepping Heavenward* (1869) as well as numerous novels for younger readers; she wrote many hymns during her lifetime, and her hymn "More Love to Thee, O Christ" remains in circulation today among numerous Protestant denominations. Though compositions by women hymnists always constituted a minority of hymns in circulation, some of the best-known, most beloved hymnists of the century were women writers, among them Sarah Flower Adams, Cecil Frances Alexander, Fanny Crosby, Charlotte Elliott, Frances Ridley Havergal, and Felicia Hemans.

The genre's tradition of egalitarian populism provided both an obstacle to and an opportunity for sentimental hymnody. Though female-authored hymns were in the main decorously modest and conservative in avowal, their sheer existence derives from and even extends the genre's tradition of egalitarianism. Despite the fact that women vastly outnumbered men in church attendance and participation in auxiliary organizations, they nonetheless were still formally barred from preaching and still had lesser social status, a subordinate condition that made them well suited to a form associated with the powerless and disadvantaged. As a genre born out of and still bearing the traces of demotic ambitions, it was accessible to everyone; one had only to be able to write about religious experience in such a way as to inspire recognition and feeling in others. Indeed, in the nineteenth century, virtually everyone did write hymns, and the form was so genuinely bottom-up that professional writers, such as William Cullen Bryant and Oliver Wendell Holmes, contributed to the genre only after amateurs had already made it popular and fashionable. The career of hymnist Phoebe Hinsdale Brown evidences how the genre's tradition of populist inclusivity directly enabled female authorship. When Asahel Nettleton compiled his *Village Hymns,* he canvassed average citizens rumored to write religious poetry and solicited their work, a detail that confirms both the inclusiveness of this genre as well as its wide use among common people. In his inquiries, he encountered Brown, a housewife whose struggles with poverty and domestic cares motivated her to write devotional poetry in her quest for divine aid and strength. In 1818, Brown wrote a poem in response to a nosey neighbor's probing query about her late-afternoon walks; originally titled "My Apology for My Twilight Rambles, Addressed to a Lady," the poem explains her need to

. . . steal awhile away
From little ones and care,
And spend the hours of setting day
In gratitude and prayer.[69]

She kept the poem private for several years before Nettleton requested samples of her lyrics, and he would eventually edit this homely poem to expunge its personal references and include it in *Village Hymns.*[70] Helped by this well-publicized narrative of private devotion, it became a genuinely popular hymn in the nineteenth century and was widely touted, if erroneously, as the first hymn published by an American woman.[71]

With few other options available for women to take an active role in the worship service, hymnody provided women with an unprecedented religious forum that extended even into the church itself. There is no discounting the genuine religious authority women acquired by writing hymns circulated in print and performed in worship service, for these lyrics allowed women to circumvent Pauline prohibition by inviting others—namely, the singing congregation—to speak their words for them. Hymns interpreted scripture, offered theology, and told readers and singers what to feel, think, and do. In that respect, sentimental hymnody contravened the very gender traditionalism and restraint it touted by providing a venue for women to express themselves and their beliefs in the worship service and to exert influence on the beliefs of others. Hymnody as a result became a popular, influential literary genre of sentimentalism, which in this form was able to move beyond the limits of the silent printed page to circulate in heretofore inaccessible locales such as churches and worship service.

But in order to violate these long-standing restrictions, women writers had to disavow altogether their aspiration to do so and publicly affirm their allegiance to social and religious convention. Sentimental refinement of populist hymnody provided one vital means by which women writers were able to confirm their traditionalist bona fides, but numerous other characteristic features of sentimentalism also proved useful in providing assurances of conservatism while also fortifying the emotional impact of their hymns. For instance, the genre's characteristic pleas for divine assistance affect a posture of frailty and dependence that both capitulates to conventional nineteenth-century notions of femininity and invites potent emotional identification in worshippers, at once defusing the hymns' impropriety and making them affectively compelling. The long literary tradition of private female poetry writing also rendered hymnody acceptable, as it constituted this endeavor not as evidence of ambition for an unseemly public audience but instead as a worthy female occupation attesting to the writers' retiring inwardness, piety, and gentility. Elizabeth Gray has observed that religious poetry was an acceptable idiom for Englishwomen because of its formal resemblance to prayer, "a passive and private undertaking in which nineteenth-century women were held to excel."[72]

Domestic seclusion, which Lauren Berlant terms "containment," also became another signature feature of sentimental hymnody that worked to conceal the extraordinary public influence these texts afforded their authors.[73] Because hymns were publicly performed during worship service and offered clerical instruction about scripture and observance, female hymnists broadcast their confinement in the home, their domestic enclosure offsetting the audacious publicity of their texts and affirming their unambitious modesty: a woman might respectably compose hymns in the privacy of her home without venturing out into the public or compromising her domestic duties.[74] The hymn thus functioned as a textual "intermediary," to use Elizabeth Maddock Dillon's term, which used the rhetoric of the private domestic sphere to justify unprecedented female authority in the public domain of theology and religious practice.[75] The many domestic uses of hymns—in family prayer, the instruction of children, or household leisure activities—only furthered this association of hymnody with domesticity. Domestic enclosure consequently became a requisite feature in works by women hymnists, and it was widely believed that a hymn composed in a private moment of retiring self-reflection was more sincere, truthful, and effective in eliciting similar sentiments in others.[76] A hymn's private, domestic composition also contributed to its public acceptance because it was believed that, unlike the more polished work of professional songwriters or the rough compositions improvised at revivals, such works were the product of personal trial, sensibility, and genuine Christian experience rather than brash ambition or the spontaneous workings of ecstatic crowds. In this respect, the private domestic setting that imparted respectability to hymns in novels by Stowe and Warner became a generic marker of hymn quality and sincerity.[77] And though, as Mary De Jong has shown, neither women nor men hymnists used such language more than the other, the pervasive references to home in hymns about the afterlife indirectly rendered this form a celebration of a traditionally female space.[78] Hymnody was thus construed not as a transgression of biblical restrictions on female participation in church but as an expression of feminine domesticity.[79] Harriet Beecher Stowe even claimed that the Christian hymn was the invention of the supreme paragon of sentimental femininity, as with her assertion that St. Mary's Magnificat in the New Testament was the first such work.[80]

The domestic seclusion of emotion also helped provide important additional justification for female-authored hymnody. In continuation of Watts's and Wesley's shared belief that hymns ought to promote emotion in worshippers, mainline denominations agreed that hymns should incite emotion, but conservatives maintained that those emotions should be temperate and receive public expression solely through the performance of the hymn. While it was believed that women were better able to access pious feelings and to craft more emotionally potent hymns, their domestic confinement served as an important reassuring counterweight that promised the preservation of public decorum: privately composed hymns about emotional trials, it was presumed, were less likely to cause unseemly emotional excesses in public worship service.[81] That is, the emotionalism that initially worried conservative critics became acceptable within the confines of domesticated feminine piety.

The biographical writings of numerous popular female hymnists evidence their willing compliance with these expectations, both by depicting their hymns as the privately composed products of domestic experience and by concomitantly disavowing any public professional ambition. For instance, in an 1870 letter, popular hymnist and novelist Elizabeth Prentiss used this rhetoric of domestic privacy, writing, "Most of my verses are too much of my own experience to be put in print now. After I am dead I hope they may serve as language for some other hearts," a statement that attests both to the use of the hymn form in private life and the perception that hymns deriving from domestic privacy are more sincere and compelling than ones written professionally.[82] Prolific and beloved professional hymnist Fanny Crosby had to reckon with this assumption, and in one of her memoirs she claimed that all her many hymns derived not from canny professional craft but from private personal experience: she wrote, "That some of my hymns have been dictated by the blessed Holy Spirit I have no doubt; and that others have been the result of deep meditation I know to be true. . . . Most of my poems have been written during the long night watches, when the distractions of the day could not interfere with the rapid flow of thought."[83] This belief gave rise to the enduring subgenre of hymn histories, such as Nicholas Smith's *Songs from the Hearts of Women* (1903), which, by revealing the biographical details behind famous female-authored hymns, purported to verify their authenticity.

In their many hymn compositions, sentimental women writers explicitly enlisted all these generic conventions so as to justify and authenticate their poems. Just as sentimental novels portrayed hymnody as fully compatible with pious restraint, so sentimental hymns are discernibly informed by this same cultural ethos, visibly referencing such generic hallmarks as modesty, authenticity, private domesticity, and aspiration for self-betterment.[84] In effect, the hymns of sentimental writers infused a long-peripheral religious genre with the qualities and beliefs that gave sentimentalism such profound cultural purchase. The end results were mutually beneficial: sentimental discourse helped hymns become respectable in the eyes of mainline denominations in spite of sentimentalism's adoption of numerous features of revivalism (as discussed in the preceding chapter), and hymns enabled sentimentalism and sentimental writers in particular to acquire genuine religious authority.

Stowe's hymns provide a vital example. Of the writers in her cohort, none had a stronger imprimatur to contribute to hymnody than did she. As a daughter of Lyman Beecher, sister to numerous ministers (including Henry Ward Beecher), and the wife of a seminary professor, Stowe had an impeccable religious pedigree, and the sensation that was *Uncle Tom's Cabin* positioned her as a significant evangelical voice. Her contributions to hymnody began at the behest of her brothers Henry and Charles, who set three of her poems to music composed by Charles and included them in the *Plymouth Collection*, the hymnbook born out of the famous singing at Henry's Brooklyn congregation. Her oft-reprinted hymns were revered equally for their religious sentiment and literary caliber. As was typical of the form, the private personal experiences behind some of Stowe's hymns would garner attention, as with her hymn "The Secret," which was incorrectly reputed to derive from her grief following her son's brain injury at Gettysburg, despite the fact that it was first published nearly a decade earlier.[85]

Stowe's "Still, Still with Thee" was perhaps her most popular hymn, appearing in at least ten different hymn collections by the end of the century.[86] Hymnologist E. E. Ryden has claimed that "for sheer poetic beauty there is probably not a single American lyric that can excel 'Still, Still with Thee.'"[87] The hymn visibly incorporates many of the same generic standards that permeate fictional depictions as well as more genteel female-authored hymns. Like Phoebe Brown's "Twilight Ramble," the hymn was reputed to have originated in Stowe's own solitary walks: Edward Ninde claimed that in 1853 Stowe shared the hymn's lyrics with a companion during an early morning stroll and described them as "verses which she had written at such an hour."[88] As a consequence, the hymn was cloaked in the mantle of biographical authenticity, a presumption that invites the hymn to be received not as a literary composition crafted with professional expertise but as a homely, modest expression of personal faith, born out of private experience and feeling rather than the expectation of the public eye. The hymn's contents fortified this autobiographical reading, for the hymn itself describes the prayerful pursuit of divine communion during an early morning walk, "when the bird waketh and the shadows flee." Over the course of six stanzas, the hymn repeatedly affirms its sentimentality and its subscription to polite standards of class, taste, and respectability. For example, it extols the devotional merits of quiet repose and solitude, as the speaker regards the early morning as a special occasion to feel "nearness to Thee and heaven." Whereas revival or camp-meeting hymns often invited singers to shout or publicly proclaim God's praises, as with Fanny Crosby's lyric assertion that "the children of the Lord have a right to shout and sing," Stowe's hymn instead celebrates the spiritual rewards of private, silent reflection.[89] The fifth stanza, for instance, describes the virtues of praying silently while abed at night, for such practices, she suggests, afford rest and relief from life's burdens:

> When sinks the soul, subdued by toil, to slumber
> Its closing eye looks up to Thee in prayer,
> Sweet the repose beneath Thy wings o'ershading.

And just as mid-century novels depict hymnody as a vehicle for self-improvement and refinement, so Stowe's hymn interprets daybreak as a reminder that every day provides another opportunity for spiritual rejuvenation and betterment: she writes,

> As to each new-born morning
> A fresh and solemn splendor is given,
> So does this blessed consciousness awaking.

In the logic of the hymn, this pursuit of self-improvement is implicitly associated with the development of a finer, more attentive aesthetic sensibility, as the speaker's growing spiritual reverence is both activated and signaled by a keen appreciation for beauty. In its delight in the "purple morning" and the "calm dew and freshness of the morn," the hymn presumes that, in engendering mindfulness and gratitude, faith enables the detection of beauty in the commonplace. In heightening aesthetic receptivity in this fashion, piety cultivates the sensibilities and thereby implicitly furthers the refinement of the faithful.

Alcott's hymn "My Kingdom" acquired renown because it similarly broadcast its fidelity to the normative pious femininity that coursed through much of Alcott's fiction. Though *Under the Lilacs* is remembered merely as a minor work in Alcott's corpus, "My Kingdom" became a beloved and successful hymn, set to several different musical arrangements and included in both hymnbooks and children's poetry collections well into the twentieth century. Alcott promoted "My Kingdom" by publicly emphasizing its origins in personal experience and private reflection. Alcott began to circulate the poem several years before the 1877 publication of *Under the Lilacs*, when such works—hymns written by amateur women in moments of private reflection—had already developed particular currency. Eva Munson Smith, herself an amateur composer and philanthropist, contacted Alcott in research for her mammoth work, *Woman in Sacred Song: A Library of Hymns, Religious Poems, and Sacred Music by Woman* (1888), a comprehensive anthology that suggests that by the late century women were already recognized and even celebrated as hymnists of high caliber. Alcott responded by submitting "My Kingdom," which she described in 1875 as "the only hymn I ever wrote. It was composed at thirteen, and as I still find the same difficulty in governing my kingdom, it still expresses my soul's desire, and I have nothing better to offer."[90] In this description, Alcott bolsters the hymn with public professions of modesty and imperfection: by undercutting her public stature and openly admitting her shortcomings, Alcott trumpets the hymn's origins in private domestic experience and emotional sincerity. Though the publication of Smith's volume was delayed for over a decade, "My Kingdom" was published that same year, 1875, in the children's collection *The Sunny Side*, edited by Unitarian minister Charles W. Wendté and H. S. Perkins. Alcott submitted "My Kingdom" with a note that identified the poem as a product of her own youth: "I send you a little piece which I found in an old journal, kept when I was about thirteen years old. . . . Coming from a child's heart, when conscious of its wants and weaknesses, it may go to the hearts of other children in like mood."[91] Lest her readers interpret the poem's childlike voice as imitative pandering, Alcott here clarifies that the hymn had been composed during her own youthful private reflections in a scenario very much like that of contemporary fiction depicting the uses of hymns for struggling young people. Wendté and Perkins were clearly aware that they were in possession of something special, and on their title page they heralded the hymn as an "original poetic contribution" and reprinted this personal explanation as the head note to the poem itself, taking care to identify this narrative as coming from "*a private letter*" (italics in original) to publicize its humble derivation from a private moment of trial and, by extension, its authenticity. Alcott further burnished the hymn's modest origins by attributing it, two years later in *Under the Lilacs*, to the character Miss Celia, who makes a similar confession to youthful authorship: she tells Ben, "I feel very proud to think you chose that [hymn], and to hear you say it as if it meant something to you. I was only fourteen when I wrote it; but it came right out of my heart, and did me good. I hope it may help you a little."[92]

Similar beliefs suffuse the hymns of Anna Warner, a well-regarded evangelical author of several novels as well as jointly written works with her sister, Susan. Her fiction is seldom remembered today, even by specialists in nineteenth-century women's literature, but several of her hymns remain in active circulation worldwide. In her memoir of her sister, *Susan Warner* (1909), Anna reprinted a lengthy passage from Susan's diary to describe the beginnings of her career as a hymnist. Susan wrote, "The next day, Sunday, in the afternoon, A. [her shorthand for Anna] had been copying off some hymns . . . and left them with me to look over. I had not read two verses of 'We Would See Jesus,' when I thought of Anna, and merely casting my eye down[,] the others so delighted and touched me that I left it for tears and petitions. I wished A. might prove the author—and after found out she was, I sat by her a little while with my head against her crying such delicious tears. It seemed to me as if other people find pleasure on the earth, and as if A. and I go skimming through the air to get it,—more refined and pure. Thank God for this."[93] Though Anna at the time of the memoir's publication had already acquired international acclaim for her children's hymn "Jesus Loves Me," this excerpt depicts her as a retiring female hymnist whose verses derive from private heartfelt yearnings and piety rather than unseemly public ambition. Notably, Susan's final remarks in this diary entry candidly state her belief that feminine piety and private religious reflection are innately more "refined and pure" than worldly ambition or pleasure, beliefs that plainly underlie her portrayal of hymnody in *The Wide, Wide World*. In publishing this entry, Anna suggests as well that the hymn "We Would See Jesus" would have remained private had it not received the approval of her famous sister, and Anna would make the hymn public, albeit as discreetly as possible, by including it in her novel *Glen Luna; or, Dollars and Cents* (1852). As was typical of nineteenth-century women writers looking to preserve their modesty and respectability, she published the novel pseudonymously under the name Amy Lathrop, and she inserted the hymn in the novel without any attribution of authorship or invitation of acclaim.[94] In the novel, two sisters, Katy and Grace, sing hymns to their beloved friend Miss Easy on her deathbed; she requests that they sing her "favourite" hymn, and they comply with the words of Anna's own hymn "We Would See Jesus" about the yearnings for intimacy with Christ amid worldly travails.[95] The elision of Anna's own authorship emerges as a supreme gesture of modesty and self-control, subordinating her ego and ambition out of an apparent desire to proffer a hymn that might provide comfort to those in need during times of trouble. In this respect, she models the self-effacement, privacy, and unassuming restraint that her female contemporaries upheld as the chief consequences of hymnody and of sentimentalism more generally.

"Jesus Loves Me" was published under similar circumstances. In the novel *Say and Seal*, the main character, Faith Derrick, observes the seminarian John

Linden singing a simple children's hymn to a dying orphan boy. As with "We Would See Jesus," she included the hymn with no introduction and with no clear attribution of authorship. Though both hymns would circulate widely and be included in denominational hymnals designed for public congregational worship, both novels present the hymns in the most intimate and withdrawn of domestic spaces, at the bedsides of the dying. As an extension of this enclosure of hymns in private domestic spaces, Anna suggests that hymns are invaluable resources for trials of the most solitary kind, as the dying prepare to face the unknown in the afterlife and seek assurances that they will meet their maker. That is, although these hymns are sung to the dying by well-meaning caregivers, they gain purchase in the private interiority of those undergoing the most introverted and personal of experiences. Through these novelistic introductions, Anna Warner shrouded her hymns, as it were, in privacy, solitude, and modesty, all of which affirm her own feminine respectability and her qualification to write such works.

The modesty and humility of "Jesus Loves Me" are inversely proportional to the extraordinary international renown that the hymn would achieve, and this suggestive ratio may elucidate the larger function of these generic registers. To be sure, these affirmations of privacy, humility, and conservatism helped craft an image of hymnody that neutralized the form's very publicity and egalitarian origins, using assurances and displays of feminine refinement to moderate the hymn's capacity to upset social norms. These assurances of privacy and domesticity provided the necessary ballast that enabled the hymn eventually to find inclusion in public worship, serving as a counterweight that ensured that public performance would never devolve into an unseemly spectacle like that of the revival meeting. At the same time, these declarations of conservatism enabled these women to work in a form that for the first time gave them a genuine voice in American Christianity and allowed them to create and shape religious views and experience.[96]

Though today hymns are no longer touted for their importance, there is no discounting the potency and power afforded by hymnody in the nineteenth century. Hymns were not simply poems set to music but were interpreted as theological works in their own right, refined in the crucible of personal experience to transmit essential religious doctrine about the nature of divinity, human beings, and faith, as well as the responsibilities of the believing Christian. According to Henry Ward Beecher, "Hymns are worship, and should be respected as such."[97] In affirming beliefs presumably learned from trial or offering thanks or praise, hymns modeled behaviors as well as ways of engaging with divinity, and, in the opinion of nineteenth-century observers and clergy, the influence of hymns on believers and nonbelievers alike was substantial. Hymns were widely credited with inciting conversion and moral reform, and they were upheld as important foundations of childhood education and character building.[98] Children were urged to memorize hymns out of the belief that religious verses learned in youth could exert moral influence throughout life.[99] In the mindset of the nineteenth century, hymns had the power to shape or change a person's life, sending them on the road to righteousness and salvation. The religious impact and theological content of hymnody are at the fore of Beecher's remark that "with a Bible and a hymn-book a man has a whole library; and if he knows how to use those two things, he knows enough to be a missionary, or to be a minister anywhere."[100] Though literary women may have endorsed conventional notions of propriety, it is by no means a humble thing to elect to work in a form with such transformational power and authority. The hymn enabled sentimentalism to acquire a genuine foothold in formal religious ritual, and it likewise enabled literary women to become legitimate religious authorities. They did so, however, by participating in a campaign to divest the form of its activist energies and allocating those insurrectionary powers exclusively for themselves.

CHAPTER 3

The Christian Plot

Stowe, Millennialism, and Narrative Form

Blessed is he that readeth, and they that hear the words of this prophecy, and keep those things which are written therein: for the time is at hand.
—Revelation 1:3

THROUGHOUT THE nineteenth century, it was a widely held belief that the millennium was imminent. Established denominations and new religious movements alike shared the belief that the divine kingdom would soon be established on Earth, and religious leaders as diverse as Lyman Abbott, Henry Ward Beecher, Horace Bushnell, Alexander Campbell, Lorenzo Dow, Dwight L. Moody, John Humphrey Noyes, and Joseph Smith all maintained that the religious fulfillment of human history was impending.[1] The evangelism of the American Home Missionary Society, one of the era's leading Protestant organizations, was openly motivated by the desire to prepare humankind for the impending millennium, and revivalist Charles Finney assured an audience in 1835 that "if the church will do all her duty, the millennium may come in this country in three years."[2] William Miller, a Baptist minister from Upstate New York, created a veritable frenzy of millennialist fervor with his conviction that Christ would return by March 1844, but the failure of his projection in no way dimmed widespread millennialist expectation. Americans interpreted both the economic collapse of 1837 and the revolutions of Europe in the 1840s as signs of the coming apocalypse.[3] Even Lincoln's second inaugural address registered the widespread belief that the

United States would play a pivotal role in the coming millennium, as with his assertion that the nation remains "the last, best hope of earth."[4]

Millennial anticipation was everywhere visible in the United States in the mid-nineteenth century, and, unsurprisingly, it surfaces in contemporary religious literature by women writers. As Herbert Ross Brown observed in 1940, "The ebullient prophets of the sentimental generation were confident that the millennium was just around the corner."[5] In Catharine Sedgwick's 1835 novel, *Home*, Mr. Barclay interprets the spread of democracy and the erosion of class hierarchies as "some heralds of this millennium."[6] In Susan Warner's *Wide, Wide, World*, John Humphreys testifies to his millennialist conviction: "I know that a day is to come when those heavens shall be wrapped together as a scroll—they shall vanish away like smoke, and the earth shall wax old like a garment;—and it and all the works that are therein shall be burned up."[7] Sarah Josepha Hale's *Northwood* (1852) anticipates that the millennium will enable "great elements of human progress," such as the "change [of] man's heart" and the imprisonment of Satan.[8] The closing chapter of Harriet Beecher Stowe's *Uncle Tom's Cabin* offered the most famous literary avowal of millennialist belief in the entire century, let alone among nineteenth-century women's writing. Insisting that the impending millennium necessitates the abolition of slavery, Stowe enlists the thundering oratory of the pulpit to urge readers to "read the signs of the times!"[9] The imminence of the millennium, she proclaims, is evident in the revolutionary upheaval sweeping Europe and encroaching on the United States. "This is an age of the world when nations are trembling and convulsed. A mighty influence is abroad," she insists, "surging and heaving the world, as with an earthquake. . . . Every nation that carries in its bosom great and unredressed injustice has in it the elements of this last convulsion."[10] The source of this international turmoil, she contends, is the "the spirit of HIM whose kingdom is yet to come," an event that will soon transpire in a "*day of vengeance*" [emphasis in original] in which Americans will have to face the "wrath of Almighty God" for the collective national sin of slavery. Similar rhetoric pervades *Dred: A Tale of the Great Dismal Swamp* (1856), in which the novel's titular character, the fugitive slave Dred, prophesies the vengeance that will be enacted with Christ's return. Where *Uncle Tom's Cabin* only foretells the imminent destruction of American civilization, *Dred* dramatizes such an event, as slavery unleashes chaos and lawlessness that ravage the basic structures of civilized society, among them family, law, and religion. In fulfillment of biblical prophecy, the high in *Dred* are laid low, forced to live as fugitives in a grisly swamp, while the most loathsome, base elements of society become the new ruling class, all while Dred preaches from the book of Revelation to herald the end of times.

Despite the heated intensity of these anticipations of the millennium, such concerns seem to recede from view in Stowe's later fiction. With their folksy idiom, light humor, and affectionate depiction of domestic life, Stowe's later domestic novels seem free of the weighty eschatology of *Uncle Tom's Cabin* and *Dred*. Consequently, scholarly attention to the presence of millennialism in Stowe's work—and in sentimental literature as a whole—has focused exclusively on these two early novels, *Uncle Tom's Cabin* in particular.[11] The suspension of slavery in 1863 seems to be the implicit explanation for this putative disappearance of millennialist anticipation, for the elimination of the social instigator of Stowe's fear seemingly coincides with the apparent evaporation of apocalyptic terrors from her fiction. However, this assumption is deficient, for in the years between *Dred* and the Emancipation Proclamation, Stowe published three novels—*The Minister's Wooing* (1859), *The Pearl of Orr's Island* (1862), and *Agnes of Sorrento* (1862)—that are strikingly devoid of pronouncements heralding the arrival of the divine kingdom on Earth. Nor do Stowe's papers evidence a diminution of millennialist expectation. In *The American Woman's Home* (1869), a domestic manual she coauthored with her sister Catharine Beecher, the two Beecher women envision "a dawning day to which we are approaching, when a voice shall be heard under the whole heavens, saying 'Alleluia'—the 'kingdoms of this world are become [sic] the kingdoms of our Lord and of his Christ, and he shall reign forever and ever.'"[12] In *Footsteps of the Master* (1877), she extended this Adventist vision by asserting, "It may be . . . that in assemblies of his people Jesus will suddenly stand, saying, 'Peace be unto you!'"[13] In *He's Coming Tomorrow* (1874), Stowe envisioned public reaction to the news that Christ would fulfill prophecy and return to Earth on the following day. At the vision's close, a "band of clergymen" congregates on the steps of a church and proclaims, "It's no matter now about these old issues [of sectarian conflict]. . . . *He* is coming: He will settle all. Ordinations and ordinances, sacraments and creeds, are but the scaffolding on the edifice. They are the shadow: the substance is CHRIST!"[14]

Amid this abundance of extra-literary expressions of millennialist expectation, the seeming disappearance of such sentiment from Stowe's fiction may be due less to the abolition of slavery than to the insufficiency of our assumptions about nineteenth-century millennialist belief. To assume that the stark fright of *Uncle Tom's Cabin* is typical of millennialism is to confuse the anomalous with the norm and to presume that nineteenth-century millennialist belief is identical to that of the early twenty-first century. A few high-profile exceptions aside—such as Millerism and its progeny, Seventh-Day Adventism—millennialism of the nineteenth century was generally characterized not by heated prophecies of the end of the world but by the optimistic expectation of progress in both spiritual and worldly matters. At its essence, millennialism is a philosophy of human history that produces narratives forecasting the eventual destination of human civilization, and American Protestants across denominations in the nineteenth century believed that civilization was steadily heading not toward destruction but toward a new age characterized by enlightenment, improvement, and the elimination of all worldly ills. It is in this form, as a Protestant theology of divinely ordered progress, that millennialism chiefly exerted influence, both on Stowe's fiction and on the nineteenth century writ large. Though more subtle than the eruptions of terror that close *Uncle Tom's Cabin*, this form of millennialism resulted in a hopeful worldview that everywhere saw signs of progress and indications that a new age was imminent. The panicked proclamations of end times in *Uncle Tom's Cabin* have eclipsed the more conventional millennialism of Stowe's domestic fiction, which relies more heavily on narrative form than on explicit exhortation to affirm the widespread belief that biblical prophecies are everywhere being fulfilled. In novels published both before and after emancipation in 1863, Stowe's novels diverge from the traditional millennialist genre of the jeremiad to demonstrate the effects of Christianity in creating resolution, reunion, and improvement out of tattered, estranged families and social disorder.[15] Stowe's novels demonstrate the nineteenth-century expectation that Christian faith can and will exert predicable results on individuals and communities, changing the very course and vector of human civilization. In this regard, her novels, including *Uncle Tom's Cabin* and *Dred*, are manifestly organized according to what one religious historian has termed the "Christian plot" but that, in Stowe's work, could be more accurately described as the "Protestant plot": the expectation that human history will inevitably result in redemption and restoration.[16]

Stowe's narrative engagement in millennialism highlights the scriptural antecedents of sentimental narrative convention. Attention to nineteenth-century millennialist belief can help us see in a new light the happy endings and narrative resolutions that characterized much of Stowe's fiction, as well as that of her female sentimental contemporaries, and that has long jeopardized the seriousness with which they were regarded by critics. In their formulaic disentanglement of complex plots into neat matrimonial pairings and newly restored happy families, sentimental novels adapted and modernized religious prophecy to show not only that human beings are indeed marching incrementally toward the predicted new age but also that white, middle-class, North Atlantic Protestant housewives—and not ordained clergy—are chiefly responsible for the fulfillment of scriptural prophesy. This argument builds on the foundational work of Nina Baym, Gillian Brown, and Jane Tompkins on the sacrality of domesticity in sentimental literature, and it seeks to show in particular how the contemporary theological preoccupation with millennialism provided narrative forms and tropes that imparted particular religious currency to women's work, both literary and domestic.[17] This consideration aims to transpose somewhat the formulation offered by these predecessors, who have analyzed the ways in which sentimentalism imparted a religious character to domesticity; the stimulus of millennialism causes Stowe, I argue, to impart instead a domestic character to Protestantism. The workings of divine providence, Stowe repeatedly suggests, may be discerned not just in the grand sweep of political history, as with the revolutions of the 1840s, but in the private recesses of homes and families, both overseen by women.[18] And in situating these millennialist plots in the recent American past, Stowe's novels suggest that the new age may already be upon them.

For those of us old enough to remember the outright global panic that preceded the year 2000, the term *millennium* connotes images of mass destruction and civic chaos, with the expectation that human society as we know it will disintegrate. In this respect, the millennium is widely conflated with the apocalypse, a term that is also widely taken to mean a cataclysmic end to civilization. The outbursts of millennialist anxiety in Stowe's early fiction would seem to accord with these popular assumptions, though both millennialism and Stowe's promotion of eschatological theology are significantly more complicated than popular opinion would suggest. The word *millennium* itself simply means a thousand-year period, while the word *apocalypse* merely denotes the disclosure of clandestine information; over time, *apocalypse* has become the label for an entire literary genre that purports to divulge the most supremely privileged secret of all: the fate of human civilization. Apocalyptic literature predicting the conclusion of human history was common in antiquity among both Jewish and Christian communities, but the Revelation attributed to John of Patmos in the New Testament has become the most canonical of apocalypses, offering a highly elaborate vision of last things in which a period of a thousand years would figure prominently. In Revelation 20:4–6, John envisioned that Satan would be imprisoned in a pit for a thousand years, during which time Christian martyrs would be resurrected and reign at the side of Christ. At the close of this period, Satan will be released to wage a final battle for supremacy, and Satan's defeat will be followed by the judgment of all human beings. Death itself will be vanquished with the establishment of the magnificent city of New Jerusalem, from which Christ himself will reign in perfect peace and order.

It is an understatement to say that this prophecy has yielded a wealth of various theological interpretations, but common among them is the belief that the thousand-year period described in Revelation will be a new age of unprecedented peace and harmony. The precise nature and timing of that period, however, remain an unsettled question, and it was by no means clear even to early church fathers whether John's prediction forecast either a literal thousand-year period or the physical return of Christ to Earth. By the same token, theologians debated whether the millennium would be accompanied by an actual bodily resurrection of Christian martyrs or instead by a more symbolic resurrection, as with a resurgence of religious faith. Augustine, for instance, maintained that the thousand-year era had already begun with Christ's life on Earth, while others argued that the millennium commenced with the Christian conversion of Constantine and the Roman Empire. Both Martin Luther and John Calvin rejected the notion of a literal millennium, deeming it a relic of Jewish messianic hopes for worldly redemption and one unsuited to the new dispensation of Christianity.[19]

In the modern era, millennialist belief is typically classified into two types distinguished by their predicted chronologies of events and accompanying worldviews. The belief known as premillennialism is characterized by the expectation that the projected thousand years of peace can occur only after the catastrophic destruction of the current world order and the execution of divine wrath in Judgment Day. According to premillennialist interpretation, society stands at the very threshold of obliteration, and the worsening of human affairs is regarded as a hopeful sign of the imminence of the millennium and the literal return of Christ to Earth.[20] Though some aspects of premillennialism have seen a revival among evangelical Christians in the United States in the late twentieth and early twenty-first centuries and have become virtually synonymous with popular understandings of millennialism, it was by and large a minority belief in the United States in the nineteenth century. In its stead, the theology known as postmillennialism dominated eschatological belief. Whereas premillennialists associated the millennium with ruin and eternal condemnation, postmillennialists conceived of the millennium as the worldly perfection of human civilization, characterized by the elimination of human conflict and the reign of peace, prosperity, and abundance.[21] It is only after this thousand-year period of peace and prosperity that the predicted Judgment Day and the ultimate resolution of human history may occur. Just as premillennialists perceived decline as the chief sign of the imminent millennium, so postmillennialists saw progress as an indicator that the new age was approaching.[22] Moreover, postmillennialists believed that, with the help of divine inspiration, human beings themselves may inaugurate the millennium through social reform and ministry, for the resurrection envisioned in Revelation was interpreted as denoting the rebirth of religious faith rather than the literal rising of the dead. In a similar vein, postmillennialists often expected the global reign of the church rather than that of Christ himself. The belief that human society would continue during the millennium was supported by apocalyptic statements in the New Testament, as with Jesus's assertion in the Gospel according to Luke that "the Kingdom of God is not coming with signs to be observed; nor will they say, 'Lo, here it is!' or 'There!' for behold, the kingdom of God is in the midst of you" (Luke 17:20–21). That is, postmillennialists believed that the establishment of the divine kingdom on Earth will take place in, and will not destroy, modern society.

Though postmillennialism may seem like a highly liberal contemporary interpretation of scriptural prophecy, it had strong advocates in North America among such august, influential theologians as Jonathan Edwards (1703–58) and Samuel Hopkins (1721–1803), both of whom conceived of the millennium in secular, worldly terms. Edwards roundly rejected the premillennialist expectation of a literal reign of Christ on Earth and asserted instead that the millennium would be overseen by worldly authority figures and extend rather than conclude the annals of human history.[23] As he envisioned it, the millennium will not be preceded by catastrophe, nor will it be confined to the thousand-year time period allotted in Revelation, but it will instead arrive gradually. The millennium, he believed, promised to be a period of worldly, material improvement marked by agricultural bounty, human betterment, and comfort: it "will be a time of the greatest temporal prosperity," he asserted.[24] In lieu of a literal resurrection, Edwards envisioned the church itself reaching a new state of glory, made possible by the unification of disparate denominations and the wide dispersal of the gospel. The millennium, he wrote, will promote "health and long life, . . . to procure ease, quietness, pleasantness, and cheerfulness of mind, also wealth, and a great increase of children."[25] Samuel Hopkins concurred with these forecasts, anticipating that all sources of division—poverty, inequity, war, denominational sectarianism, and even language differences—would dissolve amid a climate of Christian unity, munificence, and peace. Developments in agriculture and engineering, he imagined, would dramatically enhance the overall quality of life in the millennium and relieve human beings of many of their responsibilities, leaving them free to spend their time in leisure and activities of self-improvement.[26]

The first Great Awakening proved fertile soil for postmillennialism, the rapid rise in religious converts suggesting to many that systematic efforts to promote conversion could prove the tipping point in ushering in a new age.[27] Once the zeal of the Awakening had ebbed, international political events rekindled widespread belief that a new age was at hand. Political revolutions in the late eighteenth and early nineteenth centuries repeatedly aroused millennialist hopes among observers who discerned in these conflicts a fulfillment of scriptural prediction that the millennium would be preceded by a war between a vast army, whose number is likened to "the sands of the sea" (Rev. 20:8), and a small number of righteous believers. The American and French revolutions were respectively interpreted as fulfillments of biblical predictions of a final battle heralding the new age.[28] A decade later, the Napoleonic wars again activated millennialist expectation; Napoleon's defeat of Pope Pius VI in particular suggested to many in the Protestant world the overthrow of the Antichrist described in Revelation. The ensuing migration of many European Jews to Palestine likewise seemed to fulfill prophecies of the postexilic return of Jews to the Holy Land.[29] In a similar line of reasoning, the European revolutions of the 1840s were also widely interpreted as a fulfillment of biblical prophecy predicting the overthrow of tyrannical, satanic forces, an interpretation that visibly informed Stowe's assertions in *Uncle Tom's Cabin* that "this is an age of the world when nations are trembling and convulsed. A mighty influence is abroad," causing widespread social upheaval.

The impact of European politics in rekindling American millennialism evidences the unambiguously sectarian character of this resurgent theology, for nineteenth-century postmillennialism was overwhelmingly Protestant and thus anti-Catholic in its sympathies. Amid growing fears about Catholic influence, it provided theological ammunition to anti-Catholic agitators, who argued that Catholicism was a recursive impediment to the advance of progress. This interpretation found ample support in the book of Revelation, as with the widespread understanding of the Whore of Babylon as a repudiation of the Catholic Church. As Jenny Franchot has shown, this belief derived from the perception of human history through the narrowly nationalist lens of American history, a constriction that designated Catholicism, by virtue of its association with the European Old World, as a primitive, obsolete relic of an outmoded past.[30] This teleological historical narrative, which Nina Baym has dubbed "history from the divine point of view," appointed Protestantism as an emancipatory liberator because of the beliefs that it both unseated the repression, authoritarianism, and enforced ignorance of Catholicism and enabled instead new religious freedom, knowledge, and self-determination.[31] As a nation famously founded amid the Protestant pursuit of religious autonomy, the United States—or, more particularly, New England—emerges by association as the apotheosis of religious progress and as the triumphant culmination of the divine will. By extension, Catholicism is understood in this formulation as a threat to both progress and the fulfillment of providential history.

Aversion to Catholicism underlay the millennialist fervor of numerous outspoken proponents, as with the efforts of the American Home Missionary Society to prepare the United States for the millennium primarily by arresting the spread of Catholicism. Harriet Beecher Stowe's father, famed revivalist Lyman Beecher, repeatedly denounced Catholicism as an impediment to the millennium; in *A Plea for the West* (1835), for instance, he asserted that the Midwest needed to be secured as a stronghold of Protestantism so as to repel active Catholic missionary efforts there and to ensure the centrality of the United States in "providential developments."[32] Catholicism was even portrayed as inimical to history itself, a depiction that derives from the Church's "self-identification as the unchanged and unchanging religion founded by Christ," as Susan Griffin has described it.[33] While the assertion of an unbroken apostolic succession, passed from Christ to every subsequent pope, elevated Catholicism as a faithful replica of the original church of the first century, it also conferred authority to the church on the basis of stasis and permanence. In the eyes of American Protestants, this avowal merely consolidated the association of Catholicism with stagnation, degeneration, and even regression. Catholicism was thus the very entity that the progressive march of Protestant history was expected to outrun and leave behind amid the discarded ashes of antiquity, but its tenacious survival and aggressive missionary efforts were understood as threats poised to obstruct and even reverse the forward course of the United States and human history itself.

For the most part, Stowe did not engage explicitly in the anti-Catholic disposition of millennialism, although it does underlie her discussion of recent

European revolutions at the close of *Uncle Tom's Cabin* as well as her depiction of a proto-Protestant revolution in *Agnes of Sorrento*. However, the foundation of postmillennial fervor in anti-Catholicism imparts an ineluctable
sectarian character to Stowe's millennialist narratives. Though her novels may
not directly depict the defeat of Catholicism at the hands of Protestant conquest, the millennialist narrative form of these texts implicitly situates these
novels within that context. As I will show, Stowe's domestic novels narrate the
fulfillment of scriptural prophecy and the culmination of human progress,
but, in so doing, she also dramatized the triumph of a theology freighted
with anti-Catholic overtones and uses. The narrative realization of that Protestant theology is coterminous in nineteenth-century thinking with the final,
conclusive defeat of Catholicism in its supposed effort to frustrate progress.
Moreover, in narrating the powers of middle-class New England housewives
to enable improvement and usher in the millennium, Stowe designated these
women as vital, effective warriors in the campaign toward progress and
against Catholic obstructionism. And though her domestic novels often seem
to withdraw from the public political exhortations of *Uncle Tom's Cabin* and
Dred, this context appoints the home as the front on which this sectarian war
will be won, with housewives leading the charge.

The paper trail documenting Stowe's immersion in contemporary post-
millennial theology is considerable. As a daughter of Lyman Beecher, Stowe
was reared in a household steeped in both anti-Catholicism and sectarian
postmillennialist expectation. During her childhood, her father daily offered a prayer for the second coming of Christ, and the entire Beecher family
attended a monthly prayer meeting for the commencement of the millennium.[34] In an 1827 sermon delivered to the American Board of Missions,
Beecher informed his audience of missionaries that their own efforts could
bring about the millennium. "From the beginning," he insisted, "the cause
of God on earth has been maintained and carried forward only by the most
heroic exertion. Christianity, even in the age of miracles, was not propagated
but by stupendous efforts. And it is only by a revival of primitive zeal and
enterprise that the glorious things spoken of the city of our God can be accomplished."[35] Throughout her life, Stowe would associate her mother, who
died when Stowe was a toddler, with the millennialist promise of Hebrews
12:22–23, a passage that she recalled her father reciting on her mother's
deathbed: "Ye are come unto Mount Zion, the city of the living God, to the
heavenly Jerusalem, and to an innumerable company of angels; to the general
assembly and Church of the first born, and to the spirits of just men made

perfect."[36] When Harriet was sixteen years old, her father pronounced his conviction that the millennium would be presaged by "revolutions and [so-cial] convulsions . . . until every despotic government shall be thrown down and chaos resume its pristine reign, and the Spirit of God shall move upon the face of the deep and bring out a new creation," a belief evident in the closing chapter of *Uncle Tom's Cabin*.[37]

Though she was raised amid postmillennialism, she was heavily affected by the premillennialist Millerite movement of the early 1840s, and she re-solved to redouble her religious devotion amid anxious concern that she would be unprepared for Christ's imminent return.[38] After the suicide of her brother George in 1843, the year in which Millerite anticipation was at its peak, Stowe wrote a stream of heartfelt letters enjoining her loved ones to pre-pare themselves for the return of Christ to Earth.[39] The concluding chapter of *Uncle Tom's Cabin* undeniably registers the temporary influence of premillen-nialist anxiety, but elsewhere Stowe extensively expressed postmillennialist convictions, among them the belief that the new age would be characterized by the perfection of worldly conditions and the suspicion that Christ's reign might not be a literal one per se. For instance, in *Footsteps of the Master*, a collection of assorted religious writings, Stowe offered a pragmatic inter-pretation of Adventist expectation, suggesting that Christ's return might be of a more spiritual, symbolic turn. She wrote, while it "is believed by many Christians that Christ is yet coming to reign visibly upon this earth," such an event is logistically "suggestive of grave difficulties," such as problems of crowd control. The circumstances of modernity, such as population density in urban locations, make it necessary that Christ find more orderly means of returning to Earth, and she imagines that it "may be possible that the barrier between the spiritual world and ours will be so far removed that the presence of our Lord and his saints may at times be with us, even as Christ was with the disciples in this interval."[40] It is thus likely that the millennium will be an era characterized by the spiritual, rather than the bodily, presence of Christ. In a more private setting, Stowe voiced her postmillennialist conviction that the future would be marked not by destruction and decline but by the absence of woes and grief. In an 1879 letter to Oliver Wendell Holmes, she inquired, "Does not the Bible plainly tell us of a time when there shall be no more pain? That is to be the end and crown of the Messiah's mission, when God shall wipe all tears away. My face is set that way, and yours, too, I trust."[41]

Despite her outburst of premillennialist anxieties in *Uncle Tom's Cabin* and *Dred*, Marie Caskey observed that the eschatological beliefs of Stowe's husband, seminary professor Calvin Stowe, provided theological ballast for Stowe, and his postmillennialist beliefs are well documented.[42] In *Origin and History of the Books of the Bible* (1867), a volume produced with assistance from his wife, Calvin Stowe offers a distinctively optimistic interpretation of Revelation, contending that "the general object of [Revelation is] to excite and encourage Christians in times of depressions and persecution"; consequently, it should be interpreted "as it was designed to be used, for comfort and encouragement."[43] These prophecies, he asserts, should be regarded as assurances of future improvement rather than indications of impending suffering. In a previous work of biblical exegesis, he warned readers against looking for fulfillments of those prophecies in contemporary events, implicitly expressing a postmillennialist belief that Revelation ought to be approached holistically rather than atomistically, which was the favored interpretive technique of such premillennialists as William Miller, who used the numerical specifics of Revelation to calculate the precise date of Jesus's return.[44] In an 1875 letter, Harriet expressed receptivity to the postmillennialist message of her husband's Easter sermon: she writes, "Mr. Stowe preached a sermon to show that Christ is going to put everything to right at last, which is comforting. So the day was one of real pleasure, and also, I trust, of real benefit, to the poor souls who learned from it that Christ is indeed risen for them."[45] Christianity, the Stowes aver, enables progress, improvement, and resolution of worldly ills.

Indeed, this distillation of postmillennialist belief neatly summarizes the larger plot trajectory of Stowe's fiction, which unwaveringly narrates how Protestantism can "put everything to right at last." To be sure, Stowe's novels often document how fervently Americans of the early national period cleaved to such a belief. Stowe's historical novels express nostalgic yearning for a time long gone, when men still wore powdered wigs and knee breeches, when clergy were regarded as veritable royalty and front doors were kept unlocked. Postmillennialist optimism was a key ingredient in her portraits of a past era of putatively greater simplicity and sincerity, when one could expect that devotion and effort would reliably result in reward, whether in eliciting material riches or in instigating the new age. In *Oldtown Folks* (1869), for instance, the millennium is a recurring subject of conversation among the novel's characters. The minister Mr. Avery was "a warm believer in the millennium," in particular the postmillennial expectation that "the poor old earth should produce only a saintly race of perfected human beings . . . [as] compensation for the darkness and losses of the great struggle." Avery remains certain that the millennium is imminent and sees its signs in "every political and social change. [The American] Revolution was a long step towards it, and the French Revolution, now in progress, was a part of that distress of nations which heralded it."[46] Conversations throughout the novel likewise make passing reference to this expectation, as with the dialogue between Sam Lawson, the sometime handyman and town idler, and Miss Lois, an irascible older woman, about a clock that she wants fixed. "Now this 'ere's a 'mazing good clock," he observes. "Give me my time on it, and I'll have it so 't will keep [time] straight on to the Millennium." In response to Miss Lois's incredulity at this remark, Sam attempts to engage her in conversation about theology instead of having to commit to a deadline for his repair work, asking her opinion about the millennium. She retorts by using theology to spur Sam to get back to work: "My opinion . . . is that if folks don't mind their own business, and do with their might what their hand finds to do, the Millennium won't come at all." He overlooks this postmillennialist barb insinuating that his own laziness is keeping the millennium at bay, and he instead tries to explain some of the finer points of theology: "Wal, you see, Miss Lois, it's just here,—one day is with the Lord as a thousand years, and a thousand years as one day." Her rejoinder is pointed: "I should think you thought a day was a thousand years, the way you work," she replies (32). Similarly, the villainous character Miss Asphyxia is particularly inclined to reference premillennialist anticipation of divinely ordained violence, as with her offhand remark about the novel's hero, Harry Percival, in which she justifies keeping him permanently separated from his sister and her ward, Tina: "I'd jest as soon have the great red dragon in the Revelations a comin' down on my house as a boy!" (102). Shortly thereafter, she accuses Tina of lying by referencing Revelation 19:20: "Don't you know where liars go to, you naughty, wicked girl? 'All liars shall have their part in the lake that burns with fire and brimstone,'—that's what the Bible says; and you may thank me for keeping you from going there" (105). In *Poganuc People* (1878), Stowe parodied premillennialist pessimism, as with the "lugubrious" efforts of Mother Jones to squelch the joys of a young couple with her remark that "this 'ere's a dyin' world," and by contrast Stowe portrays the hopefulness of postmillennialism as well suited to an era of American history replete with promise. For example, in a portrayal of Sunday worship services, she documents the era's belief in a prophesied new age of peace and prosperity as well as the belief that the United States would play a central role in the fulfillment of this prophecy:

After the singing came Dr. Cushing's prayer—which was a recounting of God's mercies to New England from the beginning, and of his deliverances from her enemies, and of petitions for the glorious future of the United States of America—that they might be chosen vessels, commissioned to bear the light of liberty and religion through all the earth and to bring in the great millennial day, when wars should cease and the whole world, released from the thraldom of evil, should rejoice in the light of the Lord. The millennium was ever the star of hope in the eyes of the New England clergy: their faces were set eastward, towards the dawn of that day, and the cheerfulness of those anticipations illuminated the hard tenets of their theology with a rosy glow. They were children of the morning.[47]

This fond portrait infuses postmillennialism with warmth and patriotism, suggesting that this belief has noble historical precedent and cultivates a forward-looking optimism well worth emulating.

In confirmation of Jenny Franchot's observation that "to write history is to reenact it," Stowe's historical novels are supported by plots that, over the lengthy span of a novel, affirm the legitimacy of these beliefs by demonstrating the workings of divinely inspired progress in human affairs.[48] In this way, the novels' plots dramatize the ongoing betterment of civilization and human nature. A narratological x-ray of Stowe's fiction demonstrates how closely she relied upon a postmillennialist philosophy of history in plotting her novels. Where Stowe's novels typically commence with families and communities in disarray—whether through fragmentation, bereavement, or poverty—so these families are typically restored by novels' end, with the reunion of loved ones and the restitution of worldly resources to their proper stewards. While this narrative propulsion toward reconciliation and resolution complies with prevailing novelistic conventions of eighteenth- and nineteenth-century English-language novels, in Stowe's novels the chief narrative pivot enabling the transformation of confusion and estrangement into propriety and affiliation is Christian belief. To be sure, Stowe's novels typically employ the same novelistic conventions as her contemporaries in resolving entangled plots, such as intensification of crisis and the disclosure of withheld information, but it is the transformation afforded by Christian faith that ultimately causes the narrative conditions of resolution. In this way, she adapts a largely secular literary genre to corroborate the religious belief in the advent of divinely inspired progress.

Such a trajectory can be discerned in *The Minister's Wooing*, which tracks the aftereffects of the apparent death at sea of James Marvyn, an impetuous young man in eighteenth-century Newport.[49] His widowed mother, now left fully alone by her son's premature death, falls into a deep depression, unable to reconcile herself to the harsh Calvinist doctrine that condemns James to perdition unless signs of his religious conversion can be found. In his absence, his beloved cousin Mary Scudder, a devout young woman, attracts the attention of two inappropriate suitors, the dissolute Aaron Burr and the well-meaning, if blundering and theologically rigid, minister Samuel Hopkins, whom Mary agrees to marry out of a sense of duty. Mary's engagement to Hopkins seems to resolve the familial fragmentation and isolation caused by James's death, but James unexpectedly reappears in Newport on the eve of Mary's marriage, thereby unsettling this engagement. The novel clarifies that James is alive entirely because of the literal saving power of Christianity: in the midst of a shipwreck, James spontaneously recalled a passage from the Gospel according to Mark in which Jesus quells a storm at sea, and this remembrance enables him to retain his courage and the presence of mind to survive this catastrophe. Just as Christianity enables James's survival and remedies familial fragmentation, so Christian faith similarly enables the resolution of the marriage plot. In Christ-like selflessness, Hopkins gives Mary up after reflecting on the similarity of the marriage bond to the relationship between Christ and the church. He comes to understand that "whenever there is a cross or burden to be borne by one or the other, that the man, who is made in the image of God as to strength and endurance, should take it upon himself . . . even as Christ for his church." Hopkins imitates Christ and releases Mary from their engagement, and James likewise interprets this sacrifice through the lens of faith, commenting that this gesture "tells on my heart more than any sermon you ever preached": the resolution of the marriage plot enables Hopkins's ministry to reach new heights of effectiveness.[50] In these interlocking narratives of bereavement and matrimony, Stowe adapts the marriage plot to suggest that Christianity brings out the best in people and enables the resolution of suffering. In thus facilitating courage, selflessness, and mindfulness, Christianity enables the correction of worldly ills and the gradual perfection of society.

While the correspondences between postmillennialist optimism and novelistic form may seem merely coincidental, Stowe often inserted explicit references to apocalyptic prophecy at precisely the narrative turning points, drawing attention to this similarity and inviting readers to consider who is really causing the narrative's events to unfold as they do. For instance, in a letter to Mary in which James describes his religious conversion at sea, he calls the shipwreck the "crisis of his life," a common evangelical phrase widely used to describe the state of profound desperation that was believed to precede conversion. This life-threatening calamity, he confesses, was "as dreadful as the Day of Judgment," as he witnesses "the hopeless rocks before" them.[51] To be sure, this allusion to apocalyptic prophecy comports with Stowe's efforts to show how millennial expectation pervaded early American life, as characters interpret the events of their lives through the lens of scriptural typology. At the same time, this comparison of the shipwreck to Judgment Day highlights how the events of the novel fulfill simultaneously novelistic convention and religious belief. While resolving the marriage plot, James's reappearance also literalizes evangelical understanding of conversion as a kind of rebirth, and it likewise invokes apocalyptic prediction that the millennium will be accompanied by the resurrection of the dead. The primary result of such allusions at pivotal moments in the narrative is the suggestion that it is the deity and not mere novelistic convention that enables the changes and miraculous turns of events that provide the structure of her novel. Stowe famously remarked that "God wrote" *Uncle Tom's Cabin*, but her adherence to postmillennialist theology no less demonstrates the workings of divine providence in dictating and overseeing the events in her domestic novels. Stowe makes this point explicit in *The Pearl of Orr's Island* in the remark of the pious heroine, Mara Lincoln, on her deathbed: in reflecting back on her life, she observes, "How plainly we can see that our heavenly Father has been guiding our way!"[52] The hand that moves the plot toward resolution is not that of the novelist but that of the divine, whom Stowe in *The Minister's Wooing* terms the "great Author" of all human life.[53]

The compliance of *The Minister's Wooing* with postmillennialist belief is made even more explicit by the novel's inclusion of Samuel Hopkins, a vigorous proponent of postmillennialism, as one of the central characters. Hopkins's advocacy of postmillennialism is by no means an incidental footnote to the novel, but rather the topic is Hopkins's default subject of conversation, one that he discourses upon so widely that it becomes the subject of humor. For instance, at the early-morning breakfast table, the day's first cup of coffee launches Hopkins into an impromptu homily about the millennium. He intones to a patient and indulgent Mary, "In the Millennium, I suppose, there will be such a fulness and plenty of all the necessaries and conveniences of life, that it will not be necessary for men and women to spend the greater part of their lives in labor in order to procure a living. It will not be necessary for each one to labor more than two or three hours a day,—not more than will conduce to health of body and vigor of mind; and the rest of their time they will spend in reading and conversation, and such exercises as are necessary and proper to improve their minds and make progress in knowledge" (76). By way of explanation for this unprompted sermon, Stowe comments that the "fact of a future millennium was a favorite doctrine of the great leading theologians of New England, and Dr. Hopkins dwelt upon it with a peculiar partiality. Indeed, it was the solace and refuge of his soul" (77). While this spontaneous outpouring of millennialist doctrine at the breakfast table sketches a droll portrait of Hopkins's abstracted unworldliness, it is nonetheless a faithful distillation of Hopkinsian theology, evidencing Stowe's own research in the service of historical, doctrinal fidelity.[54]

The influence of postmillennialist belief on Stowe's narrative form is evident in her use of other suggestive literary devices. As was the case with *The Minister's Wooing*, Stowe's fiction often turns on disclosures of information long kept secret. With the discovery of suppressed information, wrongs are set to right, and estranged families are restored. In *The Minister's Wooing*, for instance, the revelation that James Marvyn is alive enables the renewal of his suffering mother's faith and the union of the virtuous Mary Scudder with a suitable mate. *Uncle Tom's Cabin* similarly finds resolution with disclosure: a chance conversation onboard ship leads to the reunions of George Harris with his long-lost sister, Emily de Thoux, and of Cassy with her daughter, Eliza, thereby effectively undoing the work of slavery in compromising the integrity of the American family. In addition, Harry Percival of *Oldtown Folks* learns at novel's end that he is the son and heir of an English lord, both his identity and property now restored to him. For readers familiar with English-language novels of the eighteenth and nineteenth centuries, such devices are common fare, linking such disparate canonical works as *Pride and Prejudice*, *Jane Eyre*, *The House of Seven Gables*, *The American*, and *The Rise of Silas Lapham* in their narrative reliance on suspension and disclosure both to fabricate and resolve crises. For readers conversant with nineteenth-century evangelical belief, this commonplace novelistic device has a decidedly theological inflection, one that Stowe openly exploits so as to emphasize the larger cosmological significance of her narrative forms. While narrative disclosure may be a common novelistic device, within the evangelical lexicon it functioned as an explicit scriptural allusion to apocalyptic prophecy, for the very word *apocalypse* literally means an unveiling or disclosure of hitherto secret information. It is for this reason that the title of the most famous work of apocalyptic literature, the biblical account of John of Patmos, is frequently translated as Revelation precisely because it purports to divulge clandestine information of the highest order. In this regard, Stowe's novels and those of her sentimental contemporaries generally are in and of themselves literally apocalyptic, for their novels hinge on the revelation of concealed information that, as with biblical Revelation, both illuminates the unfortunate current state of affairs and enables the correction of a world in disarray.

Though the widespread use of disclosure in nineteenth-century fiction was likely inadvertently rather than deliberately typological, Stowe often couples this narrative form with cues that suggest her deliberate structural reliance on millennialist prophecy. In this way, Stowe does not graft theology onto her narratives so much as demonstrate the inherent religious inflections of the narrative form she uses. At the heart of *The Pearl of Orr's Island*, for instance, is a mystery about the origins of a young boy who washes up on the shore of a peaceful Maine island, his body and that of his dead mother affixed to a spar in an apparent attempt to save them from shipwreck. The only clue to the boy's identity is the mother's monogrammed and jeweled bracelet, which is entrusted for safekeeping to the care of the local minister, Mr. Sewell, who, the novel strongly intimates, has privileged information about the boy's origins. With no known living relatives, the boy, fittingly named Moses, is taken in by a local family, and the novel charts his development and maturation, attending in particular to his relationship with Mara Lincoln, another orphan raised by parental surrogates. As Moses reaches adulthood, the question of his identity remains an unsettled mystery until late in the novel, when Moses inquires for information from the minister. Mr. Sewell confesses that, having recognized the bracelet, he has always known the truth about Moses's identity and planned on informing him at an appropriate time. What follows are several chapters in which Mr. Sewell divulges a wealth of long-hidden secrets, about his own past and that of Moses's family. As a young man, Mr. Sewell worked as a tutor in the household of the Mendoza family, an unhappy aristocratic Spanish family living in Florida; there, he fell in love with Dolores, the pious older daughter betrothed to a wealthy but abusive older man. When the patriarch of the Mendoza family learns of his ardor for Dolores, Sewell flees and remains ever after a bachelor out of his abiding love for Dolores, a state that had long provided fodder for speculation and gossip among his congregation. Sewell learns later that Dolores, after marrying Don Guzman and residing in Cuba, has disappeared with her family en route to the United States after an attempted slave insurrection on their plantation. All these years, Sewell has kept abreast of the Guzman estate and has arranged for Moses to collect the full inheritance of his long-lost family, if he so chooses.

This narrative immediately transforms Moses from an unidentified, orphaned foundling into the scion of an aristocratic Spanish family and the heir to a considerable estate in Cuba, thereby restoring his kinship, status, and fortune. There is nothing immediately remarkable about this narrative trajectory, which employs common novelistic tropes of hidden identity and social reversals that pervade nineteenth-century fiction, structuring, for instance, such contemporary works as Maria Susanna Cummins's *The Lamplighter* (1854) and E. D. E. N. Southworth's *The Hidden Hand* (1859), in which indigent orphan children are revealed to be well-born and affluent. However, *The Pearl of Orr's Island* repeatedly alludes to the supreme scriptural precedent for narratives of disclosure—the biblical book of Revelation—to suggest that Stowe's novel is shaped less by prevailing novelistic convention than by millennialist belief. The most obvious of these references is that of Moses's given name, which alludes to the biblical story of Moses, who was also rescued from the water to be reared among familial surrogates and who, in his role as prophet, is widely understood by Christians as a scriptural antecedent for Christ himself by ushering in a new revelation of divine will and enabling a new age of freedom and behavioral self-governance. This straightforward use of typology aside, Stowe frames the central mystery of the novel, the question of Moses's identity, within the context of millennialist anticipation. Captain Kittredge, the local teller of tall tales, marvels that no other traces of the sunken ship have been found, and Miss Roxy, an opinionated older woman, replies with the assertion that the ship's identity, fate, and location "won't be known till the sea gives up its dead."[55] That is to say, Moses's origins will not be known definitively until the onset of the resurrection, predicted in Revelation, that heralds the thousand-year era of peace; the resolution of the novel's central problem functions as a veritable synecdoche of the resolution of human history as predicted in the Bible.

And in fulfillment of Miss Roxy's prediction, Mr. Sewell's narrative contains several references to apocalyptic literature to suggest that the resolution of this mystery coincides with the commencement of the new age predicted in the New Testament. For instance, the central chapter of Sewell's account is suggestively entitled "Hidden Things," a phrase widely used in translations of the opening verse of Revelation, in which John of Patmos announces his intention of sharing the "hidden things" shown to him by an angel of the Lord. Likewise,

Sewell prefaces his lengthy narrative with an allusion to one of the distinctive features of apocalyptic literature: the announcement of its paramount confidentiality in relaying privileged information known only to the deity, a convention evident in the opening assertion of Revelation that what follows is the "Revelation of Jesus Christ, which God gave him to show to his servants what must soon take place; he made it known by sending his angel to his servant John" (Rev. 1:1). Mr. Sewell references this scriptural convention with the announcement, "I am going to show you . . . what only you and my God know that I possess," suggesting that the narrative is literally apocalyptic in revealing secrets known only to the divine.[56] Nor is it incidental that a clergyman, the Minister Sewell, issues the revelation of Moses's secret identity, a narrative fine point that takes this novelist convention out of its traditional secular frame and expressly locates it within a religious context. Finally, as is the case with *The Minister's Wooing* and is believed to be the case with apocalyptic literature, Sewell's revelation ushers in progress and growth. Before learning his identity, Moses had been literally and spiritually wayward, his itinerant life as a sailor reflecting his morally adrift state. Knowledge of his origins calms his rootless drifting and enables him to settle: he completes the construction of the ship he has longed to build since boyhood and, after years of evasion, finally admits his love for pious Mara, to whom he becomes betrothed. In both respects, Moses moves from a holding pattern of prolonged adolescent self-absorption toward an adulthood steadied by companionship and responsibility. Similar to the refinement and maturity James Marvyn acquires after conversion, the novel concludes with Moses a mature married man.

To be sure, the anti-Catholic undertones of millennialism come into view in *The Pearl of Orr's Island*. The mysterious, inscrutable nature of the Guzman family is fortified by their affiliation with the Catholic Church, which Protestants have long denounced as murky and unintelligible because of its ritual reliance on Latin and because of the belief that Catholic clergy operate in shadowy, underhanded ways. It is not accidental that the intervention of the Protestant minister in these muddled family affairs contributes directly toward their resolution. His involvement similarly enables Moses to acquire greater knowledge and self-determination, and these consequences derive from the millennial equation of Catholicism with ignorance and obstruction and of Protestantism with enlightenment and liberty. That Moses declines to claim his patrimony and decides instead to remain in Protestant New England signals, on a minute level, the victory of New England Protestantism over Old World Catholicism.

In all of these ways, Stowe's domestic fiction often works to affirm post-millennial conviction that, with the help of Protestantism, the world is steadily progressing and improving. This fulfillment of prophecy occurs not solely through divine will, as was believed by the premillennialists, but with the agency of Christian faith, which betters human beings and engenders righteous actions that move the human race ever closer to the millennium. The private morality and piety of the most common person, she suggests, bear witness to the gradual fulfillment of prophecy and have the power to effect change on an enormous, cosmological scale. The movements of divinely ordered sacred time, her novels propose, can be discerned in the workings of the everyday and the commonplace. Also implicit in these domestic novels is the persistent suggestion that, in thus revealing the presence of divine influence in human lives, Stowe herself functions as a prophet, who reveals hidden truths to a readership otherwise ignorant of these divine mysteries.[57] She made this suggestion explicit in her assertion that "God wrote" *Uncle Tom's Cabin*, proclaiming herself a vessel of divine revelation, but her domestic novels repeatedly suggest that they are no less informed by special access to divine secrets. In this way, Stowe tacitly assumed extraordinary religious and moral authority, and she likewise posited her novels as a form of modern scripture through which readers might gain access to the divine will.[58]

This implication is consistent with Stowe's repeated interest in demonstrating the particular significance of women in enabling the fulfillment of Christian eschatology. Moreover, it can explain why fiction about domesticity so often provided the setting for these postmillennialist narratives. There is little doubt that women occupy a deeply vexed role in this prophetic tradition, and Stowe's fiction often rehabilitates the status of women in the Christian apocalypse, striving to demonstrate that women are better able than anyone else to inaugurate the millennium. Stowe took her cues from the explicitly gendered visions that pervade Revelation, in which women of varying virtue function as embodied prophecies and warnings. The very name of this genre and prophetic tradition has an explicitly gendered valence: the Greek word *apokalypsis*, which is translated into English interchangeably as "revelation" and "apocalypse," is etymologically akin to the word *anakaluptō*, which means "unveiling," a term that frequently reoccurs in English translations and commentaries on the Revelation of John.[59] To be sure, unveiling has decidedly female-specific connotations. In both the ancient Near East and the American nineteenth century, veils are typically reserved for women to shield their faces and identities from public view, and the veil is thus metonymically associated with feminine privacy as well as the protection of the female body from improper advances. Unveiling evokes at once the preservation of female modesty and the erotics of undress, the act of exposure by which one may achieve intimate access to the female body.[60] While "to unveil is to remove mystery," in the words of biblical scholar Tina Pippin, unveiling also connotes the public presentation of womanly secrets, bodily or otherwise, that are usually invisible to view.[61] Such a connotation infused uses of this term in the United States of the nineteenth century, as with Lydia Maria Child's description of Harriet Jacobs's controversial 1861 account of the sexual violence perpetrated against slave women, *Incidents in the Life of a Slave Girl*, as a literary unveiling of a long-secret atrocity.[62] The veil was also marked by sectarian connotations. As apparel traditionally worn by women during Catholic worship and by Catholic women who have entered a convent—in popular parlance, by women who have "taken the veil"—this garment became a nineteenth-century metonym for Catholicism, one that denoted in particular the disquieting opacity and inscrutability of Catholicism, signaling what Jenny Franchot has termed "the spectacular obscurities of Rome."[63] In this instance, the veil connoted a worrisome and problematic secretiveness that stood in sharp contrast with the Protestant self-identification with transparency and enlightenment.

The Revelation of John is deeply preoccupied with the propriety of female exposure and the consequences of public female unveiling. Revelation describes four female iconic figures characterized chiefly by their relative degrees of modesty and willingness to recede from public view. Two villainous female figures are distinguished by their publicity and indiscriminate sexuality: the Whore of Babylon, who fornicates with the "kings of the earth" (Rev. 17:2), and Jezebel, a false prophet who incites her followers to "commit adultery with her" (Rev. 2:22). Critics have interpreted both instances of profligate female sexuality as metaphors for the immorality of leaders and institutions governed by worldly desires for power, and, as mentioned earlier, since the Reformation the Whore of Babylon has been widely interpreted as a stand-in for the Catholic Church and its political aspirations. As these two figures suggest, Revelation constitutes unrestrained access to the female body as the height of immorality and a veritable threat to the public welfare.[64] Implicit in the description of these two women is the assumption that female virtue requires the withdrawal from public view and the restriction of bodily access, and Revelation proffers two examples of such ideal femininity: the Woman Clothed with the Sun (Rev. 12) and the New Jerusalem (Rev. 21:2). Described as a portent, the Woman Clothed with the Sun cries "out in birth pangs, in the agony of giving birth" (Rev.12:1–3). Menaced by a giant red dragon seeking to devour her baby, she bears a boy "who is to rule all the nations with a rod of iron. But her child was snatched away and taken to God and to his throne; and the woman fled into the wilderness, where she has a place prepared by God" (Rev. 12:5–6). Though this vision exposes to public view the private anguish of childbirth, the text affirms her feminine modesty by maintaining that she is "clothed with the sun," nature itself providing a protective shield. She is then secreted to a private refuge prepared by the deity, returned to the shelter of retiring invisibility expected of respectable women. The second icon of proper femininity is the image of the New Jerusalem, the lavish homeland promised at the completion of Christian eschatology. The New Jerusalem is described as "a bride adorned for her husband," a comparison that implies that, according to bridal customs of the ancient Near East, she is veiled and shielded from view for all but her rightful husband, who alone may unveil her and gain access to the body that the Whore and Jezebel so freely proffer.[65] This bridal metaphor implicitly likens the long-promised entrance of the faithful into New Jerusalem to the intimacy the bridegroom may now enjoy with his modest bride.[66]

All of these examples attest that, in the logic of Revelation, the public exposure of private female affairs figures prominently in eschatological prophecy about the fate of human history.[67] Within Revelation, such transgression is acceptable only if it complies with conventional domestic constraints on female authority and contributes to the well-being of the church. This precept implicitly underwrites much of Stowe's fiction, which also airs to public view the private lives of women. As feminist historians have long observed, domestic circumscription has resulted in the invisibility of women's lives in the historical record, which has until recently been largely preoccupied with the events of public life from which women were excluded. In this larger disciplinary context, Stowe's fiction is especially important in part because it habitually traverses the historical erasure of women by laying bear what would normally go unseen because of domestic enclosure. Most famously, in *Uncle Tom's Cabin* she exposed the clandestine effects of slavery on the homes and families of slaves, showing the private anguish of mothers whose children have been sold away, the stunted character of slave children reared without parents, and the effects of concubinage on women. In this respect, *Uncle Tom's Cabin* is explicitly apocalyptic in its revelation of the many secret domestic sins of slavery, and, where Revelation permits limited female exposure for the greater spiritual good, so Stowe clarifies that she offers these unseemly revelations in the hope that "Christendom may be delivered from so great an evil as slavery."[68]

Though her later domestic novels lack the robust moral imprimatur of *Uncle Tom's Cabin*, they no less expose to view the private lives of women by documenting the inner workings of domesticity that usually remain unseen: the thrifty processes by which old dresses are recut and "turned," the home manufacture of candles, the vast undertaking required to produce the requisite pies of early winter, and the seasonal rotation of domestic chores. In this respect, her domestic novels offer a glimpse behind the public showroom of the parlor into the private responsibilities that give shape to women's lives. Though these literary portraits of behind-the-scenes housekeeping may seem tepid in comparison to the high stakes of *Uncle Tom's Cabin*, Stowe's domestic writings elsewhere clarify that they are no less vital to the fulfillment of millennialist prophecy. Though women's work may be sequestered behind closed doors, Stowe intimates that the very hopes of human civilization depend on the daily labors of women in rearing children and running households.[69] For instance, in the *American Woman's Home*, the Beecher sisters occasionally interrupt their advice about décor and cookery with ecstatic millennial rhapsodies, intermittently envisioning "a dawning day to which we are approaching . . . [when] 'there shall be no more death, neither sorrow, nor crying; neither shall there be any more pain.'"[70] The implicit connective link between these effusions of millennial anticipation and domestic advice is the presumption that diligent, pious housewifery contributes in a meaningful way to the advent of the millennium.[71] Catharine Beecher would make this point explicit in her introduction to the volume, in which she pronounces that the "duties of woman are as sacred and important as any ordained to man," and she strongly suggests that in their daily domestic labors, women enable the progress that signals the coming new age. She writes, "During the upward progress of the age, and the advance of a more enlightened Christianity, the writers of this volume have gained more elevated views of the true mission of woman—of the dignity and importance of her distinctive duties, and of the true happiness which will be the reward of a right appreciation of this mission, and a proper performance of these duties."[72] Beecher's phrasing suggests both that the advent of the millennium has enabled the two Beecher women to recognize the larger cosmic import of women's domestic work and that the successful implementation of their own domestic manual will contribute further to the arrival of the promised new age.

In the first pages of the next chapter, they elaborate on the millennial contributions of women, declaring that "the family state . . . is the aptest earthly illustration of the heavenly kingdom, and in it woman is its chief minister."[73] To be sure, this assertion capitulates to widespread mid-century perception of the home as a kind of heaven on earth, a perception that imputes sacred authority to women in creating an environment of happiness that portends that of the millennium and the afterlife.[74] Furthermore, they assert that, although female labor may be confined to the private recesses of the household, the woman is no less a "minister" than are ordained clergy: as homemakers and mothers, women dictate the future moral direction of human civilization, determining whether it will progress quickly toward the new age or languish in its current state of acute imperfection. Later in the volume, they conclude a chapter on "The Christian Neighborhood" with an eruption of millennialist anticipation, contending that "this life is but the infant period of our race," an assertion that not only breathlessly anticipates the fullest culmination of human maturation in the millennium but also implies that the female caregiver of the infant is also the steward of the entire human race. They follow this statement with a reprint of William Cowper's poem "Task," which elatedly details the "bliss," "abundance," "harmony and love" of the coming millennium, and the implicit thesis of this discussion is the suggestion that women, in the domestic duties that take place behind closed doors, enable this state of worldly perfection. Moreover, in providing the instruction that enables female readers to perform these duties more ably, the volume itself contributes to the perfection of human civilization and the advent of the millennium.[75]

Stowe's *House and Home Papers* expresses similar beliefs. Serialized in the *Atlantic Monthly* in 1864, *House and Home Papers* is composed of a series of essays on housekeeping from the perspective of the middle-class married man Christopher Crowfield, as he recounts his experiences with prudent domestic economy, in opposition to the unfettered consumerist desires of his daughters. In the third essay, "What Is a Home?" Stowe, in the voice of her male persona, diverges from the book's materialist pragmatics, with its discussions of redecorating and upholstery, to intimate that domesticity contributes directly to the fulfillment of millennialist prophecy. In explaining that love is what makes a house a home, Stowe tethers her discussion of domesticity to a grander context: love, the quality that best typifies home life, "is the jeweled foundation of this New Jerusalem descending from God out of heaven, and takes as many bright forms as the amethyst, topaz, and sapphire of that mysterious vision." Thus, the New Jerusalem, she alleges, will be built on the groundwork laid by domesticity, and not that of politics or ministry, and she thereby attributes extraordinary importance to the work that women do in making homes loving and efficient: they make possible the cardinal conditions of affection and altruistic affinity from which all other millennial developments will spring. She subsequently reiterates that the happy home is itself a figuration of the New Jerusalem promised in Revelation: "New Jerusalem of a perfect home cometh down from God out of heaven. But to make such a home is ambition high and worthy enough for *any* woman, be she what she may."[76] In this latter passage, Stowe overtly declares that through homemaking, women forge the New Jerusalem and enable the fulfillment of millennial prophecy.[77]

In *Footsteps of the Master*, her foray into biblical exegesis, Stowe went further, arguing that Christ himself was a superlative housekeeper, for "many little incidents in Christ's life show the man of careful domestic habits." She sees abundant traces of Christ's domestic facility in the gospels:

> He would have the fragments of the feast picked up and stored in the baskets, "that nothing should be lost." His illustrations show the habits of a frugal home. His parable of the kingdom of heaven, likened to the leaven hidden in three measures of meal, gives us to believe that he had often watched his mother in the homely process of bread-making. The woman, who, losing one piece of money from her little store, lights a candle and searches diligently, brings to our mind the dwelling of the poor where every penny has its value. . . . Many little touches indicate, also, the personal refinement and delicacy of his habits, the order and purity that extended to all his ways.[78]

This apparent attention to domestic matters figures as a cornerstone in her larger argument that Christ is the fullest apotheosis of traditional womanliness.[79] Where "mighty, mysterious, terrible" God is a divine father, so Christ is the divine mother, loving, attentive, and patient. Stowe makes this assertion repeatedly, as with her comparison of Christ's conduct on the eve of his arrest to that of "a dying mother, who knows that a few hours will leave her children orphans," a comparison that invokes the death of Stowe's own mother, Roxana Foote Beecher, when Stowe herself was small. She likewise compares Christ's abiding affection for Judas to that of a "mother [who] loves and pities the unworthy son who is whitening her hair and breaking her heart." In another instance, she compares Christ's capacity to grant peace to that of a mother, stating that "whatever burden or care we take to Jesus, if we would get the peace promised, we must *leave* it with Him as entirely as the little child leaves his school troubles with his mother."[80] This elaborated conceit implicitly suggests both that the mother has special status in the new dispensation and that women's work is a potent extension of Christ's own ministry in helping human beings to arrive at their final eschatological destination.

These assertions may help us understand the larger significance of Stowe's domestic fiction as well as the shift she made in the 1850s from writings of overt political and religious significance to fiction focused on the rhythms of domestic life. Set against the backdrop of *Uncle Tom's Cabin* and *Dred*, such novels may seem slight or trivial, but her supplementary writings about the sacrality of housekeeping demonstrate that, in her mind, these novels are of equal religious import and likewise have their sights set firmly on the millennium. In writing about homemaking, Stowe pulls back the veil of domestic privacy to extol the unsung heroes who make the millennium possible, one load of laundry at a time.[81] *The Minister's Wooing* is one such case in which the correction of worldly turmoil is enabled by the order and comfort provided by a conscientious housekeeper. The novel commences by establishing the importance of such a figure, the widow Katy Scudder, who is mother to the novel's heroine, Mary Scudder, and hostess to Samuel Hopkins. Though it may be easy to overlook Mrs. Scudder's domestic labors in a novel that features a shipwreck, scenes of abject despair, and a bold antislavery address, as well as appearances from a debonair Aaron Burr, Stowe begins the novel with a lengthy discussion of Mrs. Scudder's considerable domestic aptitude and in this way invites readers to take note of the invisible, capable hands that make possible the very environment in which much of novel—and, indeed, life itself—takes place. The first thing that Stowe establishes in her novel about pious New England life of the eighteenth century is the supremacy of the female housewife: such women as Mrs. Scudder, she avers, "reign [as] queens in whatever society they move; nobody was more quoted, more deferred to, or enjoyed more unquestioned position than she." The source of this authority is none other than Mrs. Scudder's admirable domestic skill, which, among "shrewd people, commands more esteem than beauty, riches, learning, or any other worldly endowment." These domestic skills directly yield religious authority: "her energy of character, her vigor and good judgment, caused her to be regarded as a mother in Israel; the minister boarded at her house, and it was she who was first to be consulted in all matters relating to the well-being of the church."[82] Her adept housekeeping interpreted as evidence of her character as well as her judgment as a manager, she becomes the minister's trusted counselor, advising him how best to oversee the church that provides religious inspiration and instruction for the wider public. In this respect, Mrs. Scudder's supervisory influence extends beyond the confines of her well-managed home into the religious lives of the community, enabled solely by her domestic proficiency.

In the aftermath of James Marvyn's presumed death at sea, the community of Newport undergoes a series of complications and controversies worsened by misguided priorities and ineffective leadership. Though the novel takes place in a devout culture that reveres its clergy, Mr. Hopkins's well-meaning effort to undermine the local slave trade only serves to alienate his parishioners and jeopardize his own status. This failure of clerical leadership coincides with the appearance of a different kind of male authority, embodied by the rakishly charming Aaron Burr, whose sycophantic, insincere praises mask his private contempt and desires to seduce the vulnerable women in his sights. Likewise, the normally pious, tough-minded Mrs. Marvyn experiences a crisis of faith that the abstracted Mr. Hopkins is wholly incapable of resolving. In this crucible of venality and confusion, Mrs. Scudder's housekeeping provides a rare safe haven of orderliness that gives stability and consolation to those otherwise derailed by these disappointments and failures; as Lora Romero has observed, Mrs. Scudder's housekeeping provides a more effective moral influence than that of the venerable Mr. Hopkins.[83] For instance, immersion in the traditional womanly housekeeping of the Scudder residence enables the French aristocrat Virginie de Frontignac to strengthen her moral resolve and embark on a more righteous life, terminating her affair with Burr and returning to her lawful husband after embracing the domestic labors promoted by the Scudders; in addition, the successes of the Scudder women in reforming Virginie also implicitly suggest the moral triumph of womanly Protestant influence over the moral corruption of Catholicism, which in the logic of the novel, has compromised both matrimony and womanly domesticity. Even Aaron Burr observes that the Scudder household is a more convincing testament to the looming millennium than Hopkins's academic theology. Himself a grandson of renowned postmillennialist theologian Jonathan Edwards, Burr as a diversion lures Hopkins into a discussion of millennialism, and, after listening indifferently to Hopkins expound at length, Burr responds to the entrance of the Scudder women with the remark that "we sometimes find ourselves in company which enables us to believe in the perfectibility of the human species. We see family retreats, so unaffected, so charming in their simplicity, where industry and piety so go hand in hand! One has only to suppose all families such, to imagine a Millennium."[84] Diligent, pious house-keeping is a more convincing proof of millennialism than Hopkins's arguments, and the happy family home provides a glimpse of the perfection that Hopkins can only imagine. Mrs. Scudder's domesticity provides a bulwark of rectitude in a morally compromised world and enables the gradual improvement of those with whom it comes into contact, facilitating the triumph of virtue over sin and order over chaos. In this way, her tidy, well-ordered home makes Newport a better place and enables the steady march of progress and enlightenment over the forces of greed and carnality.

A similar phenomenon occurs in "The Minister's Housekeeper," a short story included in *Sam Lawson's Oldtown Fireside Stories* (1871), in which effective housekeeping again prevails over traditional ministry. The recently widowed Parson Caryl hires the eminently capable seamstress Huldy to oversee his household, and, as was the case with Mrs. Scudder, Stowe appreciatively details Huldy's many accomplishments, from laundering and baking to gardening and animal husbandry. A cheerful singer in the church choir who is courted by numerous local bachelors, Huldy exerts a beneficent influence on the minster and, by extension, the entire congregation. In the colloquial voice of Huldy's cousin, town idler and raconteur Sam Lawson, Stowe explicates this influence:

> And when her work was done arternoons, Huldy would sit with her sewin' in the porch, and sing and trill away till she'd draw the meadow-larks and the bobolinks, and the orioles to answer her, and the great big elm tree overhead would get perfectly rackety with the birds; and the parson, settin' there in his study, would git to kind o' dreamin' about the angels, and golden harps, and the New Jerusalem. . . . Folks noticed, about this time, that the parson's sermons got to be like Aaron's rod, that budded and blossomed: there was things in 'em about flowers and birds, and more 'special about the music o' heaven. And Huldy, she noticed, that ef there was a hymn run in her head while she was 'round a workin' the minister was sure to give it out next Sunday.[85]

Huldy's joyful sewing songs directly inspire the minister to reflect on the prophesied new age and contemplate the glories that lie ahead. In this instance, Huldy's domesticity provides the minister with a glimpse of the happiness and prosperity predicted in Revelation, and these private reflections result in more jubilant sermons that likewise invite congregants to perceive the world around them as thriving and blossoming as it moves toward this state of fulfillment. In this chain of events, the influence of Huldy's domestic mien extends outward, not only enabling order and domestic reconstruction after Parson's Caryl's bereavement but also reminding the clergy and the congregation that the world is moving toward a state of perfection. In both ways, women's work enables the attainment of millennial perfection, functioning directly as a form of community ministry.

In thus endearing her to the minister, Huldy's domestic skills result in his marriage proposal. In this respect, "The Minister's Housekeeper" fulfills the waylaid marriage plot between the minister and his beautiful young housekeeper in *The Minister's Wooing*, and it likewise invokes Stowe's own marriage to Calvin Stowe, an older widowed clergyman.[86] For readers conversant with domestic literature and novels of the nineteenth century, this matrimonial development is practically obligatory, in fulfillment of the marriage plot that pervaded English-language narrative literature beginning in the eighteenth century and that has long shaped reader expectation. Scholars over the last thirty years have provided important analyses of marriage-plot fiction, tracing its roots in contemporary economic and social developments, but Stowe's fiction necessitates that we also consider marriage-plot fiction in the context of religious theology.[87] Frank Kermode has contended that narrative endings are inherently influenced by eschatology, the theology of the world's end, and Stowe's fiction communicates that this influence also extends to marriage-plot literature of the nineteenth century.[88] In this instance and in countless others of its kind, the marital union signals a new beginning after an ordeal and the creation of a new society rooted in better values than the preceding one (the first Mrs. Caryl seems to have been a joyless, ornery woman). The novelistic convention of the marriage plot is in and of itself inherently millennial: it provides reassurances of ongoing improvement and renewal, and it does so by enabling the reproduction of the homes and families overseen by female labor. Indeed, in both Jewish and Christian religious traditions, marriage is theologically understood as enabling the perfection of the world and the onset of the promised new age. Of paramount significance to the history of the marriage-plot narrative is the book of Revelation, which is among the oldest works of narrative literature to conclude with a marriage marked as signaling regeneration and resolution. At the close of his lengthy vision of last things, after the description of innumerable trials of celestial scale and significance, John envisions peace, restoration, and reunion in the person of a bride readied for marriage: he sees "the holy city, new Jerusalem, coming down out of heaven from God, prepared as a bride adorned for her husband. And I heard a loud voice from the throne saying, 'See, the home of God is among mortals. He will dwell with them; they will be his peoples, and God himself will be with them; he will wipe every tear from their eyes. Death will be no more; mourning and crying and pain will be no more, for the first things have passed away.' And the one who was seated on the throne said, 'See, I am making all things new'" (Rev. 21:2–5). The New Jerusalem is imagined here as a bride, and the long-awaited resolution of human history is configured as a glorious marriage celebration.

The book of Revelation thus provides the longest-lived and most influential work of narrative literature to conclude in triumphant matrimony, and, while it remains unclear whether other leading popularizers of English-language marriage-plot fiction were directly influenced by this apocalyptic scriptural narrative antecedent, Stowe clarifies in "The Minister's Housekeeper" that her execution of the marriage plot was determined above all else by Christian eschatological prophecy. Huldy's joyful sewing songs cause Parson Caryl to contemplate the New Jerusalem, a reverie that reinvigorates both his and his congregations' millennial hopes. While this scene illustrates how domesticity may activate millennialist aspiration, it also figures as a metonymic romantic daydream, for, in thinking about a city depicted in the Bible as a bride, Caryl also entertains a fantasy of matrimony. Huldy causes Caryl to think about both millennialism *and* marriage, and it is thus unsurprising that Huldy herself is transformed into a bride by story's end, their marriage at once affirming the powers of domesticity to effect progress and typologically enacting scriptural prophecy. In other words, the housekeeper not only enables the advent of the New Jerusalem through her domestic labors but also becomes a figuration of the New Jerusalem in the guise of the bride. With this neat allusion to scripture, Stowe is able both to satisfy secular literary convention and demonstrate its wider theological significance.

Scriptural precedent also exerts visible influence on the domestic reconstructions that typically conclude the marriage plots of Stowe's fiction. As discussed earlier, these narratives typically move from a state of familial fragmentation, isolation, and bereavement to one of reunion and familial renewal, with the triumphant restoration of the home in joy, marriage, and affiliation. In some instances, the narratives conclude with descriptions of the lush, well-appointed homes made possible by marriage, as with the final

chapter of Susan Warner's *The Wide, Wide World*, which, although removed at
her publisher's behest, describes the impeccably decorated sitting room given
to Ellen Montgomery by her new husband, a space that includes a drawer full
of money allocated for her personal use. In *St. Elmo* (1867) Augusta Evans details the extravagant appointments—such as its rare volumes, intaglios, gob-
lets, and jeweled trinkets—of the estate, Le Bocage, that the novel's penniless
orphan heroine, Edna Earl, will inherit upon marriage to St. Elmo Murray
at the novel's close. Such lavish descriptions of domestic abundance invoke
the famous conclusions of such canonical novels as *Pride and Prejudice* and
Jane Eyre in which marriage enables the penniless but virtuous heroine to
become mistress of a magnificent home. Otherwise, however, Stowe's narratives often conclude with descriptions of the rich, abundant joy of these
new homes, well-stocked with children and other loved ones. *Poganuc People*,
for instance, concludes with the novel's newly married heroine, Dolly Cushing, transformed into a beloved matron surrounded by daughters. *Oldtown
Folks* likewise concludes with the long-delayed marriage of the novel's narrator, Horace Holyoke, to his beloved childhood friend Tina Percival, their
home populated by her beautiful young daughter and numerous relatives.
The Pearl of Orr's Island, too, concludes with the creation of a loving home-
stead after a lifetime of rootless wandering, as Moses admits, "I am tired of
wandering. . . . I am coming home now. I begin to want a home of my own."[89]

Triumphant domestic restoration is thus a veritable requirement of
mid-century sentimental fiction, Stowe's in particular, and though this convention may seem to be merely a subsidiary feature of the marriage-plot tradition, it is equally rooted in ancient scriptural precedent, which habitually
promises a new home in reward for pious forbearance. The Abrahamaic covenant, for instance, promises abundant land in exchange for Abraham's faithfulness (Gen. 13:17), and Psalm 68 expressly praises the capacity of the divine
to provide homes to the needy:

Father of the fatherless and
protector of widows
is God in his holy habitation
God gives the desolate a home to
dwell in. (Ps.68:5–6)

Most famously, Job is rewarded for his loyalty with the restoration of his
property, home, and family (Job 42:10–13). This scriptural tradition reaches

its culmination in the final chapters of the New Testament, which concludes with a description of the magnificent New Jerusalem where a small selection of faithful Christians will reside at the conclusion of human history. In the penultimate chapter of Revelation, an angel shows John a vision of the "holy city Jerusalem coming down out of heaven from God. It has the glory of God and a radiance like a very rare jewel, like jasper, clear as crystal" (Rev. 21:10–11). The next twenty-five verses describe in detail the extraordinary features that characterize this promised future home, its walls made of jasper and studded with precious gems, the gates made of pearls, and the streets paved in gold. This description of the New Jerusalem functions as the climactic completion of Revelation and of the Christian Bible itself, all the many trials and battles predicted in the coming age finding ultimate resolution in a new homeland of unparalleled brilliance and wealth.

This assurance of a marvelous new home is compelling to readers and believers precisely because it resolves long-standing problems that thread throughout scripture. For instance, the domestic conclusion of Revelation provides a neat bookend to the traumatic primal domestic banishment from Eden with which Genesis begins and which much of the Hebrew Bible seeks to manage through laws and cautionary narratives of exile and return. It likewise resolves the long exile of the Israelites, as they wander homeless in the desert and await entrance into the promised land. The magnificent urban vision that concludes Revelation thus offers a new domestic dispensation, the promise of a glorious New Jerusalem replacing and even surpassing the homelands offered to both Abraham and the Israelites. Moreover, Revelation expressly identifies itself as composed from a similar state of homelessness, as John claims to have written the narrative from exile, in "patient endurance" on the Greek island of Patmos (Rev. 1:9). The plight of exile likewise makes its way into the Gospels, as with Jesus's assertion that followers abandon familial ties if they conflict with religious beliefs: "Do not think that I have come to bring peace on earth; I have not come to bring peace, but a sword. For I have come to set a man against his father, and a daughter against her mother" (Matt. 10:34–35). All of this is to say that for Christian writers of the nineteenth century such as Stowe, the narrative convention of domestic rehabilitation has far older generic antecedents than have been previously recognized. For instance, the millennialist overtones of *The Pearl of Orr's Island* produce an awareness that the exile of Moses Pennel, living on a remote Maine island far away from his family's estate in Cuba, suggestively mirrors that of John, banished to an island in the Aegean, and both narratives conclude with domestic resettlement and restoration. Moreover, the roots of these narrative conventions in sacred literature serve to elevate considerably the stakes of the marriages and homes with which nineteenth-century fiction routinely closes. For mid-century sentimental women writers intimately familiar with scripture—as was certainly the case for Cummins, Hale, Sedgwick, Stowe, and Warner, among others—these concluding literary marriages may enable not only social, marital, and economic security but also the very salvation of the human race itself.

The wealth of millennialist theology in Stowe's fiction leads inexorably to the suggestion that the inception of the new age may have already commenced.[90] While the bumbling and unworldly ministers Samuel Hopkins and Parson Caryl dreamily imagine the millennium in a distant future, Stowe's fiction repeatedly suggests that one has only to look around to see the signs that betoken its commencement. Where such figures as William Miller discerned signs of the millennium in contemporary political events, Stowe's fiction adheres more closely to scriptural assertions that the new age will arrive without fanfare, "like a thief in the night" who breaches the sanctum of the home without attracting notice (1 Thess. 5:2). In depicting the reconstruction of families and the correction of error in renewed Christian piety, Stowe's fiction narrates the advent of this much-anticipated progress, which she shows as occurring in the here and now and not in the hereafter. *The Pearl of Orr's Island*, for instance, implicitly establishes its own narrative resolution as a sign of millennial realization. Miss Roxy's prediction that Moses's identity will remain unknown until the onset of the millennium implicitly posits Mr. Sewell's confession as an indication that the new age has already begun: the novel's own narrative resolution portends the healing, improving effects of religious faith and resolute striving. Elsewhere in the novel Stowe suggests that the predictions forecast in Revelation are being fulfilled not in grand public spectacles but in private, personal ways. After Miss Roxy predicts that the mystery will be solved in the far-flung cosmic future, Captain Kittredge is inspired by her reference to Revelation to relay a tall tale about his travels, telling his daughter Sally about seeing a man in India wear spectacular jewels who "looked like something in the Revelations—a real New Jerusalem look he had." He here references Revelation 21:18–21, which describes the precious materials out of which the New Jerusalem is made, the walls decorated with such gems as sapphires and amethysts and the streets paved with gold. When his wife objects to his use of scripture in support of his yarn, Kittredge replies, "Don't it tell about all sorts of gold and precious stones in the Revelations? . . . that's all I meant. Them ar countries off in Asia ain't like our'n,—stands to reason they shouldn't be; them's Scripture countries, and everything is different there."[91] This jauntily inventive use of eschatological prophecy conveys a belief that scriptural promises may be fulfilled in worldly, pragmatic terms: abundance and prosperity may be awarded in the here and now, and the New Jerusalem promised in scripture may already exist.

Otherwise, though, the novel repeatedly seeks to show the ways in which personal relationships and private moral triumphs, rather than the public forum of politics, may register the fulfillment of biblical prophecy. For example, during a childhood quarrel between Mara and Moses about the ethics of his stealing eggs from an eagle's nest, Stowe comments on the features of Mara's personality that make her able to maintain moral certainty amid Moses's brazen casuistry. Stowe writes, "Reader, there are some women of this habit; and there is no independence and pertinacity of opinion like that of these seemingly soft, quiet creatures, whom it is so easy to silence, and so difficult to convince. Mara, little and unformed as she yet was, belonged to the race of those spirits to whom is deputed the office of the angel in the Apocalypse, to whom was given the golden rod which measured the New Jerusalem. Infant though she was, she had ever in her hands that invisible measuring-rod which she was laying to the foundations of all actions and thoughts."[92] Stowe here references Revelation 21:15–17, in which an angel shows John a vision of the New Jerusalem and, equipped with a "rod of gold," measures the city's dimensions in detail. Firmly resisting Moses's cunning arguments in defense of plunder, Mara enforces stable norms of morality amid the pressures of sophistry, and Stowe perceives in this moral resolve a worldly figuration, in miniature, of the assessments that will precede entrance into the New Jerusalem. Mara contributes in a commonplace, functional way to the preservation of the moral standards without which salvation cannot take place, and Stowe suggests that it is through small daily victories and fervent loyalty to uprightness that common people—white, Protestant, middle-class women in particular—may bring about the peace and virtue that characterize the promised new age. In addition, this metaphor suggests that the New Jerusalem Mara measures is not a physical space but instead Moses's own "actions and thoughts": the New Jerusalem she describes may not a place per se, but a moral, spiritual state of union with the divine. That is, *The Pearl of Orr's Island* conveys a belief that "the kingdom of God is among you" and not a literal physical space to be created at a later date (Luke 17:21).

Stowe similarly depicts Judgment Day as a private, personal experience rather than an imminent, collective reckoning from on high. Often the centerpiece of premillennialist visions of the apocalypse, Judgment Day is frequently depicted in visual illustration and literary portraiture as the cataclysmic conclusion of human history, with the public tallying of virtue and settling of moral scores, in which the sinful are exposed for their crimes and subjected to grave punishments while the righteous are publicly recognized and sanctified. In *The Pearl of Orr's Island*, however, Judgment Day is woven into the normal fabric of human life and is depicted not as the end of human affairs but as a customary occurrence in which moral inventory enables self-knowledge. As described in the novel, every day has the potential to be Judgment Day if we are able to reflect honestly about our transgressions, and it is only through such examination that we may effect change and foster the progress on which the new age depends. For instance, Mara's grave illness causes Moses to take stock of his conduct toward her, and he realizes with considerable agony that there is no time left for him "to make amends" for his many misdeeds against her. Though he understands that "all had been a thousand times forgiven and forgotten between them," he comes to learn that "nothing in the soul's history ever dies or is forgotten," so that "when the beloved one lies stricken and ready to pass away, comes the judgment-day of love, and all the dead moments of the past arise and live again."[93] In her analysis of Moses's self-reproach, Stowe ventures into theology here, proffering a postmillennialist interpretation of Revelation not as a depiction of a spectacular supernatural event but instead as a description of the workings of the divine in commonplace, personal incidents. Judgment Day occurs whenever we honestly examine our behavior and consciences, and it is imposed from within and not from without, the product of love rather than vengeance, as it is often interpreted in premillennialism. In this way, Stowe revises the private revelation of self-recognition that so often functions as the narrative pivot of nineteenth-century fiction and renders it a miniaturized, personalized fulfillment of apocalyptic prophecy. Thus, her later fiction intimates that she may have reconsidered her attention to politics as the primary theater of millennialism in the famous conclusion to *Uncle Tom's Cabin*, suggesting in such novels as *The Pearl of Orr's Island* that the millennium is indeed occurring right now, but it is taking place at home and in private.

The rich context of nineteenth-century millennialism that pervades Stowe's writings necessitates that we recognize narrative form as an agent of religious instruction and evangelism. Modern readers and critics have long grumbled that Stowe's domestic fiction seems formulaic, predictable, or derivative, but an awareness of the scriptural antecedents of her work may allow us to regard this scripted quality as a religious asset rather than as a literary liability. Lauren Berlant has noted that sentimentality is characterized by "a love affair with conventionality"; an understanding of the religious character of sentimental literary conventions enables us to see that this generic conventionality in the nineteenth century also signaled a loyalty to religious conventions and expectations.[94] What might in a secular context seem like a literary weakness emerges in a religious context as a chief indicator of scriptural fidelity and sectarian affiliation. Formulaic plots are purposeful and meaningful in Stowe's fiction, for they invited readers to see that Protestantism yields predictable, reliable results and leads inexorably toward a projected, predicted end. Formulaic predictability would doubtless have been of immense comfort to contemporary readers, who saw affirmed in methodical plots the power of Protestantism to create order out of chaos, whatever shape that chaos took. If novels may be predictable, then so may be the pious life, which Stowe repeatedly affirms will result in domestic reunion and restoration, whether in this life, the afterlife, or in the New Jerusalem.

Considered more broadly, Stowe's domestic fiction also occupies an important place in the history of feminist theology. Contemporary feminist biblical scholars, such as Catherine Keller, Tina Pippin, and Lee Quinby have argued that Christian eschatology is inherently masculinist and misogynist: Revelation constitutes the future world as a place free of women and female authority as wanton, immoral, and destructive.[95] According to Tina Pippin, "The Apocalypse is not a safe space for women."[96] The nineteenth century, however, was characterized by numerous diverse efforts to secure a central place for women in eschatology. For instance, Elizabeth Cady Stanton marveled at the apparent misogyny of Christian eschatology and in her commentary on Revelation in the *Woman's Bible* (1898), declared, "Verily, we need an expurgated edition of the Old and the New Testaments before they are fit to be placed in the hands of our youth to be read in the public schools and in theological seminaries, especially if we wish to inspire our children with proper love and respect for the Mothers of the Race."[97] Several female religious leaders were lauded as worldly figurations of the Woman Clothed with the Sun, among them Mother Ann Lee of the Shakers and Mary Baker Eddy, founder of Christian Science. Within the history of nineteenth-century feminist interventions in Christian eschatology, Stowe's domestic fiction plays a vital role. Stowe significantly revised the genre of apocalyptic literature, loosening it from its long-standing moorings in the jeremiad denouncing the sinfulness and corruption of the current world. Instead, Stowe reshaped apocalyptic literature into an ebullient, hopeful domestic novel that celebrates rather than decries daily life and sees signs not of decline but of progress.[98] In this effort, her numerous novels and writings highlighted and dramatized the powers of women—and their traditional domestic work—to create the progress widely heralded as a chief indicator of millennial inception but that was typically sought in the public world of politics and commerce rather than in the private, domestic sector. We are looking for the millennium in the wrong place, Stowe seems to suggest: in a world riven by death and disorder, it is women who enable restoration and reunion and thereby carry out the ministry of Christ. Moreover, she reformed the vexed status of the female prophet, transforming it from that of the promiscuous Jezebel (as well as her American legatee, Anne Hutchinson) to that of the dutiful, domestic housewife. As she constituted it, the new age promises to be characterized by the supreme ascendency of the home itself, as all human beings return from their exilic wanderings to their rightful homes and families. But where such female religious leaders as Ann Lee, Jemima Wilkinson, and Mary Baker Eddy would attract controversy for their indecorous assumption of public roles of authority, Stowe's theological interventions evaded controversy because they were packaged in the guise of warm, nostalgic fiction that veiled their controversial contents, as it were, in celebrations of family, marriage, and the traditional womanly art of domesticity. For Stowe, it is the traditionally womanly facilities and roles—and not clerical authority or politics—that enable the fulfillment of prophecy and the destined culmination of human history.

Nor is there any doubt that Stowe's writings were prescient, even progressive in appointing women's work a vital agent of the millennium, for these ideas would become foundational in several theological systems that would become popular in the second half of the nineteenth century. For instance, Ellen G. White, founder of the Seventh-Day Adventist movement born out of Millerite millennialism, wrote extensively about the central role of domesticity in bringing about the new age, as with such works as *An Appeal to Mothers* (1864), *Health, or How to Live* (1865), and *Important Facts of Faith: Laws of Health, And Testimonies* (1864). In *The Ministry of Healing* (1905), for instance, White channeled Stowe in her assertion that the "restoration and uplifting of humanity begins [sic] in the home."[99] The linkage between Stowe and Ellen White is visible in the numerous mentions that White made to Stowe's fiction in her own theological writings; for instance, she referenced *Uncle Tom's Cabin* alone in at least three different texts. The frequency with which she referenced Stowe indicates Ellen White's perception of Stowe as a useful point of reference for her own theological assertions. The two chapters that follow—on the embrace of sentimentalism in both Mormonism and Christian Science, respectively—examine the ways in which these two immensely popular new faiths of the nineteenth century developed theologies of domesticity that systematize the religious ideas put in wide circulation by mid-century women writers. Both used sentimentalism to evidence their respectability, but they also used sentimentalism as the foundation for theologies that similarly imputed supreme religious authority to women. What had been merely a fictional suggestion in Stowe's novels became canon doctrine among these two later sects.

CHAPTER 4

═══════

Derelict Daughters and Polygamous Wives

Mormonism and the Uses of Sentiment

IN 1872, a bimonthly women's periodical began publication in Salt Lake City, Utah. In its mission statement, *Woman's Exponent* announced its twofold ambition both to promote the "diffusion of knowledge" among its Mormon readers and to correct the poor public image of Mormon women, who are "grossly misrepresented through the press by active enemies who permit no opportunity to pass of maligning and slandering them."[1] In response to these alleged misrepresentations, *Woman's Exponent* presented itself as a venue by which Mormon women may "represent [them]selves" and in so doing keep up with current events and receive information on subjects ranging from recipes to international politics. Patterned after the suffragist periodical *Woman's Journal* founded two years earlier, *Woman's Exponent* primarily contained content composed by local Mormon women, but it was not averse to reprinting material originally published in the mainstream press, such as *Hearth and Home* and *Appleton's Journal*.[2] Literature figured prominently in this dual endeavor to reshape the Mormon woman's public image and to circulate "interesting and valuable" information, and *Woman's Exponent* represented the Mormon woman as a knowledgeable, discerning reader interested in keeping up with contemporary literary developments. In support of such an image, the periodical featured announcements of new literary releases, biographical sketches of such distinguished writers as Alice Cary and George Eliot, and bon mots by such writers as Fanny Fern. *Woman's Exponent* also cultivated female literary ambition by hiring Mormon women to serve as writers, editors, and compositors, and it likewise published the occasional work of locally authored fiction.

Poetry was especially significant in this effort to remake the Mormon woman's public image, for each issue featured a poem, usually by a local woman, in the upper-left corner of the second page. This poet's corner participated in this effort of image correction by offering abundant evidence of the sensibility, literary taste, and education of Mormon women. Lu Dalton's poem "A Mother's Resignation," published in November 1872, typifies the kind of poetry published in *Woman's Exponent*. Composed of seven octaves, it employs the familiar poetic idiom of sentimental consolation verse and recounts the efforts of a grief-stricken mother to reconcile herself to the death of a child. With faultless meter and elegant diction, Dalton's poem communicates her full command of convention, both literary and cultural. For instance, in describing the "beauty of the tender face,/Small fingers, clasping flowers pale and sweet," Dalton demonstrates at once her personal composure in the face of grief as well as her command of literary genre, for her poem participates in the widespread nineteenth-century poetic form of the child elegy, a genre that also produced such works as Lydia Sigourney's "Death of an Infant" (1827) and Henry Wadsworth Longfellow's "Resignation" (1849).[3] After several anguished stanzas, the poem concludes with a reiteration of the conventional language of feminine resignation amid worldly suffering, which appears in countless works of nineteenth-century women's literature: despite her profound sorrow, the poem's speaker resolves to embrace and submit to "God's will," because it

> . . . is wiser than our frail desires,
> His mercy tenderer than our purest love;
> And I can yield to this since He requires [my son].[4]

For readers of literature composed in the sentimental mode, this is familiar rhetoric used widely to express both the struggle of emotional self-control amid life's heartbreaking vicissitudes and the belief that proper, pious femininity mandates the acceptance of divine will, however hurtful or seemingly unjust. This poem thus advances the stated ambitions of *Woman's Exponent* by presenting an image of Mormon womanhood that is both familiar and normative, her command of poetic forms evidencing her sensibility and the poem's contents expressing her full absorption of sentimental notions of proper feminine response to grief.

Dalton's poem and *Woman's Exponent* highlight the centrality of sentimental discourse to nineteenth-century efforts to refashion the public image of Mormon women. This effort is particularly noteworthy because sentimentalism proved one of the most damaging rhetorical weapons leveled against Mormonism in the mid-century. The runaway success of Harriet Beecher Stowe's *Uncle Tom's Cabin* inspired the publication of countless novels that similarly depicted the sufferings of women under the yoke of Mormon polygamy. And just as anti-Catholic novels depicted young women cruelly seduced and abused by lascivious priests, so these later works presented Mormonism as an equivalent new menace that threatened to enslave and exploit vulnerable young women. After decades of such portraits, Mormon advocates sought to redress their public image by enlisting sentimental rhetoric and iconography. In particular, they sought to alter the public understanding of Mormon domesticity and marriage as practiced through the controversial institution of polygamy. Sentimental rhetoric enabled Mormon defenders to assert the compliance of Mormon home life with familiar, normative belief and to rehabilitate the public image of the Mormon woman by presenting her as the paradigmatic sentimental woman: pious, well-read, and refined. Sentimentalism, in other words, provided the terms by which Mormon domesticity was chiefly criticized and by which it would ultimately be defended and normalized by its advocates.

As I will show, the complex Mormon engagement in sentimentalism is significantly enriched by the substantial contributions of this literary discourse to foundational Mormon theology about the divinity of motherhood. Sentimental ideals were thoroughly absorbed and reified among the Latter-day Saints, who, in the mid-nineteenth century, would come to interpret a conventionally sentimental poem by Eliza R. Snow—a beloved, prolific writer as well as an immensely capable administrator—as containing revealed truths about the afterlife, divinity, and the inherent holiness of motherhood. As shown in both Snow's career and the reception of her most famous poem, sentimentalism directly contributed to the establishment of female religious authority among the Latter-day Saints.

Sentimental Rhetoric and the Defense of Polygamy

Initially, the Church of Jesus Christ of Latter-day Saints plainly opposed polygamy, the practice that permits men to have more than one wife at a time. In an evocation of Levitical prohibition, the *Book of Mormon*, first published in 1830, declared that such practices were strictly forbidden: Mormon scripture reads, "There shall not any man among you have save it be one wife; and concubines he shall have none" (Jacob 2:27). However, as early as 1835, rumors began to circulate that Joseph Smith, the founder of Mormonism, and members of his inner circle had secretly taken additional wives. In 1843, Joseph Smith recorded a revelation instituting the new doctrine of "Celestial Marriage," which asserted both the everlasting endurance of marriages consecrated in the Mormon church as well as the righteousness of polygamy. Section 132 of *Doctrine and Covenants*, the Mormon scripture of continuing revelation, states, "If any man espouse a virgin, and desire to espouse another, and the first give her consent; and if he espouse the second, and they are virgins, and have vowed to no other man, then is he justified; he cannot commit adultery with that belongeth unto him and to no one else."[5] This revelation remained clandestine throughout Smith's life, though he and members of his inner circle took numerous additional wives, with Smith's own plural wives numbering in the dozens, according to biographer Fawn Brodie.[6] In 1852, eight years after Smith's violent death at the hands of an Illinois mob, Brigham Young, Smith's successor, finally disclosed this revelation, making it official church doctrine. What had long been an open secret was thus made public, and it soon sparked an outcry in the mainstream press.[7]

Brigham Young's timing was somewhat unfortunate, for that same year Harriet Beecher Stowe created a national sensation with the publication of *Uncle Tom's Cabin*, a novel that effectively consolidated sentimentalism's status as a potent public discourse that might be deployed to decry the injustices perpetrated against women and children and elicit reader sympathy on behalf of the oppressed. Stowe's novel also confirmed the public uses of sentimentalism as a heuristic of gender normalcy, for she used the contented domesticity at the heart of sentimentalism as a rubric of morality and social justice; in particular, she transformed sentimental discourse into a public standard assaying the ethics of a household's arrangements.[8] The publication of *Uncle Tom's Cabin* had immediate consequences for Mormons as its successes inspired scores of opportunistic writers to attempt to harness the same reader concern by drawing attention to the plight of white women outside the bounds of the United States in the Western territories. Whereas Stowe identified slavery as an egregious violation of sentimental femininity, a host of copycat writers found an analogous peril in Mormonism and published literally dozens of narratives warning readers and their daughters from succumbing to the appeals of Mormon missionaries, which, they aimed to show, could only lead them away from their families and to lives of polygamy and abuse.[9] Characterizing polygamy as a form of white slavery that preyed upon respectable, middle-class girls from good East Coast families, writers of anti-polygamy novels closed the gap of race, class, and region that necessarily estranged Stowe's white, middle-class readers from such characters as Topsy and Eliza, and instead portrayed polygamy as an even more pernicious form of slavery that stalked among readers on the East Coast, protected by law and looking to abduct the readers' own daughters.

Literally dozens of such narratives were published by the end of the century. Some of the better-known and more popular novels include Orvilla Belisle's *The Prophets: Or, Mormonism Unveiled* (1856); Alfreda Eva Bell's *Boadicea* (1855); Metta Fuller's *Mormon Wives* (1856); and Maria Ward's immensely popular *Female Life Among the Mormons* (1855), which went through numerous editions by the end of the century.[10] Another impetus behind this sudden wave of novels may have been the culture of rabid, compulsory polygamy that swept Mormonism in the mid-1850s in the period known as the Mormon Reformation, when Mormon leaders promoted polygamy with particular intensity and which consequently led to a dramatic increase in polygamous marriages.[11] These novels were composed using sentimental convention and comprise a subgenre of sentimentalism that manipulated these formulas to effect a somewhat different end. Anti-Mormon novels constituted a hybrid combining tropes from both the eighteenth-century sentimental seduction narrative about the perils that befall young women who allow themselves to be seduced, such as Susanna Rowson's *Charlotte Temple* (1791), and the later nineteenth-century sentimental form narrating the trials of solitary, pious young women. While these novels derived from the immediate stimulus of *Uncle Tom's Cabin*, the anti-Mormon novel generically also stemmed from the many anti-Catholic exposés that became popular in the second quarter of the nineteenth century. As with such works as Maria Monk's *Awful Disclosures of the Hotel Dieu Nunnery* (1836), Rebecca Reed's *Six Months in a Convent* (1835), and Josephine Bunkley's *The Testimony of an Escaped Novice* (1855), these works typically recount the trials of an impressionable young woman who falls prey to the allures of Catholic influence and innocently joins a convent, only to endure terrible abuse and imprisonment.[12] The symmetry between anti-Catholic and anti-Mormon narratives is striking, and both genres depict their respective denominational target as tyrannical, oppressive, and sexually licentious, for vulnerable young women in both genres become subject to the rapacious sexual demands of men who falsely present themselves as moral stewards, whether Catholic priests or Mormon missionaries and husbands. The generic overlap between the two forms is particularly visible in the career of sensational novelist Orvilla Belisle, who authored works in both genres: in 1855, she published *The Arch Bishop; Or, Romanism in the United States* and a year later she published *The Prophets: Or, Mormonism Unveiled.*

Following the narrative precedent of anti-Catholic novels about white women in religious captivity, anti-Mormon novels typically follow the trials of a newly converted woman, usually from a mainline Protestant background on the East Coast, who converts to Mormonism under the influence of a husband or fiancé and without any previous knowledge of the Mormon doctrine of polygamy. Once she does learn about it, her husband promises to remain faithful, only to take another wife later due to pressure from religious authorities, a generic quality that bears witness to the influence of anti-Catholic novels, which similarly critique the excessive power of Catholic clergy. The addition of another wife results in the collapse of the heroine's faith and health, and the novels typically end with the heroine's apostasy and departure from the Mormon fold, either by death or flight. Along the way, the novels describe the travails of numerous other women whose spirits have likewise been broken by polygamy, who have also been abandoned to poverty by faithless husbands, and who lose their will to live. The rest of the narrative recognizably adheres to the sentimental blueprint by depicting the trials of this good-hearted heroine, separated from her beloved family, and her struggles with faith, submission to authority, and the creation of a new family amid coreligionists. Though the main character is a standard iteration of the conventional sentimental heroine, these novels nonetheless invert sentimental formula by presenting her not as a role model to be emulated, as was typical in the traditional sentimental form, but as an example that readers should categorically avoid, as was the case with eighteen-century seduction narratives and anti-Catholic novels. These texts depict female suffering not to inspire conversion but instead to dissuade it; faith in these novels functions as the source of anguish, not as the panacea to it, and they consequently strive to instill female readers with the religious skepticism usually depicted as improper and unwomanly in conventional sentimental novels.

Anti-Mormon novels often derive their moral and literary authority from explicit comparisons to Stowe's *Uncle Tom's Cabin* and the attendant context of slavery. For example, Alfreda Bell argued that in Utah "women are treated as but little better than slaves; they are in fact white slaves; are required to do all the most servile drudgery; are painfully impressed with their nothingness and utter inferiority, in divers ways and at all seasons."[13] To consolidate this association, she depicts runaway polygamous women hunted by mobs of men with dogs, lynched, hanged, and beaten to death. Writers of these novels, too, similarly framed their books as incitements to political action. For example, Catharine Waite opened her 1866 book, *The Mormon Prophet and His Harem*, with a preface announcing her hope that readers would take action to dismantle this institution. Another writer, Metta Fuller, compared her *Mormon Wives* to Stowe's antislavery novel. Fuller wrote, "As citizens of this country, we owe it as a duty [to the Constitution and to humanity to] . . . sternly oppose slavery in all its forms," thereby recasting polygamy as a subset of slavery and her own book as a quasi-sequel to *Uncle Tom's Cabin*.[14] Stowe's unmistakable influence is also apparent through countless analogous scenes and set pieces that pay explicit homage to *Uncle Tom's Cabin*. These novels, for example, habitually featured exciting scenes of escape patterned after Eliza's flight from slavery, as with Maria Ward's closing scene of the narrator fleeing into the wilderness to evade recapture from a mob of Mormon men. Likewise, they routinely imitate the famous death of Eva St. Clare with heartrending deaths of spiritually enlightened women and girls who reject specious religious doctrine and return to the Protestantism of their childhoods. For example, the climactic scene of Fuller's novel *Mormon Wives* portrays the melodramatic death of its long-suffering heroine, Margaret, who has had to endure her husband's faithless polygamy. With her family surrounding her deathbed, she doles out forgiveness to her disloyal husband and sister wife, urging them to atone because "God forgives—only—those who repent. . . . I have prayed for you," she murmurs with boundless compassion.[15] And in honor of the central preoccupation of *Uncle Tom's Cabin*, these novels repeatedly depict the deleterious effect of polygamy on homes and mother-child bonds: once their husbands take new wives, loving mothers lose their will to live and neglect their children and homes. Within just a few years, polygamy has been so firmly conflated with slavery that the Republican Party, during its 1856 national convention, formally committed to the abolition of what they termed the "twin relics of barbarism," polygamy and slavery.[16]

The most striking example of Stowe's influence is Jennie Switzer's novel *Elder Northfield's Home* (1882), the very title of which constitutes an homage to Stowe's novel and similarly emphasizes the injurious effects of polygamy on the home front. Switzer's novel is virtually a character-for-character adaptation of *Uncle Tom's Cabin* to polygamous Utah: it has an unruly, neglected Mormon child in need of socializing, modeled after Topsy; a well-meaning but hapless husband forced to make unpleasant sacrifices, modeled after Shelby; and a bitter polygamous wife who has endured terrible trials, modeled after Cassy. And like *Uncle Tom's Cabin,* the novel concludes with the revelation that all the righteous characters are estranged relatives and closes with their reunion and collective departure to New York, which, as the novel's beacon of liberty, functions as an analogue to Stowe's Liberia. Anti-polygamy writings became so entangled with *Uncle Tom's Cabin* that by the 1870s, Harriet Beecher Stowe herself was actively enlisted as a voice in the cause, writing a preface to Fanny Stenhouse's 1872 memoir of her own experiences of polygamy, *Tell It All.* In that preface, Stowe asked readers to regard Stenhouse's appeal as a successor to her own *Uncle Tom's Cabin,* writing, "Our day has seen a glorious breaking of fetters. The slave-pens of the South have become a night-mare of the past; the auction-block and whipping-post have given place to the church and school-house; and the songs of emancipated millions are heard through our land. Shall we not then hope that the hour is come to loose the bonds of a cruel slavery whose chains have cut into the hearts of thousands of our sisters—a slavery which debases and degrades womanhood, motherhood, and the family?"[17] Though sentimentalism contributed to the efforts to eliminate slavery in the American South, its vestiges endure among the Mormons, and, Stowe suggests, readers ought to continue the work begun in *Uncle Tom's Cabin* by seeking the similar eradication of polygamy.

In their depictions of Mormon life, these narratives pay particular attention to the day-to-day domestic lives of polygamous wives, describing how they raise their children, maintain their homes, and interact with their spouses (sister wives included). In so doing, these texts uphold a decidedly sentimental benchmark for appropriate female behavior, presuming in particular that a woman's commitment to her household duties indexes her religious faith. In the logic of sentimentalism, a devout housekeeper is a contented, scrupulous housekeeper.[18] Unsurprisingly, anti-Mormon novels persistently contend that Mormonism, and polygamy in particular, violate this sentimental ethos by rendering women ineffective household managers. In his 1857 account, *The Husband in Utah,* Austin Ward remarked on the laziness of polygamous wives, commenting that polygamy induced "a state of apathetic indifference and no respect for their husbands." After interviewing men in both polygamous and monogamous households, Ward claimed that "most men found it more difficult to get a button sewed on a shirt, where their houses were filled with wives, than to have the whole shirt made where there was only one" wife.[19] According to these accounts, Mormon women, thus deprived of a husband's undivided attention and rendered disposable, lack any personal investment in homes they share with rival wives. Mormon doctrine, in effect, transforms the home from the sphere of female dutifulness to an expression of her indifference, both to her husband and to her responsibilities. While this emotional apathy results in untidy homes, it also results in neglected children, and images of unattended, unkempt children pervade these novels. Furthermore, these texts contend that Mormonism not only transforms devoted husbands into faithless philanderers, but it also causes women in droves to abandon their homes, husbands, and children to follow seductive missionaries to Utah.[20] In both of these ways, these novels suggest that Mormonism precipitates the very conditions of abandonment and familial fragmentation that usually commence sentimental novels, which, as discussed in previous chapters, narrate the process by which families and homes may be reconstructed. One has only to read the following passage about a young Mormon convert leaving her home for Utah from John Russell's 1853 novel, *The Mormoness*, to witness how explicitly Mormonism was held accountable for the crisis of derelict girls that sentimentalism sought to resolve: "She had now no home. Henceforth she must be a pilgrim upon the face of the wide and unfriendly world. No hopes but such as spring from a faithful discharge of stern duties of life were before her. Toil and suffering and even martyrdom itself might be her lot."[21] Russell's phrasing "wide and unfriendly world" in this passage references the title of Susan Warner's paradigmatic sentimental novel, *The Wide, Wide World*, but he also specifies that the religious faith that typically corrects female homelessness in standard sentimental fare here only contributes to this plight.

In all of these ways, sentimental narrative convention, tropes, and ideology posed very real problems in public relations for nineteenth-century Mormons. And in the vein of Mary Henderson Eastman's *Aunt Phillis's Cabin* (1852), which rewrote Stowe's novel in defense of slavery, Mormon writers and leaders coopted sentimental discourse in an attempt to defend polygamy and proffer a countervailing public image of the private life of the Mormon wife. This use of sentimentalism became particularly strenuous in the third quarter of the nineteenth century, as Mormons attempted to assimilate into mainstream American culture in pursuit of statehood for Utah and formal admission to the United States.[22] Polygamy remained an intractable sticking point in this campaign, and Mormons would eventually renounce polygamy in 1890 so that might Utah might receive statehood in 1896. But in the years leading up to this compromise, sentimental defenses of polygamy and Mormon femininity proliferated. As Nancy Bentley has observed, the public outcry against polygamy evidenced how the "currency of domestic fiction . . . was converted into political currency," and, in pursuit of the latter, Mormon advocates coopted the former.[23] For instance, Mormon critic and writer Edward Tullidge would rely explicitly on sentimental rhetoric in *Women of Mormondom* (1877), a text composed in direct response to the publication of Fanny Stenhouse's memoir, *Tell It All*, in which she detailed her misery as a polygamous wife. Stenhouse's autobiography posed a grave publicity problem for Mormons not only because of the public endorsement of Harriet Beecher Stowe but also because Stenhouse and her husband had had direct access to the highest-ranking leadership of the church, thereby endowing them with a great deal of privileged information. Beginning with its opening pages, Stenhouse's narrative sounded familiar sentimental notes and corroborated some discomfiting suspicions. As a young Englishwoman raised a devout Baptist, Stenhouse first encountered Mormonism upon the conversion of her parents while she was working as a teacher in France. Once she returned to England, she found herself the subject of attention from an eager Mormon missionary, who intermingled his religious petitions with romantic appeals and soon made her his wife. In this way, Stenhouse's conversion was enabled by the very circumstances of familial separation, economic need, and female itinerancy that, as discussed in a previous chapter, thrust young women out into the world and engaged the attention of sentimental narrative.

The rest of Stenhouse's narrative details her anguished efforts to reconcile with her husband's decision to take another wife. Stenhouse's terms in relaying this struggle directly reference sentimental convention. The sentimental narrative hinges on the heroine's resolution to tolerate and even embrace the burdens that plague her, to "kiss the chastening rod," to use stock sentimental language.[24] Taking her cue from this sentimental trope of female resignation, Stenhouse initially interprets her loathing of polygamy as a sign that her character needs reforming and that she must learn joyful submission to divine will. "How I strove against my rebellious nature: how I battled with myself!" she wrote. "That God had sent the Revelation [instituting polygamy] I never questioned, and all rebellion to His will I knew must be sinful. I had no thought of evading the responsibility: my heart must be subdued. . . . I tried to reason with myself and to persuade myself that it was I who was to blame and not the Revelation. If the Lord required me to submit, it must be for some good purpose."[25] Stenhouse here describes her efforts to embrace her hardship under the assumption that it, as well as the doctrine of polygamy that produced it, is divinely ordained and therefore purposefully engineered for her own betterment. Just as Lu Dalton's poem describes her gradual acquiescence to "God's will [which] is wiser than our frail desires," Stenhouse here expresses her commitment to the self-discipline and emotional management central to sentimental accounts of female maturation.[26] In so doing, this passage chronicles Stenhouse's efforts to abide by the sentimental script of character reform. After years of struggle, her efforts at sentimental resignation ultimately fail, and she takes this failure as conclusive evidence of the absolute injustice of polygamy: "A woman," she writes, "can nerve herself to endure almost anything, and outwardly she may conceal her feelings, but there are limits beyond which endurance is not possible."[27] Within Stenhouse's logic, her inability to venerate polygamy after protracted efforts of self-betterment evidences not the limitations of sentimental resignation but the iniquity of polygamy. As with the many scenes of righteous rebellion that interleave sentimental narration, sentimental discourse maintains that there is a fine line separating beneficial suffering from outright abuse, and there are some things that a sentimentalized woman cannot and should not tolerate: for example, while Ellen Montgomery in Warner's *Wide, Wide World* is expected to endure her aunt's sharp tongue and callousness, her sentimentality forbids her from submitting to the violence of Mr. Saunders, a vicious salesman who threatens her and beats her horse. With *Uncle Tom's Cabin*, Harriet Beecher Stowe charted some of the outer limits of intolerable abuse, and Stenhouse's narrative follows this generic precedent by maintaining that religiously sanctioned marital infidelity is equally intolerable. To expect women to abide and even celebrate their husband's dalliances with other women is to exploit the doctrine of resignation for ungodly, obscene, and decidedly unsentimental purposes.

In all of these ways, Stenhouse's narrative employs sentimental convention to impugn the abuse of Mormon women, and its published rebuttal, Tullidge's *Women of Mormondom*, responded by seeking to repair the legitimacy of Mormonism by showing its compliance with sentimentalism. In imitation of the imploring appeals for Mormon women that prefaced Stenhouse's narrative as well as *Uncle Tom's Cabin*, Tullidge begins with the exclamation, "Long enough, O women of America, have your Mormon sisters been blasphemed! From the day that they, in the name and fear of the Lord their God, undertook to 'build up Zion,' they have been persecuted for righteousness sake."[28] Turning these sentimental critiques on their head, Tullidge agrees that Mormon women are indeed oppressed and in need of help, but the perpetrators who assail them are not callous Mormon husbands intent on marital cruelty but defamatory writers such as Maria Ward and Fanny Stenhouse, who, in depicting Mormon women as powerless victims, undercut their character, influence, and leadership. Tullidge's account seeks to square these claims with the historical record, and to that end he relays chapter by chapter the history of Mormonism through portraits of women who proved important along the way. For example, his chapters covering the earliest years of Mormonism provide an opportunity to depict and extol such women as Lucy Mack Smith, Joseph Smith's mother, and poet Eliza Snow. Through innumerable examples of Mormon women's sterling character and piety, Tullidge portrays them as willing and even indispensable leaders in Mormon life. In contrast to Stenhouse's claims that Mormonism denigrates women and renders them silent, passive, and scorned, he counters that Mormonism is the apotheosis of female-centered religion. Mormon women, he claims, are genuine leaders and sources of moral authority: he writes that the Mormon woman

> became the high priestess and prophetess. She was this *officially*. The constitution of the Church acknowledged her divine mission to administer for the regeneration of the race. The genius of a patriarchal priesthood naturally made her the apostolic help-meet for man. If you saw her not in the pulpit *teaching* the congregation, yet was she found in the temple, *administering* for the living and the dead. . . . She held the keys of the administration of angels and of the working of miracles and of the "sealings" pertaining to "the heavens and the earth" [the sealing ritual binds families together for eternity]. Never before was woman so much as she is in this Mormon dispensation![29]

While preserving women's traditional place as church helpmeet, Mormonism in Tullidge's formulation sanctifies women's conventional roles, hailing their guardianship of children as a divine mission and interpreting their caretaking work as a private extension of the Mormon priesthood's duties.[30] These womanly roles, Tullidge claims, may be separate from those of men, but they are more than equal, their separateness evidencing their doctrinal holiness and their sacrosanct separateness from every day public life. He does concede the suffering of Mormon women but seeks to recuperate its sentimental credentials: "The Mormon women have borne the cross and worn the crown of thorns for a full lifetime; not in their religion, but in their experience. Their strange destiny and the divine warfare incarnated in their lives, gave them an experience matchless in its character and unparalleled in its sacrifices."[31] These women, he avers, suffer not because of the cruelties inherent in Mormonism but because of their true womanhood, willingly embracing their ordeals in the patient forbearance requisite to sentimental femininity. While acknowledging the idiosyncratic circumstances—that is, their frontier travels and persecution from hostile outsiders—that set Mormon women apart from their peers, this passage is nonetheless intent on minimizing the differences in belief and practice that set Mormon women apart from Tullidge's presumably non-Mormon readership and emphasizes instead the commonalities that might make Mormon women seem more familiar, such as their adulation of Christ and their adherence to sentimental resignation.

Tullidge's book is replete with similar rhetoric designed to confirm the full adherence of Mormon women to pious, sentimental femininity and the usefulness of sentimentalism in rhetorically constituting womanly domesticity as a form of religious stewardship. Another such instance is his reiteration of an oft-repeated anecdote from the Mormon archives that rebuts the widespread assertion that Mormon missionaries specifically targeted ignorant, uneducated women lacking sophistication or judgment. This anecdote, about the early life of Eliza Snow, implicitly undermines such a claim by evidencing the literary sensibility and gentility of one early female convert. As a veteran of the earliest days of Mormonism who survived several difficult westward migrations and played an instrumental role in the development of the church, Snow was by the end of her life a living legend and a repository of a wealth of historical lore. In the 1870s, she composed a brief autobiographical sketch in which she recounted some memories of those early days. Her autobiography tellingly lingers on the details of her literary achievements before her conversion to Mormonism in 1835 at the age of thirty-one. In the 1820s, she explains, she'd acquired some local literary acclaim in Ohio, where she lived at the time, and, around 1826, she received "eight volumes of 'Godey's Lady's Book'" as an award for an unspecified poem.[32] Snow's timeline is noteworthy, for *Godey's* did not begin publication until 1830, well after 1826, around which time she claims to have won this prize. This patchiness may have been due to Snow's advanced age at the time she wrote this record, but her discernible pride in recalling this prize discloses an eagerness to showcase her familiarity with one of the most important brand names of women's literature and to depict herself as fully sophisticated and educated at the time of her conversion. It would seem that this intent was fully shared by her contempo-

raries, who retold this story repeatedly to counter widespread characterizations of Mormon women as ignorant and simpleminded and to depict them
instead as fully conversant with contemporary literature and properly social-
ized in sentimental letters and normative femininity.[33] In Edward Tullidge's
version of this narrative, he makes this aim clear, remarking on her respectable New England heritage, devout patriotism, modesty (her early poems, he
clarifies, were published under a pseudonym so as to avoid a vulgar public
reputation), and expertise in such traditional feminine arts as "needlework
and home manufactures."[34] Eliza Snow and, by extension, Mormon women
in general, Tullidge aims to show, are the fullest apotheosis of conventional
sentimental womanhood: knowledgeable, dutiful, and fully compliant with
traditional gender norms.

The use of sentimental literary tropes and rhetoric is equally visible in
Helen Mar Whitney's 1884 pamphlet *Why We Practice Plural Marriage*,
which, like Tullidge's book, broadcasts its intent to alter public opinion about
the effects of polygamy on Mormon women. She begins by making this aim
clear: "My purpose in publishing [this] pamphlet on the subject of plural
marriage is to throw more light upon it, and to show forth the foolishness
and inconsistency of those who hold it up as a 'foul stain that pollutes the
very soil where it exists.'"[35] Instead, she presents polygamy as a solution designed to provide homes and families to women who would otherwise have
no means of self-support. In the normal state of affairs, Whitney maintains,
"there would have been husbands and homes for all womankind," but under
current conditions "women are denied these privileges and are forced to seek
employment outside of home," a circumstance that she openly suggests may
lead to prostitution.[36] Polygamy, she maintains, helps right the social wrongs
that render women economically vulnerable and restores them to their proper
place in the private, domestic sphere. Indeed, there seems to have been some
truth to Whitney's claims, for numerous studies of nineteenth-century Mormon polygamous families have confirmed that the majority of women who
became plural wives (that is, women who married into households that already included at least one wife) did so out of dire economic need: plural
wives tended to be orphaned, widowed, divorced, aged, or otherwise vulnerable. Many, too, tended to be foreign converts, women from northern Europe especially in need of community and aid.[37] In offering "a solution for
helping the fatherless and widows," as Kathryn Daynes recently put it, polygamy constituted an effort, however uncommon, to a perceived crisis afflicting
young women.[38]

In this respect, Helen Whitney presented polygamy as a solution to the crisis of homelessness and isolation that persistently served as the opening narrative prompt of sentimental narration. As with the wanderings of Gerty Flint in Maria Cummins's *Lamplighter* (1854), Edna Earl in Augusta Evans's *St. Elmo* (1867), and the eponymous heroine of Fanny Fern's *Ruth Hall* (1855), sentimental novels habitually commence with a family in disarray and its children—typically a daughter—thrust into the world to make their own way. What follows is often a string of relocations and displacements, moving from residence to residence, before she is ultimately able to settle into a home of her own, a culmination that usually transpires through marriage. Few conditions are as dire as that of rootless transition in sentimental literature, and, in moving transitorily from place to place, unprotected girls typically fall prey to the designs and carelessness of others: Edna Earl suffers a train wreck in *St. Elmo*, Capitola Black becomes subject to a lecherous highwayman in E. D. E. N. Southworth's *Hidden Hand* (1859), and Ellen Montgomery endures abuse from shopkeepers and fellow travelers alike in Susan Warner's *Wide, Wide, World.* Nancy Cott's research in the gender demographics of the Second Great Awakening, discussed in Chapter 1, sheds considerable light on this persistent narrative about homeless young women by revealing that the first decades of the nineteenth century really did see the dislocation of countless young women, who were forced by the advent of industrial textile manufacture to seek work outside the traditional enclosure of the home.[39] These young women, Cott shows, commonly turned toward religion to find community and moral guidance, and, in support of Helen Whitney's defense of polygamy as a structure of support for such young women, Mormonism did indeed present itself as a safe haven for dislocated, disadvantaged women.

The economic circumstances that underwrote the narrative premise of sentimentalism proved instrumental to the growth of Mormonism, which succeeded in attracting many of these independent single women in search of faith and community. Nineteenth-century commentators often remarked on the high density of young female converts to this new religion, and disapproving observers accused Mormons of taking undue advantage of these transient young women and using missionary work as a pretext for seduction.[40] For example, in her best-selling account *Female Life Among the Mormons*, Maria Ward describes being approached by a Mormon missionary while traveling without a chaperone, a circumstance that made her especially vulnerable to his appeals; the solitude that makes her receptive to his religious proposals also makes her vulnerable to his romantic overtures, and she ends up marrying him and relocating to Utah.[41] Ann Eliza Young, an apostate plural wife of Brigham Young, also suggested that such women were special targets of Mormon missionaries.[42] Though such critics as Ward and Young contended that conversion provided a pretext for seduction, Whitney presents polygamy within the larger context of female dislocation that would also preoccupy sentimental fiction, constituting polygamy as a practical, functional realization of the suggestion in sentimental fiction that religious affiliation serves as a gateway to much-needed social affiliation: it is through Mormonism and its doctrines governing marriage, Whitney suggests, that sentimental ideals may become lived realities. The Mormon women's periodical *Woman's Exponent* made a similar claim in its mission statement, which maintained that Mormon women "are engaged in the practical solution of some of the greatest social and moral problems of the age."[43] Though it declines to explain, this statement implies that, as participants in polygamy, Mormon women are engaging in an important social experiment designed to correct the problem of female dislocation that so preoccupied women's narrative literature at the time.

Whitney concludes her pamphlet with an explicit invocation of sentimental literary discourse: she closes by reprinting the poem "The Women of Everlasting Covenant," written by her son, Orson F. Whitney, a Mormon worthy who would achieve renown as a hymnist, journalist, and an apostle in the highest order of the Mormon priesthood. That Helen Whitney would give this poem the last word in her polemic, let alone include it all, communicates her public relations savvy about the usefulness of sentimental literary discourse to a political debate about the protection of vulnerable young women. By enveloping polygamy within sentimental poetics, this poem not only constitutes it within a normative and normalizing discourse but also characterizes polygamy as the ultimate fulfillment of sentimental femininity. A lengthy poem composed of 274 lines in seventeen stanzas, Orson Whitney's poem narrates with lofty diction the celestial revelation instituting the doctrine of polygamy, which he calls, "Abrahamic Covenant, restored."[44] Overturning public assumptions about the sexual immorality of both polygamy and monogamy, the poem characterizes monogamy as

> Concomitant of empire-crumbling vice,
> Immolating Virtue at the shrine of Price. . . .
> Let marriage vows be honorable in all
> Untrammeled by a monogamic wall
> Of selfishness and rank hypocrisy. (70)

According to Orson Whitney, polygamy heralds "glad tidings, from above" by providing "God-given boon to homeless innocence": that is, it provides shelter and moral defense to single women who would otherwise be vulnerable to sexual endangerment and abandonment (71, 70).

This angle places Whitney's argument within a recognizable sentimental context of female protection, but Whitney reserves his most explicit engagement in sentimental discourse for his final stanza, when he suddenly diverges, without transition, from general assertions about the holiness of polygamy to an encomium to his own mother, the pamphlet's author and the poem's dedicatee:

> My mother! On thy pale and care-lined brow,
> O'erhung with sorrow's wreath of silver snow,
> Outvying fabled splendor's fairest gem,
> Shall shine, in heaven's light, a diadem;
> Thy tear-dimmed eye shall be forever bright,
> Thy form renewed and robed in living light,
> Where souls redeemed immortal glories share,
> And God is near, and love is everywhere. (72)

This stanza, at once highly specific and broadly general, is fully saturated in sentimental discourse, which crowds out any other mode of perceiving Helen Mar Whitney. Though the reader knows Helen Mar Whitney through the medium of her pamphlet as an opinionated woman capable of mustering strong argument and wielding sophisticated rhetoric, Orson Whitney's stanza transforms her utterly into a patient, careworn woman who has endured trials silently and without complaint. In thus wedging his outspoken mother into a sentimental prototype, this stanza is literally incapable of perceiving the mother through any other lens, taking the normal signs of aging, such as her lined brow and graying hair, as the bodily signs of patient, womanly forbearance. As with the inarticulate cry "My Mother!" that begins the stanza, sentimentalism here enables Orson Whitney to reduce his mother to a broad, inclusive stereotype crafted to be emotionally stirring and instantly recognizable. In this way, Orson Whitney—and, by implication, Helen Mar Whitney, for reprinting this poem in such a context—deploys sentimentalism to elide the specificities of Mormon life, history, and personhood; to situate Mormon doctrines governing women within the normalizing frame of sentimentalism; and to constitute polygamy as a new dispensation that will enable dutiful women to achieve full sanctification and thus fulfill the sentimental narrative promise of eternal salvation.[45]

The Institutionalization of Sentiment

The Mormon adoption of sentimentalism extended well beyond the production of public rhetoric in defense of polygamy. Although for much of the nineteenth century the Latter-day Saints were a separatist sect seeking economic and social secession from mainstream American culture, this disconnection apparently did not include literary severance. Nor did other contemporary separatist religious groups, such as the Oneida Perfectionists and the Shakers, employ similar literary discourse in writings about their own equally radical innovations in marital and family structures. Instead, the archives evidence a long-standing Mormon affinity for and embrace of mainstream women's literature in the sentimental vein. Mormon homilies, periodicals, and poetry of the nineteenth century are replete with references to sentimental literature, all of which affirm that Mormon readers had access to such texts and avidly consumed them. Mormon enthusiasm for sentimental literature seems to have been so keen that Brigham Young, Mormon president from 1847 to 1877, addressed it in several speeches, enjoining his listeners not to shirk their duties in favor of reading and urging them to select more "useful" reading materials than the novels that caused unabashed readers to have "tears running down their cheeks, until their books become perfectly wet."[46] In his study of the literary tastes of the western frontier, Richard Clement has observed a marked yearning for such reading material among female pioneers, who hoped to relieve the tedium of their lengthy journeys with novels about courtship and domesticity.[47] *Woman's Exponent* offers abundant evidence of the particular appeal of sentimental literature to Mormon readers. The bimonthly magazine filled its pages with abundant literary content, such as snippets of literary gossip, announcements of new publications, and the occasional author biography. More narrowly, however, the magazine's editors presumed their readers to be principally interested in sentimental writers and thus paid special attention to the lives and works of such writers as Louisa May Alcott, Alice and Phoebe Cary, Fanny Fern, Harriet Beecher Stowe, and Susan Warner, treating them like beloved intimates who require no introduction and who could be spoken of familiarly. For example, the "About Women" column mentioned in 1872 that "Mrs. Stowe is announced for public readings at New Haven in the Fall. She is spending the Summer at Hampton Beach," a notice that presumes that readers required neither Harriet Beecher Stowe's full name nor an explanation of her importance to take an interest in her travel itinerary and lecture schedule.[48] As the primary literary organ of Mormon women in the nineteenth century, *Woman's Exponent* kept sentimentalism a vibrant literary mode well into the first decades of the twentieth century, long after it had ceded its literary prominence to other genres and aesthetics in mainstream popular literature. Its pages filled with countless poems and articles celebrating motherhood, eulogizing deceased children, and extolling the virtues of domesticity, *Woman's Exponent* helped make sentimentalism the semiofficial literary register of Mormon women.

The popularity of sentimental forms within this particular religious setting was fostered by such renowned women as Eliza Snow, a revered poet and highly successful organizer of numerous women's causes, and Emmeline B. Wells, editor of *Woman's Exponent* and as a result a leading literary tastemaker.[49] Both well-read and reared in the middle class, they respectively became models of proper decorum and discerning taste, and in that capacity they influenced the literary predilections and styles of their coreligionists. That two such powerful public women could shape the reading preferences of their peers illustrates one of the contradictions of sentimental literature and perhaps one of the primary grounds for its appeal among Mormon women of the nineteenth century. In addition to running the Relief Society, the long-standing Mormon women's benevolence organization, Snow also published such conventional sentimental fare as "My Own Home" (1856), a poem in which she denounces the "paltry worth" of "fame" and "Mammon's vot'ries" to extol the virtues of a humble home, "where love and pure affection meet/In plain simplicity."[50] In this particular case, Snow's public life as an accomplished administrator was coupled with publications that celebrated the private, womanly sphere of the home. Though she was married to Joseph Smith and later to Brigham Young, neither marriage produced children, and neither was characterized by the domestic intimacy celebrated in sentimental literature. As a plural wife to both men, her spousal role was largely ceremonial, and she spent the later decades of her life living in a dormitory-like setting with Young's dozen or so other wives in his famously large home. This contrast between what Snow promoted in her writing and how she actually lived was further complicated by the fact that her sentimental tributes to modesty and dutifulness also contributed to her public prominence among her fellow Mormons. In this way, Snow's dual roles as sentimental author and civic leader communicate the religious authority conferred by the writing of sentimental lyric. At the same time, it expresses the complex social function of sentimental literature, which, on the one hand, instructed female readers in genteel femininity while, on the other hand, it authenticated the normative credentials of women whose own lives differed profoundly from the domestic ideals they propounded, as was the case with such sentimental writers as Louisa May Alcott, Fanny Fern (the pseudonym of Sarah P. W. Parton), Lydia Sigourney, and Susan Warner. As was the case for female readers and writers elsewhere and of different sectarian affiliations, sentimental literature among Mormon women contributed to the discursive construction of gendered separate spheres even while it enabled women readers and writers to traverse such a fictive binary.[51] While the sentimental idiom offered some of these writers a vehicle through which they could earn a living while working respectably within the home, sentimentalism allowed other writers, such as Snow and Maria Cummins, to idealize traditional domestic arrangements, such as marriage and family, that they themselves would never experience.

This contrast between sentimental ideals and lived realities may partially explain the appeal of sentimental literature for nineteenth-century Mormon women, many of whom endured grueling westward migrations and were active, vital leaders in the development of a pioneer society. In addition to running households and raising children, Mormon women were regularly entrusted with innumerable public-works projects designed to develop the Mormon infrastructure and economy. For example, in addition to running Relief Society, Snow helped found the first hospital in Utah and arranged for numerous women to receive formal medical training on the East Coast. Likewise, the success of *Woman's Exponent* depended upon its fleet of female editors, writers, typesetters, and sales agents.[52] Brigham Young's desire to make Mormons entirely self-sufficient led him to charge women to create and run a store for the sale of locally made goods and to generate a homegrown silk industry. Even polygamy had the potential to make women more autonomous and financially independent. Though the tribulations of polygamy are not to be trivialized, it was not unusual for plural wives, as well as the wives of traveling missionaries, to run and support their own households, a condition that fostered resourcefulness and entrepreneurship amid a sea of poverty and desertion.[53]

Within a frontier society made possible by able, effective, even mighty women, it is little wonder that sentimentalism took hold, at once reinforcing the domestic ideals Mormon women strove to create with their industrious public labors and reminding highly capable female managers and adminis- trators of their proper place and the duties that bound them to their fami- lies, communities, and faith. For pioneer women contending with less than ideal domestic circumstances, sentimental literature functioned as agents of self-improvement and aspiration, likely providing much-needed affirmation and assurance amid often trying circumstances.[54] Typically at the core of sen- timental novels of female maturation is a narrative relaying a young woman's struggle to manage and resolve affliction, which may take the form of iso- lation, poverty, powerlessness, bereavement, or some combination thereof. Through the tutelage of a benevolent older woman and the cultivation of religious faith, the sentimental heroine eventually ceases to chafe at these worldly cares and instead comes both to embrace them as providential les- sons from a loving deity and to assume a willing selflessness in providing nurturance even to her most exasperating tormentors. By "feel[ing] right," as Harriet Beecher Stowe memorably termed this magnanimous sentimental affect, and by renouncing any expectation that her own wishes be fulfilled, as did Lu Dalton in her poem "A Mother's Resignation," the sentimental woman may acquire emotional release from these worldly burdens.[55] For early gener- ations of Mormon women grappling with the dire privations that inevitably accompany pioneer life, sentimental narratives likely normalized disquieting encounters with homesickness, dissatisfaction, and destitution. By situating these hardships within a prescribed plot line that concluded in relief and piety, sentimental texts transformed these potentially disillusioning experi- ences into wholesome rites of spiritual passage and as evidence of their spe- cial favor from the divine.

As Jan Shipps, a leading scholar of Mormonism has remarked, "People live inside stories," and it would seem that Mormon female readers saw much of their own lives narrated and dramatized in sentimental fiction.[56] For Mor- mon women who abandoned comfortable lives for an arduous voyage and an uncertain future, sentimental literature likely served as a cherished reminder of the genteel sensibilities and refinements they left behind and no doubt hoped to reinstate in the West. In such a context, the domestic narrative at the core of sentimental fiction must have been particularly meaningful, for these novels typically depicted the execution of such a transformation. As with Ellen Montgomery's triumphant assumption of all household duties upon the debilitating illness of her aunt in Susan Warner's *Wide, Wide World* or Mary Scudder's tranquil housework after learning that her sweetheart has died at

sea in Stowe's *Minister's Wooing*, the sentimental narrative charts the process
by which domesticity was thought to bring civility, grace, and harmony to
an itinerant and disordered life, a narrative template that Mormon pioneer
women doubtless hoped to replicate in their own lives. In this context, the
reading of sentimental literature may have enabled Mormon women living
in the remote West to retain their command of normative feminine ideals, to
affirm their refined sensibilities amid harsh conditions, and to envision the
idealized home lives they hoped to establish.[57]

However, the relationship between the two is significantly more complicated than one of simple reader identification, for several of the beliefs
inherent in sentimental literature would be reified and institutionalized in
Mormon practice, tradition, and theology. While in some instances the correspondence derived from discursive engagement in the same shared well of
contemporary notions about piety and domesticity, in other cases sentimental literature directly provided the source material for canon doctrine. The
Relief Society is an illustrative instance of the former case. In 1842, at the
height of the popularity of women's benevolence organizations, Joseph Smith
mandated the creation of a similar women's auxiliary organization, which was
designed "to look to the wants of the poor," "to teach the female part of the
community," and "to save souls."[58] As Anne Firor Scott has noted, the earliest
leaders of Relief Society were chosen not just because of their executive abilities but also because of their origin from parts of the country where benevolence organizations were customary, and they were charged with fashioning
a sectarian replica of these mainstream women's organizations.[59] To be sure,
the proliferation of benevolence societies, as discussed in Chapter 1, was born
out of the delegation of religious authority to women amid the Second Great
Awakening, which also made possible the emergence of female-authored religious literature. Likewise, benevolence societies were built on the belief that
social service and care for the needy were suitable expressions of female piety,
a conviction that would be widely circulated and elaborated in sentimental
fiction and poetry. In both respects, the Relief Society is a practical application of the ideologies that undergird sentimentalism.

The discursive linkage between this benevolence organization and sentimentalism would be made explicit in the leadership of Eliza Snow, the
premier poet and circulator of sentimental rhetoric among the Latter-day
Saints, who led the Relief Society for decades. In her poem "The Female
Relief Society: What Is It?" (1872), she constituted that organization in a
recognizably sentimental frame. The Relief Society, she writes, is

. . . an Institution form'd to bless
The Poor, the widow, and the fatherless—
To clothe the naked and the hungry feed,
And in the holy paths of virtue, lead.[60]

Just as polygamy was touted as a practical solution to the plight of homeless young women that preoccupied sentimental literature, so the Relief Society was similarly characterized as an institutionalized structure of philanthropy that systematically provided the assistance that was otherwise left impromptu in sentimental narrative, with such sympathetic strangers as Trueman Flint of Cummins's *Lamplighter* or Nina Gordon of Stowe's *Dred* stepping in to provide care to desperately needy women and children.[61] In its narration of the kindness of strangers, sentimental literature depicted and extolled the unplanned relief work performed by everyday citizens outside of formal organizations, but the Relief Society prearranged and legislated the work of charitable support that had been left disorganized in sentimental literature. In providing food, shelter, and resources to families in need, the Relief Society directly assumes maternal caretaking responsibilities for families under stress and thereby strives to preserve the cohesiveness of homes in consequent danger of dissolution. That is, the Relief Society takes up and institutionalizes the task of familial restoration and protection that was often the object of contemporary sentimental narrative.

The institutionalization of sentimental belief is also visible in Mormon theologies of family and the afterlife. In sentimentalism in particular, the family is persistently portrayed as deeply fragile, susceptible to dissolution with the slightest pressure. As was discussed in the previous chapter, intact nuclear families are a veritable rarity in sentimental literature, sundered just as often by such capricious forces as conspiracy, financial ruin, or confusion as by death or illness. For a literary genre that seems to revere and celebrate domestic life at every turn, sentimentalism nonetheless characterizes families as deeply vulnerable, whether in elegies that commemorate the premature deaths of children or in the many novels that depict children left to rear themselves. Through migratory wanderings in search of a home, the forsaken daughter at the sentimental novel's center comes to develop Christian piety, to learn the circumstances that inadvertently led to her abandonment, and to reconstruct the family, either through marriage to a loving fellow Christian or through her literal reunion with these missing parents. In both scenarios, these novels clarify that families need connective tissues other than affections and kinship to bind them together. Through the gradual narrative reconstruction of the family, it becomes clear that the bond missing is often faith, whether in the divine or in each other. In sentimentalism, it is largely through faith that families may be restored and the conditions that render single young women homeless may be eradicated. One has only to recall how readily Ellen Montgomery's new faith in Warner's *The Wide, Wide World* transforms her domestic circumstances to see how Christian faith renews the family in sentimental consciousness: after Ellen is left by her parents to be raised by a cold, begrudging aunt, her newfound Christian piety suddenly renders her a desirable charge, and she is in quick succession adopted by a devout family of ministers, reclaimed by long-lost relations in Scotland, and ultimately married to her beloved adoptive brother. In brief, piety enables the reconstruction of the family, and faith is rewarded by a return home.

For nineteenth-century readers, this assertion that faith enables the reunion of long-lost family members had some powerful implications and applications. As was discussed in Chapter 3, Harriet Beecher Stowe used this narrative of familial restoration to offer reassurance of a coming millennium. Otherwise, though, the conclusion of sentimental narrative in family reunion suggestively evoked widespread conception of the afterlife, which was, and is still, widely believed to enable the restoration of families separated by death. It is only through shared religious belief that families may be restored in the afterlife; without belief, they remain just as fragmentary in death as they were in life. The eighteenth-century visions of Emanuel Swedenborg significantly contributed to this widespread belief, his visions confirming belief that heaven is in fact a real city composed of actual houses inhabited by genuine families.[62] Within nineteenth-century popular understanding, heaven was by no means an ethereal, dematerialized realm, but rather possessed a tactile, concrete character; family would again function normally, with married life continuing unabated and all relationships interrupted by death now restored. Within such a cultural and religious context, sentimental narratives about the capacity of Christian faith to restore broken homes functioned simultaneously on two planes, at once offering readers instructions in how they might improve their own current domestic lives and simultaneously dramatizing popular beliefs about the afterlife. By concurrently depicting these two domains of Christian existence, sentimental texts implied that faithfulness and obedience in the former could effect a joyful family reunion in the latter. Elizabeth Stuart Phelps's *The Gates Ajar* was the era's most popular and influential articulation of this belief. The novel charts the struggles of a young woman, Mary Cabot, bereaved by the Civil War death of her beloved brother, to adopt the resignation and acceptance of divine will elaborated in such poems as Dalton's "Mother's Resignation." Calvinist clergy only aggravate further resistance, but she finds consolation in the assurances of her widowed aunt that she will not only be reunited with her brother in the afterlife but will also enjoy a rich domestic life in heaven, augmented with sundry material amenities. Heaven, her Aunt Winifred pledges, is a continuation of our lives on Earth, with families and homes restored. Readers responded with such avidity to Phelps's conception of the afterlife that she wrote three sequels, and it likewise inspired several imitations, such as Louis H. Pendleton's *The Wedding Garment: A Tale of the Afterlife* (1894).

Of all the literary qualities that may have drawn Mormon readers to sentimentalism, this narrative of faith-based familial reconstruction may have been the most meaningful and resonant for Mormon readers, for whom dislocation and familial disruption may have been vividly lived realities. They certainly were for early Mormons, as converts in the 1830s and 1840s migrated repeatedly, moving from Upstate New York to Ohio, Missouri, and Illinois before eventually settling in Utah. In addition to the many single young women who found kinship and community by converting to Mormonism, new converts often found themselves leaving their families to travel in considerable discomfort and peril across the continent (and even the Atlantic Ocean) to Utah to participate in the great "Gathering to Zion," the relocation of all fellow believers to this new religious colony on the frontier. The trials of travel were by no means over for Mormons once they arrived in Utah, however, for Mormon men were often required to embark without any financial support—"without purse or scrip" as they termed it—on lengthy missions to distant locations, usually leaving their wives and families behind in equally precarious financial straits.

And just as sentimentalism narrates the process by which religious faith may conclusively bind families together, so Mormonism similarly created a doctrine by which religious rite may enable the eternal preservation of the family. What had largely been a typological suggestion of religiously sanctioned family reunion in sentimentalism became bedrock doctrine in Mormonism, which, from the first decades of Mormon history, similarly touts religious faith as the primary connective glue binding family together. Beginning in the 1840s, Joseph Smith instituted a doctrine that enabled Mormons of good standing to participate in a Temple ritual that binds families together even into the afterlife. This sacrosanct rite, known as the sealing ceremony, promises to preserve families for all eternity and render them impervious to separation even after death. This doctrine, drawn from the same nineteenth-century well of religious inquiry and innovation as sentimentalism, has been characterized by scholar Douglas Davies as the essential, core teaching of Mormonism, which he describes as "above all else, a theology of death's conquest."[63] The Mormon vision of the afterlife likewise formalized nineteenth-century popular visions of heaven as fully corporeal and material so that the Mormon family reunited after death may expect to enjoy such perquisites as lavish estates and attentive servants. In the Mormon conception of the afterlife, the most exalted state of glory is available only to righteous, observant people with families, those who have been married in the Temple and have raised children. In this way, Mormonism doctrinally formalized what had been merely hinted at in sentimentalism: that is, a belief in the literal sanctity of family.[64] Thus, in Mormonism as in sentimentalism, faith and family are wholly reciprocal and mutually dependent: just as piety enables family to endure in eternity, so family enables the individual believer to achieve salvation. In her 1865 poem "Immortality," published in the Mormon newspaper *Deseret News*, Eliza Snow summarized these beliefs in her assertion that

> To the faithful Saints of God,
> Who live to do His will, death has no sting:
> 'Tis a kind porter to conduct us where
> A realm of light and beauty shines around—
> A world of glorious immortality! . . .
> T' enjoy life's sweet associations, such
> As parents, children, husbands, wives and friends—
> With Gods and Goddesses—with the noblesse
> Of all eternities.[65]

The Mormon afterlife, as Snow describes it, promises the companionship of departed loved ones, abundant material resources, and relief from household cares, and it is in this respect the doctrinal culmination or realization of a belief that heretofore had been a widespread popular aspiration circulated chiefly through the medium of sentimental literature.

Eliza R. Snow and the Divinity of Motherhood

But literary sentimentalism exerted its most direct, immediate influence on Mormon theology through the poetry of Eliza Snow. Though she has been forgotten in the annals of American literary history, Snow was a beloved exemplar of moral rectitude who held a position of rank and honor that few nineteenth-century women could ever hope to attain.[66] Raised in Ohio to a farming family originally from New England, she converted to Mormonism in 1835 and spent the rest of her life committed to the development of Mormon belief and culture. Around 1838, Joseph Smith designated her the poet laureate of the Latter-day Saints, and in 1842, she was among the first to learn of the new doctrine of polygamy, which was confided to her by Joseph Smith, and she soon thereafter became one of Smith's first plural wives; in nineteenth-century Mormon lore, she was rumored, albeit incorrectly, to have been Smith's first plural wife.[67] Several months after Smith's death in 1844, she became a plural wife of his successor, Brigham Young, although she remained devoted to Smith's memory throughout her life. Her privileged marital status, in combination with her keen administrative abilities and literary talents, enabled her to occupy innumerable leadership positions—such as president of the Relief Society from 1868 to 1887, board member of the *Woman's Exponent*, and an organizer of the Deseret Hospital, Utah's first such facility—that proved indispensable to the growth of Mormonism. Her status also extended into religious spheres, for she participated in the Mormon Endowment ordinance, playing the role of Eve in the highly secretive, sacrosanct initiation ceremony.[68] According to a few accounts, she also seems to have functioned as an informal advocate of polygamy, paying social calls to reluctant women and persuading them to comply with church teachings.[69] Dubbed variously the Prophetess, Priestess, and Presidentess of Mormonism as well as "Zion's Poetess," she was described by Apostle John W. Taylor at her 1887 funeral as "a mother to this people," an assertion seconded by Elder Milo Andrus, who concurred that "in regard to her being Mother, I bear my testimony that thousands and tens of thousands will call her Mother in Israel."[70] By 1890, Mormon primary-school teachers were advised to cultivate "a reverence" for Snow in their young pupils.[71] She was so iconic during her lifetime that she occasionally appears as a character in anti-Mormon novels, as with her comic presence in Austin Ward's 1857 *The Husband in Utah*, in which she is portrayed as a "silly-looking girl" with laughable literary pretensions and a marked romantic interest in the novel's narrator.[72] That Snow was in her fifties at the time of the novel's publication, had already been married to both Smith and Young, and had already achieved considerable renown for her poetry clearly undercuts Ward's claims to documentary accuracy.

While holding all these leadership positions, she was also a prolific poet who published literally hundreds of poems about Mormon life, often using sentimental prosody, imagery, and scenarios. Mormon women who read no literary texts other than Snow's poems in the pages of such Mormon periodicals as the *Deseret News*, the *Nauvoo Wasp*, *Juvenile Instructor*, *Times and Seasons*, and *Woman's Exponent* would have received a full education in the sentimental literary idiom, with poems on such iconic sentimental topics as motherhood, domesticity, childhood innocence, matrimony, infant mortality, and the struggles of faith amid suffering. By writing in the sentimental idiom, Snow presented this literary aesthetic as both fully compatible with Mormon orthodoxy and as suitable for the literary expression of female experience. Snow was for decades the cynosure of Mormon literary life, and her status as a revered icon of refinement helped imbue sentimentalism with the air of gentility among Mormon women eager to embrace the trappings of sophistication amid the hardship of pioneer life.[73] Her poetry consequently occupies a special place in Mormon culture, functioning at once as evidence of Mormon artistic and cultural achievement, as a valued chronicle of Mormon history from the perspective of a true insider, and as devout expressions of Mormon faith.

However, Eliza Snow's literary legacy extends beyond merely shaping Mormon literary taste, for her sentimental poetry exerted direct influence on Mormon doctrine. To trace the influence of Snow on nineteenth-century Mormonism is to document the reach of sentimentalism beyond the printed page and, as channeled by this particularly powerful interpreter, into the beliefs and religious observances of its readers. A thorough accounting of her influence necessitates a wider reconsideration of the intellectual roots of Mormon doctrine more generally. Intellectual historians of this religious movement tend to focus on philosophical and spiritual influences on Joseph Smith, but such a narrow focus on Smith's own intellectual heritage ignores the other literary influences in circulation at the time, which, in shaping key figures in his inner circle, also affected Smith and early Mormonism.[74] Though we do not know the extent of Smith's own personal familiarity with sentimentalism, he certainly encountered it through the medium of Snow's poetry, which he praised in the highest terms.

Snow's influence is visible in one particular poem that has profoundly shaped how Mormons understand the afterlife and their cosmology. A highly conventional sentimental lyric composed of eight ballad stanzas, it was originally published in 1845 under the title "My Father in Heaven" in the Mormon journal *Times and Seasons*; it was later retitled "Invocation, or The Eternal Father and Mother," but it finally came to be known popularly by its first line, "O My Father." Snow's poem was swiftly recognized as an original contribution to Mormon theology and hailed by Mormon leadership as a religious revelation, with Snow herself celebrated as a seer.[75] In this respect, Snow constitutes yet another instance of a sentimental woman writer hailed as a prophet, an intimation that Harriet Beecher Stowe famously made for herself, and Snow's poem "O My Father" was likewise recognized as a sacred text for its ability to reveal secret divine truths. Snow's poem was set to music and incorporated in a volume of Mormon hymns published in 1851; today it can be found in the Mormon hymnal as hymn 292, with music composed by James McGranahan.[76] It has been recorded literally dozens of times, set to numerous different tunes and arrangements, and sung, whether by a soloist or a congregation, by millions of people worldwide. Today "O My Father" is habitually sung at Mormon funerals, and homilies and essays on the topic of mortality commonly feature recognizable excerpts from Snow's poem. For example, Mormon President Spencer W. Kimball discussed Snow's "O My Father" in his 1978 address "The True Way of Life and Salvation," a talk published in *Ensign,* the official magazine of the Church of Jesus Christ of Latter-day Saints. In all of these ways, Snow's "O My Father" has been fully absorbed and assimilated into Mormon doctrine, observance, and liturgy.

Central to this poem of theological revelation is its deep engagement in innumerable sentimental tropes and conventions, which take on a wealth of new connotations when read in this denominational, doctrinal context.[77] As one of the most influential poems of the American nineteenth century, "O My Father" merits reproduction in its entirety.

O my Father, thou that dwellest
    In the high and glorious place;
When shall I regain thy presence,
    And again behold thy face?

In thy holy habitation,
    Did my spirit once reside?
In my *first* primeval childhood
    Was I nurtur'd near thy side?

For a wise and glorious purpose
    Thou hast plac'd me here on earth,
And withheld the recollection
    Of my former friends and birth:
Yet oft times a secret something
    Whispered you're a stranger here;
And I felt that I had wandered
    From a more exalted sphere.

I had learn'd to call thee father,
    Through thy spirit from on high;
But until the key of knowledge
    Was restor'd, I knew not why.
In the heav'ns are parents single?
    No, the thought makes reason stare;
Truth is reason—truth eternal
    Tells me I've a mother there.

When I leave this frail existence—
    When I lay this mortal by,
Father, mother, may I meet you
    In your royal court on high?
Then at length, when I've completed
    All you sent me forth to do,
With your mutual approbation
    Let me come and dwell with you.[78]

When read purely at face value, Snow's poem appears to be a poetic condensation of the stock sentimental narrative. With its opening invocation of a beloved but absent parent, the poem, true to form, portrays the family as fragmentary and broken, with the poem's speaker left to fend for herself in an unfamiliar and confusing world. Expressing an anguished yearning for reunion, the speaker relays the process by which she has come to understand

and even embrace this estrangement and, just as important, to envision with definitive clarity their pending reunion. As is typical in sentimental narration, the pivot enabling the reconstruction of the family is the heroine's mounting spiritual conviction, and, in the fifth stanza, the "spirit from on high" enables the speaker to understand the larger providential purpose behind her isolation and to visualize the true nature of her family, which functions as a metonymic placeholder for a time, outside the scope of the poem, when such a reunion will occur. In asking, "In the heav'ns are parents single?" Snow engages the contemporaneous debate about the endurance of human attachments in the afterlife, and her definitive reply—"No, the thought makes reason stare"—conveys a belief that marriages and family structures persist in the afterlife, opinions that concur with widespread nineteenth-century belief as well as core Mormon doctrine.

In compliance with standard sentimental convention, "O My Father" narrates the spiritual alchemy that restores familial affections and intimacy. But what is particularly complicated about Snow's poem is that it transforms this canonical sentimental narrative into a distinctively sectarian typology depicting the state and potential of every human soul in Mormon theology. Within Mormon doctrine, all human beings first begin as infant spirits who reside in loving intimacy with their heavenly parents. So that these spirits may participate in the Mormon ordinances that enable them to proceed toward salvation, it is incumbent upon Mormons to bear children and thus endow these spirit children with bodily forms. Once incarnate in human bodies, these spirits may achieve reunion in the afterlife with both their worldly families, to whom they have presumably been sealed, and their divine families, the heavenly parents who first gave them birth in what Mormons call "premortal" existence. If they live exemplary lives and pass through all ritual requirements, they may pass on to the supreme celestial realm of the afterlife, in which they, too, may become gods and heavenly parents who also reproduce their own spirit children.

Thus, the yearning for parental reunion that infuses Snow's "O My Father" revises that of typical sentimental narrative, for the poem's speaker longs less for a worldly parent than for a divine one, the Heavenly Father. The hint of heavenly reunion that underlay sentimental scenes of family gathering was thus moved to the fore and made explicit in Snow's poem, in which worldly quests for kinship and shelter now denote divine epiphany and postmortem communion.[79] Much of the poem relays the speaker's growing perception that this familial title is less an affectionate honorific for the divine than a literal description of her filial relationship with the divine parent who made her in the premortal world: as the fifth stanza relates, the speaker had wondered why human beings "call thee father," but, until her awakening to Mormon cosmology, she "knew not why." Though Judeo-Christian readers of countless denominations might recognize traditional parental language describing divinity in this poem, it more specifically derives from the Mormon belief that the deity is literally a divine Father who sires spirits in need of bodily form. Thus, in imagining a return to her rightful place in her long-lost parent's home, Snow transforms the sentimental domestication of wayward girls into a narrative about the exilic condition of all human beings and implicitly touts the Mormon dispensation as the means by which human beings may achieve these dual reunions.

Though the apostrophic subject of Snow's poem is this divine Father, the poem was groundbreaking because of its invocation of a divine Mother, again making literal and explicit what had been largely implicit in conventional sentimental writings. For readers familiar with sentimentalism but unfamiliar with Mormon doctrine, the assertion that "truth eternal/Tells me I've a mother" in heaven would seem to comply with the sentimental veneration of motherhood, which perceived angelic virtues in motherly sacrifice, patience, and constancy.[80] Within this figuration, the devout, selfless mother functions as the paragon of sentimental femininity, whose example and moral tutelage enable the sentimental reformation and consequent salvation of her loved ones. As Eve Cherniavsky puts it, the sentimental mother is, "literally and symbolically, not of this world," characterized by a "perfectly loving" "angelic presence."[81] In invoking a saintly and ethereal mother in heaven, Snow's poem thus seems to employ the pervasive sentimental trope of the "angel in the home," the saintly "domestic savior," to use Paula Bennett's phrase, whose piety and forbearance under worldly travail make her a potent Christian missionary and a decorporealized, divine presence on Earth.[82] As evidenced by Orson Whitney's poem and countless others by Dianthe Baker, Hannah T. King, and Emmeline B. Wells, the sentimental canonization of motherhood found widespread literary expression in nineteenth-century Mormonism, but Snow takes this contemporaneous cultural preoccupation to another plane altogether. In its perception of a heavenly mother, Snow's "O My Father" affirms not only that worldly families may endure in the afterlife—confirming that we retain our relationships with our mothers even after death—but also that the Heavenly Father's parentage logically requires that he have a spouse, a female partner who could conceive and bear the spirit children who eventually take bodily form through human reproduction. In thus relying on "reason," "O My Father" introduced the Mormon doctrine of the Heavenly Mother, the beloved consort of the Heavenly Father and the mother of all earthly souls. Based as it was in a literary aesthetic that habitually attributed angelic, even Christ-like qualities to mothers, "O My Father" concretized and institutionalized the sentimental belief in the divinity of motherhood.

Reputed to have had considerable gifts of prophecy, Snow reportedly experienced a mystical revelation that came to inspire this poem, although multiple counternarratives credit Joseph Smith as its original source, even though he did not formally record it.[83] According to one such account, Snow is said to have overheard an 1839 conversation in which Smith sought to console Zina Huntington, one of Smith's wives and Snow's successor as president of the Relief Society, on the death of her mother by assuring her not only that she would meet her mother again in the afterlife but that she would also meet her "eternal Mother, the wife of your Father in Heaven."[84] In 1895, Joseph F. Smith, a nephew of Joseph Smith who would become Mormon president in 1901, told a stake convention that "God revealed [the doctrine of Heavenly Mother] to Joseph Smith; Joseph Smith revealed it to Eliza Snow Smith, his wife; and Eliza Snow was inspired, being a poet, to put it into verse" in the poem "O My Father."[85] These various explanations of origin notwithstanding, Heavenly Mother remains a somewhat elusive, mysterious figure who has gone largely unexamined in Mormon theology.[86] Though Heavenly Mother is elevated as the supreme role model for Mormon women and as justification for their sacred obligation to bear children, she receives little formal attention in Mormon life and observance; she is nowhere visible in Mormon portraiture or illustration, and her divine nature remains a topic unexplored by theologians and untaught in Mormon Sunday schools.[87] In recent decades, Mormon feminists have advocated greater attention to Heavenly Mother, much to the concern of Mormon leadership, and in some instances their campaigns have led to their excommunication.[88] In 1991, Mormon President Gordon B. Hinckley formally forbade prayers to Heavenly Mother, describing those who did so as "well-meaning but . . . misguided." He responded to feminist objections that the relative invisibility of Heavenly Mother evinced theological gender bias, remarking that the "fact that we do not pray to our Mother in Heaven in no way belittles or denigrates her."[89]

The canonical stature of Snow's poem derives from its transmission of this new sacrosanct doctrine, and, in this capacity, it functions as de facto religious scripture, for in no other Mormon sacred text can this teaching be found. This truly unusual reception history makes analyzing Snow's poem a delicate business, but we must take seriously Snow's decision to relay this revelation using recognizably sentimental tropes, not only because she brought a wealth of familiar literary conventions to bear on this new religious doctrine but also because it may help explicate the shroud of mystery that cloaks Heavenly Mother. Jill Mulvay Derr, a prominent scholar of Mormon women's history, has observed that Snow's poem has exerted considerable influence on Mormon conceptions of Heavenly Mother, and as such it should be noted that "O My Father" is noticeably silent about the nature of Heavenly Mother, merely deducing her existence and requesting reunion once the speaker "leave[s] this frail existence."[90] This reticence is coupled with the poem's fuller portrait of Heavenly Father, whom Snow portrays as loving, wise, and resolute. Though the poem is renowned for its revelation of Heavenly Mother, the poem is directed to Heavenly Father, and in this way the poem retains highly traditional gender divisions, positing the male deity as a public entity, amenable to human contact and capable of visibly intervening in human lives. By contrast, Heavenly Mother recedes into the background behind her more famous spouse, and her depiction solely as a mother creates a logical framework for this invisibility: whereas Heavenly Father conducts his divine business somewhat in the public eye, Heavenly Mother's work as deliverer and nurturer of infant spirits instead justifies her invisibility, both in the poem and in the earthly plane altogether, for her tasks are traditionally performed in privacy and within the confines of the home, however divine it may be. In thus implicitly imputing separate, gendered spheres to these two deities, Snow drew upon sentimental norms to set a denominational precedent for secreting Heavenly Mother outside the public eye. Her domestic and familial responsibilities presumably of paramount importance, Heavenly Mother declines public attention, and in so doing she evinces her supreme modesty, humility, and selfless service to those in her care.

Spencer Kimball explicitly interpreted the poem and its depiction of Heavenly Mother in accordance with sentimental notions of female humility and selflessness: he remarked, "When we sing that doctrinal hymn and anthem of affection, 'O My Father,' we get a sense of the ultimate in maternal modesty, of the restrained, queenly elegance of our Heavenly Mother, and knowing how profoundly our mortal mothers have shaped us here, do we suppose her influence on us as individuals to be less if we live so as to return there?"[91] Her obscurity interpreted to denote her "modesty" and self-sacrifice, Heavenly Mother in Kimball's interpretation is by no means invisible but is instead abundantly perceptible both in her profound influence on her charges and in the earthly mothers who similarly assume the trappings of sentimental womanliness. According to Kimball, we publicly honor Heavenly Mother when we preserve her privacy and when we live righteous lives designed to conclude in family reunions in the afterlife. To demand that Heavenly Mother move into the public spotlight is to compromise her full womanliness and to subject her to the vulgarities and injuries that sentimental heroines traditionally encounter once they leave home and openly embark on the wide world that Susan Warner took as the title of her most famous novel. This sentimental investment in protecting the purity of both Heavenly Mother and the family she presides over has long functioned as an explanation for the secrecy surrounding her. Her invisibility thus derives from a custodial desire on the part of both her divine consort and Mormon leadership to shield her from mistreatment in the public sector, whether by the disrespectful taking of her name in vain or by mockery or insult.[92] She remains outside public view not only out of her own selfless devotion to her duties in the private, domestic domain but also out of a wider administrative effort to protect the sanctity of domesticity, one designed in part to resolve the crisis of familial endangerment that infused sentimentalism more generally and Snow's most famous sentimental poem in particular. In all of these ways, Snow's sentimental forms profoundly shape both her poem's content and the new doctrine they helped establish, enduring in the relative invisibility of Heavenly Mother and her continued seclusion in the celestial home.

Snow's delivery of this revelation in the medium of sentimentalism is all the more significant in light of the considerable spiritual powers ascribed to Mormon women of the nineteenth century, who were believed to have had special aptitudes for prophecy and divination; Snow herself was renowned for her ability to speak in tongues.[93] Because Mormon women, Snow included, already had a public platform and an audience for the recitation of religious revelation, her decision to frame the revelation of Heavenly Mother within a literary idiom seems purposeful and calculated. As the recent agitations of Mormon feminists have shown, the doctrine of Heavenly Mother is indeed potentially divisive and has the power to challenge and even overturn established convention, and in so doing to challenge traditional gender roles and even possibly contribute to the proliferation of self-reliant, itinerant women. As it was, these traditional gender roles were already somewhat tenuous in nineteenth-century Mormonism, as the demands of pioneer life required that women couple their domestic responsibilities with more public ones, such as tending the farms and businesses left behind by missionary husbands or contributing to Mormon efforts to develop an autonomous economy fueled by home manufacture. The revelation of Heavenly Mother had the potential to upset the balance even further by throwing into question both the patriarchal leadership of the priesthood and that of the household more generally. The potential for upheaval was further compounded by the climate of social and political instability in which Snow composed "O My Father." Written in the year after the assassination of Joseph Smith and when mounting hostilities with non-Mormon neighbors in Illinois made it increasingly likely that Mormons would have to decamp and migrate further westward, "O My Father" was composed during an era when the stability of the Mormon home was never in greater peril.

Set against this backdrop of volatility, Snow's enlistment of sentimental tropes emerges as an attempt to stabilize, reassure, and reaffirm. This generic engagement is most clearly apparent in the relative invisibility of Heavenly Mother, whose modesty and dutifulness make her the divine apotheosis of sentimental maternity rather than an affront to it and the concomitant patriarchal religious authority. Likewise, in accessing a familiar scenario of homeless daughters in search of loving homes, Snow situated the speaker's dilemma, and that of migratory Mormons more generally, within a recognizable narrative template that reliably concludes in the restoration of the home, a story line that would have been especially meaningful for Mormons preparing to relocate in Utah or temporarily encamped in Winter Quarters in 1846. Though the poem's speaker, and the 1840s Mormon reader, may feel dispossessed, Snow follows sentimental practice by reshaping migratory homelessness from a state of decline into a divinely ordained transition to a better world, thereby assuring readers of promising futures both in the earthly realm of Utah and in the afterlife. The poem likewise dramatizes the process of sentimental character reform, with the speaker's doubts and questions about her relationship with Heavenly Father in the first two stanzas giving way to affirmations of faith and requests for intimate reunion in the final stanzas. Along the way, she comes to embrace sentimental resignation, interpreting suffering as evidence of Heavenly Father's "wise and glorious purpose" and recounting her efforts to discern that larger plan amid isolation and confusion. In all of these ways, the speaker models sentimental dutifulness and characterizes resistance and inquiry as signs of ignorant faithlessness, thereby implicitly coaxing the reader to assume a similar posture of trust, fidelity, and submission in the face of tribulation and potentially disruptive new revelations.

In addition, the poem's formal regularity—for example, its use of such devices as tetrameter and rhyme scheme—conveys a commitment to established convention, if merely generic ones. The poem's conventional form is in some tension with the visionary, expansive revelation documented in it, and this conflict results in the plodding, workmanlike form coming to seem like a cage, containing and reining in the speaker's cosmic vision. For example, the poem's fifth stanza conveys such a strain between form and content:

> I had learn'd to call thee father,
> Through thy spirit from on high;
> But until the key of knowledge
> Was restor'd, I knew not why.

This stanza provides the poem's turning point, when the speaker finally comes to understand her true familial relationship with the Heavenly Father, a revelation inspired by the Holy Spirit. In describing the restoration of this "key of knowledge," Snow employs enjambment with some visible discomfort, the poem's syntax spilling over from the stanza's third line to the fourth. The syntactical break that would traditionally close the third line instead interrupts the fourth, with a resoundingly awkward caesura falling before the resumption of the clause that began in the third line, "I knew not why." The end result of this enjambment is the impression of a celestial revelation that overflows and even breaches the highly scripted poetic structure in which Snow works. With the form thus working to enforce containment and self-censure, the poem radiates a heroic effort to maintain restraint and adherence to normative convention amid considerable temptations otherwise. In this way, the poem models the very discipline and self-control that Snow and her literary cohort made characteristic of sentimental womanliness and that later interpreters would perceive embodied in Heavenly Mother.

The poem's store of poetic forms works to temper and even defuse its potentially inflammatory content. For example, there is something to be said about the sentimentality inherent in Snow's decision to work within tetrameter rather than the more traditional pentameter. Tetrameter was a common form for English-language hymns and likely contributed to the ease with which it was adapted to music, and, as Chapter 2 demonstrated, Snow thus employed a devotional literary form that was in the process of becoming a gendered one associated in particular with sentimental femininity. That said, tetrameter also requires that she use two fewer syllables and thereby limits her poetic options quite significantly. In the dual context of the speaker's ample self-control and decision to embrace her exile from her beloved parents, this omission of a poetic foot contributes to the poem's portrait of the speaker as someone able to do without, to make sacrifices willingly, and even to elect them freely and without imposition. That is to say, Snow's tetrameter works to generate a sentimental poetics of sacrifice and resourcefulness, uncomplainingly making the best of what she has and without the desire for more. In this way, the meter implicitly dampens any suspicions of radical or subversive leanings in the poem.

Similarly, Snow's use of the quatrain rhyme scheme ABAB allows her to build a poetic structure that audibly emphasizes pairing and mimetically reproduces the poem's own narrative of delayed reunion. While the two pairs of rhyming lines in each stanza reflect the poem's preoccupation with the divine pair that rules heaven, the poem also delays the resolution of each rhyming pair, interrupting it with the commencement of a new rhyme. In both cases, the interpolated new rhyme may temporarily interrupt and even obscure the conclusion of the previous rhyme, but it cannot prevent its final and ultimate resolution: the rhyme structure, that is, communicates the futility of forestalling the inevitable. In this respect, Snow chose poetic forms that on the one hand acknowledge delay and obstruction but confirm an expected outcome, implications that mimic the speaker's own delayed reunion with her heavenly family and that would have been sorely needed by Mormon readers in need of reassurance amid grave uncertainty. On the other hand, the rhyme scheme introduces a sense of constant renewal and refreshment, with the repeated introduction of new rhyming pairs. This poetic device lyrically conveys a sense of optimism and regeneration that doubtless would have been welcome to Mormon readers of 1845. While the poem's use of rhyming pairs rhythmically invokes the divine couple that is at the poem's center, the infusion of new pairs also works as a poetic allusion to the Mormon belief that the pantheon of divine couples may be infinitely expanded. That is to say, Snow's rhyme scheme offers a rhythmical elaboration on the doctrine of divinization, the doctrine that all Mormon married couples may undergo deification and join the ranks of celestial, divine couples.

The Mormon attraction to sentimentalism may have derived from its uses as a public affirmation of female domestic duty amid a culture that found such traditional gender norms imperiled by any number of different threats, from hostile critics to polygamy to civil-service commitments. Sentimentalism both camouflaged and enabled the leadership and authority of Mormon women, Eliza Snow among them, whose organizational abilities and independence proved essential to the establishment of this new American religion: in this particular instance, it enabled Snow to be recognized as a prophet, and it likewise enabled her poem to be received as religious scripture. As it did with women throughout the United States and of innumerable religious affiliations, sentimentalism functioned as a wishful corrective to the social ills that threatened to uproot the American woman and endanger the American home, attempting to teach readers how things *ought* to be and how faith might restore the broken and reunite the estranged.

Within this context, "O My Father" emerges as the most definitive example of the ambivalence of sentimentalism, for it envisions the supreme expression of female religious authority in the person of Heavenly Mother, only to conceal her from public view in conformity with conventional notions of female modesty. Through the revelation of Heavenly Mother, the poem attempts to render the home finally, permanently, whole and unassailable, impervious to disturbance of any kind. What had been an impossible fantasy of perfect domesticity in literature and in the wider world became cosmological reality in Snow's poem. In the form of Heavenly Mother, Snow envisioned a sentimental woman whose allegiances could never be divided, who could never be wrested from her home. Her invisibility a sign of her total commitment to her duties, Heavenly Mother's family remains permanently intact, even into the afterlife. Furthermore, the Mormon doctrine of divinization makes it possible for all women to achieve this state of supreme religious authority and perfect domestic completeness: if Mormon women live righteously and follow all required ordinances, they too may one day become divine and assume the powers and role of Heavenly Mother. In this one denominational setting, the powers of self-improvement that so motivate sentimentalism may lead women to a state of absolute cosmological authority, albeit one deferred to the afterlife and one in which they will be confined in a celestial home for all eternity.

CHAPTER 5

The Mother Church

Mary Baker Eddy and the Practice of Sentimentalism

CHRISTIAN SCIENCE was among the most controversial and alluring new sects of the American nineteenth century, and its founder, Mary Baker Eddy, was by extension among the most provocative public figures of the last quarter of the nineteenth century, her vexed reputation enduring well after her death in 1910. As the author of *Science and Health with Key to the Scriptures* (first published in 1875 but reissued in revised form numerous times) and the leader of Christian Science, Eddy became an international celebrity and the object of both veneration and condemnation. Her followers exalted her as a divinely inspired prophet whose religious revelations offered relief from bodily ailments, and her detractors denounced her as a barely literate charlatan and plagiarist. Mark Twain, one of her most dedicated critics, acknowledged these competing public perceptions when he stated that, although he deemed her a crook and a fraud, she was nonetheless "the most interesting woman that ever lived, and the most extraordinary."[1] Eddy's theological ideas were partially responsible for these divergent public opinions, for, in asserting that "a sick body is evolved from sick thoughts" and that bodily healing could be effected through prayer and theological instruction, she ran afoul of the late-century professionalization of medicine and its attendant efforts to eradicate alternative healing techniques and practitioners; all the same, Eddy's ideas found favor amid the late-century New Thought movement, which concurred with Eddy in the belief that thoughts may exert profound influence on the body and on the material world.[2] Primarily, however, Eddy's own life and persona were the chief sources of this public disagreement about her legitimacy as a religious authority. Mark Twain's 1902 remarks evidence this preoccupation with Eddy's public persona: he wrote, "I am not combating [Christian] Science. . . . I haven't a thing in the world against it. Making fun of that shameless old swindler, Mother Eddy, is the only thing I take any interest in."[3] Central to Twain's admission is his telling use of Eddy's honorific, Mother, a term widely used by Eddy's followers to describe her and one that Eddy freely employed in both published writings and in private correspondence, as with the valediction "With love, Mother" that she used to close her 1896 Message to the Annual Meeting of the Church of Christ, Scientist.[4] The sting of Twain's statement derives from its pointed contrast between this affectionate appellation and his counterclaim that Eddy was a brazen con artist altogether undeserving of this sobriquet.[5] Her public presentation, Twain suggests, is decidedly at odds with the reality of her true private nature.

Twain was justified in highlighting this moniker, for maternity figured prominently in Eddy's public image and in her theological writings. She wrote extensively about the religious significance of mothers, as with her assertion that the Virgin Mary was a prophet in her own right and her claim that the mother figure in religious scripture symbolically denotes "God; divine and eternal Principle; Life, Truth, and Love" (*Science and Health* 592:16–17).[6] As an institutional extension of this public elevation of maternity, the monumental Boston church and headquarters that Eddy commissioned in the 1890s was dubbed the Mother Church, an edifice that contained a well-appointed chamber reserved for Eddy called Mother's Room. The room contained numerous visual markers of Eddy's maternal authority: she requested that the words "MOTHER" and "LOVE" be engraved over the room entrance, and the chamber contained a stained-glass window adorned with the words "Suffer Little Children to Come unto Me," from Matthew 19:14.[7] As it had with Twain, Eddy's maternal persona elicited considerable ire among critics who suspected a disconnection between this maternal public image and Eddy's private reality. According to such critics as Twain and Georgine Milmine, Eddy was in no way the embodiment of maternity, with its allied associations with caregiving, domesticity, and selflessness: rather, they claimed, Eddy was a self-absorbed malingerer, a slattern, and a liar. Furthermore, critics alleged that Eddy had been an indifferent, even neglectful mother incapable of caring for her own son, who had been raised by surrogates and came to know his mother only in adulthood. Her motherhood, they maintained, was little more than a fiction.

The object of this chapter is not to rehearse this heated turn-of-the-century debate about Mary Baker Eddy's legitimacy or to determine the precise correspondence between her public image and private life. Rather, this chapter takes its cue from the preoccupation of Eddy's critics with her maternity and examines Eddy's explicit use of sentimentality in constituting her religious authority.[8] As previous chapters have argued, sentimental literature of the nineteenth century advocated for female religious authority while complying with normative expectation. On its own terms, the medium of sentimental literature, which is both composed and consumed within the confines of the private domestic sphere, enabled women writers themselves to exert religious influence, offer scriptural interpretation, and endorse emergent religious theology while complying with the standards of modesty and propriety that they helped circulate.[9] For instance, the hymn form, as previously discussed in Chapter 2, enabled women to assume a public religious voice while honoring the Pauline edict barring women from public speech during Christian worship. In the same vein, Harriet Beecher Stowe's fiction repeatedly suggested that traditional housewifery offered women an important medium by which they might actively contribute toward the fulfillment of millennial prophecy; similarly, Eliza Snow envisioned the supreme female religious authority in the form of Heavenly Mother, only to secrete her from public view in conformity with feminine decorum.

This negotiation between the indecorous assumption of public religious authority and the normative compliance with feminine modesty reaches its fullest expression in the life and work of Mary Baker Eddy, a female religious leader who persistently engaged sentimental rhetoric, tropes, and forms to moderate her status as a pioneer of female religious leadership and to package herself as the apotheosis of the pious, loving mother rendered iconic by innumerable works of sentimental literature.[10] Eddy's biographer Gillian Gill has argued that because of Eddy's remarkable authority, her life "rewrites the female plot"; this chapter will amend that salient claim to argue that precisely because Eddy's life so diverged from the stereotypical "female plot," she was at great pains to demonstrate her conformity with it.[11] As this chapter will show, Eddy attempted to control her public image by circulating innumerable stories and poems in which she actively employed sentimental rhetoric of maternity, domesticity, and love, and repeatedly portrayed herself as a stock character in a sentimental narrative. In invoking literary tropes of feminine modesty and selflessness to camouflage her unprecedented authority and fame, Eddy presents her controversial life story as an iteration of a familiar sentimental narrative of the triumph of piety over suffering. In this respect, Eddy's efforts at image control constitute an important public attempt to implement and execute what had largely been a discursive, literary mode of constituting female religious authority. In characterizing herself as the apotheosis of the sentimental mother, Eddy presented herself as the literary word made flesh.

Attention to Eddy's avowed, explicit sentimentality may help us understand why she attracted so many outspoken critics when other female religious leaders, such as Phoebe Palmer (founder of the Holiness movement) and Ellen G. White (founder of Seventh-Day Adventism), did not receive such widespread outpourings of rancor. Eddy's use of sentimentality is comparable to that of the Latter-day Saints a generation before, as both used sentimentalism to answer their critics and present themselves as familiar and appealing. However, the vitriol of Eddy's critics demonstrates that her literary rhetoric failed to be convincing to nonbelievers and was even perceived as a ruse. This incredulity may be due to the fact that by the late century, the sentimental literary idiom had become old-fashioned and was derided for its perceived mawkishness and unoriginality. By the time she reached the apex of her celebrity and power in the 1890s, the dutiful, compliant, sentimental female prototype of the mid-century had given way to the New Woman of the late century, whose independence, mobility, and self-reliance made the sentimental ideal seem stodgy and saccharine by comparison.[12] An avid reader and writer of sentimentalism since her own girlhood, Eddy misjudged the literary and cultural climate of the late century and failed to recognize that the era's culture of the New Woman provided her with an opportunity to present herself as the fulfillment of the new feminine ideal: with her managerial authority, business acumen, and unconventional marital history, Mary Baker Eddy was the apotheosis of the late-century New Woman, yet she sought to camouflage these features by marketing herself as the fulfillment of the feminine ideal of a previous generation: modest, domestic, and retiring. Her critics suspected her of being a phony, and, to a degree, they were correct: Eddy was a modern New Woman masquerading as an old-fashioned sentimental one.

The harsh response to her sentimentality also derived from changing literary aesthetics. It is telling that two of her most vociferous, damaging critics were literary writers associated with the turn-of-the-century literary aesthetic of realism that prized documentary verisimilitude and constituted itself in opposition to the emotionalism and formulaic predictability of sentimentalism: Mark Twain and Willa Cather, who, it is now recognized, was the chief author of a notorious series of articles about Eddy that appeared in *McClure's* in 1907 and 1908.[13] Both Twain and Cather attacked Eddy by taking particular aim at her writing ability; influenced by the contemporary literary climate that elevated "life-likeness" over "book-likeness," to use the influential formulation of arch-realist William Dean Howells, they respectively interpreted her literary sentimentality as evidence of her dishonesty and inanity.[14] Twain, for instance, lampooned Eddy's poems for their very sentimentality: they are characterized, he claimed, by their "affectation, [and] artificiality; their make-up is a complacent and pretentious outpouring of false figures and fine writing, in the sophomoric style."[15] Eddy's engagement with stock sentimental tropes, Twain assumes, indicates her literary incompetence and moral duplicity. Cather, in collaboration with Georgine Milmine, similarly conflated Eddy's literary sentimentality with dishonesty and affectation:

> She spent many hours in her room "composing poetry," which sometimes appeared in the poet's corners of local newspapers, and there is a tradition that she wrote a love story for *Godey's Lady's Book*. This literary tendency was a valuable asset, which Mrs. Glover [Eddy's name after her first marriage] made the most of. It gave her a certain prestige in the community, and she was not loth to pose as an "authoress." Perhaps it was this early habit of looking at herself as a literary authority which led her to take those curious liberties with English which have always been characteristic with her. She drew largely upon the credit of the language, sometimes producing a word or evolving a pronunciation which completely floored her hearers.[16]

These two notorious criticisms communicate that Eddy's beleaguered reputation derived in part from late-century skepticism about the idiom of literary sentimentalism, which had so influenced Eddy's own sensibilities as a young woman but that in her old age had become the object of derision and prompted critics to question her integrity. This suspicion that Eddy's writings were unoriginal resulted in an accusation charging her with plagiarizing *Science and Health* from the manuscripts of Phineas Quimby, a mesmerist and healer with whom she studied in the 1860s. This accusation has never been substantiated, and Gillian Gill has recently acquitted Eddy on the grounds that Quimby was likely illiterate, but this accusation communicates a recognition that Eddy's writings had an unattributed antecedent, although that antecedent was largely generic and discursive rather than factually based: that is, she relied heavily on the conventions of literary sentimentalism rather than on a particular textual source.

To analyze Mary Baker Eddy's tireless enlistment of sentimental rhetoric and tropes is to see how profoundly this literary register was absorbed into the church that she founded. As is evident in the sentimental poems that would be included in the Christian Science hymnal and the transformation of Eddy's life story into sectarian typology, Eddy's own literary habits and narratives became that of the Christian Science church. In metamorphosing into the avatar of pious sentimental maternity, Eddy helped channel sentimentalism into an institutionalized, organized religion in which some core sentimental ideals—the transformational power of love, the sacred import of the home, and the belief that woman will usher in the new age—became theological doctrine. As such, this indigenous American religion of the nineteenth century constitutes one important instance of the "concrete social institutionalization" of sentimentalism, to use Laura Wexler's phrasing, and demonstrates another instance in which sentimentalism exerted direct influence on theology and religious belief.[17] As formulated by Eddy, Christian Science can be construed as a literalization of the "sentimental love religion" famously envisioned by Leslie Fiedler.[18]

Sentimental Biography: Mary Baker Eddy's Self-Narration

The suspicion that Eddy had drawn too liberally from auxiliary sources also resulted in the accusation that her maternal public persona was itself a copy, drawn from the unattributed example of Ann Lee, the charismatic female leader of the Shakers who was similarly called Mother by her followers.[19] The original "Mother Church" was not the stately Boston edifice built by Christian Scientists in the 1890s but the central Shaker meetinghouse, which shared this same moniker. The correspondences between Christian Science and the Shakers are not inconsiderable. The Shakers developed a similar theology of divinity that constituted the divine not as a single-gender Father but as Father-Mother, a theological teaching that Eddy herself would advocate in *Science and Health*. Both Eddy and Lee claimed healing powers, characterized themselves as Christ's female successor, and identified with the Woman Clothed with the Sun in the New Testament book of Revelation. The two faiths also disallowed spoken prayer in favor of silent meditation and shared deep skepticism about the theological status of the body, a belief that led the Shakers to renounce sexual intercourse in favor of celibacy and that led Eddy to renounce the materiality of the body altogether. When confronted with the accusation that she had liberally borrowed from Shakerism, Eddy conceded her similarity to Mother Ann but responded with a straightforward disavowal: "I never was especially interested in the Shakers."[20] Beyond these overlaps, later scholars, such as Susan Hill Lindley and Robert Peel, have failed to find substantial evidence of Eddy's deliberate appropriation of Shaker doctrine and iconography, concluding instead that any derivations were accidental and born out of Eddy's exposure to the Shakers while growing up in close proximity to the Shaker village of Canterbury, New Hampshire.[21] This accusation also overlooks the fact that motherhood had long been a fixture of Eddy's professional reputation, well before she became known as Mother Eddy, in particular because of her work as a healer specializing in obstetrical and gynecological maladies and her renown for easing her patients' labor pains and difficulties conceiving children. Her own biological motherhood, a condition resolutely discouraged in Shakerism, was the primary source for her maternal public persona, and, as I will soon show, she actively engaged sentimentalism to provide rhetorical justification and impart literary luster to this status, however vexed and controversial. Moreover, by the time Christian Science attained national prominence at the turn of the century, the Shakers had dwindled to a single colony, and Eddy's public persona owed less to this dwindling sect than to her enlistment of scenarios, structures of feeling, and discourse rendered familiar and appealing in sentimental literature.

However, unlike the scant evidence binding Eddy to the Shakers, the ties linking Mary Baker Eddy to literary sentimentalism are direct, literal, and abundant. Born in 1821 to a Calvinist farming family in New England, Mary Baker acquired a taste for literary sentimentalism during her girlhood, and in early adolescence she wrote numerous poems that demonstrate her efforts both to master this literary idiom and to emulate sentimental expectations of self-governance and self-improvement. In one childhood poem, "Alphabet and Bayonet," she urged a daydreaming classmate to

> . . . fix thy restless mind
> On learning's lore and wisdom's might,
> And live to bless mankind.[22]

A poem in praise of self-improvement, it characterized education as the fulfillment of personal independence and moral autonomy, signaling her command of this sentimental value even at this young age. Her early embrace of sentimental ideals and forms is particularly visible in the poem "Resolutions

for the Morning," which she authored at age twelve. Composed of eight qua-
trains, the poem is a catalogue of resolutions of self-betterment, as with the
assertion in the fifth stanza,

> I'll greatful remember the blessings I've shared,
> And make this my daily request;
> Increase thou my faith, my vission enlarge,
> Clothe me with the garment of peace [sic].[23]

While this imperfectly spelled and rhymed poem evidences her childhood
engagement and compliance with sentimental forms and moral expectations,
it also communicates her full awareness that sentimental attestations of piety
were modulated by tacit desires for public authority and power. Even while
she pledges to "go to the altar of God and pray," her yearnings for virtue are
accompanied by the explicit ambition for literary skill as well as a public audience. The poem begins by resolving first to cultivate the aesthetic sensibilities
that evidence female refinement and respectability: she vows to

> . . . rise in the morn and drink in the dew,
> From flowers that bloom in the vale—
> So mildly dispensing their charms ever new,
> Over hillocks, and flowery dales.

In the next stanza, she explains that careful attention to nature may not
only "enlighten the spiritual eye" but also "inspire my pen as I write": that is,
self-betterment will enable her to develop the skills and sensitivities needed
to fulfill her literary ambitions. From the very outset, sentimental discourse
provided her, as it did to so many women, with a vehicle by which she might
acquire public status while also tempering it with assertions of piety.

   In her adult life, she attempted to make a career out of sentimental literature. In 1844, her husband of only a few months died suddenly, leaving her
pregnant and penniless. In the years that followed and at the peak of sentimentalism's mid-century popularity, she struggled to support herself and
her son by attempting to live by her pen, a struggle undertaken by countless
contemporary women, few of whom found financial security in so doing.
She published innumerable poems and stories in the sentimental vein, such
as the poems "A Fragment" and "My Mother" in *The Floral Wreath, and Ladies' Magazine*. She even succeeded in placing a poem in *Godey's Lady's Book*

in 1853, but the majority of her prolific publications were in such regional New England venues as the *New Hampshire Patriot and State Gazette*. Her poems engage the typical topics that occupy sentimental literature: motherhood, childhood, domesticity, and bereavement. Though her poems may initially seem like unremarkable iterations of the sentimental literary corpus, they are notable in part because so many of them derive explicitly from the struggles that afflicted much of her life. For instance, the poem "The Widow's Prayer" bears particular witness to her use of sentimental rhetoric and forms to impart order and purposefulness to personal turmoil. Published in 1845 in the *Freemason's Monthly Magazine*, it is the prayer of a widow seeking help from the divine, and it is thus visibly informed by her own dire woes.[24] With its aestheticization of bereavement and invocation of familiar literary tropes of grief, the poem is a typical example of the sentimental genre of consolation verse, as the speaker attempts to find solace from grief and reconcile herself to a divine will that is so at odds with her own. The poem reads,

> Forgive my frailties, Lord,
> That I should dare repine,
> Though lone, amid a stranger land,—
> At dealings such as thine.[25]

The poem's sentimental vocabulary is particularly evident in the second verse, which articulates the familiar sentimental perception of woe as an expression not of divine disfavor but of divine love; despite the considerable influence of Methodism and other contemporary religious movements on sentimentalism, this common sentimental belief derived from the Calvinist doctrine of affliction and contends that ordeals may remove impediments to one's faith and provide an opportunity for spiritual growth.[26] The second verse uses the typical phrasing commonly used in sentimental literature to describe this belief: just as Emily Graham in Maria Susannah Cummins's *Lamplighter* (1854) remarks to Gerty Flint that only "those who, in the severest afflictions, see the hand of a loving Father, and, obedient to his will, kiss the chastening rod," so her poem describes the struggle to arrive at this resignation:

> Hast thou not said, thy grace shall prove
> Sufficient for thy rod,
> Hope gives to Faith a view of love,
> Mid chastenings of a God![27]

She used the same sentimental vocabulary of willing affliction in the 1849 poem "To My Mother in Heaven," which was likewise composed in response to a personal crisis, in this case the death of her mother. In its depiction of her mother as a kindly angel watching over her loving daughter, the poem is a typical example of sentimental consolation verse and of the generic adulation of maternity. The poem's fifth stanza, for instance, describes the efforts to perceive this loss as a reminder of the joys that wait in heaven, where the departed mother now resides. The stanza reads,

> Yet round the sad, forsaken hearth,
> At vesper hour, sweet prayer
> On trembling pinions soars to Heaven
> To mingle with thee there;
> And bless thee for this glorious hope,
> And meekly kiss the rod,
> As when *thy* spirit once did lift
> The trust of *mine* to God![28]

In this poem, she seeks to discern a beneficent larger purpose behind this sorrow, an event that caused her not only grief but also considerable trouble, for her father's consequent remarriage required her to leave her childhood home and find a residence for herself and her son elsewhere.

These several examples of Eddy's considerable poetic corpus demonstrate her active participation and fluency in sentimental forms, which she repeatedly employed to constitute the events that transpired in her own life. Amid the poverty, loss, and isolation that plagued so much of her life, sentimental aesthetics and tropes transformed her sufferings into conventional, even predictable events rendered familiar by considerable literary precedent. What might seem to be cruel and random is transformed by sentimental convention into a deliberate and purposeful occasion for self-betterment and invigorated faith. Sentimental discourse also offered assurance that her sufferings, like those of the sentimental heroine, will reliably conclude in joy and reunion, whether in this world or in the afterlife. More significant, these poems also illustrate that from a very young age, she regarded sentimental prototypes as suitable models for her own character and public persona. As early as 1833, she consistently fashioned her public presentation according to recognizable, stock sentimental paradigms, modeling herself after a trope drawn from a corresponding life stage, whether the determined girl intent on self-improvement;

the isolated, penurious young woman seeking community and income; or the bereaved daughter finding consolation in prayer and faith. These numerous poems function as etiologies of Eddy's later public image, in which she presented herself as yet another sentimental paradigm in an appropriate life stage, as the wise, loving apotheosis of sentimental womanhood in the form of Mother Mary. For Eddy, the reliance on sentimental femininity in fashioning her public persona was a lifelong habit learned in childhood.[29]

While it is uncertain whether she actually attempted to adopt the private emotional register of pious resignation that the poems aspire to, the historical record documents that her emulation of sentimental temperament had not been confined to poetic lyric, for she seems to have affected a literary public image well before she founded Christian Science. Acquaintances from her early life allege that as a young woman, Eddy attempted to fashion a literary public image as an "authoress," a persona that imparted status and glamour to her desperate efforts to support herself and her son through writing. Cather and Milmine, Eddy's most hostile biographers, contend that Eddy fostered this reputation by deliberately cultivating an image of quirky eccentricity: for instance, they quote a witness who recalls Eddy's presentation as an "authoress" during her first meeting in the 1860s with Phineas Quimby, who first introduced Eddy to the idea of mind cure that would prove so essential to Christian Science theology. According to this observer, Eddy cultivated this literary reputation by wearing purposely unconventional outfits designed to make her stand out and seem artistic: "She wore a poke bonnet and an old-fashioned dress, but my impression was that her costume was intended to be a little odd, as in keeping with her 'literary character.'" They also contend that Eddy's public literary pretension resulted in attempts at eloquence, which too often yielded unfortunate malapropisms: "Perhaps it was this early habit of looking upon herself as a literary authority which led her to take those curious liberties with English which have always been characteristic of her. She drew largely upon the credit of the language, sometimes producing a word or evolving a pronunciation which completely floored her hearers. Some of these words and phrases have passed into local bywords. 'When I vociferate so loudly, why do you not respond with greater alacrity?' she sometimes seriously demanded of her attendants. She referred to plain John Varney as 'Mr. Ve-owney,' and few ordinary words were left unadorned."[30] In telling this story, Cather and Milmine suggest that Eddy's infamous inclination to misuse words, for which her critics would attack her viciously, derived from a lifelong affectation of literariness.[31] While any accusation by Cather and

Milmine should be taken with a grain of salt, the bemusement of their un-named witness suggests that even during the height of sentimentalism's popularity in the mid-century, Eddy's literary public performance already met with skepticism. As the attacks from Twain and Cather in the early twen-tieth century demonstrate, this response would only increase in vitriol as sen-timentalism waned in literary esteem.

Eddy's supporters responded to these accusations of literary affectation by seeking to bolster her sentimental bona fides. She is no imposter, these de-fenders maintain; rather, they argue, Mary Baker Eddy is the real thing, the perfect embodiment of sentimental femininity and true womanhood. There are innumerable examples in which Eddy's loyal supporters countered public criticisms by reaffirming her full adherence to the now-old-fashioned norms of female piety and selflessness. Irving Tomlinson, a long-time follower and aide, actively drew upon sentimental tropes in his literary memoir of Mary Baker Eddy. In his depiction of Mary Baker as a child, Tomlinson invoked the familiar sentimental prototype of the selfless, saintly child, Eva St. Clare of Stowe's *Uncle Tom's Cabin*. For instance, he writes, "Little Mary Baker often gave away her mittens, her cap, and even her warm coat to some poor, shiver-ing child at school less fortunate than herself. She just could not bear to wit-ness any kind of distress without doing something to remove it." And like Eva St. Clare, Eddy's sensitivities made her physically frail and vulnerable, Tom-linson claims, thereby employing the long-standing sentimental conflation of piety with bodily weakness to explain Eddy's nonattendance of school, which her critics often cited to attack her intelligence, fitness for religious leadership, and capacity for authorship: Eddy's truancy was caused by her selflessness and virtue, he suggests, and not by laziness or stupidity. Eddy was also an impec-cable housekeeper, he maintains, a devoted adorer of children, and a woman of sterling taste. Whereas Cather and Milmine depicted Eddy as ruthlessly ambitious, Tomlinson instead depicts her authority as the expression of her supreme femininity and womanliness: "Over the infant Cause of Christian Science she faithfully watched as a mother watches over her babe. While oth-ers slept, Mrs. Eddy beheld grave dangers threatening the newborn Cause, and in the long night hours she asked God to give her the means of protecting that which had been entrusted to her care."[32] Her formidable authority is merely that of a mother protecting her offspring, and this sentimental comparison renders her untraditional power both orthodox and normative.

Sybil Wilbur, who was hired to write a competing portrait of Eddy in direct response to the Cather and Milmine biography, repeatedly depicts

Eddy in conformity with sentimental tropes.[33] For instance, she mitigates Eddy's controversial second marriage by enlisting sentimental formula. In 1853, the widowed Mary Baker Glover married dentist Daniel Patterson, a man who would prove a neglectful and even adulterous spouse and whom Eddy would divorce on the grounds of abandonment in 1873. Critics used this unfortunate episode to attack Eddy's judgment, their condemnations callously forgetting that marriage offered the impoverished and homeless widow a rare chance of security. That Eddy would marry a third time, to Asa Gilbert Eddy in 1877, only contributed to the imputation that Eddy was a modern-day American Jezebel, whose fraught conjugal history undermined the legitimacy of her role as prophet. Years later, when the unsavory details of her second marriage emerged in the public eye, Eddy and her biographer Wilbur countered these criticisms by arguing that Eddy married Patterson specifically because he promised to reunite her with her son, George, who was being raised elsewhere because of her poverty. It was love of her son, Eddy and her autobiographical deputy Wilbur claimed, that compelled her to accept Patterson's hand, and it was his refusal to reclaim George that first tipped off his new wife that he was not the gallant man he claimed to be. In this respect, Wilbur implicitly aligns Eddy with the familiar literary prototype of the wronged woman; as with such novels as Susanna Rowson's *Charlotte Temple* (1791) and Hannah Webster Foster's *The Coquette* (1797), these early iterations of the sentimental novel habitually narrate the sufferings of young women lured by unfaithful, treacherous rakes who lack the constancy to be dutiful husbands. This literary formulation allows Wilbur to present Eddy as a victim of her own naïveté and optimism rather than of poor character judgment, who was willing to sacrifice her marital felicity for the chance of reclaiming her son. Wilbur similarly sought to correct the contentions of such critics as Cather and Milmine that Eddy had been an apathetic mother by presenting her as the paradigmatic sentimental mother, a loving companion beloved by all children. This affinity, Wilbur claims, caused "a gentle rumor of saintliness [to] spread through that region, and . . . some dwellers of the countryside came to think of Mrs. Patterson [as was her married name at the time] as a saint and to go to her for advice and comfort. Among those who sought her aid was a mother carrying her infant, a child whose eyes were badly diseased. The mother was a simple working woman, so simple that she could still believe there was a relation between piety and power. She wept as she laid her babe on Mrs. Pattersons's knees and implored her to ask God to cure its blindness."[34] She successfully cured the

child, and this episode not only affirms the widespread sentimental belief in
the capacity of love and faith to effect healing, but it also figures as an early
episode in Eddy's development of Christian Science theology.

Wilbur also sought to burnish Eddy's literary status by bolstering her importance in sentimental literary circles. Eddy, she maintains, was a prolific,
respectable, and sought-after writer well before the theological epiphany that
occasioned the founding of Christian Science. According to Wilbur, Eddy's
closest analogue in the literary climate of the mid-century was none other
than Harriet Beecher Stowe, who, according to Wilbur, essentially scooped
Eddy with the serialization of *Uncle Tom's Cabin* in 1851. Eddy was a keen
critic of slavery due to her brief residence in South Carolina in the 1840s, and
she was poised, Wilbur suggests, to become the leading female literary voice
in its opposition. Wilbur explains,

> Mary Baker was an unusually intellectual woman; where did she stand
> in this hour? Conceive her position. She who might have effectively
> wielded her pen in this cause must allow it to lie idle. She must be-
> hold another woman do that which, with her family behind her, as
> the Beechers were behind Harriet Beecher Stowe, she, too, might have
> done. She was like a soldier paroled on honor whose sword is rest-
> less in its scabbard. Moreover, she was deprived of independence by
> these circumstances, for, throttled on the subject for which she felt
> the greatest interest, she could not write on sugary nothings as many
> another genius, struggling against its environment, has discovered.[35]

According to Wilbur, Mary Baker Eddy might have become the leading writer
of literary sentimentalism if she, too, had had the support and reputation of
a prominent family as Stowe had. Instead, Wilbur suggests, Eddy had to wait
several decades for her writings to enable the liberation of the entire human
race from the thrall of bodily suffering. In this respect, Eddy's writings constitute a fulfillment of the promise of freedom merely foreshadowed in Stowe's
earlier literary success. Another biographer claimed that Eddy's sentimental
sympathy for the plight of slaves led her to sacrifice her own financial security
on their behalf; according to Ella Hay, Eddy freed her first husband's slaves
upon his death, a gesture that left her entirely penniless and instigated the
dire poverty that characterized the majority of Eddy's adult life.[36] Her sympathy for the sufferings of others surpassed her concern for her own financial
welfare, Hay suggests.

The sentimentalization of Eddy's public image is also evident in the widespread effort to portray Eddy as an exemplary housekeeper and homemaker, an endeavor undertaken by both Eddy and her sympathetic chroniclers. This campaign seems to have emerged in response to two prompts. First, Christian Science was dogged by the public assumption that its practice necessitated the neglect of bodily hygiene and inevitably resulted in uncleanliness. Eddy's own writings contributed to this impression, as with her infamous assertion in *Science and Health* that "the daily ablutions of an infant are no more natural nor necessary than would be the process of taking a fish out of water every day and covering it with dirt in order to make it thrive more vigorously in its own element" (413:12–16). This statement not only suggested that Eddy encouraged the neglect of children, but it also depicted the abnegation of traditional maternal duty as religiously righteous behavior; in this respect, Eddy herself fueled the rumors about her maternal and domestic inadequacies. Second, this campaign sought to refute accusations that Eddy's ambition rendered her an indifferent housekeeper, for Eddy's critics gleefully repeated rumors about her slatternly homemaking and neglect of her domestic duties as a young widow.[37] While a similar accusation today would carry little weight, such an attack in the late nineteenth century implicitly impugned her morality, decency, and fitness for public recognition as the beloved Mother Mary. To neutralize both criticisms, testimonies of Eddy's domestic gifts work to demonstrate her private qualifications for public leadership, and she herself repeatedly emphasized the spiritual merits of domesticity, thereby reifying long-standing sentimental understandings of the religious significance of housekeeping.

Because of its concentrated attention to household affairs, sentimentalism has often been described as domestic literature, and the central narrative of spiritual transformation is often effected by the heroine's education in household management.[38] As discussed in previous chapters, an unruly household in sentimental literature indexes moral disorder and the consequent need for ethical reform, as with the disarray of Dinah's kitchen in *Uncle Tom's Cabin* and the March sisters' domestic struggles in *Little Women*; by the same token, Ruth Hall's clean and cheery household registers her innate goodness in Fanny Fern's *Ruth Hall* (1855) as does Huldy's efficient housekeeping in Stowe's short story "The Minister's Housekeeper."[39] Sentimentalism teaches the spiritual rewards of a clean, well-ordered household, and by example, Eddy likewise taught that domestic hygiene was expected of Christian Scientists. She did not hesitate to channel this value into her theological writings, thereby transmuting sentimental ideals into formal religious theology. In *Science and Health*, her theological magnum opus, she strongly advocated for domestic cleanliness in her strong assertion, "I insist on bodily cleanliness within and without. I am not patient with a speck of dirt" (*Science and Health* 413:20–21). Irving Tomlinson discussed at considerable length Eddy's particular gifts for housekeeping, observing that, "In spite of the thousand and one demands on her time, Mrs. Eddy found opportunity to oversee the management of her home and thoroughly to train the workers whom she called there. The executive ability she so ably manifested in the conduct of the Christian Science movement, she applied with equal effectiveness to the running of her home. So smoothly adjusted was the domestic machinery of her household that the maximum of results was obtained with a minimum of labor." According to Tomlinson, Eddy's religious leadership is merely an extension of her domestic gifts and the fulfillment of her womanly nature. The effort to establish Eddy's domestic cleanliness caused Tomlinson to resort to quoting her former landlady, a Mrs. Sally Wentworth, with whom Eddy lodged for two years, to affirm that "'Mrs. Eddy was a very neat person and always kept her room in good order."[40] Her enthusiasm for housekeeping was such that it was the subject of a monograph, Elbert Hubbard's *Little Journeys to the Homes of Great Teachers—Mary Baker Eddy* (1908), which remarked on the cleanliness of Eddy's home, the propriety of her household meals, and the orderliness of her household routine. Hubbard noted that Eddy's followers overwhelmingly complied with Eddy's insistence on domestic order, noting that "all these things are seen in the homes of Christian Scientists. Always in the home of a good Christian Scientist the bath room is as complete as the library, and both are models of good house-keeping, seemingly always in order for the inspection committee."[41]

In presenting Eddy as the exemplar of sentimental womanhood, these supporters were only following Eddy's example, for her own writings provide the richest illustrations of her enlistment of sentimental literary tropes in the constitution of her authority and public persona. The very title of Eddy's 1891 autobiography, *Retrospection and Introspection*, engages sentimental tropes. While the memoir itself somewhat constitutes a violation of feminine norms of modesty and domestic enclosure, the title tempers these implications by broadcasting Eddy's conformity with sentimental femininity: characterized as the product of her "Introspection," it publicizes her inwardness and capacity for self-reflection, qualities requisite to sentimental character reform and self-governance. Otherwise, the contents of this memoir everywhere en-

gage sentimental tropes. Though she may not have had any formal education, religious training, or official ordination to justify her religious authority,
she instead presents her own life and character as her chief qualifications for
sectarian leadership, and in this way she was a late-century extension of the
tradition of the self-styled, populist religious leadership that commenced
with the Second Great Awakening, as discussed in Chapter 1. Eddy nonetheless used sentimental tropes to establish her credentials, suggesting that,
even from early life, signs of her specialness have always been evident: in
particular, the trappings of sentiment often function in her autobiographical
writings as visible markers indicating that her calling as the founder of a new
religion had been evident even from childhood. Furthermore, these allusions
to sentimental literary convention helped create the impression of Eddy as
the fulfillment of long-standing religious expectation that had heretofore
been confined to literary transcription. In so doing, she relies on the same
dynamic of intertextual typology that casts the New Testament as the realization of the promises and expectations of the Hebrew Bible: in reiterating the
contents of an earlier text, the later text emerges as the fulfillment of the previous text's ambitions. For instance, the massacre of the innocents narrated
in the Gospel according to Matthew strikingly echoes a similar incident in
Exodus 1:22 in which Pharaoh orders the slaughter of all Israelite male in-
fants; the outcome of this narrative dependence is the suggestion that Jewish
history and messianic prophecy have finally found resolution in the birth of
Christ. A similar dynamic operates in Eddy's autobiographical writings in
which the precedent of sentimental literature functions as a kind of literary
herald anticipating her advent, thereby allowing her to present herself as the
fulfillment of a familiar, more modern literary typology. Whereas Christ was
touted as the completion of Jewish prophecy, so Eddy positions herself as the
fulfillment of sentimental yearning for a loving mother figure who can afford
relief from worldly suffering.

To be sure, Eddy on numerous occasions presented herself as the fulfillment of literary prediction in the traditional scriptural manner. In her memoir, for instance, she claimed to have repeatedly heard her name called by an
unknown voice, an event that places Eddy in the biblical tradition of Abraham and Samuel, as a similarly summoned prophet. She likewise claimed
that the biblical book of Revelation explicitly predicted Christian Science and
intimated that the scroll held by the angel in Revelation 10 is none other than
Science and Health, her own magnum opus.[42] But, in her extra-theological
writings, she drew upon popular sentimental literature to characterize her-

self as the incarnation of a different scriptural tradition. This invocation of sentimental convention is visible, for instance, in her portrait of herself as a girl. Though her critics depicted her as a spoiled, tantrum-prone child, her self-portrait visibly conscripts the recognizable sentimental paradigm of the loving, pious child whose pure-hearted religious wisdom exceeds that of more theologically sophisticated adults, a stock trope evident in such characters as Willie Barclay in Catharine Sedgwick's *Home* (1835), Eva St. Clare in Stowe's *Uncle Tom's Cabin* (1852), Fleda in Susan Warner's *Queechy* (1852), and Mara Lincoln in Stowe's *Pearl of Orr's Island* (1862). According to Eddy in *Retrospection and Introspection*, she was a theologically precocious child preoccupied with religious questions from an early age, listening avidly while her Calvinist father engaged in heated religious debate with more liberal relatives. While other children merely memorized and recited the catechism, Eddy recalls being fixated on the Calvinist doctrine of election, which caused her to worry so deeply about the damnation of her friends and family that she fell ill. It was only her mother's loving reassurance that caused her to cease pondering her father's harsh theology: "My mother, as she bathed my burning temples, bade me lean on God's love, which would give me rest, if I went to Him in prayer, as I was wont to do, seeking His guidance. I prayed; and a soft glow of ineffable joy came over me."[43] Cynthia Schrager has commented on the sentimental overtones of this moment, in which Eddy renounces a harsh paternalistic doctrine in favor of a more loving, maternal theology.[44] At the same time, it also provides another instance in which a sentimental woman writer rejects the Calvinism of her upbringing to adopt progressive, even radical doctrines, and it thus places Eddy in the company of such fellow writers as Sedgwick, Stowe, and Warner. While this moment provides an early foreshadowing of her later theological conviction that faulty theology can yield bodily ailments and that healing can be engendered by theological correction, it uses this familiar trope of the sympathetic pious child to demonstrate that Eddy's concerns about the welfare of others were pronounced even in early childhood, and it implicitly characterizes the Christian Science theology of healing as the culmination of this lifelong sympathy for suffering.

Her account of childhood makes numerous other references to sentimental tropes. When undergoing the doctrinal examination requisite to Congregationalist church membership, for instance, she refused to profess predestinarian beliefs she did not hold and "stoutly maintained that I was willing to trust God, and take my chance of spiritual safety with my brothers and sisters . . . even if my creedal doubts left me outside the doors." Likewise, when asked by clergy to name the precise moment of her spiritual regeneration, she declined to answer directly and responded with a recitation of Psalm 139, "Search me, O God, and know my heart."[45] This moment of doctrinal indifference strikingly echoes the Warner sisters' refusal to answer the questions posed in their own doctrinal examination, and in this way it evokes the professions of ecumenism in sentimentalism, discussed in Chapter 1, that regard denominational confessions and creedal divisions as misguided and potentially harmful impediments to faith. In conformity with the sentimental denunciation of Calvinism, Eddy implies that, even as a child, she recognized the shortcomings of these doctrinal attributions of wrath and injustice to the divine, and asserted instead a more modern, sentimental understanding of the divine as loving and beneficent. This depiction of a remarkably brave moment of childhood religious conviction also evokes the paradigm of the pious sentimental child whose enlightened religious wisdom allows him or her to stand up to stern and faulty religious authority, such as Jane in Catharine Sedgwick's *New-England Tale* (1822), whose broad ecumenical piety allows her to discern the faults of her aunt's harsh Calvinism, or Ellen Montgomery of Warner's *Wide, Wide World,* whose faith compels her to disobey the religious edicts of her uncle, Mr. Lindsay.

In this literary convention, the innocent moral clarity of the pious child enables him or her to see through the errors of adult theology, but Eddy's account raises the stakes of this recognizable sentimental trope, for Christian Science contends that theological error causes not only misunderstanding but also bodily illness, suffering, and death: as she explains it, erroneous belief in the primacy of matter rather than spirit causes human illness, and a corrective theological reeducation may enable bodily healing and the relief from corporeal suffering. The sentimental precedent of the doctrinally precocious child thus figures as a portent anticipating Eddy's theological innovations and demonstrates that she has always possessed a special gift of theological insight that well qualifies her for religious leadership. Though she may not have attended seminary, sentimental convention positioned Eddy within a different tradition of religious leadership, one born out of natural ability, wholesome character, divine inspiration, and sympathy rather than mere training or human-made ritual. Just as Stowe and Warner used sentimental tropes both to assume and conceal their religious authority, so Eddy also used sentimental narrative precedent as an authenticating credential affirming her legitimate claim to religious leadership.

Expressions of her ardent love for domesticity likewise abound. In *Science and Health*, she proclaimed, "Home is the dearest spot on earth, and it should be the centre, though not the boundary, of the affections" (58:21–23). In *Retrospection and Introspection*, for instance, Eddy inserts her poem "The Country-Seat," written in her youth, as a transition from her childhood to the discussion of her brief first marriage; an ode to the beauties of nature, the poem's larger narrative function is apparent in the last stanza, which expresses her yearning for a home of her own:

> Oh, give me the spot where affection may dwell
> In sacred communion with home's magic spell!
> Where flowers of feeling are fragrant and fair,
> And those we most love find a happiness rare;
> But clouds are a presage,—they darken my lay:
> This life is a shadow, and hastens away.[46]

This desire for a loving home, she suggests, directly resulted in marriage. She later uses her love of domesticity as explanation for her grief at the prospect of her son's removal, commenting that "my home I regarded as very precious." The chronicles of her followers are similarly replete with instances of Eddy's particular enthusiasm for domesticity; Tomlinson quotes Eddy as saying, "The strongest tie I have ever felt . . . next to my love of God, has been my love for home."[47]

This engagement in conventional womanly rhetoric is all the more noteworthy because it so diverges from Christian Science teachings, which disavow the material world altogether and strongly encourage adherents to divest their attention and care from bodily concerns. Even Hubbard, Eddy's domestic chronicler, remarked on the disconnection between Eddy's doctrinal teachings and the scrupulousness she maintained, commenting that "you could never work out [this insistence on domestic order] of 'Science and Health with Key to the Scriptures' in a lifetime of study."[48] Ardent domesticity and housekeeping comprise serious attachments to the specious world of material forms, which may result not only in the belief that the body is subject to the same depredations as matter but also in the realization of that belief through the eruption of illness. Elsewhere, Eddy spoke stridently against the necessity of cleanliness to health, insisting that "drugs and hygiene cannot successfully usurp the place and power of the divine source of all health and perfection" (*Science and Health* 167:12–14.). She even commented that the true home was not a material, physical place at all but a spiritual state: she observed, "Home is not a place but a power. We find home when we arrive at the full understanding of God. Home! Think of it! Where sense has no claims and Soul satisfies."[49] Similarly in a public address, she declared that the "home of the Christian Scientist is in the understanding of God. His affection and interests are there, and his abiding place is there."[50] Her writings contain some striking moments of contradiction, as with her competing assertions that "we need a clean body and a clean mind,—a body rendered pure by Mind as well as washed by water" (*Science and Health* 383:3–4), a remark undermined by the earlier repudiation of infant bathing. The end result of this incongruity between doctrine and rhetoric is the implication that the sentimental rehabilitation of Eddy's public image was deemed important enough to compromise the very integrity of Christian Science theology.

Eddy's sentimental self-presentation reaches its zenith with the depiction of her separation from her son, George, who at the age of four was taken from her custody to reside with the Baker family's longtime nurse. Critics used this episode to impugn her character and womanly nature, but Eddy portrayed this incident using the familiar literary tropes of bereaved maternity that figured so prominently in women's literature of the nineteenth century. In their condemnations, Eddy's turn-of-the-century critics failed to recall that earlier in the century adoption and parental surrogacy had been common for the children of the poor, who were often taken in by relatives, community members, or tradesmen (the latter in the case of apprenticeships) when the nuclear family proved unable to support them.[51] Furthermore, this delegation of parental responsibility frequently provided the initial prompt of sentimental narrative, as with the decision to transfer custody of Ellen Montgomery from her parents to that of her aunt in Warner's *Wide, Wide World*, the adoption of the orphan Lilly Benton by Mrs. Grayson in Augusta Evans's *Beulah* (1859), the long-standing residency of Elsie Dinsmore with her father's family while he travels abroad in Martha Finley's *Elsie Dinsmore* (1867), and Jo Bhaer's adoption of the orphan Nat Blake in the opening scene of Alcott's *Little Men* (1871).[52] Though such events were commonplace in the nineteenth century, the literature of this period commonly featured maternal distress in the face of this separation. For instance, Mrs. Montgomery grieves piteously in anticipation of her separation from her daughter, Ellen, and Mrs. March, of Alcott's *Little Women*, vigilantly refuses the offer of her husband's Aunt Josephine to take in one of her children in response to the collapse of their family's finances. Ruth Hall, the heroine of Fanny Fern's 1855 autobiographical novel of the same name, is forced to give up her daughter Katy to the care of her late husband's parents, and the novel charts her tireless efforts to accrue enough capital to reclaim her. Consolation verse figured as the extreme example of maternal anguish amid the dislocation of children, although in this genre reunion may occur only postmortem in the afterlife. In a genre that spanned much of the century, from Lydia Sigourney's "Death of an Infant" (1827) to Sarah Piatt's "Death Before Death" (1870), this form often implicitly engaged the contemporary culture of parental surrogacy by constituting the divine as the ultimate parent, the great Father who in the afterlife now cares for the child in the mother's stead.

Eddy actively engages the literary constitution of maternal grief in her autobiographical account. Like so many literary mothers before her, she attributes this estrangement to her poverty, acknowledging, "I had no training for self-support." Her account is exceedingly abbreviated, with no details or designation of the antagonists behind this removal, and she describes only her own patient faith amid this ordeal: "The night before my child was taken from me, I knelt by his side throughout the dark hours, hoping for a vision of relief from this trial." She declines to express directly whether she found any such solace and instead she proffers a stanza from her poem "Mother's Darling," which she says was composed in the aftermath of this separation:

> Thy smile through tears, as sunshine o'er the sea,
> Awoke new beauty in the surge's roll!
> Oh, life is dead, bereft of all, with thee,—
> Star of my earthly hope, babe of my soul.[53]

The unrelieved sorrow portrayed here suggests that she found no consolation from prayer, but what is remarkable in this account is the use of the sentimental elegy as a proxy for prose elaboration. Just as she had at earlier intervals in her life, this episode documents Eddy's continuing reliance on sentimental prototypes as models for her own public persona, and here she uses poetry to characterize herself as the bereaved mother made recognizable by so much poetry. This interpolation of lyric frames this biographical episode within a familiar, normative structure of female suffering, and she invites the reader to perceive this incident within an established literary tradition and thereby to regard it as both piteous and conventional. The inclusion of this stanza also implicitly burnishes Eddy's own character by suggesting that even amid dire anguish, she possessed the judgment, composure, and taste to craft poetry. In thus publicizing this moment of personal anguish, Eddy constitutes herself as the apotheosis of sentimentality while flouting one of its bedrocks tenets: its transformation of suffering, especially that wrought by political or social inequity, into a "world of private thoughts, leanings, and gestures," in the words of Lauren Berlant.[54] The poem's engagement in the world of the private and domestic is useful only insofar as it helps her to shape her public persona and legitimize her religious authority.

Nor was "Mother's Darling" the only poem she circulated to consolidate the sentimental underpinning of this episode in her life. Perhaps her most famous poem was "Mother's Evening Prayer," which was also composed in response to this crisis. Like "The Widow's Prayer," the poem is in the form of a prayer beseeching the deity to safeguard the speaker's child in her absence. Though it is said to have been composed in the 1840s at the time she was forced to relinquish her son, Eddy first publicly circulated this poem after Cather and Milmine accused her of being a neglectful mother, giving it prominent place in a collection of poems she issued in 1910. The poem directly counters this accusation by characterizing Eddy as a devoted mother who struggles not only to retain her son despite poverty but also to adopt the familiar posture of sentimental resignation in the face of suffering.

> O Gentle presence, peace and joy and power;
> O Life divine, that owns each waiting hour,
> Thou Love that guards the nestling's faltering flight!
> Keep Thou my child on upward wing tonight.

> Love is our refuge; only with mine eye
> Can I behold the snare, the pit, the fall:
> His habitation high is here, and nigh,
> His arm encircles me, and mine, and all.

> O make me glad for every scalding tear,
> For hope deferred, ingratitude, disdain!
> Wait, and love more for every hate, and fear
> No ill,—since God is good, and loss is gain.

> Beneath the shadow of His mighty wing;
> In that sweet secret of the narrow way,
> Seeking and finding, with the angels sing:
> "Lo, I am with you always,"—watch and pray.

No snare, no fowler, pestilence or pain;
   No night drops down upon the troubled breast,
When heaven's aftersmile earth's tear-drops gain,
   And mother finds her home and heav'nly rest.[55]

This conventional sentimental poem expressly refutes public accusations of maternal negligence and provides biographical justification for Eddy's public image as a benevolent, kindly matriarch. As was the case with her inclusion of a stanza from "Mother's Darling," the poem also corroborates Eddy's composure and taste amid calamity, and its formal regularity and generic predictability give the impression of Eddy as striving to maintain poise and self-control when events transpired against her.

Sentimental Love Religion

"Mother's Evening Prayer" also evidences that Eddy's strategic use of sentimentalism left visible traces on the religion that she founded. Unlike "Mother's Darling," this sentimental poem acquired considerable sectarian stature, for Eddy had the poem adapted to music and included within the Christian Science hymnal in 1910, the same year it was issued in her poetry collection; the fact that this poem was publicly rolled out in two different settings in the same year suggests a calculated effort to distribute the poem as widely as possible and thereby consolidate Eddy's motherly image amid a flood of criticism.[56] In addition, the decision to adapt the poem into a hymn, despite its divergence from traditional hymn forms, demonstrates Eddy's awareness of the uses of hymnody in both confirming the female hymnist's normative femininity and in affording her religious authority, a phenomenon discussed in Chapter 2. Her familiarity with sentimental hymnody of the mid-century is also evident in the inclusion of such foundational works as Harriet Beecher Stowe's "Still, Still with Thee" in the Christian Science hymnal, in addition to works by Lydia Sigourney and numerous other sentimental nineteenth-century women hymnists.

   In transforming this poem from a private, personal lyric into a collective, publicly performed hymn, Eddy clearly believed that it was of denominational value, and it has been interpreted thus by Christian Science adherents. Church by-laws ensured the longevity and circulation of this poem and hymn, for Christian Science congregations are required to sing Eddy's hymn compositions at least once a month, and they are likewise required to announce Eddy's authorship every time one of her hymns is sung (the hymnal includes six hymns by Eddy). The hymn has consequently acquired considerable status: for instance, in the current edition of the Christian Science hymnal, "Mother's Evening Prayer" is adapted to six different musical arrangements. As was the case with Eliza Snow's "O My Father," the sentimental tropes of Eddy's "Mother's Evening Prayer" acquired a host of additional theological valences in this religious setting. In the first place, Christian Science worshippers likely discern in the poem's title a reference to Eddy's own familiar honorific, hearing in its title less an invocation of generic sentimental elegy than a reference to Mother Mary herself; consequently, the hymn functions as an expression of Eddy's own sectarian wishes in general rather than as an expression of bereaved motherhood in particular. This interpretation is supported by Eddy's public honorific, "Mother," and her inclination to portray her followers as her children; in fact, she was particularly prone to do so in verse, as with the poem "Mother's New Year Gift to the Little Children."[57] The sectarian embrace of the poem likewise highlights aspects of the poem that would otherwise seem conventionally sentimental. For instance, the poem's formal invocation of prayer acquires particular significance in the context of the Christian Science doctrine that reprieve from suffering can be found in prayer and spirituality; indeed, this context highlights the poem's confirmation that prayer alone enables succor and bodily protection from worldly ills, as with the speaker's assertion that in God "No snare, no fowler, pestilence, or pain" can be found. In portraying a mother's entreaty and attendant consolation, the poem uses sentimental convention to dramatize a scene of Christian Science healing, in which prayer affords comfort and relief. And in invoking Eddy's own personal history, the poem simultaneously evokes the very starting point of Christian Science, in her originary revelation that prayer can effect healing.

A 1914 article about Eddy's hymns in the *Christian Science Journal* confirms this interpretation of "Mother's Evening Prayer." Mary Louise Baum extols the hymn as "perhaps the most complete poetic expression of Mrs. Eddy's religious ideal and also of her own human experience and hope. We find her asking protection for her fledgling idea, and in affirming her assurance of this protection, she says: 'His arm encircles me, and mine, and all.'"[58] According to Baum, this poem has value less as a document of biographical significance than as an expression of Eddy's broader worry about the future of Christian Science itself: in particular, Baum interprets the child who is the subject of prayerful worry not as an allusion to George Glover, Eddy's estranged son, but as the still incipient Christian Science church, Eddy's most famous progeny. This interpretation seems to have been widely accepted and was endorsed by the church itself, for Baum's essay would be included within the official, church-issued *Concordance to Christian Science Hymnal.*

This reading has a number of implications and functions. Eddy died a year after the text's publication as both a poem and a hymn, and this context imparts a poignantly valedictory character to the text, as Eddy offers a final public prayer for the church she founded and will soon leave leaderless. At the same time, the text invokes a number of other contexts and concerns. In the first place, it addresses Eddy's somewhat controversial removal from her followers: in 1889, Eddy moved from Boston to Concord, New Hampshire, where she effectively retreated from public life, although she continued to write, publish, and correspond as well as take regular daily drives. Critics attacked her for this relocation, positing her as reclusive, unapproachable, and aloof; Twain, for instance, characterized her as virtually imperial in her inaccessibility, writing, "When Mrs. Eddy is not dictating servilities from her throne in the clouds to her official domestics in Boston or to her far-spread subjects round the planet, but is down on the ground, she is kin to us and one of us: sentimental as a girl, garrulous, ungrammatical, incomprehensible, affected."[59] The context of Eddy's maligned removal from Boston, the Church's center of activities, to New Hampshire imparts a particular resonance to the poem, suggesting that this separation was a source of considerable anxiety and trouble for Eddy, who yearned to guide and steer her church just as a mother longs to raise her child. The poem confirms Eddy's continuing devotion to the church, despite her physical estrangement (though, to be sure, distance did not prevent her from continuing to exert control over its daily operations). At the same time, this denominational reading interprets Eddy's beset biological maternity through the lens of typology, at once memorializing this traumatic moment in Eddy's life and positing it as an etiology of Eddy's later religious leadership: her experience as a biological mother figures in the hymn as a prefiguration or herald anticipating the fulfillment of her maternity with the founding of Christian Science. Implicit in this typological interpretation is the notion that Eddy channeled her frustrated, obstructed maternal sentiments outward: without a child to care for, she became a mother at large, offering care and healing to all through her religious teachings.

These readings also impart particular significance to the public performance of this poem through collective hymn singing. Hymn adaptation transformed a private, silent literary form into a public, communal, and audible one, but the public performance of a hymn interpreted as an expression of Eddy's worry about the church's survival implicitly works as confirmation that the church has indeed survived. The public performance of "Mother's Evening Prayer" functions in ways similar to the Passover Seder in Judaism, in that both commemorate a dire episode that threatened the future of a persecuted religious minority and, in the act of commemoration, celebrate their respective survivals. In all these ways, Eddy's stock sentimental poem acquires an array of denominational connotations while characterizing Eddy's religious authority as a public expression of private maternal feeling.

There are numerous other examples that evidence the Christian Science absorption of sentimentalism, as with Mother's Room, the space designed especially for Eddy in the Mother Church. At the level of furnishings, the room presented a serious public-relations problem, for it was lavishly appointed even by Gilded Age standards: with marble walls, a rare onyx mantle, and even gold-plated water pipes, the room contained an abundance of valuable decorative objects, such as ancient Persian carpets, a table carved out of onyx, tapestry pillows, and numerous imported lamps. Mother's Room put Eddy's power and affluence on extravagant public display, and as such it attracted notice not only for its excesses but also for its apparent incompatibility with Christian Science theology, which denounced materialism as sinful and even dangerous to the health. Such critics as Mark Twain castigated Christian Science for this discrepancy, juxtaposing, for instance, its theological repudiation of materialism with the high fees charged by practitioners. Mother's Room inherently suggested that the renunciation of worldliness did not extend to Eddy herself, and the end result was the allegation that Eddy was enriching herself through the theological denial of materiality.

In response, sentimental ideology was once again enlisted to address this public-relations problem, and the room was rhetorically refashioned from the lush chamber of a wealthy potentate to a snug, maternal den patterned after the familiar sentimental construction of maternal space. Whether "Marmee's Corner" in Alcott's *Little Women* or Mrs. Scudder's cozy kitchen in Stowe's *Minister's Wooing*, sentimental discourse limns the maternal space as distinctive in its integration of duty with comfort, its homely contents evidencing both the execution of female responsibilities, such as needlework, and the inviting environment suited to quiet self-reflection and nurture. Though its marble walls and gold-plated pipes remained intact, the room was discursively renovated to function as a spatial expression of Eddy's warm motherliness. As mentioned earlier, Eddy requested that the words "MOTHER" and "LOVE" be engraved over the room entrance, and the room contained a stained-glass window inscribed with the words "Suffer Little Children to Come unto Me," thereby articulating Eddy's particular affection and affinity for children. The room entrance also contained a mosaic that reads "THE CHILDREN'S OFFERING" to offer public proclamation that the funds for Mother's Room derived not from Eddy's or the church's abundant wealth but from the dedicated fundraising efforts of the "Busy Bees," the children's auxiliary organization. This acknowledgment invites the visitor to perceive the room as the product of collective filial devotion rather than Eddy's personal power and wealth, as Twain would allege. In addition, the church circulated a disclaimer dissociating Eddy from the room's opulent interior: in a church-commissioned narrative of the Mother Church, Joseph Armstrong asserts that Eddy rejected the original plan for lavish furnishings and opted instead for modest, comfortable appointments that more accurately reflect her sensible, homely taste. Armstrong substantiates this assessment with an elaborate description of the room's unpretentious contents, which included "a handkerchief, a tiny pincushion, dressing gown, slippers and every needful toilet article." He similarly clarified that the room's many valuable decorations derived not from extravagant church expenditure but from donations from grateful parishioners: "Loving touches still continue to be added to this room, and ever will be, as long as hearts turn in gratitude to the one who gave her life for them and the world."[60] Armstrong here transforms the material trappings of Eddy's power and prominence into expressions of private devotion and sentiment: Mother's Room contains these objects not because Eddy is prosperous but because she is helpful, selfless, and beloved. To consolidate this association with the sentimental construction of maternal domestic space, Eddy herself donated to Mother's Room a large six-by-five-foot painting of the homely rocking chair in which Eddy habitually sat during the years of reflection and composition that generated *Science and Health* and that itself became a beloved, iconic emblem of Eddy's maternal authority.[61] This painting provides a visual reminder of the humble, comfortable domestic spaces from which Christian Science emerged and on which it discursively relies in the construction of Eddy's public image.

Having constituted herself as a devoted mother patterned after sentimental iconography, Eddy repeatedly affirmed that the connective link binding her to her followers was not power or obedience but simple love: as a loving mother attends carefully to the needs and development of her children, so

Mary Baker Eddy governed her church, striving to help it grow to sturdy independence and maturity. Her 1899 poem "To the Sunday School Children," for instance, begins with a declaration of this love: alluding to Anna Warner's iconic hymn "Jesus Loves Me," it reads, "Jesus loves you! so does mother," a line that likens Eddy's own love for her child followers to the unconditional love of Christ and that of mothers for their children.[62] Likewise, the prominent engraving of the words "MOTHER" and "LOVE" before the entrance of Mother's Room also give public testimony to this identification of Eddy with maternal love. Irving Tomlinson credits Eddy's inherently loving, maternal nature for his abiding affection for her, observing, "I shall never forget that [first] visit or Mrs. Eddy's graciousness and consideration. She expressed such tender, loving, motherly solicitude that I was instantly drawn to her."[63] Calvin Hill, who also authored an account of his relationship with Eddy, evidenced the use of this rhetoric of maternal love among Eddy's own followers, who freely describe themselves as devoted children guided by a loving mother in Eddy. For instance, he reprints an 1899 letter to Eddy from "First Members of the Mother Church": "As 'them of old time' were guided, encouraged, and uplifted by trope, metaphor, and symbol, so are you, in this age, being shown the way whereby you and your children are drawn by the band of unity into the great Heart of love"; the letter was likewise signed from "Your loving children."[64] Eddy even suggested that her healing abilities derived expressly from her extraordinary capacity for love: love, she maintained, "is the secret of all healing, the love which forgets self and dwells in the secret place, in the realm of the real. But it is not mere human love that heals . . . not a love for a person nor for anything—it is Love itself. The realization of this love for a moment will heal the sick or raise the dead."[65] In affirmation of this claim, Tomlinson included the testimony of a woman whose child Eddy cured: "I wish I could make the world know what I saw when Mrs. Eddy looked at those children [of mine]. It was a revelation to me. I saw for the first time the real Mother-Love, and I knew that I did not have it. I had a strange, agonized sense of being absolutely cut off from the children. It is impossible to put into words what the uncovering of my own lack of real Mother-Love meant to me."[66] This passage presumes Eddy's own maternal love to be the source of her therapeutic healing powers, and it likewise attributes the child's illness to the mother's own hardheartedness.

    This depiction of Eddy as a loving mother had some important theological implications. While on the one hand it posits her authority as selfless and beneficent, it also tacitly elevated her to extraordinary spiritual heights. This

implication derives from Eddy's unequivocal assertion that love is the essential, elemental attribute of divinity; indeed, she habitually used the word *Love*
as a synonym for the divine. For instance, in her poem "Love," which speaks
in apostrophic address to the divine, she repeatedly defines divinity simply as
love, as with this line from the final stanza, "For Love alone is Life."[67] In *Science and Health*, she flatly proclaimed that "God is love" (2:23), an assertion
she would widely repeat, as with the 1891 text *No and Yes*.[68] She supported
this belief with a decidedly gendered portrait of the divine as a doting, tender
mother: for instance, she states, "Love feeds, clothes, and shelters every one
of His dear ones. Love is a Mother tenderly brooding over all Her children.
This Mother guards each one from harm, nourishes, holds close to Herself,
and carefully leads along the upward way."[69] She furthered this gendered association in her interpretive claim that mothers in the Bible are symbolic representations of divine love in its purest form; as she summarizes it, "Love [is]
represented by Mother" (*Science and Health* 569:2–3). With this depiction
of the deity as a loving mother, Eddy extends the sentimental tradition of
divinizing motherhood, which derives from the figure of the Virgin Mary,
who was so closely associated with Catholicism, and which is also evident in
Stowe's perception of Christ as a loving, maternal housekeeper and in Eliza
Snow's revelation of Heavenly Mother.[70] But where these previous sentimental writers offered a feminized vision of the divine to highlight the religious
significance of women and women's traditional work, the chief beneficiary
of Eddy's vision of a feminized deity seems to be none other than Eddy herself. To put it baldly, she characterizes the divine in her own image: as a loving mother. And, by sheer virtue of her public status as benevolent, loving
Mother Mary, her portrait of the divine implicitly constitutes herself as both
godly and godlike.

The Rise and Fall of Apocalyptic Motherhood

The broader implications of this likeness are nothing short of extraordinary. Eddy not only depicted herself as fully sanctified but she also directly
suggested that, as such, she was the long-awaited fulfillment of millennial,
apocalyptic prophecy.[71] To make that case, she drew on the same apocalyptic
imagery and prophecy that underlay Stowe's domestic fiction and its attendant insinuation that women will play a crucial role in the instigation of the
millennium. Though it remains uncertain whether Eddy's interpretation of

Revelation was directly influenced by Stowe, with whose works she was familiar, Eddy nonetheless extends Stowe's feminist millennialism to intimate that a woman—presumably herself—had indeed ushered in the new age, which arrived with the initial publication of *Science and Health* in 1875. She would make this suggestion explicit on a number of occasions. As mentioned earlier, Eddy interpreted the scroll held by the angel in Revelation 10 as a biblical portent anticipating *Science and Health*. She also paid special attention to the strong presence of women in Revelation, taking them to presage the vital contribution of women to the fulfillment of prophecy.[72] She perceived Revelation 12 as especially significant, noting that "the twelfth chapter of the Apocalypse, or Revelation of St. John, has a special suggestiveness in connection with the nineteenth century. In the opening of the sixth seal, typical of six thousand years since Adam, the distinctive feature has reference to the present age" (*Science and Health* 559:32–560:1–5). Eddy paid particular attention to the figure in Revelation 12 of the Woman Clothed with the Sun— who suffers in childbirth while being menaced by a red dragon—to intimate that she is a figuration of Eddy herself. The envelopment of this woman in the sun, Eddy claims, symbolizes her revelation of "spiritual Truth," while the moon under the woman's feet expresses the woman's subordination of matter (*Science and Health* 561:27). This comparison was furthered by the fact that this biblical figure is defined exclusively by her status as a mother whose child is taken away from her, for Revelation 12:5 specifies that after the conclusion of this birth, "her child was snatched away and taken to God and to his throne," a detail that evokes Eddy's own complicated maternal authority. Eddy also interpreted the child as a prophetic sign of her own theological ideas, a metaphor that, we have seen, she and such followers as Mary Louise Baum and Irving Tomlinson habitually used. She made this claim explicit: "The spiritual idea [that is, the Christian Science belief in the supremacy of spirit over matter] is typified by a woman in travail, waiting to be delivered of her sweet promise, but remembering no more her sorrow for joy that the birth goes on; for great is the idea, and the travail portentous" (*Science and Health* 562:24–28). This latter comment references the great difficulty Eddy experienced in bringing Christian Science to fruition; that the child will eventually "rule all the nations" she takes as confirmation of the imminent dominion of Christian Science.

In addition, Eddy intimated that she herself completed and fulfilled the work begun by Jesus Christ. In her interpretation of Revelation, she wrote, "As Elias [which she interprets as a symbol for prophecy] presented the idea

of the fatherhood of God, which Jesus afterwards manifested, so the Revela-
tor completed this figure with woman, typifying the spiritual idea of God's
motherhood" (*Science and Health* 562:3–7). The worldly manifestation of the
deity as a mother, she suggests, "complete[s]" the portrait that commenced
with the life of Christ. In *Retrospection and Introspection*, she would make this
assertion more explicit with her outspoken claim that the "second appearing
of Jesus is, unquestionably, the spiritual advent of the advancing idea of God,
as in Christian Science": her own ideas, that is, constitute the second coming of Christ heralded in Revelation.[73] She likewise defined the New Jerusalem to "[represent] the light and glory of divine Science" (*Science and Health*
575:9–10), and she revised the Lord's Prayer so that it reads, "Thy kingdom
is come" rather than "Thy kingdom come" (*Science and Health* 16:31). Irving
Tomlinson seconded this belief in his stunning Christological description of
Eddy as "the one who gave her life for them and the world."[74]

   While Eddy's millennialist interpretations may seem to the nonbeliever
like a theological curiosity or a feat of egoism, it is the supreme culmination
or realization of sentimental piety. Where Eliza Snow concealed the divine
mother behind the cloaks of modest decorum, Eddy used sentimentality to
bolster and authenticate her religious authority. Eddy transforms the sentimental trope of the loving mother into the supreme figure of anointed religious authority, positing herself as the fulfillment of the prophecies that
Stowe wrote into her fiction and appointed as the bringer of a new dispensation. Motherhood was no longer valued merely discursively or culturally, but
its supreme status here was made official and without apology.

   And where women a generation before had to write hymns, poems, and
novels to excerpt religious influence, Eddy literally wrote scripture, for her
Science and Health with Key to the Scriptures is regarded among Christian Science adherents as a sacred, divinely inspired text. Christian Science worship
services ritually constitute *Science and Health* as a companion piece to the
Bible, thereby replicating a long-standing textual convention. Jewish worship
services typically entail the reading of two sacred texts, one taken from the
Torah, or from the first five books of the Hebrew Bible, and another from
the Haftorah, the words of the prophets. Christian Sabbath services follow
the same pattern, although the readings derive from the Hebrew Bible and
then from the New Testament, thereby positioning the New Testament as
the fulfillment or culmination of the promises of the Hebrew Bible. Christian
Science worship services are structured after this pattern, with readings taken
from the Christian Bible, which includes both the Hebrew Bible and the New

Testament, and from *Science and Health*. In this ritual practice, *Science and Health* is positioned as the fulfillment of the promises of both previous biblical texts. And following the chapter and verse notations of the Bible, each sentence in *Science and Health* has a numerical notation listing its page and line numbers, this apparatus offering a visual cue to the text's sacrality.

Christian Science also formalized the religious importance of female literary authority. Sentimentalism reaffirmed the centrality of reading to religious instruction and practice, and Christian Science institutionalized this belief. Church by-laws stipulate that Eddy herself could never be replaced with another individual church leader, and Christian Science did away with the clerical hierarchies critiqued in sentimentalism, for Christian Science has no formal ordained clergy. Instead, worship services are led by two Readers, positions that are regularly alternated among congregants. To ensure the continuation of female leadership within the church, Church by-laws mandate that one reader must be female, one male. Worship services include no sermons, but they are entirely scripted and composed of readings, announcements, and the singing of hymns. Other than prayer, the central ritual act for Christian Scientists is the act of reading, in particular the reading of the works of the most influential, famous, and successful sentimental woman writer, for much of the worship service consists of readings of selections from *Science and Health*. Textual access and literary engagement are central to Christian Science practice, and thousands of Christian Science Reading Rooms were established in the twentieth century to make Eddy's many writings available to the public, including her poems and autobiography, for it is through her writings that she continues to perform the pastoral duties of instruction and consolation. In this respect, Christian Science institutionalized the role of the literary text as a platform for female religious authority, and it likewise designates the reading of female-authored religious texts as essential to spiritual development, ideas that circulated in mid-century sentimentalism and that became canon doctrine and formal practice in Christian Science.

Unsurprisingly, Eddy received considerable criticism for her bold claims to authority as well as her uses of sentimentality in effecting them. Just as mid-century sentimental writers used Catholicism as the benchmark of religious iniquity, so Mark Twain repeatedly enlisted Catholic tropes to impugn Eddy's ethics and sincerity. For instance, he criticized her for presenting herself as the "Voice of God," and he predicted that she would become a "thousand times" as rich as the pope.[75] He focused in particular on the discrepancy between Eddy's godlike persona and the lavishness of Mother's Room. He

wrote, "As a picturesquely and persistently interesting personage, there is no
mate to Mrs. Eddy, the accepted Equal of the Saviour. But some of her tastes
are so different from His! I find it quite impossible to imagine Him, in life,
standing sponsor for that museum there, and taking pleasure in its sumptu-
ous shows. I believe He would put that Chair [Eddy's famous rocking chair]
in the fire. . . . I think He would break those electric bulbs, and the 'mantle-
piece of pure onyx,' and say reproachful things about the golden drain-pipes
of the lavatory, and give the costly rug of duck-breasts to the poor, and sever
the satin ribbon and invite the weary to rest and ease their aches in the consecrated chairs." The extravagant appointments of Mother's Room simply
cannot be squared with Eddy's Christological claims, Twain avers. He likewise accused her of using the honorific Mother to stage an elaborate con
game in which she acquired religious authority by specifically invoking the
first Mother Mary, the mother of Christ who acquired insuperable authority
among Catholics. He asked, "How long will it be before they place her on
the steps of the Throne beside the Virgin,—and, later, a step higher? First,
Mary the Virgin and Mary the Matron; later, with a change of precedence,
Mary the Matron and Mary the Virgin." He reserved his most vicious attack
for her old-fashioned sentimental poetry, marveling at her inability to notice
the weakness of the poems she wrote in the mid-century: "That she could
still treasure up, and print, and manifestly admire those Poems, indicates
that the most daring and masculine and masterful woman that has appeared
in the earth in centuries has the same soft, girly-girly places in her that the
rest of us have."[76] Twain wonders here at the disconnection between Eddy's
tough-mindedness as a leader and the inherent sentimentality of her poems,
to suggest that her authoritative persona is designed to conceal her inner
sentimentality. What he overlooks in this formulation is that Eddy actively
employed literary sentiment to conceal a toughness of character and resolve
that look altogether modern today but that Eddy herself seems to have found
a potential impediment to her public persona.

Twain's blows landed, and Eddy reacted more decisively and defensively
to his attacks than she would to her other public critics. She issued a public
statement disavowing the honorific Mother, arguing that it had been imposed
on her against her will by particularly strident followers. She wrote, "It is a fact,
well understood, that I begged the students who first gave me the endearing
appellative 'Mother' not to name me thus. But, without my consent, that word
spread like wildfire."[77] She also responded by amending Church by-laws to
stipulate a formal name change. Article XXII, section 1 reads as follows:

In the year eighteen hundred and ninety-five, loyal Christian Scientists had given to the author of their textbook, the Founder of Christian Science, the individual, endearing term of Mother. At first Mrs. Eddy objected to being called thus, but afterward consented on the ground that this appellative in the Church meant nothing more than a tender term such as sister or brother. In the year nineteen hundred and three and after, owing to public misunderstanding of this name, it is the duty of Christian Scientists to drop the word *mother* and to substitute Leader, already used in our periodicals.[78]

In addition, she ordered that Mother's Room be permanently closed and unavailable to the public, its evocatively sentimental name expunged, for section 17 of Article XXII describes the room as the one "formerly known as 'Mother's Room.'"[79]

Eddy would live for several more years after this public repudiation of her maternal authority, but the remaining years would be characterized by an even more dire public challenge to her leadership. In 1907, a faction that included former associates as well as her own son waged a lawsuit charging that Eddy was mentally incompetent to lead the church, and they argued that, among other things, her domestic seclusion evidenced her incapacity as well as her ineffectiveness as a leader. Her publicized domesticity, which had been designed as a visible expression of Eddy's wholesomeness and maternal familiarity, was construed as a sign of her inability, for religious leaders are expected to assume public duties and offer public religious instruction, not spend their time sitting in rocking chairs in comfortable parlors. Though the "Next Friends" suit, as it was called, was decided in Eddy's favor, it signaled increasing skepticism about this brand of sentimental religious leadership, which mitigated the seeming vulgarity and impropriety of public religious authority by couching it in the rhetoric of family, domesticity, and love. The Next Friends suit and Twain's attacks communicate that sentimentalism had outlived its usefulness as a rhetoric of female religious authority: it had helped Eddy portray Christian Science as respectable, but it had become a public liability amid the skepticism and literary tastes of the turn of the century, making her the subject of open public mockery. This brand of conflicted female religious leadership had already become obsolete, as firebrands like Carry Nation aggressively pursued temperance campaigns and evangelist Aimee Semple McPherson would soon brazenly court media attention. Though these women would assume public religious authority without apology, they were able to do so because of the contributions of sentimentalism, which, for the better part of the nineteenth century, provided a discourse of feminine respectability that enabled women for the first time to assume genuine religious leadership, and it likewise provided a vehicle by which controversial religious movements could be assimilated into the American mainstream. The sentimental affirmation of respectability and religious subservience enabled American women such as Mary Baker Eddy to traverse social norms, religious custom, and even biblical injunction, and thereby stake a place for themselves in American religious life and leadership.

NOTES

Introduction

1. Ann Douglas, *The Feminization of American Culture,* 2nd ed. (New York: Anchor, 1988), 44.

2. David S. Reynolds, *Faith in Fiction: The Emergence of Religious Literature in America* (Cambridge, Mass.: Harvard University Press, 1981), 94.

3. Jane Tompkins, *Sensational Designs: The Cultural Work of American Fiction, 1790–1860* (New York: Oxford University Press, 1985), 125-40.

4. Nina Baym, *American Women Writers and the Work of History, 1790–1860* (New Brunswick, N.J.: Rutgers University Press, 1995); Dawn Coleman, *Preaching and the Rise of the American Novel* (Columbus: Ohio State University Press, 2013); Tracy Fessenden, *Culture and Redemption: Religion, the Secular, and American Culture* (Princeton: Princeton University Press, 2007); Sharon Kim, "Puritan Realism: *The Wide, Wide World* and *Robinson Crusoe,*" *American Literature* 75 (December 2003): 783–812; Abram Van Engen, "Puritanism and the Power of Sympathy," *Early American Literature* 45.3 (Fall 2010): 533–64.

5. Laura Wexler, "Tender Violence: Literary Eavesdropping, Domestic Fiction, and Educational Reform," in *The Culture of Sentiment: Race, Gender, and Sentimentality in Nineteenth-Century America*, ed. Shirley Samuels (New York: Oxford University Press, 1992), 9.

6. This assumption was widespread in early studies of sentimentalism, such as E. Douglas Branch, *The Sentimental Years: 1836–1860* (New York: D. Appleton-Century, 1934), 125; Herbert Ross Brown, *The Sentimental Novel in America, 1789–1860* (Durham, N.C.: Duke University Press, 1940); Helen Waite Papashvily, *All the Happy Endings* (New York: Harper & Brothers, 1956); Barbara Welter, "The Cult of True Womanhood: 1820–1869," *American Quarterly* 18 (Summer 1966): 151–74.

7. Mark S. Massa, S.J., *Anti-Catholicism: The Last Acceptable Prejudice* (New York: Crossroad, 2003), 23–24.

8. John Corrigan and Lynn S. Neal, *Religious Intolerance in America: A Documentary History* (Chapel Hill: University of North Carolina Press, 2010), 51.

9. Carleton Beale, *Brass-Knuckle Crusade: The Great Know-Nothing Conspiracy: 1820–1860* (New York: Hastings House, 1960), 9–10; Massa, *Anti-Catholicism*, 28.

10. Fessenden, *Culture and Redemption*, 6.

11. Marianne Noble, *The Masochistic Pleasures of Sentimental Literature* (Princeton: Princeton University Press, 2000), 52ff.

12. Nancy Bentley, "Marriage as Treason: Polygamy, Nation, and the Novel," in *The Futures of American Studies*, ed. Donald E. Pease and Robyn Wiegman (Durham, N.C.: Duke University Press, 2002), 343–70; Bruce Burgett, *Sentimental Bodies: Sex, Gender, and Citizenship in the Early Republic* (Princeton: Princeton University Press, 1998); Elizabeth Maddock Dillon, *The Gender of Freedom: Fictions of Liberalism and the Literary Public Sphere* (Stanford, Calif.: Stanford University Press, 2004); Julia A. Stern, *The Plight of Feeling: Sympathy and Dissent in the Early American Novel* (Chicago: University of Chicago Press, 1997).

13. Dillon, *Gender of Freedom*, 49; Amy Schrager Lang, *Prophetic Woman: Anne Hutchinson and the Problem of Dissent in the Literature of New England* (Berkeley: University of California Press, 1987); Papashvily, *All the Happy Endings*, 103–104.

14. Gillian Brown, *Domestic Individualism: Imagining Self in Nineteenth-Century America* (Berkeley: University of California Press, 1990), 7.

15. Lora Romero, *Home Fronts: Domesticity and Its Critics in the Antebellum United States* (Durham, N.C.: Duke University Press, 1997), 5.

16. Laura Wexler, "Seeing Sentiment: Photography, Race, and the Innocent Eye," in *American Literary Studies: A Methodological Reader*, ed. Michael A. Elliott and Claudia Stokes (New York: New York University Press, 2003), 63–94.

17. Terryl L. Givens has analyzed this depiction of Mormons in *The Viper on the Hearth: Mormons, Myths, and the Construction of Heresy* (New York: Oxford University Press, 1997), 23ff. Similar suspicions pervade the claims of anti-Catholic agitators, such as that of Edward Beecher, who asserts that Catholicism "is organizing seductive and proselyting systems of education, and aims by means of them to corrupt and enlist in their vast schemes the children of Protestant parents." See *The Papal Conspiracy Exposed, and Protestantism Defended, in the Light of Reason, History and Scripture* (Boston: Stearns, 1855), 15.

18. Philip Fisher, *Hard Facts: Setting and Form in the American Novel* (New York: Oxford University Press, 1985), 8.

19. Jennifer L. Brady, "Theorizing a Reading Public: Sentimentality and Advice About Novel Reading in the Antebellum United States," *American Literature* 83 (December 2011): 724.

20. Paul J. Griffiths has considered the broader role of reading in religious observance. See *Religious Reading: The Place of Reading in the Practice of Religion* (New York: Oxford University Press, 1999).

21. Cited in Candy Gunther Brown, *The Word in the World: Evangelical Writing, Publishing, and Reading in America, 1789–1880* (Chapel Hill: University of North Carolina Press, 2004), 121.

22. Brown, *Word in the World*, 88–95.

23. John Bunyan, "The Author's Apology for His Book," in *The Pilgrim's Progress*, ed. N. H. Keeble (1678; repr., Oxford: Oxford University Press, 1990), 7.

24. Suzanne M. Ashworth, "Susan Warner's *The Wide, Wide World*, Conduct Literature, and Protocols of Female Reading in Mid-Nineteenth-Century America," *Legacy* 17 (2000): 141–64.

25. For a fuller discussion of the influence of *Pilgrim's Progress* on these works, see Ruth K. MacDonald, *Christian's Children: The Influence of John Bunyan's* The Pilgrim's Progress *on American Children's Literature* (New York: Peter Lang, 1989).

26. James D. Bratt, "The Reorientation of American Protestantism, 1835–1845," *Church History* 67 (March 1998): 52–82, 67; Nathan O. Hatch, *The Democratization of American Christianity* (New Haven: Yale University Press, 1989), 125–26.

27. For a fuller history of nineteenth-century evangelical publishing, see Candy Gunther Brown, *The Word in the World,* and David Paul Nord, *Faith in Reading: Religious Publishing and the Birth of Mass Media in America* (New York: Oxford University Press, 2004).

28. Quoted in Hatch, *Democratization,* 126.

29. Quoted in David S. Reynolds, *Faith in Fiction,* 209.

30. Numerous critics have elaborated on this belief. See Ray Allen Billington, *The Protestant Crusade, 1800–1860: A Study of the Origins of American Nativism* (Chicago: Quadrangle, 1964), 143, 157; Fessenden, *Culture and Redemption,* 60–83; Jenny Franchot, *Roads to Rome: The Antebellum Protestant Encounter with Catholicism* (Berkeley: University of California Press, 1994), 23.

31. Henry F. May, "The Recovery of American Religious History," *American Historical Review* 70.1 (October 1964): 80, 79.

32. Lawrence Foster has offered a study of the broader nineteenth-century intersection of innovations in religion and gender relations: see *Women, Family, and Utopia: Communal Experiments of the Shakers, the Oneida Community, and the Mormons* (Syracuse, N.Y.: Syracuse University Press, 1991).

33. Nathaniel Hawthorne, "The Scarlet Letter," in *Nathaniel Hawthorne: Collected Novels* (1850; repr., New York: Library of America, 1983), 344–45.

Chapter 1. Revivals of Sentiment

1. Ann Douglas, *The Feminization of American Culture,* 2nd ed. (1977; New York: Anchor, 1988), 13.

2. Jane Tompkins, *Sensational Designs: The Cultural Work of American Fiction, 1790–1860* (New York: Oxford University Press, 1985), xvii.

3. Sharon Kim, "Puritan Realism: *The Wide, Wide World* and *Robinson Crusoe,*" *American Literature* 75 (December 2003): 783–812; Marianne Noble, *The Masochistic Pleasures of Sentimental Literature* (Princeton: Princeton University Press, 2000); Abram Van Engen, "Puritanism and the Power of Sympathy," *Early American Literature* 45.3 (Fall 2010): 533–64.

4. Nathan O. Hatch, *The Democratization of American Christianity* (New Haven: Yale University Press, 1989), 4

5. Hatch, *Democratization*, 10; Richard Carwadine, "The Second Great Awakening in the Urban Centers: An Examination of Methodism and the 'New Measures,'" *Journal of American History* 59 (September 1972): 329; Roger Finke and Rodney Stark, *The Churching of America, 1776–2005: Winners and Losers in Our Religious Economy* (New Brunswick, N.J.: Rutgers University Press, 2005), 57, 71, 121; A. Gregory Schneider, *The Way of the Cross Leads Home: The Domestication of American Methodism* (Bloomington: Indiana University Press, 1993), xx; John H. Wigger, *Taking Heaven by Storm: Methodism and the Rise of Popular Christianity in America* (New York: Oxford University Press, 1998), 3.

6. Noble, *Masochistic Pleasures*, 52ff.

7. William G. McLoughlin, *Revivals, Awakenings, and Reform: An Essay on Religion and Social Change in America, 1607–1977* (Chicago: University of Chicago Press, 1978), 98.

8. Finke and Stark, *Churching*, 56.

9. Ray Allen Billington, *The Protestant Crusade, 1800–1860: A Study of the Origins of American Nativism* (Chicago: Quadrangle, 1964), 118–19; Jenny Franchot, *Roads to Rome: The Antebellum Protestant Encounter with Catholicism* (Berkeley: University of California Press, 1994), 5.

10. Catherine A. Brekus, *Strangers and Pilgrims: Female Preaching in America, 1740–1845* (Chapel Hill: University of North Carolina Press, 1996), 140; Nancy A. Hardesty, *Woman Called to Witness: Evangelical Feminism in the Nineteenth Century* (Nashville, Tenn.: Abingdon, 1984), 65; Schneider, *Way of the Cross*, xviii.

11. Barbara Leslie Epstein, *The Politics of Domesticity: Women, Evangelism, and Temperance in Nineteenth-Century America* (Middletown, Conn.: Wesleyan University Press, 1981), 6.

12. Jon Butler, *Awash in a Sea of Faith: Christianizing the American People* (Cambridge, Mass.: Harvard University Press, 1990), 4.

13. This claim derives from Roger Finke and Rodney Starke's recent research re-evaluating religious statistics of the nineteenth century. Such critics as Jenny Franchot and Susan Griffin have argued that Catholicism was the nation's largest denomination, but Finke and Starke compellingly argue that scholars have dramatically overestimated the numbers of Catholics in the United States throughout the nineteenth century, and they contend that Catholicism became the largest denomination only by 1890, with Methodism the largest denomination until then. See Finke and Starke, *Churching*, 121; Franchot, *Roads to Rome*, xx; Susan M. Griffin, *Anti-Catholicism and Nineteenth-Century Fiction* (Cambridge: Cambridge University Press, 2004), 3. Though Nathan Hatch gives a different number, he agrees that Methodism was the most populous denomination of the mid-century. See "The Puzzle of American Methodism," in *Methodism and the Shaping of American Culture*, ed. Nathan O. Hatch and John H. Wigger (Nashville, Tenn.: Kingswood, 2001), 27, 28. John Corrigan and Lynn S. Neal, *Religious Intolerance*

in America: A Documentary History (Chapel Hill: University of North Carolina Press, 2010), 51.

14. Butler, *Awash*, 236–37; Hatch, "Puzzle," 37; Schneider, *Way of the Cross*, xx.

15. Keith J. Hardman, *Charles Grandison Finney, 1792–1875: Revivalist and Reformer* (Syracuse, N.Y.: Syracuse University Press, 1987), 190–91.

16. McLoughlin, *Revivals*, 11.

17. Douglas, *Feminization*, 28–32; Donald M. Scott, *From Office to Profession: The New England Ministry, 1750–1850* (Philadelphia: University of Pennsylvania Press, 1978), 53–75.

18. Robert V. Remini, *Andrew Jackson and the Course of American Democracy*, vol. 3 (New York: Harper & Row, 1984), 6–7; Arthur M. Schlesinger, Jr., *The Age of Jackson* (Boston: Little, Brown, 1950), 133–42; Harry L. Watson, *Liberty and Power: The Politics of Jacksonian American* (New York: Hill and Wang, 2006), 11–13; Sean Wilenz, *Andrew Jackson* (New York: Times Books, 2005), 6–9.

19. Hatch, *Democratization*, 40ff; Winthrop S. Hudson, "A Time of Religious Ferment," in *The Rise of Adventism: Religion and Society in Mid-Nineteenth-Century America*, ed. Edwin S. Gaustad (New York: Harper & Row, 1974), 3–5; Ira L. Mandelker, *Religion, Society, and Utopia in Nineteenth-Century America* (Amherst: University of Massachusetts, 1984), 41–42. Edwin Gaustad summarizes the relationship between political populism and religious populism as follows: "The Age of Jackson was also an Age of Finney as men sought or reveled in a direct confrontation with God—their sacred if not their democratic right." See "Introduction," in *Rise of Adventism*, xv.

20. Hatch, *Democratization*, 10; Ann Taves, *Fits, Trances, and Visions: Experiencing Religion and Explaining Experience from Wesley to James* (Princeton: Princeton University Press, 1999), 20–46.

21. A. Gregory Schneider has extensively analyzed the ways in which Methodism's success was made possible by its active recruitment of the sentimental discourse of domesticity and maternity, but the relationship between Methodism and sentimentalism was markedly reciprocal. See *Way of the Cross*, 122–208. See also Butler, *Awash*, 281.

22. Mary P. Ryan, *Cradle of the Middle Class: The Family in Oneida County, New York, 1790–1865* (Cambridge: Cambridge University Press, 1981), 12. Paul E. Johnson and Sean Wilentz have similarly observed that the era's revivalism initiated a dramatic change in domestic and marital relations. See *The Kingdom of Matthias* (New York: Oxford University Press, 1994), 7–8.

23. For a discussion of the religious status of early American women, see Laurel Thatcher Ulrich, *Good Wives: Image and Reality in the Lives of Women in Northern New England, 1650–1750* (New York: Random House, 1982), and Amanda Porterfield, *Feminine Spirituality in America: From Sarah Edwards to Martha Graham* (Philadelphia: Temple University Press, 1980).

24. Though modern scholars dispute the authenticity of this letter, it has nonetheless informed denominational strictures about the role of women in instruction and leadership.

25. Carroll Smith-Rosenberg, *Disorderly Conduct: Visions of Gender in Victorian America* (New York: Knopf, 1985), 129–30; Wigger, *Taking Heaven*, 152–72. For studies of female preachers, see Brekus, *Strangers and Pilgrims;* Catherine A. Brekus, "Female Evangelism in the Early Methodism Movement, 1784–1845," in *Methodism and the Shaping of American Culture*, 135–73; Paul Wesley Chilcote, *John Wesley and the Women Preachers of Early Methodism* (Metuchen, N.J.: Scarecrow, 1991); Elizabeth Elkin Grammer, *Some Wild Visions: Autobiographies by Female Itinerant Evangelists in Nineteenth-Century America* (New York: Oxford University Press, 2003); Jean Miller Schmidt, *Grace Sufficient: A History of Women in American Methodism, 1760–1939* (Nashville, Tenn.: Abingdon, 1999), 29–32, 99ff.

26. Ryan, *Cradle*, 83ff.

27. According to Elizabeth Elkins Grammer, evangelicalism also "invited women to undertake new roles as social workers, teachers, managers, missionaries, and writers." See *Some Wild Visions*, 6. See also Douglas, *Feminization*, 28–32; Scott, *From Office to Profession*, 53–75.

28. Anne M. Boylan, *Sunday School: The Formation of an American Institution, 1790–1880* (New Haven: Yale University Press, 1988), 114–23; Lois A. Boyd and R. Douglas Brackenridge, *Presbyterian Women in America: Two Centuries of a Quest for Status* (Westport, Conn.: Greenwood, 1993), 7; Brekus, *Strangers and Pilgrims*, 124; Nancy F. Cott, *The Bonds of Womanhood: Woman's Sphere in New England, 1780–1835* (New Haven: Yale University Press, 1977), 154; Karin E. Gedge, *Without Benefit of Clergy: Women and the Pastoral Relationship in Nineteenth-Century American Culture* (New York: Oxford University Press, 2003), 198–99, 202; Lori D. Ginzberg, *Women and the Work of Benevolence: Morality, Politics, and Class in the Nineteenth-Century United States* (New Haven: Yale University Press, 1990), 14; Leonard I. Sweet, *The Minister's Wife: Her Role in Nineteenth-Century American Evangelism* (Philadelphia: Temple University Press, 1983), 31–32.

29. Boyd and Brackenridge, *Presbyterian Women*, 93–94; Brekus, *Strangers and Pilgrims*, 119, 120, 133; Hardesty, *Woman Called to Witness*, 44. Mary Ryan, for instance, tracks the response in Oneida County, New York, in 1808 to a female itinerant preacher, and she likewise discerns the increasing erosion of this gendered prohibition. See *Cradle*, 72ff.

30. Hardman, *Finney*, 185.

31. Lawrence Foster, *Women, Family, and Utopia: Communal Experiments of the Shakers, the Oneida Community, and the Mormons* (Syracuse, N.Y.: Syracuse University Press, 1991), 226; Hardman, *Finney*, 101; Charles G. Finney, *Lectures on Revivals of Religion*, 2nd ed. (New York: Leavitt, Lord, 1835), 239–40.

32. Lydia Maria Child, "Speaking in the Church," in *A Lydia Maria Child Reader*, ed. Carolyn L. Karcher (Durham, N.C.: Duke University Press, 1997), 356.

33. Billington, *Protestant Crusade*, 347.

34. This claim is indebted to Elizabeth Maddock Dillon's work on the "intermediary" role of the text in enabling nineteenth-century women to comply with expectations

of domestic enclosure while still engaging in public intellectual discourse. See *The Gender of Freedom: Fictions of Liberalism and the Literary Public Sphere* (Stanford, Calif.: Stanford University Press, 2004), 4.

35. Mary Dewey, ed., *Life and Letters of Catharine M. Sedgwick* (New York: Harper, 1871), 249–50. Mary Kelley has discussed Sedgwick's religious ambitions for her writings. See Kelley, *Private Woman, Public Stage: Literary Domesticity in Nineteenth-Century America* (New York: Oxford University Press, 1984), 286, 289–91.

36. This letter, dated 31 January 1834, is included in Dewey, ed., *Life and Letters*, 239.

37. Catharine Sedgwick, *Home* (Boston: James Munroe, 1839), 65.

38. Anna B. Warner, *Susan Warner* (New York: Putnam, 1909), 264.

39. Thomas H. Skinner to Susan Warner, 24 June 1851. Special Collections of the Library of the United States Military Academy at West Point. Quoted with permission.

40. Nina Baym comments that the "most fervently pious domestic novels suggest that the women authors envisioned themselves as lay ministers, their books as evangelical sermons that might spur conversion." See *Woman's Fiction: A Guide to Novels by and About Women in America, 1820–1870*, 2nd ed. (Urbana: University of Illinois Press, 1993), 44.

41. Dawn Coleman has ably analyzed Stowe's use of ministerial oratorical technique in her essay "The Unsentimental Woman Preacher of Uncle Tom's Cabin," *American Literature* 80 (June 2008): 265–92.

42. Quoted in Charles Edward Stowe, ed., *Life of Harriet Beecher Stowe, Compiled from the Letters and Journals* (Boston: Houghton Mifflin, 1889), 335. This letter is dated 4 February 1859.

43. Harriet Beecher Stowe, *My Wife and I: or, Harry Henderson's History* (New York: J. B. Ford, 1871), 92.

44. Augusta J. Evans, *St. Elmo: A Novel* (1867; repr., New York: Arno, 1974), 292, 293.

45. Herbert Ross Brown similarly comments on the position of sentimentalism amid these secular spiritual enthusiasms. See *The Sentimental Novel in America, 1789–1860* (Durham, N.C.: Duke University Press, 1940), 181–200. Barbara Epstein's findings likewise concur with this assessment. See *Politics of Domesticity*, 89.

46. Ralph Waldo Emerson, "New England Reformers, Lecture at Amory Hall," in *Ralph Waldo Emerson: Essays and Lectures*, ed. Joel Porte (New York: Library of America, 1983), 592, 591.

47. Mabel Baker, *Light in the Morning: Memories of Susan and Anna Warner* (West Point, N.Y.: Constitution Island Association, 1978), 44.

48. Nancy Cott estimates that women outnumbered men by a third in these settings, although Richard Brown contends that women outnumbered men by a ratio of three to one. See Cott, "Young Women in the Second Great Awakening," *Feminist Studies* 3 (Autumn 1975): 15–16; Richard D. Brown, *Knowledge Is Power: The Diffusion of Information in Early America, 1700–1865* (New York: Oxford University Press, 1989), 162; Brekus, *Strangers and Pilgrims,* 124; Cott, *Bonds*, 127; Epstein, *Politics of Domesticity*, 45; Paul E. Johnson, *A Shopkeeper's Millennium: Society and Revivals in Rochester, New York,*

1815–1837 (New York: Hill & Wang, 1978), 108; Ryan, *Cradle*, 12, 61. Ann Douglas has also commented on the effects of disestablishment on what she termed the "feminization" of American Protestantism. See *Feminization*, 17–43.

49. Olivia Egleston Phelps Stokes, *Letters and Memories of Susan and Anna Bartlett Warner* (New York: Putnam, 1925), 26.

50. Quoted in Anna Warner, *Susan Warner*, 283.

51. Helen Papashvily has also attributed the publication of Warner's novel to the sensibilities of a previous generation of women, although she characterizes this generation by its exposure to the novels of Susanna Rowson. See Papashvily, *All the Happy Endings* (New York: Harper & Brothers, 1956), 10–11.

52. David Paul Nord, *Faith in Reading: Religious Publishing and the Birth of Mass Media in America* (New York: Oxford University Press, 2004), 115–18.

53. Quoted in Nord, *Faith in Reading*, 119. Unless specified otherwise, all italics in quotations replicate the formatting of their original publications.

54. Mary Ryan has observed the proliferation of this genre. See *Cradle*, 87–88. See also Schmidt, *Grace Sufficient*, 40ff.

55. Helen Papashvily, in an early study of sentimentalism, makes a similar claim, remarking that "tracts in quantity masqueraded as fiction." See *All the Happy Endings*, 4.

56. Nord, *Faith in Reading*, 115–22.

57. Tompkins, *Sensational*, 153–55.

58. Nord, *Faith in Reading*, 119–20.

59. Ginzberg, *Women and the Work of Benevolence*, 17, 54.

60. Warner, *Susan Warner*, 214–16.

61. In studying library loans records of the mid-century, Ronald J. Zboray concludes that men also read such works. This conclusion, however, does not undermine the explicit gendering of these novels and their direction to a young female readership. See "Reading Patterns in Antebellum America: Evidence in the Charge Records of the New York Society Library," *Libraries & Culture* 26 (Spring 1991), 301–33.

62. Baym, *Woman's Fiction*, ix.

63. Eve Cherniavsky, *That Pale Mother Rising: Sentimental Discourse and the Imitation of Motherhood in Nineteenth-Century America* (Bloomington: Indiana University Press, 1995), 106.

64. Cott, "Young Women," 17–18, 23.

65. According to Eve Cherniavsky, "sentimental attachment is governed by the logic of economic dependence." See Cherniavsky, *That Pale Mother*, 36.

66. For instance, Tracy Fessenden observes that the sentimental emphasis on domesticity "conspicuously defused revivalist energies," which seemed poised to become culturally disruptive. See *Culture and Redemption: Religion, the Secular, and American Culture* (Princeton: Princeton University Press, 2007), 90–91.

67. Dewey, ed., *Life and Letters*. For letters in which Sedgwick expresses annoyance, see, for example, letters dated 19 November 1824 and 15 September 1933, in which she refers to "religious agitators" and "fanatics."

68. In one letter, Benjamin Adams urges Susan Warner to attend an upcoming meeting, giving her advice about accommodations, but a letter later confirms that neither she nor her sister attended. See Benjamin Adams to Susan Warner, 9 August and 21 August 1864, Special Collections of the Library of the United States Military Academy at West Point. Quoted with permission.

69. Fred Louis Pattee, *The Feminine Fifties* (New York: Appleton, 1940), 8.

70. Brown, *Sentimental*, 81.

71. Papashvily, *All the Happy Endings*, 8.

72. Philip Fisher, *Hard Facts: Setting and Form in the American Novel* (New York: Oxford University Press, 1985), 95.

73. Joanne Dobson, "Reclaiming Sentimental Literature," *American Literature* 69 (June 1997): 268; Karen Sánchez-Eppler, *Touching Liberty: Abolition, Feminism and the Politics of the Body* (Berkeley: University of California Press, 1993), 26.

74. Lauren Berlant, *The Female Complaint: The Unfinished Business of Sentimentality in American Culture* (Durham, N.C.: Duke University Press, 2008), 35.

75. Some important works in this scholarly tradition include Elizabeth Barnes, *States of Sympathy: Seduction and Democracy in the American Novel* (New York: Columbia University Press, 1997); Bruce Burgett, *Sentimental Bodies: Sex, Gender, and Citizenship in the Early Republic* (Princeton: Princeton University Press, 1998); Elizabeth Maddock Dillon, "Sentimental Aesthetics," *American Literature* 76 (September 2004): 495–524; Julie Ellison, *Cato's Tears and the Making of Anglo-American Emotion* (Chicago: University of Chicago Press, 1999); Shirley Samuels, *Romance of the Republic: Women, the Family, and Violence in the Literature of the Early American Nation* (New York: Oxford University Press, 1996); Julia A. Stern, *The Plight of Feeling: Sympathy and Dissent in the Early American Novel* (Chicago: University of Chicago Press, 1997); and Van Engen, "Puritanism," 533–64.

76. June Howard, "What Is Sentimentality?" *American Literary History* 11 (Spring 1999): 69.

77. Walter L. Lingle and John W. Kuykendall, *Presbyterians: Their History and Beliefs* (Atlanta: John Knox, 1988), 106.

78. Quoted in Hardman, *Charles Finney*, 115–16. This passage also appears in Perry Miller, *The Life of the Mind in America: From the Revolution to the Civil War* (New York: Harcourt, Brace, 1965), 26.

79. Finney, *Lectures*, 339.

80. Charles E. Hambrick-Stowe, *Charles G. Finney and the Spirit of American Evangelicalism* (Grand Rapids, Mich.: Eerdmans, 1996), 158–59.

81. Though she declines to speculate why, Barbara Epstein has shown that early-nineteenth-century women tended to find these orthodox interrogations particularly grating, which may explain why women gravitated in remarkable numbers to the new heart-centered evangelicalism propounded in revivalism. See *Politics of Domesticity*, 55–57.

82. Warner, *Susan Warner*, 202.

83. Hatch, *Democratization*, 137.

84. Elisabeth Jay, *The Religion of the Heart: Anglican Evangelicalism and the Nineteenth-Century Novel* (Oxford: Clarendon, 1979), 104.

85. Boyd and Brackenridge, *Presbyterian Women*, 94; Cott, "Young Women," 21; Colleen McDannell, *The Christian Home in Victorian America, 1840–1900* (Bloomington: Indiana University Press, 1986), 128; Sweet, *Minister's Wife*, 31–32.

86. Sharon Kim has argued that Warner's *The Wide, Wide World* is influenced by Puritan theology, and this chapter diverges from that critical position by contending instead that the novel registers the influence of contemporary heterodoxy, which Warner's own papers amply evidence sympathy toward. See Kim, "Puritan Realism," 783–812.

87. Hardesty, *Woman Called to Witness*, 87–88.

88. R. Marie Griffith, *God's Daughters: Evangelical Women and the Power of Submission* (Berkeley: University of California Press, 1997), 123; Karen Halttunen, *Confidence Men and Painted Women: A Study of Middle-Class Culture in America, 1830–1870* (New Haven: Yale University Press, 1982), 57.

89. Susan Warner, *Queechy* (1852; repr., Philadelphia: J. B. Lippincott, 1907), 316.

90. Harriet Beecher Stowe, *Uncle Tom's Cabin or, Life Among the Lowly*, ed. Ann Douglas (1852; repr., New York: Penguin, 1981), 624.

91. William James, "The Varieties of Religious Experience," in *William James: Writings, 1902–1910*, ed. Bruce Kuklick (New York: Library of America, 1987), 159, 185.

92. R. Marie Griffith writes, "The first step . . . is the recognition of one's own sinfulness and profound need for forgiveness and mercy." See *God's Daughters*, 99. See also Schneider, *Way of the Cross*, 44.

93. Augusta J. Evans, *Beulah* (1859; repr., New York: Grosset & Dunlap, nd), 70.

94. Madeline Leslie, *The Household Angel in Disguise* (1857; repr., Boston: Shepard, Clark, 1860), 242.

95. Joycelyn Moody, *Sentimental Confessions: Spiritual Narratives of Nineteenth-Century African American Women* (Athens: University of Georgia Press, 2001), 10.

96. For instance, Sandra Gustafson has suggested the influence of conversion narratives, a vital narrative form of the Second Great Awakening, on sentimentalism. See "Margaret Fuller and the Forms of Sentiment," *American Quarterly* 47 (March 1995): 36–37.

97. Griffith, *God's Daughters*, 17; Susan F. Harding, "Convicted by the Spirit: The Rhetoric of Fundamental Baptist Conversion," *American Ethnologist* 14 (February 1987): 167–81; Elaine J. Lawless, "Rescripting Their Lives and Narratives: Spiritual Life Stories of Pentecostal Women Preachers," *Journal of Feminist Studies in Religion* 7 (Spring 1991): 54. This phenomenon is indebted to the sympathetic identification that Glenn Hendler has characterized as endemic to sentimental literature. See *Public Sentiments: Structures of Feeling in Nineteenth-Century American Literature* (Chapel Hill: University of North Carolina Press, 2001), 3–13.

98. Harding, "Rescripting," 167, 169. This practice comports with Elizabeth Barnes's observation that "sentimental fiction's evocation of personal feeling becomes a necessary precondition for participating in the feeling of others." See *States of Sympathy*, 18.

99. Maria Susanna Cummins, *The Lamplighter*, ed. Nina Baym (1854; repr., New Brunswick, N.J.: Rutgers University Press, 1988), 322.

100. Paul J. Griffiths, *Religious Reading: The Place of Reading in the Practice of Religion* (New York: Oxford University Press, 1999), 3.

101. James D. Bratt, "The Reorientation of American Protestantism, 1835–1845," *Church History* 67 (March 1998): 52–82; Mandelker, *Religion, Society, and Utopia*, 43–45; Mark Noll, *America's God: From Jonathan Edwards to Abraham Lincoln* (New York: Oxford University Press, 2002), 341; Schmidt, *Grace Sufficient*, 51.

102. Hardman, *Charles Finney*, 51; Mandelker, *Religion, Society, and Utopia*, 43–45; Noll, *America's God*, 341.

103. Hardman, *Charles Finney*, x, 14; Johnson, *Shopkeeper's Millennium*, 3, 5, 96; William G. McLoughlin, *Modern Revivalism: Charles Grandison Finney to Billy Graham* (New York: Ronald, 1959), 11.

104. Finney, *Lectures*, 9, 188.

105. Miller, *Life of the Mind*, 32.

106. Quoted in Miller, *Life of the Mind*, 33.

107. Cushing Strout discusses the influence of Finneyite Arminianism on Stowe in his essay "*Uncle Tom's Cabin* and the Portent of Millennium," *Yale Review* 57 (Spring 1968), 380. This argument also diverges from Nina Baym's assertion that Warner's *Wide, Wide World* is "Calvinist fiction." See Baym, *Woman's Fiction*, xxiv.

108. Noble, *Masochistic Pleasures*, 52ff. Sedgwick mocks Calvinism chiefly with her portrait of Mrs. Wilson, a sanctimonious but utterly selfish and cruel Calvinist who is convinced not only of her election but also that this divine favor exempts her from ever having to perform good works. Stowe, on the other hand, took aim at this older theology with a brief aside in *My Wife and I*: she wrote, "If you are ever to be married, your wife is probably now in the world; some house holds her, and there are mortal eyes at this hour to whom her lineaments are as familiar as they are unknown to you. So much for the doctrine of predestination" (127).

109. Caroline Chesebro', *Victoria; or, The World Overcome* (New York: Derby and Jackson, 1856), 42.

110. Maria J. McIntosh, *Woman in America: Her Work and Her Reward* (New York: Appleton, 1850), 63–64.

111. Warner, *Queechy*, 166-67.

112. Susan Warner and Anna Warner [pseudonymously as Elizabeth Wetherell and Amy Lathrop], *Say and Seal*, vol. 1 of 2 (Philadelphia: J. B. Lippincott, 1860), 76.

113. John Seelye offers a different take on this quality of sentimentalism, finding in it a "strong antinomian undercurrent." In my view, the obedience and scriptural attachments inherent in sentimentalism undercut such a claim. Nina Baym, however, acknowledges the relative impotence of ministers in this literary canon, observing that "ministers appeal to the heroine not in their official capacity, however, but as loving friends." Barbara Epstein's formulation is particularly germane here, for she contends that "popular women's culture in nineteenth-century America . . . expressed a complex

amalgam of reactions to male power: protest, resentment, disapproval, fear, accommo-dation." See John Seelye, Jane Eyre's *American Daughters from the* Wide, Wide World *to* Anne of Green Gables: *A Study of Marginalized Maids and What They Mean* (Newark: University of Delaware Press, 2005), 94; Baym, *Woman's Fiction*, 44; Epstein, *Politics of Domesticity*, 9.

114. Maria J. McIntosh, *Charms and Counter-Charms* (New York: D. Appleton, 1848), 185.

115. Nina Baym has made a similar observation, noting that the "the task of guiding souls to God is no longer restricted to, indeed becomes quite separated from, those who have been ordained in the patriarchal social institution." Baym, *Woman's Fiction*, 44.

116. Barbara Welter, "The Cult of True Womanhood," *American Quarterly* 1 (Sum-mer 1966): 151–74; Noble, *Masochistic Pleasures*, 55ff; Laura Wexler, "Seeing Sentiment: Photography, Race, and the Innocent Eye," in *American Literary Studies: A Methodolog-ical Reader*, ed. Michael A. Elliott and Claudia Stokes (New York: New York University Press, 2003), 63–94.

117. John Wesley, *A Plain Account of Christian Perfection* (1872; repr., Kansas City: Beacon Hill Press, 1966), 19.

118. Hardman, *Finney*, 324.

119. R. Newton Flew, *The Idea of Perfection in Christian Theology: An Historical Study of the Christian Ideal for the Present Life* (London: Oxford University Press, 1934), 313–41. My definition of mysticism comes from Catherine Albanese, who defines it as "a total union with God in which, traditionally, normal and everyday consciousness disappears. . . . The goal of the mystic is a totality and completion in which he or she no longer lives as a separate human being, but God utterly engulfs the individual. . . . The mystic, in short, *becomes* God." See "Mormonism and the Male-Female God: An Explo-ration in Active Mysticism," *Sunstone* 6 (March–April 1981): 55.

120. Finney, *Lectures*, 389.

121. Quoted in Fessenden, *Culture and Redemption*, 93.

122. Cummins, *Lamplighter*, 194, 291, 249.

123. Quoted in Cummins, *Lamplighter*, 127.

124. Dewey, ed., *Life and Letters*, 197.

125. Bratt, "Reorientation," 79; Marie Caskey, *Chariot of Fire: Religion and the Beecher Family* (New Haven: Yale University Press, 1978), 141; Joan D. Hedrick, *Harriet Beecher Stowe: A Life* (New York: Oxford University Press, 1994), 145.

126. Gordon Campbell, *Bible: The Story of the King James Version, 1611–2011* (Ox-ford: Oxford University Press, 2010), 158–59.

127. Billington, *Protestant Crusade*, 42–43.

128. Ibid., 157.

129. Rebecca Theresa Reed, *Six Months in a Convent* (1835; repr., New York: Arno, 1977), 133.

130. Maria Monk, *Awful Disclosures of the Hotel Dieu Nunnery*, ed. Ray Allen Bill-ington (1836; repr., Hamden, Conn.: Archon, 1962), 99.

131. Edward Beecher, *The Papal Conspiracy Exposed, and Protestantism Defended, in the Light of Reason, History and Scripture* (Boston: Stearns, 1855), 231.

132. Billington, *Protestant Crusade*, 143; Fessenden, *Culture and Redemption*, 60–83.

133. Susan Warner, *The Wide, Wide World* (1850; repr., New York: Feminist, 1987), 73.

134. Ibid., 352.

135. Warner, *Queechy*, 133.

136. Paul C. Gutjahr, *An American Bible: A History of the Good Book in the United States, 1777–1880* (Stanford, Calif.: Stanford University Press, 1999), 2–3, 16; Hatch, *Democratization*, 44ff; Lefferts Loetscher, *A Brief History of the Presbyterians*, 4th ed. (Philadelphia: Westminster, 1983), 90; Noll, *America's God*, 379–82; Nord, *Faith in Reading*, 27–40.

137. Paul K. Conklin, *American Originals: Homemade Varieties of Christianity* (Chapel Hill: University of North Carolina Press, 1997), 1–3; Gutjahr, *American Bible*, 101ff. This summary of Campbellite doctrine is indebted to Edwin R. Groover, *The Well-Ordered Home: Alexander Campbell and the Family* (Joplin, Mo.: College Press, 1988), 12–14; Stephen V. Sprinkle, *Disciples and Theology: Understanding the Faith of a People in Covenant* (St. Louis: Chalice, 1999), 13–46.

138. Bratt, "Reorientation," 66; Fessenden, *Culture and Redemption*, 92; Hatch, *Democratization*, 63–64; Hudson, "Time of Religious Ferment," 8; Richard T. Hughes, "Christian Primitivism as Perfectionism: From Anabaptists to Pentecostals," in *Reaching Beyond: Chapters in the History of Perfectionism*, ed. Stanley M. Burgess (Peabody, Mass.: Hendrickson, 1986), 213–55.

139. Catharine Maria Sedgwick, *Hope Leslie; or, Early Times in the Massachusetts*, ed. Mary Kelley (1827; repr., New Brunswick, N.J.: Rutgers University Press, 1995), 123.

140. Catharine M. Sedgwick, *A New-England Tale, and Miscellanies* (1822; repr., New York: Putnam, 1852), 35, 102, 167–68.

141. Warner, *Wide, Wide World*, 277.

142. Alice Cary, "My Creed," *American Women Poets of the Nineteenth Century: An Anthology*, ed. Cheryl Walker (New Brunswick, N.J.: Rutgers University Press, 1995), 176–77.

143. Evans, *Beulah*, 241.

144. Susan Warner to Mary Lindley, 25 January 1883. Constitution Island Research Center, Highland Falls, New York. Quoted with permission.

145. Anna Warner to David McKell, 28 October 1904 and 21 November 1904, Constitution Island Research Center, Highland Falls, New York. Quoted with permission.

146. Warner, *Queechy*, 428.

147. See, for example, the testimony in the following text: "Colonel Lathe B. Row, USMA Class 1913," *Constitution Island Annual Report* (1981): 15–16.

148. Susan Warner, "The Bought Field," Sunday School lessons, lesson 34, Box 2, np, Constitution Island Research Center, Highland Falls, New York. Quoted with permission.

149. Susan Warner, *The Law and the Testimony* (New York: Robert Carter, 1853), iii.

150. Samuels, *Culture of Sentiment*, 5.

151. Nancy Bentley, "Marriage as Treason: Polygamy, Nation, and the Novel," in *The Futures of American Studies*, ed. Donald E. Pease and Robyn Wiegman (Durham, N.C.: Duke University Press, 2002), 343–70.

152. Henry James, "The Art of Fiction," in *The Art of Criticism: Henry James on the Theory and the Practice of Fiction*, ed. William Veeder and Susan M. Griffin (Chicago: University of Chicago Press, 1986), 168.

153. Quoted in David S. Reynolds, *Faith in Fiction: The Emergence of Religious Literature in American* (Cambridge, Mass.: Harvard University Press, 1981), 1.

154. Stowe, *My Wife and I*, 2.

155. For a fuller discussion of this phenomenon, see my essay "The Religious Novel," in *The Oxford History of the Novel in English*, vol. 6, *The American Novel: 1870–1940*, ed. Priscilla Wald and Michael A. Elliott (New York: Oxford University Press, 2014), 168–83.

156. Quoted in Clifford Putney, *Muscular Christianity: Manhood and Sports in Protestant America, 1880–1920* (Cambridge, Mass.: Harvard University Press, 2001), 31–32.

Chapter 2. My Kingdom

1. Louisa May Alcott, "Little Women," *Louisa May Alcott*, ed. Elaine Showalter (New York: Library of America, 2005), 175.

2. In this respect, the sentimental constitution of hymnody adheres to the "double logic of power and powerlessness" characterized by Shirley Samuels. See "Introduction," in *Culture of Sentiment: Race, Gender, and Sentimentality in Nineteenth-Century America* (New York: Oxford University Press, 1992), 4.

3. Samuel Rogal, *A General Introduction to Hymnody and Congregational Song* (Metuchen, N.J.: American Theological Library Association, 1991), 22–23.

4. Margaret Maison, "'Thine, Only Thine!' Women Hymn Writers in Britain, 1760–1835," in *Religion in the Lives of English Women, 1760–1930*, ed. Gail Malmgreen (Bloomington: Indiana University Press, 1986), 12.

5. John Wesley, *A Collection of Hymns for the Use of the People Called Methodists*, vol. 7, *The Works of John Wesley*, ed. Franz Hildebrandt and Oliver A. Beckerlegge (Oxford: Clarendon, 1983), 765.

6. *The Bay Psalm Book, Being a Facsimile Reprint of the First Edition, Printed by Stephen Daye, at Cambridge in New England, 1640* (New York: Dodd, Mead, 1905), xviii, n.p.

7. Gareth Lloyd, *Charles Wesley and the Struggle for Methodist Identity* (New York: Oxford, 2007), 73, 74.

8. Isaac Watts, "Preface," in *Hymns and Spiritual Songs* (1707; repr., London: Strahan and Rivington, 1773), iii, iv.

9. Ibid., vii–viii.

10. Isaac Watts, *Divine and Moral Songs for Children* (1715; repr., New York: Hurd and Houghton, 1866), 9.

11. Watts, *Hymns and Spiritual Songs,* viii–ix.

12. In her landmark study of the Second Great Awakening in Oneida County, New York, Mary P. Ryan traces the presence and wide circulation of Isaac Watts's hymns within this vital center of American religious life in the first half of the nineteenth century. See Ryan, *Cradle of the Middle Class: The Family in Oneida County, New York, 1790–1865* (Cambridge: Cambridge University Press, 1981), 32–35.

13. Henry Ward Beecher, "Introduction," in *Plymouth Collection of Hymns and Tunes; For the Use of Christian Congregations* (New York: A. S. Barnes, 1855), iii.

14. Lowell Mason, Edwards Park, and Austin Phelps, eds., *The Sabbath Hymn and Tune Book, for the Service of Song in the House of the Lord* (New York: Mason Brothers, 1865), iv.

15. Anna Warner, "Preface," in *Hymns of the Church Militant* (New York: Robert Carter, 1865), iv.

16. Emma R. Pittman, *Lady Hymn Writers* (London: T. Nelson, 1892), 64.

17. S. Paul Schilling, *The Faith We Sing* (Philadelphia: Westminster, 1983), 44, 48.

18. A. J. Lewis, *Zinzendorf, The Ecumenical Pioneer: A Study in the Moravian Contribution to Christian Mission and Unity* (Philadelphia: Westminster, 1962), 168.

19. J. Taylor Hamilton and Kenneth G. Hamilton, *History of the Moravian Church: The Renewed Unitas Fratrum, 1722–1957* (Bethlehem, Pa.: Moravian Church of America, 1967), 164, 169.

20. Lewis, *Zinzendorf,* 169.

21. Quoted in Schilling, *Faith We Sing,* 25.

22. Quoted in Lewis, *Zinzendorf,* 163.

23. Lewis, *Zinzendorf,* 13, 12.

24. Ibid., 182ff.

25. Ibid., 164.

26. Lloyd, *Charles Wesley,* 74; Franz Hildebrandt, Introduction to "A Little Body of Practical Divinity," in *The Works of John Wesley,* vol. 7, *A Collection of Hymns for the Use of the People Called Methodists,* ed. F. Hildebrandt and Oliver A. Beckerlegge (Oxford: Clarendon, 1983), 22.

27. Quoted in Lloyd, *Charles Wesley,* 74.

28. Quoted in Lewis, *Zinzendorf,* 17.

29. Wesley, *Collection of Hymns,* 74; Watts, *Preface to Hymns and Spiritual Songs,* vi.

30. Wesley, *Collection of Hymns* 75.

31. Ibid., 765.

32. Mark A. Noll corroborates this argument in *America's God: From Jonathan Edwards to Abraham Lincoln* (New York: Oxford University Press, 2002), 336–37; Jon Butler, *Awash in a Sea of Faith: Christianizing the American People* (Cambridge, Mass.: Harvard University Press, 1990), 239–40.

33. A. Gregory Schneider, *The Way of the Cross Leads Home: The Domestication of American Methodism* (Bloomington: Indiana University Press, 1993), xx.

34. For a fuller history of this phenomenon, see Catherine A. Brekus, *Strangers and*

Pilgrims: Female Preaching in America, 1740–1845 (Chapel Hill: University of North Carolina Press, 1996), and Nancy A. Hardesty, *A Woman Called to Witness: Evangelical Feminism in the 19th Century* (Nashville, Tenn.: Abingdon, 1984).

35. Ann Taves, *Fits, Trances, and Visions: Experiencing Religion and Explaining Experience from Wesley to James* (Princeton: Princeton University Press, 1999), 76–117.

36. Nathan O. Hatch, *The Democratization of American Christianity* (New Haven: Yale University Press, 1989), 151–53.

37. Louis F. Benson, *The English Hymn: Its Development and Use in Worship* (New York: Hodder & Stoughton, 1915), 359, 360; William J. Reynolds, *A Survey of Christian Hymnody* (Carol Stream, Ill.: Hope, 1987), 87.

38. Sandra S. Sizer, *Gospel Hymns and Social Religion: The Rhetoric of Nineteenth-Century Religion* (Philadelphia: Temple University Press, 1978), 66-67; Reynolds, *Christian Hymnody*, 92.

39. William G. McLoughlin, *Revivals, Awakenings, and Reform: An Essay on Religion and Social Change in America, 1607–1977* (Chicago: University of Chicago Press, 1978), 11.

40. In 1830, both the Presbyterians and Congregationalists issued hymnals, and the Baptists followed in 1843. See Susan VanZanten Gallagher, "Domesticity in American Hymns, 1820–1870," in *Sing Them Over Again to Me: Hymns and Hymnbooks in America*, ed. Mark A. Noll and Edith L. Blumhofer (Tuscaloosa: University of Alabama Press, 2006), 239–40.

41. Jon Butler observes that denominations in the antebellum era sought to strengthen their authority with the publication of sectarian texts. Denominational hymnbooks certainly functioned in that capacity. See *Awash*, 277. Candy Gunther Brown also discusses the contribution of hymnals to denominationalism. See *The Word in the World: Evangelical Writing, Publishing, and Reading in America, 1789–1880* (Chapel Hill: University of North Carolina Press, 2004), 221–26.

42. Mary De Jong, " 'Theirs the Sweetest Songs': Women Hymn Writers in the Nineteenth-Century Unites States," in *A Mighty Baptism: Race, Gender, and the Creation of American Protestantism*, ed. Susan Juster and Lisa MacFarlane (Ithaca, N.Y.: Cornell University Press, 1996), 149.

43. Henry Wilder Foote, *Three Centuries of American Hymnody* (Cambridge, Mass.: Harvard University Press, 1940), 203.

44. Benson, *English Hymn*, 375–76.

45. Gallagher, "Domesticity," 240.

46. Asahel Nettleton, "Preface," in *Village Hymns for Social Worship, Selected and Original*, 2nd ed. (New York: Goodwin, 1824), v–vi. In the latter portion of these remarks, Nettleton quotes from, and agrees with, an unattributed letter from a "much respected correspondent" (vi).

47. This reactive gesture comports with Mary Ryan's observation that the nineteenth-century "reverence for quiet, seclusion, and privacy was usually portrayed in popular

literature as a reflexive reaction to repellent developments outside the household." See Ryan, *Cradle*, 147.

48. Susan Warner, *The Wide, Wide World* (New York: Feminist, 1987), 241.

49. Marianne Noble has analyzed the ways in which sentimental fiction presents invisibility as a hallmark of feminine piety. See *The Masochistic Pleasures of Sentimental Literature* (Princeton: Princeton University Press, 2000), 33.

50. Joan Shelley Rubin, *The Making of Middle-Brow Culture* (Chapel Hill: University of North Carolina Press, 1992), 4–5; Ryan, *Cradle*, 146ff; Ronald J. Zboray, *A Fictive People: Antebellum Economic Development and the American Reading Public* (New York: Oxford University Press, 1993), 84; Thomas Augst, *The Clerk's Tale: Young Men and Moral Life in Nineteenth-Century America* (Chicago: University of Chicago Press, 2003), 177–91.

51. For a more extensive discussion of the centrality of self-control in sentimental narrative, see Jane Tompkins, *Sensational Designs: The Cultural Work of American Fiction, 1790–1860* (New York: Oxford University Press, 1985), 165ff.

52. Harriet Beecher Stowe, *Agnes of Sorrento* (Boston: Ticknor and Fields, 1862), 247, 151.

53. Stowe," The First Christmas of New England," *Betty's Bright Idea* (New York: J. B. Ford, 1876), 93.

54. Stowe, *Oldtown Folks* (1869; reprint, New Brunswick, N.J.: Rutgers University Press, 1987), 331.

55. Lyman Beecher's involvement in the changing attitudes and practices of devotional music are described in an anecdote by important hymnist Lowell Mason in *The Autobiography, Correspondence, &c. of Lyman Beecher*, vol. 2, ed. Charles Beecher (London: Sampson Low, Son and Marsden, 1863), 150–51.

56. Harriet Beecher Stowe, *Uncle Tom's Cabin or, Life among the Lowly*, ed. Ann Douglas (1852; repr., New York: Penguin, 1981), 44.

57. Ibid., 77, 78.

58. Nina Baym has analyzed the ways in which sentimentalism generally advocates this perception of suffering as temporary trials diminished by the awareness of a broader spiritual context. See *Woman's Fiction: A Guide to Novels by and About Women in America, 1820–1870*, 2nd ed. (Urbana: University of Illinois Press, 1993), 42.

59. Stowe, *Uncle Tom's Cabin*, 554.

60. Ibid., 555. According to Jonathan Aitken, Stowe made some editorial changes to these verses, switching the first lines of the first two stanzas. In addition, Stowe contributes a new final verse to the hymn and inserts a line from the hymn "Jerusalem, My Happy Home" as well as elements from revival hymnody. See Aitken, *John Newton: From Disgrace to Amazing Grace* (Wheaton, Ill.: Crossways, 2007), 235

61. Stowe, *Uncle Tom's Cabin*, 556.

62. Ibid., 557.

63. Ibid., 77.

64. Stowe, *Dred: A Dismal Tale of the Great Swamp*, vol. 2 of 2 (1856; repr., Gross Pointe, Mich.: Scholarly, 1968), 15.

65. Louisa May Alcott, *Under the Lilacs* (Boston: Little, Brown, 1928), 111–12.

66. Mary De Jong, "'I Want to Be Like Jesus': The Self-Defining Power of Evangelical Hymnody," *Journal of the American Academy of Religion* 54 (Autumn 1986): 461.

67. Henry Ward Beecher, "Introduction," in *Plymouth Collection*, vii.

68. In her memoir of the Cary sisters, Mary Clemmer Ames writes, "No singer was ever more thoroughly identified with her own songs than Phoebe Cary. With but few exceptions, they distilled the deepest and sweetest music of her soul." See *A Memorial of Alice and Phoebe Cary, with Some of Their Later Poems* (New York: Hurd and Houghton, 1873), 155.

69. Sources differ on the original title of Brown's poem. Some sources, such as Mary De Jong and Edward Ninde, title the poem as "My Apology for My Twilight Rambles, Address to a Lady," while others omit the possessive "My" altogether.

70. Nettleton would remove all references to personal content and replace them with more broadly inclusive lines. For example, he removed the gender-specific line "From little ones and care" and replaced it with "From every cumbering care." See De Jong, "Sweetest," 150; E. E. Ryden, *The Story of Christian Hymnody* (Rock Island, Ill.: Augustana, 1961), 472.

71. Nicholas Smith, *Songs from the Hearts of Women: One Hundred Famous Hymns and Their Writers* (Chicago: A. C. McClurg, 1903), 37; Ninde, *American Hymn*, 178-79, 181.

72. F. Elizabeth Gray, "Beatification Through Beautification: Poetry in *The Christian Lady's Magazine*, 1834–1849," *Victorian Poetry* 42 (2004): 267.

73. Lauren Berlant, "The Female Woman: Fanny Fern and the Form of Containment," in *The Culture of Sentiment: Race, Gender, and Sentimentality in Nineteenth-Century America*, ed. Shirley Samuels (New York: Oxford University Press, 1992), 268.

74. De Jong, "Sweetest," 164. This negotiation of the private with the public comports with Amy Schrager Lang's analysis of the problem of the "public woman" in mid-century letters, one managed by the public, literary retreat into domestic confinement. See Lang, *Prophetic Woman: Anne Hutchinson and the Problem of Dissent in the Literature of New England* (Berkeley, University of California Press, 1987). It likewise confirms Elizabeth Maddock Dillon's observation that the private sphere is "constructed and articulated in the public sphere" and that the "privacy of women is the product not of women's seclusion within their homes, but of a public articulation and valuation of woman's domestic position." See Dillon, *The Gender of Freedom: Fictions of Liberalism and the Literary Public Sphere* (Stanford, Calif.: Stanford University Press, 2004), 4.

75. Dillon, *Gender of Freedom*, 6.

76. In this regard, the hymn complies with what Lauren Berlant has termed "women's intimate public": a public presentation that presents itself as confidential and private. See *The Female Complaint: The Unfinished Business of Sentimentality in American Culture* (Durham, N.C.: Duke University Press, 2008), 27.

77. June Howard has analyzed more extensively the conflicted insistence on emo-

tional authenticity in sentimental literature. See "What Is Sentimentality?" *American Literary History* 11 (1999): 65–66.

78. De Jong, "Sweetest," 154–55; Rogal, *Sisters*, xi–xii.

79. De Jong, "Sweetest," 143; Gray, "Beatification," 262.

80. She wrote that the Magnificat shows "evidence of a soul not only exalted by genius and enthusiasm, but steeped in the traditions of ancient prophecy. It's so like the Psalms of David that a verse of it, if read casually, might seem to be taken from them." See Harriet Beecher Stowe, *Footsteps of the Master* (New York: J. B. Ford, 1877), 71.

81. Hobbs, *"I Sing for I Cannot Be Silent": The Feminization of American Hymnody, 1870–1920* (Pittsburgh: University of Pittsburgh Press, 1997, 116; Elizabeth Elkin Grammer, *Some Wild Visions: Autobiographies by Female Itinerant Evangelists in Nineteenth-Century America* (New York: Oxford University Press, 2003), 5.

82. Quoted in *The Life and Letters of Elizabeth Prentiss*, ed. George Prentiss (New York: Anson D.F. Randolph, 1882), 422.

83. Fanny J. Crosby, *Memories of Eighty Years* (Boston: James H. Earle, 1906), 166–67.

84. Mary Kelley has argued that this entanglement of private and public personae is characteristic of sentimental literature more generally. See *Private Woman, Public Stage: Literary Domesticity in Nineteenth-Century America* (New York: Oxford University Press, 1984).

85. Ninde, *American Hymn*, 248–49.

86. De Jong, "Sweetest," 156.

87. Ryden, *Christian Hymnody*, 521.

88. Robert J. Morgan, *Then Sings My Soul: 150 of the World's Greatest Hymn Stories* (Nashville, Tenn.: Thomas Nelson, 2003), 129; Ninde, *American Hymn*, 245.

89. Quoted in W. McDonald, Joshua Gill, et al., *Songs of Joy and Gladness* (Boston: McDonald, Gill, 1888), 74.

90. Quoted in Eva Munson Smith, *Woman in Sacred Song: A Library of Hymns, Religious Poems, and Sacred Music by Woman* (Chicago: Standard Music, 1888), 668.

91. Quoted in Charles W. Wendté and H. S. Perkins, *The Sunny Side: A Book of Religious Songs for the Sunday School and the Home* (New York: William A. Pond, 1875), 45. Charles Hughes confuses Alcott's explanations for "My Kingdom" and attributes this preface in *Sunny Side* to a letter to Eva Smith. See Hughes, *American Hymns Old and New: Notes on the Hymns and Biographies of the Authors and Composers* (New York: Columbia University Press, 1980), 136–37.

92. Alcott, *Under the Lilacs*, 114. Critics would pursue Alcott's autobiographical claim by attempting to generate the requisite background story attesting to the hymn's creation and worth. Such a story has proved elusive but would begin the year following Alcott's death with the publication of Alcott's postmortem *Life, Letters and Journals* (1889), edited by Ednah Cheney, a New England writer and reformer who wrote the occasional hymn. In that work she reprinted Alcott's journal entry from August 1850, where at the age of eighteen, in confessing to feelings of disorderliness, she recalled a

poem she'd written years before: "I'm not a good housekeeper, and never get my room
in nice order. I once wrote a poem about it when I was fourteen, and called it 'My Little Kingdom.' It is still hard to rule it, and always will be I think" (quoted in Ednah D.
Cheney, ed., *Louisa May Alcott: Her Life, Letters, and Journals* [1889; repr., New York:
Chelsea House, 1980], 59). Cheney reproduced the poem in its entirety as an epigraph
to her chapter on Alcott's experience at Fruitlands, her father's famously unsuccessful
attempt at a Utopian commune, and subsequent critics, such as Karen Haltunnen, have
taken that placement as confirmation that Alcott wrote "My Kingdom" while at Fruitlands, although she was only ten years old at the time and she claims to have written it
in early adolescence at age thirteen or fourteen. Regardless, no definitive story has ever
emerged. See Haltunnen, "The Domestic Drama of Louisa May Alcott," *Feminist Studies*
10 (1984): 237.

93. Quoted in Anna Warner, *Susan Warner* (New York: Putnam, 1901), 342–43.

94. For elaboration on the use of self-erasure in nineteenth-century women's poetry, see Paula Bernat Bennett, *The Emancipatory Project of American Women's Poetry,
1800–1900* (Princeton: Princeton University Press, 2003), 25–27.

95. Anna Warner, *Glen Luna; or, Dollars and Cents* (London: James Nisbet, 1870),
253. This edition was published using Warner's pseudonym, Amy Lathrop, and one of
the novel's numerous alternate titles.

96. In this regard, the history of nineteenth-century hymnody echoes Jane Tompkins oft-cited observation that mid-century women writers advocated submission and
decorum as an indirect means of achieving authority. See *Sensational Designs*, 163.

97. Henry Ward Beecher, "Relations of Music to Worship," *Yale Lectures on Preaching*, vol. 2 of 3 (New York: Fords, Howard, and Hurlbert, 1896), 129.

98. Brown, *Word in the World*, 191–92; De Jong, "Sweetest," 141–42.

99. Brown, *Word in the World*, 200.

100. Beecher, "Relations of Music," 137.

Chapter 3. The Christian Plot

1. Ernest Sandeen, "Millennialism," *The Rise of Adventism: Religion and Society in
Mid-Nineteenth-Century America*, ed. Edwin S. Gaustad (New York: Harper & Row,
1974), 110; Nathan O. Hatch, "The Origins of Civil Millennialism in America: New England Clergymen, War with France, and the Revolution," *William and Mary Quarterly*
31 (July 1974): 185–88.

2. Ernest Tuveson, *Redeemer Nation: The Idea of America's Millennial Role* (Chicago:
University of Chicago Press, 1968), 83–84; James D. Bratt, "The Reorientation of American Protestantism, 1835–1845," *Church History* 67 (March 1998): 52.

3. Michael Barkun, *Crucible of the Millennium: The Burned-Over District of New
York in the 1840s* (Syracuse, N.Y.: Syracuse University Press, 1986), 52; Joshua D. Bellin,
"Up to Heaven's Gate, Down in Earth's Dust," *American Literature* 65 (June 1993): 279.

4. Jonathan M. Butler, "Adventism and the American Experience," in *The Rise of Ad-*

ventism: Religion and Society in Mid-Nineteenth-Century America, ed. Edwin S. Gaustad (New York: Harper & Row, 1974), 174.

5. Herbert Ross Brown, *The Sentimental Novel in America, 1789–1860* (Durham, N.C.: Duke University Press, 1940), 181.

6. Catharine Sedgwick, *Home* (Boston: James Munroe, 1839), 40.

7. Susan Warner, *The Wide, Wide, World* (New York: Feminist, 1987), 312.

8. Sarah Josepha Hale, *Northwood or, Life North and South* (1852; repr., Freeport, N.Y.: Books for Libraries Press, 1972), 171.

9. For a discussion of Stowe's use of sermonic styles, see Dawn Coleman, "The Unsentimental Preachers of *Uncle Tom's Cabin*," *American Literature* 80 (June 2008): 265–92.

10. Harriet Beecher Stowe, *Uncle Tom's Cabin or, Life among the Lowly*, ed. Ann Douglas (1852; repr., New York: Penguin, 1981), 629.

11. Studies of the millennialism of *Uncle Tom's Cabin* include the following sources: Bellin, "Up to Heaven's Gate," 276; Gayle Kimball, *The Religious Ideas of Harriet Beecher Stowe: Her Gospel of Womanhood* (New York: Edwin Mellen, 1982); James Moorhead, *American Apocalypse: Yankee Protestants and the Civil War* (New Haven: Yale University Press, 1978); Kevin Pelletier, "*Uncle Tom's Cabin* and Apocalyptic Sentimentalism," *Lit: Literature and Interpretation Theory* 20 (November 2009): 266–87; Cushing Strout, "*Uncle Tom's Cabin* and the Portent of Millennium," *Yale Review* 57 (Spring 1968): 374–85; Tuveson, *Redeemer Nation*, 19.

12. Catharine E. Beecher and Harriet Beecher Stowe, *The American Woman's Home or, Principles of Domestic Science* (New York: Library of Victorian Culture, 1979), 460.

13. Harriet Beecher Stowe, "Footsteps of the Master," in *Religious Studies: Sketches and Poems* (Boston: Houghton Mifflin, 1896), 182.

14. Harriet Beecher Stowe, "He's Coming Tomorrow," in *The Second Coming of Christ* (Chicago: Moody, 1976), 15.

15. The classic analysis of the jeremiad form in American religious and political rhetoric is *The American Jeremiad* by Sacvan Bercovitch (Madison: University of Wisconsin Press, 1978).

16. Ernest Lee Tuveson, *Millennium and Utopia: A Study in the Background of the Idea of Progress* (New York: Harper, 1964), 6.

17. Nina Baym, *American Women Writers and the Work of History, 1790–1860* (New Brunswick, N.J.: Rutgers University Press, 1995), 11; Gillian Brown, *Domestic Individualism: Imagining Self in Nineteenth-Century America* (Berkeley: University of California Press, 1990), 20–29; Jane Tompkins, *Sensational Designs: The Cultural Work of American Fiction, 1790–1860* (New York: Oxford University Press, 1985), 122–46.

18. This argument is built on a foundation laid by Philip Fisher, in his attention to the purposeful arrangement of literary plot elements and time scheme. He writes, "Part of what we mean by a literary form like tragedy, sentimentalism, naturalism, or the historical novel is how each excerpts highly ordered fragments of this undifferentiated

duration to create meaningful action. The historical novel, for example, reaches back to create the moment of struggle between forces that in the reader's own day has already produced a decisive outcome. The struggle itself takes on the atmosphere of destiny." See *Hard Facts: Setting and Form in the American Novel* (New York: Oxford University Press, 1985), 115.

19. Arthur W. Wainwright, *Mysterious Apocalypse: Interpreting the Book of Revelation* (Eugene, Ore.: Wipf and Stock, 2001), 12–13, 20–21, 67–68.

20. J. F. C. Harrison, *The Second Coming: Popular Millenarianism, 1780–1850* (London: Routledge, 1979), 4; Jon R. Stone, *A Guide to the End of the World: Popular Eschatology in America* (New York: Garland, 1993), 5–6, 10–11.

21. Wainwright, *Mysterious Apocalypse*, 77.

22. Barkun, *Crucible*, 58, 147.

23. Tuveson, *Millennium and Utopia*, 137, 134.

24. Quoted by H. Richard Niebuhr, *The Kingdom of God in America* (Chicago: Willett, Clark, 1937), 145.

25. Ibid., 145. See also Amy Schrager Lang, *Prophetic Woman: Anne Hutchinson and the Problem of Dissent in the Literature of New England* (Berkeley: University of California Press, 1987), 109–10.

26. Niebuhr, *Kingdom of God*, 145–46; Wainwright, *Mysterious Apocalypse*, 177.

27. Timothy P. Weber, *Living in the Shadow of the Second Coming: American Premillennialism, 1875–1925* (New York: Oxford University Press, 1979), 14.

28. Henry F. May, in his influential call for a new historiography of American religion, observes that "American Christianity should be treated not as a series of institutions but as a prophetic movement." See "The Recovery of American Religious History," *American Historical Review* 70 (October 1964): 85. See also Barkun, *Crucible*, 51; Jon Butler, *Awash in a Sea of Faith: Christianizing the American People* (Cambridge, Mass.: Harvard University Press, 1990), 217–18, 223; Hatch, "Origins of Civil Millennialism," 420–22, 426; Moorhead, *American Apocalypse*, 5.

29. Stone, *Guide*, 20; Everett N. Dick, "The Millerite Movement, 1830–1845," in *Adventism in America: A History*, ed. Gary Land (Grand Rapids, Mich.: Wm. B. Eerdmans, 1986), 2.

30. Jenny Franchot, *Roads to Rome: The Antebellum Protestant Encounter with Catholicism* (Berkeley: University of California Press, 1994), 3–15.

31. Baym, *American Women Writers*, 46.

32. Lyman Beecher, *A Plea for the West* (1835; repr., New York: Arno, 1977), 10.

33. Susan M. Griffin, *Anti-Catholicism and Nineteenth-Century Fiction* (Cambridge: Cambridge University Press, 2004), 4.

34. Marie Caskey, *Chariot of Fire: Religion and the Beecher Family* (New Haven: Yale University Press, 1978), 23.

35. Lyman Beecher, "Resources of the Adversary, and Means of Their Destruction," in *Sermons; Delivered on Various Occasions* (Boston: John P. Jewett, 1852), 429.

36. Annie Fields, ed., *Life and Letters of Harriet Beecher Stowe* (1897; repr., Detroit: Gale Research, 1970), 10.

37. Moorhead, *American Apocalypse*, 10.

38. Joan Hedrick has shown that Stowe's religious beliefs were nothing if not variable, as is visible in her trajectory from childhood Presbyterianism to late-life Episcopalianism. A lifelong spiritual seeker, Stowe embraced numerous contemporary religious fads, including spiritualism. See *Harriet Beecher Stowe: A Life* (New York: Oxford University Press, 1994), 149.

39. Ibid., 153.

40. Harriet Beecher Stowe, "Footsteps of the Master," 182.

41. This letter is dated January 1879 and is reprinted in Charles Edward Stowe, ed., *Life of Harriet Beecher Stowe, Compiled from Her Letters and Journals* (Boston: Houghton Mifflin, 1889), 415.

42. Caskey, *Chariot of Fire*, 183.

43. Calvin E. Stowe, *Origin and History of the Books of the Bible* (Hartford, Conn.: Hartford, 1867), 490, 491. The latter quotation is lifted verbatim from his introduction to *The Criticism and Interpretation of the Bible, Designed for the Use of Theological Students, Bible Classes, and High Schools*, vol. 1 of 2 (Cincinnati: Corey, Fairbank, and Webster, 1835), 152–53.

44. Stowe, introduction, *Criticism and Interpretation of the Bible*, 164.

45. Caskey, *Chariot of Fire*, 183; quoted in Fields, *Life and Letters*, 359.

46. Harriet Beecher Stowe, *Oldtown Folks*, ed. Dorothy Berkson (New Brunswick, N.J.: Rutgers University Press, 1987), 370.

47. Harriet Beecher Stowe, *Poganuc People: Their Loves and Lives* (New York: Ford, Howard, and Hulbert, 1878), 372, 197–98.

48. Franchot, *Road to Rome*, 39.

49. Critics have long remarked on the resemblance of this crisis to the 1822 death of Dr. Alexander Fisher, fiancé of Stowe's sister Catharine Beecher, who, like Mrs. Marvyn, also suffered a spiritual crisis in its wake. See Hedrick, *Harriet Beecher Stowe*, 32; Mark A. Noll, *America's God: From Jonathan Edwards to Abraham Lincoln* (New York: Oxford University Press, 2002), 325–26; Charles Edward Stowe, *Life of Harriet Beecher Stowe*, 25.

50. Harriet Beecher Stowe, *The Minister's Wooing* (1859; repr., Ridgewood, N.J.: Gregg, 1968), 313, 314.

51. Ibid., 294.

52. Harriet Beecher Stowe, *The Pearl of Orr's Island: A Story of the Coast of Maine* (1862; repr., Ridgewood, N.J.: Gregg, 1967), 320.

53. Stowe, *Minister's Wooing*, 75.

54. For a discussion of Hopkins's advocacy of these positions, see Frederic J. Baumgartner, *Longing for the End: A History of Millennialism in Western Civilization* (New York: St. Martin, 1999), 130; Niebuhr, *Kingdom of God*, 145–46.

55. Stowe, *Pearl of Orr's Island,* 60.

56. Ibid., 241.

57. Sandra Gustafson has considered the influence of prophetic literary forms on sentimentalism. See "Margaret Fuller and the Forms of Sentiment," *American Quarterly* 47 (March 1995): 34–65.

58. Wesley Kort has suggested that scripture is defined less by the claims of divine inspiration than by its instrumentality in the "construction and maintenance of the worlds people inhabit." See *"Take, Read": Scripture, Textuality, and Cultural Practice* (University Park: Pennsylvania State University Press, 1996), 6.

59. Both words derive from the root *kaluptō,* which means "conceal" or "bury." Though the two derivations have different prefixes, both words mean "reveal" or "uncover," although *anakaluptō* has a distinctively gendered connotation. One suggestive nineteenth-century use of the term in biblical criticism appears in Matilda Joslyn Gage's commentary on Revelation in *The Woman's Bible* edited by Elizabeth Cady Stanton in 1898. See Elizabeth Cady Stanton, ed., *The Woman's Bible, Parts I & II* (1898; repr., Hong Kong: Forgotten Books, 2007), 371.

60. For a discussion of ancient customs of women's dress, see Lloyd Llewllyn-Jones, *Aphrodite's Tortoise: The Veiled Woman of Ancient Greece* (Swansea, U.K.: Classical Press of Wales, 2003), 98–107; Douglas L. Cairns, "The Meaning of the Veil in Ancient Greek Culture," in *Women's Dress in the Ancient World,* ed. Lloyd Llewellyn-Jones (London: Duckworth, 2002), 73–93.

61. Tina Pippin, *Death and Desire: The Rhetoric of Gender in the Apocalypse of John* (Louisville, Ky.: Westminster, 1992), 48.

62. Child writes, "This peculiar phase of Slavery has generally been kept veiled . . . and I willingly take the responsibility of presenting [these long-hidden facts] with the veil withdrawn." See Lydia Maria Child, "Introduction by the Editor," in *Narrative of the Life of Frederick Douglass, an American Slave* and *Incidents in the Life of a Slave Girl,* ed. Kwame Anthony Appiah (New York: Modern Library, 2000), 122.

63. Franchot, *Road to Rome,* 221.

64. See, for instance, Brian K. Blount, *Revelation: A Commentary* (Louisville, Ky.: Westminster, 2009), 10, 316–17.

65. Llewellyn-Jones, *Aphrodite's Tortoise,* 101.

66. This metaphor is implicitly enabled by the overlapping connotations of the word *veil,* for the word was also used in ancient Greek poetry to denote a city's walls; in this respect, a veil signals the protection of both feminine modesty and the civic space, which is likewise perceived as vulnerable to unwanted intruders and in need of a protective border. I am grateful to Corinne Pâche for this observation.

67. For a discussion of spectatorship and pathology in Revelation, see Christopher A. Frilingos, *Spectacles of Empire: Monsters, Martyrs, and the Book of Revelation* (Philadelphia: University of Pennsylvania Press, 2004), 103.

68. Harriet Beecher Stowe, *A Key to Uncle Tom's Cabin; Presenting the Original Facts*

and Documents upon Which the Story Is Founded. Together with Corroborative State-ments Verifying the Truth of the Work. (Boston: John P. Jewett, 1853), iv.

69. Lauren Berlant has observed a related phenomenon in the writings of Fanny Fern, whose domestic writings also work to elevate "the meaning and value of female life in the quotidian: to witness it, to affirm the dignity of its unhistoric acts" performed outside the public eye and historical record. See Berlant, "The Female Woman: Fanny Fern and the Form of Sentiment," in *The Culture of Sentiment: Race, Gender, and Senti-mentality in Nineteenth-Century America,* ed. Shirley Samuels (New York: Oxford University Press, 1992), 267.

70. Beecher and Stowe, *American Woman's Home,* 460.

71. Elizabeth Elkin Grammer has discerned a similar suggestion in the autobiogra-phies of nineteenth-century female preachers. See *Some Wild Visions: Autobiographies by Female Itinerant Evangelists in Nineteenth-Century America* (New York: Oxford University Press, 2003), 59ff.

72. Beecher and Stowe, *American Woman's Home,* 14, 15–16.

73. Ibid., 19.

74. In this respect, the Beecher sisters comply with prevailing nineteenth-century perceptions of domesticity as a kind of heaven on earth, a conflation that helped Eliz-abeth Stuart Phelps's novel about the afterlife, *The Gates Ajar* (1868), to become a best seller the year before. For a history of this nineteenth-century belief, see Colleen Mc-Dannell and Bernhard Lang, *Heaven: A History* (New Haven: Yale University Press, 1988), 228–75.

75. Beecher and Stowe, *American Woman's Home,* 459, 460-61.

76. Harriet Beecher Stowe, *House and Home Papers* (1864; repr., Bedford, Mass.: Applewood, nd), 57, 78.

77. Millennialist movements of the nineteenth century, Millerism and Seventh-Day Adventism among them, often cited Daniel 8:14 to predict a purge that would separate the righteous from the sinful. This biblical passage describes the cleansing of the temple sanctuary after its prolonged defilement, and, although it has not been analyzed as such by historians, it provides a vital scriptural linchpin binding nineteenth-century millen-nial belief and domesticity. As an interested observer of Millerism, Stowe very likely en-countered this passage in such a setting. Ronald Numbers mentions the pervasiveness of this biblical passage in Millerite millennialism: see *Prophetess of Health: Ellen G. White and the Origins of Seventh-Day Adventist Health Reform,* rev. ed. (Knoxville: University of Tennessee Press, 1992), 5.

78. Stowe, "Footsteps," 68.

79. Nina Baym observes that women writers of domestic fiction typically express a "conviction that God's values were domestic, even if the concept of God himself re-mained masculine." See *Woman's Fiction: A Guide to Novels by and About Women in America, 1820–70,* 2nd ed. (Urbana: University of Illinois, 1993), 44.

80. Stowe, "Footsteps," 237, 216, 129–30.

81. Elizabeth Maddock Dillon's work on the claims to social authority made possible by the public articulation of female domestic privacy is germane here. Dillon demonstrates that the private sphere is "constructed and articulated in the public sphere" and that the "privacy of women is the product not of women's seclusion within their homes, but of a public articulation and valuation of woman's domestic position." Stowe's public revelation of female private domesticity in order to assert the larger social significance of women corroborates this assertion. Jane Tompkins has likewise commented, "By investing the slightest acts with moral significance, the religion of domesticity makes the destinies of the human race hang upon domestic routines." See Dillon, *The Gender of Freedom: Fictions of Liberalism and the Literary Public Sphere* (Stanford, Calif.: Stanford University Press, 2004), 4; Tompkins, *Sensational Designs*, 171.

82. Stowe, *Minister's Wooing*, 1, 2, 7.

83. Lora Romero makes a related observation that Hopkins is entirely ineffective as a minister and that women are better able to effect moral and spiritual change. See *Home Fronts: Domesticity and Its Critics in the Antebellum United States* (Durham, N.C.: Duke University Press, 1997), 22.

84. Stowe, *Minister's Wooing*, 148.

85. Harriet Beecher Stowe, *Sam Lawson's Oldtown Fireside Stories* (London: Sampson Low, 1871), 102–103.

86. For a discussion of the Stowe marriage, see Kimberly Van Esveld Adams, "Family Influences on 'The Minister's Wooing' and 'Oldtown Folks': Henry Ward Beecher and Calvin Stowe," *Religion and Literature* 38 (Winter 2006): 27–61.

87. Some important examples of this scholarship include Nancy Armstrong, *Desire and Domestic Fiction: A Political History of the Novel* (New York: Oxford University Press, 1987); Michael McKeon, *The Origins of the English Novel, 1600–1740* (Baltimore: Johns Hopkins University Press, 1987); Tompkins, *Sensational Designs*.

88. Frank Kermode, *The Sense of an Ending: Studies in the Theory of Fiction* (New York: Oxford University Press, 1967).

89. Stowe, *Pearl of Orr's Island*, 400.

90. This assertion is informed by Philip Fisher's trenchant assertion that culture "articulates . . . some part of the past as it can be of use to a particular present"; that is, Stowe's conception of this American past informs her implicit claims about the American present and future. See Fisher, *Hard Facts*, 3.

91. Stowe, *Pearl of Orr's Island*, 62.

92. Ibid., 163.

93. Ibid. 382–83.

94. Lauren Berlant, *The Female Complaint: The Unfinished Business of Sentimentality in American Culture* (Durham, N.C.: Duke University Press, 2008), 2.

95. See, for instance, Catherine Keller, "Ms.Calculating the Apocalypse," in *Gender and Apocalyptic Desire*, ed. Brenda E. Brasher and Lee Quinby (London: Equinox, 2006), 1–13; Tina Pippin, "Eros and the End: Reading Gender in the Apocalypse of John,"

Semeia 59 (1992): 193–210; Lee Quinby, *Millennial Seduction: A Skeptic Confronts Apocalyptic Culture* (Ithaca, N.Y.: Cornell University Press, 1999).

96. Pippin, *Death and Desire*, 80.

97. Stanton, *Woman's Bible*, 372.

98. Joycelyn Moody has analyzed the discursive overlap between sentiment and the jeremiad, arguing that the "classic jeremiad" is inherently sentimental. See *Sentimental Confessions: Spiritual Narratives of Nineteenth-Century African American Women* (Athens: University of Georgia Press, 2001), 52.

99. Ellen G. White, *The Ministry of Healing* (Mountain View, Calif.: Pacific, 1942), 349.

Chapter 4. Derelict Daughters and Polygamous Wives

1. *Woman's Exponent* 1.12 (November 15, 1872): 96.

2. Susanna Morrill, *White Roses on the Floor of Heaven: Mormon Women's Popular Theology, 1880–1920* (New York: Routledge, 2006), 29.

3. Lu Dalton, "A Mother's Resignation," *Woman's Exponent* 12 (November 15, 1872): 90. For a fuller discussion of this nineteenth-century poetic form, see Max Cavitch, *American Elegy: The Poetry of Mourning from the Puritans to Whitman* (Minneapolis: University of Minnesota Press, 2007), 144–50, 162–79.

4. Dana Luciano's analysis of consolation literature of the nineteenth century discusses how grief was perceived as a potential incitement to religious waywardness and rebellion. For this reason, it was of vital importance that child elegies such as Dalton's publicly express their resignation to divine will so as to provide public reassurance of their own religious obedience. See Luciano, *Arranging Grief: Sacred Time and the Body in Nineteenth-Century America* (New York: New York University Press, 2007).

5. Orson Pratt, ed., *The Doctrine and Covenants, of the Church of Jesus Christ of Latter-Day Saints, Containing the Revelations Given to Joseph Smith, Jun., The Prophet, for the Building Up of the Kingdom of God in the Last Days* (1880; repr., Westport, Conn.: Greenwood, 1971), 473: 61.

6. Brodie counts forty-eight wives sealed to Smith, although many of them were posthumous "proxy wives," sealed to him for eternal marriage in the Mormon endowment ceremony. See Fawn M. Brodie, *No Man Knows My History: The Life of Joseph Smith the Mormon Prophet* (New York: Knopf, 1946), 434–65.

7. Edward Whitley provides a useful summary of public outrage. See *American Bards: Walt Whitman and Other Unlikely Candidates for National Poet* (Chapel Hill: University of North Carolina Press, 2010), 82–85.

8. Gillian Brown and Karen Sánchez-Eppler have provided important analyses of the public role of sentimental discourse of domesticity. See Brown, *Domestic Individualism: Imagining Self in Nineteenth-Century America* (Berkeley: University of California Press, 1990), 13–38; Sánchez-Eppler, *Touching Liberty: Abolition, Feminism, and the Politics of the Body* (Berkeley: University of California Press, 1993), 134–35.

9. David Brion Davis glosses the specter of slavery used in anti-Mormon discourse.

See *The Fear of Conspiracy: Images of Un-American Subversion from the Revolution to the Present* (Ithaca, N.Y.: Cornell University Press, 1971), 12–15.

10. For a more extensive study of fictional representations of Mormonism, see Terryl L. Givens, *The Viper on the Hearth: Mormons, Myths, and the Construction of Heresy* (New York: Oxford University Press, 1997). Nancy Bentley also analyzes late-century sentimental anti-polygamy novels. See "Marriage as Treason: Polygamy, Nation, and the Novel," in *The Futures of American Studies*, ed. Donald E. Pease and Robyn Wiegman (Durham, N.C.: Duke University Press, 2002), 343–70.

11. Kathryn Daynes, *More Wives Than One: The Transformation of the Mormon Marriage System, 1840–1910* (Urbana: University of Illinois Press, 2001), 106.

12. For a fuller discussion of anti-Catholic literature, see Jenny Franchot, *Roads to Rome: The Antebellum Protestant Encounter with Catholicism* (Berkeley: University of California Press, 1994); Susan M Griffin, *Anti-Catholicism and Nineteenth-Century Fiction* (Cambridge: Cambridge University Press, 2004).

13. Alfreda Eva Bell, *Boadicea; The Mormon Wife. Life-Scenes in Utah* (Baltimore: Arthur B. Orton, 1855), 54.

14. Metta Victoria Fuller, *Mormon Wives; A Narrative of Facts Stranger Than Fiction* (New York: Derby & Jackson, 1856), viii.

15. Ibid., 306.

16. Sarah Barringer Gordon, *The Mormon Question: Polygamy and Constitutional Conflict in Nineteenth-Century America* (Chapel Hill: University of North Carolina, 2002), 55.

17. Mrs. T. B. H. Stenhouse, *"Tell It All": The Story of a Life's Experiences in Mormonism* (1872; repr., Hartford, Conn.: A. D. Worthington, 1876), vi.

18. Gillian Brown offers a complementary analysis of the ways in which slavery intrudes on and compromises housekeeping in sentimental literature. See *Domestic Individualism*, 14–16.

19. Austin N. Ward, *The Husband in Utah; or, Sights and Scenes Among the Mormons*, ed. Maria Ward (New York: J. C. Derby, 1857), 95, 96. This account was a sequel to Maria Ward's best-selling *Female Life Among the Mormons*. Austin Ward claimed to be the brother of Maria Ward.

20. Maria Ward's *Female Life Among the Mormons* contains numerous examples of such behavior. See *Female Life Among the Mormons* (New York: J. C. Derby, 1856), 99; Austin Ward, *Husband in Utah*, 46.

21. John Russell, *The Mormoness; or, The Trials of Mary Maverick* (Alton, Ill.: Courier Steam Press Print, 1853), 67.

22. Lawrence Foster, *Women, Family, and Utopia: Communal Experiments of the Shakers, the Oneida Community, and the Mormons* (Syracuse, N.Y.: Syracuse University Press, 1991), 210–11.

23. Bentley, "Marriage as Treason," 343.

24. This phrase appears repeatedly in sentimental narration, and its origins remain uncertain. Though the phrase "kiss the rod" appears in Caxton's fifteenth-century translation of Reynard the Fox and Shakespeare's *Two Gentlemen of Verona*, the origin of this

precise phrasing is unclear. Thomas Kelly's 1806 hymn "Zion's King Shall Reign Victorious" contains the earliest usage I have found and may have enabled the wide circulation of this language within an ecclesiastical context.

25. Stenhouse, *Tell It All*, 143.

26. Dalton, "Mother's Resignation," 90.

27. Stenhouse, *Tell It All*, 438.

28. Edward W. Tullidge, *The Women of Mormondom* (New York: Tullidge & Crandall, 1877), iii.

29. Ibid., 23.

30. It bears remarking that Mormons do not have clergy in the traditional sense but instead have a priesthood in which Mormon men of good standing may administer church rites as well as give blessings. Lawrence Foster similarly observes that nineteenth-century Mormons employed mainstream gendered rhetoric to defend their religious structures of authority: "In terms strikingly similar to those used by their Victorian contemporaries, Mormons stressed the positive and vital social role that women could play in the family and, by extension, in the larger community, which, in the Mormon case, as generally coterminous with the family." See *Women, Family, and Utopia*, 191.

31. Tullidge, *Women of Mormondom*, 68–69.

32. Eliza R. Snow, "Sketch of My Life," in *The Personal Writings of Eliza Roxcy Snow*, ed. Maureen Ursenbach Beecher (Salt Lake City: University of Utah Press, 1995), 8.

33. This story is also repeated in the following sources: Keith and Ann Terry, *Eliza: A Poetess Comes to Zion* (Orem, Utah: Kenninghouse, 1995), 13; *Eliza R. Snow: An Immortal—Selected Writings of Eliza R. Snow* (Salt Lake City: Nicholas G. Morgan, Sr., Foundation, 1957); "Pen Sketch of an Illustrious Woman," *Woman's Exponent* 9 (August 1, 1880), 33–34. Maureen Ursenbach Beecher makes a similar argument in her essay "Three Women and the Life of the Mind," in *Eliza and Her Sisters* (Salt Lake City: Aspen, 1991), 120. Lawrence Foster has observed how sentimental ideals of domesticity became self-conscious emblems of gentility for nineteenth-century Mormons at pains to counter widespread attacks of barbarism from critics and portray themselves as fully civilized Victorians. See *Women, Family, and Utopia*, 210.

34. Tullidge, *Women of Mormondom*, 29.

35. Helen Mar Whitney, *Why We Practice Plural Marriage* (Salt Lake City: Juvenile Instructor Office, 1884), 4.

36. Ibid., 6–7.

37. Daynes, *More Wives*, 119, 123, 127; Claudia Bushman, "Mormon Women," in *Encyclopedia of Women and Religion in North America*, vol. 2 of 3, ed. Rosemary Skinner Keller and Rosemary Radford Ruether (Bloomington: Indiana University Press, 2006), 721; Stephanie Smith Goodson, "Plural Wives," in *Mormon Sisters: Women in Early Utah*, ed. Claudia L. Bushman (Logan, Utah: Utah State Press, 1997), 93–94.

38. Daynes, *More Wives*, 127.

39. Nancy F. Cott, "Young Women in the Second Great Awakening," *Feminist Studies* 3 (Autumn 1975): 17–18, 23.

40. Critics who wrote sensationalist novels touted as nonfiction were particularly partial to such assertions. See, for example, Jennie Bartlett Switzer, *Elder Northfield's Home; Or, Sacrificed on the Mormon Altar: The Story of the Blighting Curse of Polygamy* (1882; repr., New York: Books for Libraries, 1971), 192–93; Maria Ward, *Female Life,* 282–83.

41. Though it claims to be a memoir, this text is clearly a work of fiction designed to depict Mormonism as a predatory threat to women. Published pseudonymously, its author has never been identified definitively, although Leonard Arrington and Jon Haupt have speculated that it was authored by Cornelia Ferris, the wife of a government employee based in Utah in 1852–53. See Arrington and Haupt, "Intolerable Zion: The Image of Mormonism in Nineteenth Century American Literature," *Western Humanities Review* 22 (Fall 1968): 243–60.

42. Ann Eliza Young, *Wife No. 19, or That Story of a Life in Bondage, Being a Complete Expose of Mormonism, and Revealing the Sorrows, Sacrifices and Sufferings of Women in Polygamy* (1875; repr., New York: Arno, 1972), 178.

43. *Woman's Exponent* 1.12 (November 15, 1872): 96.

44. Whitney, *Plural Marriage,* 69.

45. Eve Cherniavsky has more broadly observed this tendency of sentimentalism in what she calls the "dehistoricizing logic of sentimental discourse." See *That Pale Mother Rising: Sentimental Discourse and the Imitation of Motherhood in Nineteenth-Century America* (Bloomington: Indiana University Press, 1995), 106.

46. Brigham Young, "I Hope the Brethren and Sisters Will Remember What Has Been Said," in *The Essential Brigham Young* (Salt Lake City: Signature, 1992), 216. This speech was delivered on June 30, 1873.

47. Richard W. Clement, *Books on the Frontier: Print Culture in the American West, 1763–1875* (Washington, D.C.: Library of Congress, 2003), 82–83.

48. "About Women," *Woman's Exponent* 1.6 (August 15, 1887): 46.

49. Morrill, *White Roses,* 68–69; Anne Firor Scott, "Mormon Women, Other Women: Paradoxes and Challenges," in *The Mormon History Association's Tanner Lectures: The First Twenty Years,* ed. Dean L. May and Reid L. Neilson (Urbana: University of Illinois Press, 2006), 207; Marilyn Warenski, *Patriarchs and Politics: The Plight of Mormon Woman* (New York: McGraw-Hill, 1978), 11.

50. Eliza R. Snow, "My Own Home," in *Poems: Religious, Historical, and Political* (Liverpool: F. D. Richards, 1856), 71–72.

51. This discussion of the illusory nature of gendered separate spheres is indebted to Cathy Davidson's foundational essay "No More Separate Spheres!" *American Literature* 70.3 (September 1998): 443–63.

52. Kenneth W. Godfrey, Audrey M. Godfrey, and Jill Mulvay Derr, *Women's Voices: An Untold History of the Latter-day Saints, 1830–1900* (Salt Lake City: Deseret, 1987), 17.

53. Stephanie Smith Goodson, "Plural Wives," *Mormon Sisters,* rev. ed., ed. Claudia L. Bushman (Logan, Utah: Utah State University Press, 1997), 104–105.

54. Brown, *Domestic Individualism,* 13–38. Lawrence Foster has documented the

Mormon subscription to Victorian ideals of domesticity. See *Women, Family, and Utopia*, 210.

55. Harriet Beecher Stowe, *Uncle Tom's Cabin or, Life Among the Lowly*, ed. Ann Douglas (1852; repr., New York: Penguin, 1981), 624.

56. Jan Shipps, *Mormonism: The Story of a New Religious Tradition* (Urbana: University of Illinois Press, 1985), 36.

57. Richard D. Brown has documented how novel reading in the early nineteenth century provided a vital medium for such information among isolated young women in unsettled circumstances. See *Knowledge Is Power: The Diffusion of Information in Early America, 1700–1865* (New York: Oxford University Press, 1989), 160–96.

58. Jill Mulvay Derr, "Eliza R. Snow and the Woman Question," in *Life in Utah: Centennial Selections from* BYU Studies, ed. James B. Allen and John M. Welch (Provo, Utah: BYU Studies, 1996), 220.

59. Scott, "Mormon Women," 210–11.

60. Eliza R. Snow, "The Female Relief Society of Nauvoo: What Is It?" in *Eliza R. Snow: The Complete Poetry*, ed. Jill Mulvay Derr and Karen Lynn Davidson (Provo, Utah: Brigham Young University Press, 2009), 205.

61. Jill Mulvay Derr, Janath Russell Canton, and Maureen Ursenbach Beecher, *Women of Covenant: The Story of Relief Society* (Salt Lake City: Deseret, 1992), 32.

62. Gary Laderman, *The Sacred Remains: American Attitudes Toward Death, 1799–1883* (New Haven: Yale University Press, 1996), 57; Colleen McDannell and Bernhard Lang, *Heaven: A History* (New Haven: Yale University Press, 1988), 191ff, 257–75; Michael Wheeler, *Death and the Future Life in Victorian Life, Literature and Theology* (Cambridge: Cambridge University Press, 1990), 120–21.

63. Douglas J. Davies, *An Introduction to Mormonism* (Cambridge: Cambridge University Press, 2003), 91.

64. Lawrence Foster has commented on the centrality of family to Mormonism, observing that "Mormonism saw family life and the relation between family and larger kinship networks as the ultimate basis for all progression, not only on earth but throughout all eternity. To an almost unparalleled extent, the Mormon religion really was about the family; earthly and heavenly family ideals were seen as identical." See *Women, Family, and Utopia*, 233.

65. Eliza R. Snow, "Immortality," in *Eliza R. Snow: The Complete Poetry*, 699.

66. Jan Shipps, one of the premier historians of Mormonism, had described Eliza R. Snow as "arguably the most notable female Mormon in the history of the movement." See "Dangerous History: Laurel Ulrich and Her Mormon Sisters," *Christian Century* 110 (October 10, 1993): 1013.

67. Derr and Davidson, "Introduction," in *Eliza R. Snow: The Complete Poetry*, xvi; Stenhouse, *Tell It All*, 251.

68. Ann Eliza Young makes this claim in her memoir. See *Wife No. 19*, 357.

69. This episode appears in Stenhouse, *Tell It All*, 431. Though Snow admitted that she initially found polygamy "repugnant," she later came to regard it as necessary [to]

the elevation and salvation of the human family—in redeeming . . . [the] world from corruptions." See "Sketch of My Life," 16–17.

70. Eulogies of John W. Taylor and Elder Milo Andrus, *Life and Labors of Eliza R. Snow Smith. with a Full Account of Her Funeral Services* (Salt Lake City: Juvenile Instructor Office, 1888), 24, 25.

71. Jill Mulvay Derr, "The Significance of 'O My Father' in the Personal Journey of Eliza R. Snow," *BYU Studies* 36 (1996–97): 85–86.

72. Austin Ward, *Husband in Utah*, 229.

73. Derr, "Significance," 115; Morrill, *White Roses*, 68; Warenski, *Patriarchs and Politics*, 11.

74. For such an intellectual history of Mormonism, see John L. Brooke, *The Refiner's Fire: The Making of Mormon Cosmology, 1644–1844* (Cambridge: Cambridge University Press, 1994).

75. Warenski, *Patriarchs and Politics*, 45; Derr, "Significance," 98.

76. Derr, "Significance," 95.

77. Edward Whitley offers one of the few literary analyses of Snow's poem. See *American Bards*, 104–12.

78. Eliza R. Snow, "My Father in Heaven," in *Eliza R. Snow: The Complete Poetry*, 313–14. Quoted with the permission of Brigham Young University Press.

79. Susanna Morrill has similarly observed how nineteenth-century Mormon idealizations of domestic bliss often implicitly imagine an idyllic afterlife. See *White Roses*, 136.

80. Nina Baym, *Woman's Fiction: A Guide to Novels by and About Women in America, 1820–70*, 2nd ed. (Urbana: University of Illinois, 1993), 44; Catherine A. Brekus, *Strangers and Pilgrims: Female Preaching in America, 1740–1845* (Chapel Hill: University of North Carolina Press, 1996), 120; Colleen McDannell, *The Christian Home in Victorian America, 1840–1900* (Bloomington: Indiana University Press, 1986), 128; Rosemary Radford Ruether, *Goddesses and the Divine Feminine* (Berkeley: University of California Press, 2005), 250.

81. Cherniavsky, *That Pale Mother*, 44.

82. Paula Bernat Bennett, *Poets in the Public Sphere: The Emancipatory Project of American Women's Poetry, 1800–1900* (Princeton: Princeton University Press, 2003), 28.

83. J. Spencer Cornwall, *Stories of Our Mormon Hymns*, 2nd ed. (Salt Lake City: Deseret, 1963), 144; Derr, "Significance," 100; *Life and Labors*, 17–18; Morrill, *White Roses*, 82; Tullidge, *Women of Mormondom*, 187; Terry, *Eliza*, 136; Warenski, *Patriarchs and Politics*, 45.

84. Linda Wilcox, "The Mormon Concept of a Mother in Heaven," *Sunstone*, 23 (September–October 1980): 10.

85. Derr, "Significance," 99. This narrative is also repeated in the following sources: Maureen Ursenbach Beecher, "The Eliza Enigma: The Life and Legend of Eliza R. Snow," in *Sister Saints*, ed. Vicky Burgess-Olson (Provo, Utah: Brigham Young University Press,

1978), 11; Brooke, *Refiner's Fire*, 258. A stake is a regional assembly of Mormon congregations, akin to a Catholic diocese or a Presbyterian synod.

86. Wilcox, "Mother in Heaven," 9.

87. Lynn Matthews Anderson, "Issues in Contemporary Mormon Feminism," in *Mormon Identities in Transition*, ed. Douglas J. Davies (London: Cassell, 1996), 159–60; John Heeren, Donald B. Lindsey, and Marylee Mason, "The Mormon Concept of Mother in Heaven: A Sociological Account of Its Origins and Development," *Journal for the Scientific Study of Religion* 23.4 (December 1984): 405; Linda P. Wilcox, "Mormon Motherhood: Official Images," in *Sisters in Spirit: Mormon Women in Historical and Cultural Perspective*, ed. Maureen Ursenbach Beecher and Lavina Fielding Anderson (Urbana: University of Illinois Press, 1987), 212.

88. Martha Pierce, "Personal Discourse on God the Mother," in *Women and Authority: Re-emerging Mormon Feminism*, ed. Maxine Hanks (Salt Lake City: Signature, 1992), 249; Morrill, *White Roses*, 196; Shipps, "Dangerous History," 1014.

89. President Gordon B. Hinckley, "Daughters of God," *Ensign* (November 1991): 102. Margaret Toscano, one of the better-known Mormon feminists to have been excommunicated as a result of these efforts, contends that since President Hinckley's 1991 address, mentions of Heavenly Mother have vanished from official Mormon statements and publications. See Toscano, "Is There a Place for Heavenly Mother in Mormon Theology? An Investigation into Discourses of Power," *Sunstone* 133 (July 2004): 16.

90. Derr, "Significance," 98.

91. President Spencer W. Kimball, "The True Way of Life and Salvation," *Ensign* (May 1978): 4.

92. O. Kendall White, Jr., "Ideology of the Family in Nineteenth-Century Mormonism," *Sociological Spectrum* 6 (1986): 295.

93. Ian G. Barber, "Mormon Women as 'Natural' Seers: An Enduring Legacy," in *Women and Authority: Re-emerging Mormon Feminism*, ed. Maxine Hanks (Salt Lake City: Signature, 1992), 167–74; Terry, *Eliza*, 16–17; *Life and Labors*, 14.

Chapter 5. The Mother Church

1. Mark Twain, *Christian Science with Notes Containing Corrections to Date* (New York: Harper, 1907), 102.

2. Mary Baker Eddy, *Science and Health with Key to the Scriptures* (Boston: First Church of Christ, Scientist, 1994), 260:20–21; for a discussion of the relation of Christian Science to the New Thought movement, see Beryl Satter, *Each Mind a Kingdom: American Women, Sexual Purity, and the New Thought Movement, 1875–1920* (Berkeley: University of California Press, 1999), 5, 10–14.

3. Quoted in Gillian Gill, *Mary Baker Eddy* (Cambridge, Mass.: Perseus, 1998), 454.

4. Mary Baker Eddy, "Message to the Annual Meeting of the Mother Church, 1896," *Prose Works Other Than* Science and Health with Key to the Scriptures (Boston: Trustees Under the Will of Mary Baker Eddy, 1925), 128.

5. Cynthia Schrager offers a useful analysis of the gendered assumptions in Eddy's self-presentation and Twain's criticisms. See "Mark Twain and Mary Baker Eddy: Gendering the Transpersonal Subject," *American Literature* 70 (March 1998): 29–63.

6. For instance, Eddy writes of Mary as follows: "The illumination of Mary's spiritual sense put to silence material law and its order of generation, and brought forth her child by the revelation of Truth, demonstrating God as the Father of men. The Holy Ghost, or divine Spirit, overshadowed the pure sense of the Virgin-mother with the full recognition that being is Spirit. The Christ dwelt forever an idea in the bosom of God, the divine Principle of the man Jesus, and woman perceived this spiritual idea, though at first faintly developed" (*Science and Health* 29:20–29).

7. Joseph Armstrong provides an extensive description of the room's appointments as well as the building of the Mother Church. See *A History of the Building of the Original Edifice of The First Church of Christ, Scientist in Boston, Massachusetts* (Boston: Christian Science Publishing Society, 1937), 71.

8. Gail Parker offered an early inquiry into Eddy's engagement with sentimentalism, and, although that essay's quasi-psychoanalytic claims have not informed this discussion, it nonetheless provides a noteworthy precedent for this consideration. See "Mary Baker Eddy and Sentimental Womanhood," *New England Quarterly* 43 (March 1970): 3–18.

9. Elizabeth Maddock Dillon's formulation of the role of the text in mediating the female private and public is germane here. See *The Gender of Freedom: Fictions of Liberalism and the Literary Public Sphere* (Stanford, Calif.: Stanford University Press, 2004), 4.

10. Motherhood in sentimentality has received considerable scholarly analysis. See, for instance, Eve Cherniavsky, *That Pale Mother Rising: Sentimental Discourses and the Imitation of Motherhood in Nineteenth-Century America* (Bloomington: Indiana University Press, 1995), 123; Marianne Noble, *The Masochistic Pleasures of Sentimental Literature* (Princeton: Princeton University Press, 2000), 65ff; Jane Tompkins, *Sensational Designs: The Cultural Work of American Fiction, 1790–1860* (New York: Oxford University Press, 1985), 165; Catherine M. Scholten, *Childbearing in American Society: 1650–1850* (New York: New York University Press, 1985).

11. Gill, *Mary Baker Eddy*, xvii.

12. For a discussion of the New Woman, see Carroll Smith-Rosenberg, *Disorderly Conduct: Visions of Gender in Victorian America* (New York: Knopf, 1985), 245–96; June Howard, *Publishing the Family* (Durham, N.C.: Duke University Press, 2001), 158–212.

13. David Stouck, "Introduction," in Willa Cather and Georgine Milmine, *The Life of Mary Baker Eddy and the History of Christian Science* (Lincoln: University of Nebraska Press, 1993), xv–xxviii.

14. William Dean Howells, "Criticism and Fiction," in *1886–1897*, vol. 2 of *William Dean Howells Selected Literary Criticism*, ed. Donald Pizer (Bloomington: Indiana University Press, 1993), 300.

15. Twain, *Christian Science*, 115.

16. Cather and Milmine, *Life of Mary Baker Eddy*, 31.

17. Laura Wexler, "Tender Violence: Literary Eavesdropping, Domestic Fiction, and Educational Reform," in *Culture of Sentiment: Race, Gender, and Sentimentality in Nineteenth-Century America*, ed. Shirley Samuels (New York: Oxford University Press, 1992), 19.

18. Leslie A. Fiedler, *Love and Death in the American Novel* (New York: Criterion, 1960), 3.

19. Such sources include the Cather-Milmine biography, Fleda Springer's biography *According to the Flesh* (New York: Coward-McCann, 1930), as well as Ernest Sutherland Bates and John V. Dittemore's biography *Mary Baker Eddy: The Truth and the Tradition* (New York: Knopf, 1932). In 1929 Edwin Dakin attempted to build a case against Eddy by citing a letter written by sixteen-year-old Mary Baker in which she expressed interest in visiting a nearby Shaker village but was refused permission "by [her] superiors because it would be a profanation of the Sabbathe." This letter, however, evidences less an interest in Shakerism than in the "gentleman recently from Boston" who invited her on this expedition; indeed, the discussion that immediately follows, of a Mr. Bartlett whom she had met at a wedding, evidences that at the time she wrote the letter, she was more interested in men than in the Shakers. Eddy's later biographer Robert Peel glossed this letter with the suggestion that such an outing to Shaker villages was "a usual thing for the young people to do," and convincingly argues that the Shakers would have been familiar figures in Eddy's childhood hometown of Sanbornton, New Hampshire, as they regularly sold their handicrafts in neighboring villages. See Dakin, *Mrs. Eddy: The Biography of a Virgin Mind* (New York: Blue Ribbon, 1930), 13; Peel, *Mary Baker Eddy: The Years of Discovery*, vol. 1 of 2 (New York: Holt, Rinehart and Winston, 1966), 53.

20. Gill, *Mary Baker Eddy*, 48; Mary Baker Eddy, "Reply to McClure's Magazine," *The First Church of Christ Scientist and Miscellany* (Boston: Trustees under the Will of Mary Baker G. Eddy, 1941), 313:21.

21. Susan Hill Lindley, "The Ambiguous Feminism of Mary Baker Eddy," *Journal of Religion* 64 (July 1984): 322–23. It would seem, however, that the Shaker interest in Christian Science is more verifiable. In his history of Shakerism in the United States, Stephen Stein has documented the enthusiasm many Shakers showed for Christian Science belief and healing practices. See *The Shaker Experience in America: A History of the United Society of Believers* (New Haven: Yale University Press, 1992), 326.

22. Mary Baker Eddy, "Alphabet and Bayonet," in *Poems* (Boston: Trustees under the Will of Mary Baker Eddy, 1910), 60–61.

23. A holographic copy of this poem is included in *In My True Light and Life: Mary Baker Eddy Collections* (Boston: Mary Baker Eddy Library for the Betterment of Humanity, 2002), 5–7. Later in life, Eddy would significantly revise this poem, which she retitled "Resolution for the Day," and this stanza was revised to read as follows: "To daily remember my blessings and charge,/ And make this my humble request:/ Increase Thou my faith and my vision enlarge/ And bless me with Christ's promised rest." This version is included in Eddy, *Poems*, 32–33.

24. Her publication in this setting is due to the fact that her late husband, George

Washington Glover, had been a mason, a fact noted in the poem's penultimate verse. After his death, she traveled from South Carolina, where he died, back to New England because of the financial contributions of his fellow masons.

25. This poem, in its original printing in the *Freemason's Monthly Magazine*, is reproduced in *In My True Light and Life*, 53.

26. Marianne Noble has analyzed the recurrent rhetoric of the chastening rod in sentimental literature. See Noble, *Masochistic*, 29, 56.

27. Maria Susanna Cummins, *The Lamplighter*, ed. Nina Baym (1854; repr. New Brunswick, N.J.: Rutgers University Press, 1988), 104.

28. "To My Mother in Heaven," in *In My True Light and Life*, 71.

29. Citing Nancy Armstrong's foundational work *Desire and Domestic Fiction: A Political History of the Novel* (New York: Oxford University Press, 1987), Lora Romero has argued that "the appearance of the domestic woman in the early nineteenth century cannot be separated from the modern reconstruction not just of the female self but of selfhood in general." Mary Baker Eddy's deliberate reliance on sentimental rhetoric of femininity and domesticity in the construction of a public image corroborates this important claim. See Romero, *Home Fronts: Domesticity and Its Critics in the Antebellum United States* (Durham, N.C.: Duke University Press, 1997), 25.

30. Cather and Milmine, *Life of Mary Baker Eddy*, 56, 31.

31. Eddy's recent and more even-handed biographer, Gillian Gill, corroborates this overall impression, however, noting the heightened literariness of Eddy's publications during the period when she attempted to become a professional writer; her published 1847 short story "The Test of Love," for instance, used such extravagant words as "non-pareil," "n'importe," and "intransitu." See Gill, *Mary Baker Eddy*, 72.

32. Irving C. Tomlinson, *Twelve Years with Mary Baker Eddy: Recollections and Experiences* (Boston: Christian Science Publishing Society, 1945), 13, 99.

33. Cynthia Schrager has observed, "In Eddy's authorized biography, published in 1908 shortly before her death, Sibyl Wilbur makes unabashed use of the rhetorical conventions of sentimental fiction to give narrative form to her subject's life." See Schrager, "Mark Twain," 36.

34. Sibyl Wilbur, *The Life of Mary Baker Eddy* (Boston: Christian Science Publishing Society, 1941), 69–70.

35. Ibid., 50.

36. Ella H. Hay, *A Child's Life of Mary Baker Eddy* (Boston: Christian Science Publishing Society, 1942), 54.

37. An example of this enduring accusation can be found in Stefan Zweig's *Mental Healers: Franz Anton Mesmer, Mary Baker Eddy, Sigmund Freud*, trans. Eden and Cedar Paul (Garden City, N.J.: Garden City Publishing, 1932), 111–15.

38. Mary Kelley's appraisal of sentimentalism's innate domesticity has been most influential. See *Private Women, Public Stage: Literary Domesticity in Nineteenth-Century America* (New York: Oxford University Press, 1884), x–xii.

39. Gillian Brown provides a helpful gloss to sentimental domesticity. See *Domestic*

Individualism: Imagining Self in Nineteenth-Century America (Berkeley: University of California Press, 1990), 13–38, 63–95.

40. Tomlinson, *Twelve Years*, 169, 41.

41. Elbert Hubbard, *Little Journeys to the Homes of Great Teachers—Mary Baker Eddy* (East Aurora, N.Y.: Roycrofters, 1908), 142.

42. She makes this suggestion in *Science and Health* 559:1–5.

43. Mary Baker Eddy, "Retrospection and Introspection," in *Prose Works Other Than* Science and Health with Key to the Scriptures, 13.

44. Schrager, "Mark Twain," 32.

45. Eddy, "Retrospection," 14.

46. Ibid., 18, 20.

47. Tomlinson, *Twelve Years*, 158.

48. Hubbard, *Little Journeys*, 142.

49. Quoted in Tomlinson, *Twelve Years*, 156.

50. Quoted in Augusta E. Stetson, *Reminiscences, Sermons, and Correspondence: Proving Adherence to the Principle of Christian Science as Taught by Mary Baker Eddy* (New York: Putnam, 1917), 368.

51. Joseph F. Kett, *Rites of Passage: Adolescence in America 1790 to the Present* (New York: Basic, 1977), 15, 17–18.

52. Elizabeth Barnes observes that sentimental novels "redraw the boundaries of the American family to make central the socially and politically marginalized. To effect such a change, these novels actually abstract concepts of home, family, and self from their earlier biological moorings." See *States of Sympathy: Seduction and Democracy in the American Novel* (New York: Columbia University Press, 1997), 78.

53. Eddy, *Retrospection*, 20.

54. Lauren Berlant, "Poor Eliza," *American Literature* 70 (September 1998): 164.

55. Mary Baker Eddy, "Mother's Evening Prayer," in *Poems*, 4–5.

56. For a history of this 1910 collection of her poems, see William Dana Orcutt, *Mary Baker Eddy and Her Books* (Boston: Christian Science Publishing Society, 1950).

57. The poem reads as follows:"Father-Mother God,/ Loving Me, / Guard me when I sleep; / Guard my little feet / Up to Thee. / *To the Big Children* / Father-Mother good, lovingly / Thee I seek,/ Patient, meek, / In the way Thou hast,— / Be it slow or fast, / Up to Thee." See Mary Baker Eddy, "A Verse," in *Poems Including* Christ and Christmas (Boston: Trustees Under the Will of Mary G. Baker Eddy, 1938), 69.

58. Mary Louise Baum, "The Hymns of Mary Baker Eddy," in *Concordance to Christian Science Hymnal and Hymnal Notes* (Boston: Christian Science Publishing Society, 1975), 172.

59. Twain, *Christian Science*, 276.

60. Armstrong, *Mother Church*, 73.

61. Gillian Gill provides a useful analysis of Eddy's iconic rocking chair. See Gill, *Mary Baker Eddy*, 11–12.

62. Included in Eddy, *Poems*, 43.

63. Tomlinson, *Twelve Years*, 7.

64. *We Knew Mary Baker Eddy* (Boston: Christian Science Publishing Society, 1953), 16–17. This letter makes reference to the Heart of Love, a cherished Christian Science artifact that itself evidences the pervasiveness of love to sectarian discourse: the Heart of Love is a rubber band formed in the shape of a heart, which offered Eddy reassurance during a difficult period and inspired her 1899 poem "Signs of the Heart," which proclaims, "O little heart,/To me thou art/A sign that never can depart." As the poem suggests, Eddy maintained that love is all you need: "O Love divine,/This heart of Thine/Is all I need to comfort mine." See Eddy, "Signs of the Heart," in *Poems*, 24.

65. Quoted in Tomlinson, *Twelve Years*, 91.

66. Tomlinson, *Twelve Years*, 61.

67. Eddy, "Love," in *Poems*, 6–7.

68. She plainly declares, "God is Love" in "No and Yes," in *Prose Works Other Than Science and Health with Key to the Scriptures*, 19.

69. Quoted in Tomlinson, *Twelve Years*, 90.

70. Laura Wexler has commented on the basis of sentimental maternity in the Virgin Mary. See "Seeing Sentiment: Photography, Race, and the Innocent Eye," in *American Literary Studies: A Methodological Reader*, ed. Michael A. Elliott and Claudia Stokes (New York: New York University Press, 2003), 63–94.

71. Fleta Springer has offered further commentary on Eddy's self-interested interpretation of Christian eschatology. See *According to the Flesh* (New York: Coward-McCann, 1930), 304–6.

72. She makes this suggestion in *Science and Health* 559:1–5.

73. Eddy, *Retrospection*, 70.

74. Tomlinson, *Twelve Years*, 73.

75. Twain, *Christian Science*, 286, 48.

76. Ibid., 247, 48, 106.

77. Quoted in Twain, *Christian Science*, 331.

78. Mary Baker Eddy, *Manual of the Mother Church*, 89th ed. (Boston: First Church of Christ, Scientist, 1936), 64–65.

79. Ibid., 69.

BIBLIOGRAPHY

"About Women," *Woman's Exponent* 1.6 (August 15, 1887): 46.

Adams, Kimberly Van Esveld. "Family Influences on 'The Minister's Wooing' and 'Old-town Folks': Henry Ward Beecher and Calvin Stowe," *Religion and Literature* 38 (Winter 2006): 27–61.

Aitken, Jonathan. *John Newton: From Disgrace to Amazing Grace* (Wheaton, Ill.: Crossways, 2007).

Albanese, Catherine L. "Mormonism and the Male-Female God: An Exploration in Active Mysticism," *Sunstone* 6 (March–April 1981): 52–58.

Alcott, Louisa May. "Little Women," in *Louisa May Alcott*, ed. Elaine Showalter (1868; reprint, New York: Library of America, 2005), 1–517.

———. *Under the Lilacs* (1877; reprint, Boston: Little, Brown, 1928).

Ames, Mary Clemmer. *A Memorial of Alice and Phoebe Cary, with Some of Their Later Poems* (New York: Hurd and Houghton, 1873).

Anderson, Lynn Matthews. "Issues in Contemporary Mormon Feminism," in *Mormon Identities in Transition*, ed. Douglas J. Davies (London: Cassell, 1996), 159–60.

Armstrong, Joseph. *A History of the Building of the Original Edifice of the First Church of Christ, Scientist in Boston, Massachusetts* (Boston: Christian Science Publishing Society, 1937).

Armstrong, Nancy. *Desire and Domestic Fiction: A Political History of the Novel* (New York: Oxford University Press, 1987).

Arrington, Leonard J., and Jon Haupt. "Intolerable Zion: The Image of Mormonism in Nineteenth Century American Literature," *Western Humanities Review* 22 (Fall 1968): 243–60.

Ashworth, Suzanne M. "Susan Warner's *The Wide, Wide World*, Conduct Literature, and Protocols of Female Reading in Mid-Nineteenth-Century America," *Legacy* 17 (2000): 141–64.

Augst, Thomas. *The Clerk's Tale: Young Men and Moral Life in Nineteenth-Century America* (Chicago: University of Chicago Press, 2003).

Baker, Mabel. *Light in the Morning: Memories of Susan and Anna Warner* (West Point, N.Y.: Constitution Island Association, 1978).

Barber, Ian G. "Mormon Women as 'Natural' Seers: An Enduring Legacy," in *Women and Authority: Re-emerging Mormon Feminism*, ed. Maxine Hanks (Salt Lake City: Signature, 1992), 167–84.

Barkun, Michael. *Crucible of the Millennium: The Burned-Over District of New York in the 1840s* (Syracuse, N.Y.: Syracuse University Press, 1986).

Barnes, Elizabeth. *States of Sympathy: Seduction and Democracy in the American Novel* (New York: Columbia University Press, 1997).

Bates, Ernest Sutherland, and John Valentine Dittemore. *Mary Baker Eddy: The Truth and the Tradition* (New York: Knopf, 1932).

Baum, Mary Louise. "The Hymns of Mary Baker Eddy," *Concordance to Christian Science Hymnal and Hymnal Notes* (Boston: Christian Science Publishing Society, 1975), 171–74.

Baumgartner, Frederic J. *Longing for the End: A History of Millennialism in Western Civilization* (New York: St. Martin, 1999).

The Bay Psalm Book, Being a Facsimile Reprint of the First Edition, Printed by Stephen Daye, at Cambridge in New England, 1640 (New York: Dodd, Mead, 1905).

Baym, Nina. *American Women Writers and the Work of History, 1790–1860* (New Brunswick, N.J.: Rutgers University Press, 1995).

———. *Woman's Fiction: A Guide to Novels by and About Women in America, 1820–1870*. 2nd ed. (Urbana: University of Illinois Press, 1993).

Beale, Carleton. *Brass-Knuckle Crusade: The Great Know-Nothing Conspiracy: 1820–1860* (New York: Hastings House, 1960).

Beecher, Catharine E., and Harriet Beecher Stowe. *The American Woman's Home or, Principles of Domestic Science* (1869; reprint, New York: Library of Victorian Culture, 1979).

Beecher, Edward. *The Papal Conspiracy Exposed, and Protestantism Defended, in the Light of Reason, History and Scripture* (Boston: Stearns, 1855).

Beecher, Henry Ward, ed. *Plymouth Collection of Hymns and Tunes; For the Use of Christian Congregations* (New York: A. S. Barnes, 1855).

———. "Relations of Music to Worship," *Yale Lectures on Preaching*, vol. 2 of 3 (New York: Fords, Howard, and Hurlbert, 1896), 114–45.

Beecher, Lyman. *The Autobiography, Correspondence, &c. of Lyman Beecher*, vol. 2, ed. Charles Beecher (London: Sampson Low, Son and Marsden, 1863).

———. *A Plea for the West* (1835; reprint, New York: Arno, 1977).

———. "Resources of the Adversary, and Means of Their Destruction," in *Sermons; Delivered on Various Occasions* (Boston: John P. Jewett, 1852), 267–92.

Beecher, Maureen Ursenbach. "The Eliza Enigma: The Life and Legend of Eliza R. Snow," in *Sister Saints*, ed. Vicky Burgess-Olson (Provo, Utah: Brigham Young University Press, 1978), 1–20.

———. "Three Women and the Life of the Mind," in *Eliza and Her Sisters* (Salt Lake City: Aspen, 1991), 109–29.

Bell, Alfreda Eva. *Boadicea; The Mormon Wife: Life-Scenes in Utah* (Baltimore: Arthur B. Orton, 1855).

Bellin, Joshua D. "Up to Heaven's Gate, Down in Earth's Dust," *American Literature* 65 (June 1993): 275–95.

Bennett, Paula Bernat. *The Emancipatory Project of American Women's Poetry, 1800–1900* (Princeton: Princeton University Press, 2003).

Benson, Louis F. *The English Hymn: Its Development and Use in Worship* (New York: Hodder & Stoughton, 1915).

Bentley, Nancy. "Marriage as Treason: Polygamy, Nation, and the Novel," *The Futures of American Studies*, ed. Donald E. Pease and Robyn Wiegman (Durham, N.C.: Duke University Press, 2002), 343–70.

Bercovitch, Sacvan. *The American Jeremiad* (Madison: University of Wisconsin Press, 1978).

Berlant, Lauren. *The Female Complaint: The Unfinished Business of Sentimentality in American Culture* (Durham, N.C.: Duke University Press, 2008).

———. "The Female Woman: Fanny Fern and the Form of Containment," in *The Culture of Sentiment: Race, Gender, and Sentimentality in Nineteenth-Century America*, ed. Shirley Samuels (New York: Oxford University Press, 1992), 265–81.

———. "Poor Eliza," *American Literature* 70 (September 1998): 635–68.

Billington, Ray Allen. *The Protestant Crusade, 1800–1860: A Study of the Origins of American Nativism* (Chicago: Quadrangle, 1964).

Blount, Brian K. *Revelation: A Commentary* (Louisville, Ky.: Westminster, 2009).

Boyd, Lois A., and R. Douglas Brackenridge. *Presbyterian Women in America: Two Centuries of a Quest for Status* (Westport, Conn.: Greenwood, 1993).

Boylan, Anne M. *Sunday School: The Formation of an American Institution, 1790–1880* (New Haven: Yale University Press, 1988).

Brady, Jennifer L. "Theorizing a Reading Public: Sentimentality and Advice About Novel Reading in the Antebellum United States," *American Literature* 83 (December 2011): 719–46.

Branch, E. Douglas. *The Sentimental Years: 1836–1860* (New York: D. Appleton-Century, 1934).

Bratt, James D. "The Reorientation of American Protestantism, 1835–1845," *Church History* 67 (March 1998): 52–82.

Brekus, Catherine A. "Female Evangelism in the Early Methodism Movement, 1784–1845," in *Methodism and the Shaping of American Culture,* ed. Nathan O. Hatch and John H. Wigger (Nashville, Tenn.: Kingswood, 2001), 135–73.

———. *Strangers and Pilgrims: Female Preaching in America, 1740–1845* (Chapel Hill: University of North Carolina Press, 1996).

Brodie, Fawn M. *No Man Knows My History: The Life of Joseph Smith the Mormon Prophet* (New York: Knopf, 1946).

Brooke, John L. *The Refiner's Fire: The Making of Mormon Cosmology, 1644–1844* (Cambridge: Cambridge University Press, 1994).

Brown, Candy Gunther. *The Word in the World: Evangelical Writing, Publishing, and Reading in America, 1789–1880* (Chapel Hill: University of North Carolina Press, 2004).

Brown, Gillian. *Domestic Individualism: Imagining Self in Nineteenth-Century America* (Berkeley: University of California Press, 1990).

Brown, Herbert Ross. *The Sentimental Novel in America, 1789–1860* (Durham, N.C.: Duke University Press, 1940).

Brown, Richard D. *Knowledge Is Power: The Diffusion of Information in Early America, 1700–1865* (New York: Oxford University Press, 1989).

Bunyan, John. *The Pilgrim's Progress*, ed. N. H. Keeble (1678; reprint, Oxford: Oxford University Press, 1990).

Burgett, Bruce. *Sentimental Bodies: Sex, Gender, and Citizenship in the Early Republic* (Princeton: Princeton University Press, 1998).

Bushman, Claudia "Mormon Women," in *Encyclopedia of Women and Religion in North America*, vol. 2 of 3, ed. Rosemary Skinner Keller and Rosemary Radford Ruether (Bloomington: Indiana University Press, 2006).

Butler, Jon. *Awash in a Sea of Faith: Christianizing the American People* (Cambridge, Mass.: Harvard University Press, 1990).

Butler, Jonathan M. "Adventism and the American Experience," in *The Rise of Adventism: Religion and Society in Mid-Nineteenth-Century America*, ed. Edwin S. Gaustad (New York: Harper & Row, 1974), 173–207.

Cairns, Douglas L. "The Meaning of the Veil in Ancient Greek Culture," *Women's Dress in the Ancient World*, ed. Lloyd Llewellyn-Jones (London: Duckworth, 2002), 73–93.

Campbell, Gordon. *Bible: The Story of the King James Version 1611–2011* (Oxford: Oxford University Press, 2010).

Carwadine, Richard. "The Second Great Awakening in the Urban Centers: An Examination of Methodism and the 'New Measures,'" *Journal of American History* 59 (September 1972): 327–40.

Cary, Alice. "My Creed," in *American Women Poets of the Nineteenth Century: An Anthology*, ed. Cheryl Walker (New Brunswick, N.J.: Rutgers University Press, 1995), 176–77.

Caskey, Marie. *Chariot of Fire: Religion and the Beecher Family* (New Haven: Yale University Press, 1978).

Cather, Willa, and Georgine Milmine. *The Life of Mary Baker Eddy and the History of Christian Science* (Lincoln: University of Nebraska Press, 1993).

Cavitch, Max. *American Elegy: The Poetry of Mourning from the Puritans to Whitman* (Minneapolis: University of Minnesota Press, 2007).

Cheney, Ednah D. *Louisa May Alcott: Her Life, Letters, and Journals* (1889; reprint, New York: Chelsea House, 1980).

Cherniavsky, Eve. *That Pale Mother Rising: Sentimental Discourse and the Imitation of Motherhood in Nineteenth-Century America* (Bloomington: Indiana University Press, 1995).

Chesebro', Caroline. *Victoria; or, The World Overcome* (New York: Derby and Jackson, 1856).

Chilcote, Paul Wesley. *John Wesley and the Women Preachers of Early Methodism* (Metuchen, N.J.: Scarecrow, 1991).

Child, Lydia Maria. "Introduction by the Editor," in *Narrative of the Life of Frederick Douglass, an American Slave* and *Incidents in the Life of a Slave Girl*, ed. Kwame Anthony Appiah (New York: Modern Library, 2000), 121–22.

———. "Speaking in the Church," in *A Lydia Maria Child Reader*, ed. Carolyn L. Karcher (Durham, N.C.: Duke University Press, 1997), 354–57.

Clement, Richard W. *Books on the Frontier: Print Culture in the American West, 1763–1875* (Washington, D.C.: Library of Congress, 2003).

Coleman, Dawn. *Preaching and the Rise of the American Novel* (Columbus: Ohio State University Press, 2013).

———. "The Unsentimental Woman Preacher of Uncle Tom's Cabin," *American Literature* 80 (June 2008): 265–92.

"Colonel Lathe B. Row, USMA Class 1913," *Constitution Island Annual Report* (1981): 15–16.

Conklin, Paul K. *American Originals: Homemade Varieties of Christianity* (Chapel Hill: University of North Carolina Press, 1997).

Cornwall, J. Spencer. *Stories of Our Mormon Hymns*, 2nd ed. (Salt Lake City: Deseret, 1963).

Corrigan, John, and Lynn S. Neal. *Religious Intolerance in America: A Documentary History* (Chapel Hill: University of North Carolina Press, 2010).

Cott, Nancy F. *The Bonds of Womanhood: Woman's Sphere in New England, 1780–1835* (New Haven: Yale University Press, 1977).

———. "Young Women in the Second Great Awakening," *Feminist Studies* 3 (Autumn 1975): 15–29.

Crosby, Fanny J. *Memories of Eighty Years* (Boston: James H. Earle, 1906).

Cummins, Maria Susanna. *The Lamplighter*, ed. Nina Baym (1854; New Brunswick, N.J.: Rutgers University Press, 1988).

Dakin, Edwin F. *Mrs. Eddy: The Biography of a Virgin Mind* (New York: Blue Ribbon, 1930).

Dalton, Lu. "A Mother's Resignation," *Woman's Exponent* 12 (November 15, 1872): 90.

Davidson, Cathy. "No More Separate Spheres!" *American Literature* 70.3 (September 1998): 443–63.

Davies, Douglas J. *An Introduction to Mormonism* (Cambridge: Cambridge University Press, 2003).

Davis, David Brion. *The Fear of Conspiracy: Images of Un-American Subversion from the Revolution to the Present* (Ithaca, N.Y.: Cornell University Press, 1971).

Daynes, Kathryn. *More Wives Than One: The Transformation of the Mormon Marriage System, 1840–1910* (Urbana: University of Illinois, 2001).

De Jong, Mary. "'I Want to Be Like Jesus': The Self-Defining Power of Evangelical Hymnody," *Journal of the American Academy of Religion* 54 (Autumn 1986): 461–93.

———. "'Theirs the Sweetest Songs': Women Hymn Writers in the Nineteenth-Century United States," in *A Mighty Baptism: Race, Gender, and the Creation of American Protestantism*, ed. Susan Juster and Lisa MacFarlane (Ithaca, N.Y.: Cornell University Press, 1996), 141–67.

Derr, Jill Mulvay. "Eliza R. Snow and the Woman Question," in *Life in Utah: Centennial Selections from* BYU Studies, ed. James B. Allen and John M. Welch (Provo, Utah: BYU Studies, 1996), 219–36.

——. "The Significance of 'O My Father' in the Personal Journey of Eliza R. Snow," *BYU Studies* 36 (1996–97): 85–126.

Derr, Jill Mulvay; Janath Russell Canton; and Maureen Ursenbach Beecher. *Women of Covenant: The Story of Relief Society* (Salt Lake City: Deseret, 1992).

Dewey, Mary, ed. *Life and Letters of Catharine M. Sedgwick* (New York: Harper, 1871).

Dick, Everett N. "The Millerite Movement 1830–1845," in *Adventism in America: A History*, ed. Gary Land (Grand Rapids, Mich.: Wm. B. Eerdmans, 1986), 1–35.

Dillon, Elizabeth Maddock. *The Gender of Freedom: Fictions of Liberalism and the Literary Public Sphere* (Stanford, Calif.: Stanford University Press, 2004).

——. "Sentimental Aesthetics," *American Literature* 76 (September 2004): 495–524.

Dobson, Joanne. "Reclaiming Sentimental Literature," *American Literature* 69 (June 1997): 263–88.

Douglas, Ann. *The Feminization of American Culture,* 2nd ed. (New York: Anchor, 1988).

Eddy, Mary Baker. *Manual of the Mother Church*, 89th ed. (Boston: First Church of Christ, Scientist, 1936).

——. "Message to the Annual Meeting of the Mother Church, 1896," in *Prose Works Other Than* Science and Health with Key to the Scriptures (Boston: Trustees Under the Will of Mary Baker Eddy, 1925), 125–28.

——. *Poems* (Boston: Trustees under the Will of Mary Baker Eddy, 1910).

——. *Poems Including* Christ and Christmas (Boston: Trustees Under the Will of Mary G. Baker Eddy, 1938).

——. "Reply to McClure's Magazine," in *The First Church of Christ Scientist and Miscellany* (Boston: Trustees Under the Will of Mary Baker G. Eddy, 1941), 308–16.

——. "Retrospection and Introspection," in *Prose Works Other Than* Science and Health with Key to the Scriptures (Boston: Trustees Under the Will of Mary Baker Eddy, 1925), 1–95.

——. *Science and Health with Key to the Scriptures,* rev. ed. (Boston: First Church of Christ, Scientist, 1994).

Ellison, Julie. *Cato's Tears and the Making of Anglo-American Emotion* (Chicago: University of Chicago Press, 1999).

Emerson, Ralph Waldo. "New England Reformers, Lecture at Amory Hall," in *Ralph Waldo Emerson: Essays and Lectures*, ed. Joel Porte (New York: Library of America, 1983), 589–609.

Epstein, Barbara Leslie. *The Politics of Domesticity: Women, Evangelism, and Temperance in Nineteenth-Century America* (Middletown, Conn.: Wesleyan University Press, 1981).

Evans, Augusta J. *Beulah* (1859; reprint, New York: Grosset & Dunlap, nd).

——. *St. Elmo: A Novel* (1866; reprint, New York: Arno, 1974).

Fessenden, Tracy. *Culture and Redemption: Religion, the Secular, and American Culture* (Princeton: Princeton University Press, 2007).

Fiedler, Leslie A. *Love and Death in the American Novel* (New York: Criterion, 1960).

Fields, Annie. ed. *Life and Letters of Harriet Beecher Stowe* (1897; reprint, Detroit: Gale Research Company, 1970).

Finke, Roger, and Rodney Stark. *The Churching of America, 1776–2005: Winners and Losers in Our Religious Economy* (New Brunswick, N.J.: Rutgers University Press, 2005).

Finley, Martha. *Elsie Dinsmore* (1867; reprint, New York: Arno, 1974).

Finney, Charles G. *Lectures on Revivals of Religion*, 2nd ed. (New York: Leavitt, Lord, 1835).

Fisher, Philip. *Hard Facts: Setting and Form in the American Novel* (New York: Oxford University Press, 1985).

Flew, R. Newton. *The Idea of Perfection in Christian Theology: An Historical Study of the Christian Ideal for the Present Life* (London: Oxford University Press, 1934).

Foote, Henry Wilder. *Three Centuries of American Hymnody* (Cambridge, Mass.: Harvard University Press, 1940).

Foster, Lawrence. *Women, Family, and Utopia: Communal Experiments of the Shakers, the Oneida Community, and the Mormons* (Syracuse, N.Y.: Syracuse University Press, 1991).

Franchot, Jenny. *Roads to Rome: The Antebellum Protestant Encounter with Catholicism* (Berkeley: University of California Press, 1994).

Frilingos, Christopher A. *Spectacles of Empire: Monsters, Martyrs, and the Book of Revelation* (Philadelphia: University of Pennsylvania Press, 2004).

Fuller, Metta Victoria. *Mormon Wives; A Narrative of Facts Stranger Than Fiction* (New York: Derby & Jackson, 1856).

Gallagher, Susan VanZanten. "Domesticity in American Hymns, 1820–1870," in *Sing Them Over Again to Me: Hymns and Hymnbooks in America*, ed. Mark A. Noll and Edith L. Blumhofer (Tuscaloosa: University of Alabama Press, 2006), 235–52.

Gaustad, Edwin S. "Introduction," in *The Rise of Adventism: Religion and Society in Mid-Nineteenth-Century America*, ed. Edwin S. Gaustad (New York: Harper & Row, 1974), xi–xx.

Gedge, Karin E. *Without Benefit of Clergy: Women and the Pastoral Relationship in Nineteenth-Century American Culture* (New York: Oxford University Press, 2003).

Gill, Gillian. *Mary Baker Eddy* (Cambridge, Mass: Perseus, 1998).

Ginzberg, Lori D. *Women and the Work of Benevolence: Morality, Politics, and Class in the Nineteenth-Century United States* (New Haven: Yale University Press, 1990).

Givens, Terryl L. *The Viper on the Hearth: Mormons, Myths, and the Construction of Heresy* (New York: Oxford University Press, 1997).

Godfrey, Kenneth W.; Audrey M. Godfrey; and Jill Mulvay Derr. *Women's Voices: An Untold History of the Latter-day Saints, 1830–1900* (Salt Lake City: Deseret, 1987).

Goodson, Stephanie Smith. "Plural Wives," in *Mormon Sisters: Women in Early Utah*, ed. Claudia L. Bushman (Logan, Utah: Utah State Press, 1997).

Gordon, Sarah Barringer. *The Mormon Question: Polygamy and Constitutional Conflict in Nineteenth-Century America* (Chapel Hill: University of North Carolina, 2002).

Grammer, Elizabeth Elkin. *Some Wild Visions: Autobiographies by Female Itinerant Evangelists in Nineteenth-Century America* (New York: Oxford University Press, 2003).

Gray, Elizabeth F. "Beatification Through Beautification: Poetry in *The Christian Lady's Magazine*, 1834–1849," *Victorian Poetry* 42 (2004): 261–82.

Griffin, Susan M. *Anti-Catholicism and Nineteenth-Century Fiction* (Cambridge: Cambridge University Press, 2004).

Griffith, R. Marie. *God's Daughters: Evangelical Women and the Power of Submission* (Berkeley: University of California Press, 1997).

Griffiths, Paul J. *Religious Reading: The Place of Reading in the Practice of Religion* (New York: Oxford University Press, 1999).

Groover, Edwin R. *The Well-Ordered Home: Alexander Campbell and the Family* (Joplin, Mo.: College Press, 1988).

Gustafson, Sandra. "Margaret Fuller and the Forms of Sentiment," *American Quarterly* 47 (March 1995): 34–65.

Gutjahr, Paul C. *An American Bible: A History of the Good Book in the United States, 1777–1880* (Stanford, Calif.: Stanford University Press, 1999).

Hale, Sarah Josepha. *Northwood or, Life North and South* (1852; reprint, Freeport, N.Y.: Books for Libraries Press, 1972).

Halttunen, Karen. *Confidence Men and Painted Women: A Study of Middle-Class Culture in America, 1830–1870* (New Haven: Yale University Press, 1982).

——. "The Domestic Drama of Louisa May Alcott," *Feminist Studies* 10 (1984): 233–54.

Hambrick-Stowe, Charles E. *Charles G. Finney and the Spirit of American Evangelicalism* (Grand Rapids, Mich.: Eerdmans, 1996).

Hamilton, J. Taylor, and Kenneth G. Hamilton. *History of the Moravian Church: The Renewed Unitas Fratrum, 1722–1957* (Bethlehem, Pa.: Moravian Church of America, 1967).

Hardesty, Nancy A. *Woman Called to Witness: Evangelical Feminism in the Nineteenth Century* (Nashville, Tenn.: Abingdon, 1984).

Harding, Susan F. "Convicted by the Spirit: The Rhetoric of Fundamental Baptist Conversion," *American Ethnologist* 14 (February 1987): 167–81.

Hardman, Keith J. *Charles Grandison Finney, 1792–1875: Revivalist and Reformer* (Syracuse, N.Y.: Syracuse University Press, 1987).

Harrison, J. F. C. *The Second Coming: Popular Millenarianism, 1780–1850* (London: Routledge, 1979).

Hatch, Nathan O. *The Democratization of American Christianity* (New Haven: Yale University Press, 1989).

——. "The Origins of Civil Millennialism in America: New England Clergymen, War with France, and the Revolution," *William and Mary Quarterly* 31 (July 1974): 407–30.

———. "The Puzzle of American Methodism," in *Methodism and the Shaping of American Culture*, ed. Nathan O. Hatch and John H. Wigger (Nashville, Tenn.: Kingswood, 2001), 23–40.

Hawthorne, Nathaniel. "The Scarlet Letter," in *Nathaniel Hawthorne: Collected Novels* (1850; reprint, New York: Library of America, 1983), 116–345.

Hay, Ella H. *A Child's Life of Mary Baker Eddy* (Boston: Christian Science Publishing Society, 1942).

Hedrick, Joan D. *Harriet Beecher Stowe: A Life* (New York: Oxford University Press, 1994).

Heeren, John; Donald B. Lindsey; and Marylee Mason. "The Mormon Concept of Mother in Heaven: A Sociological Account of Its Origins and Development," *Journal for the Scientific Study of Religion* 23.4 (December 1984): 396–411.

Hendler, Glenn. *Public Sentiments: Structures of Feeling in Nineteenth-Century American Literature* (Chapel Hill: University of North Carolina Press, 2001).

Hildebrandt, Franz. "Introduction to 'A Little Body of Practical Divinity,'" in *The Works of John Wesley*, vol. 7, *A Collection of Hymns for the Use of the People Called Methodists*, ed. F. Hildebrandt and Oliver A. Beckerlegge (Oxford: Clarendon, 1983), 1–22.

Hinckley, President Gordon B. "Daughters of God," *Ensign* (November 1991): 97–102.

Hobbs, June Hadden. *"I Sing for I Cannot Be Silent": The Feminization of American Hymnody, 1870–1920* (Pittsburgh: University of Pittsburgh Press, 1997).

Howard, June. *Publishing the Family* (Durham, N.C.: Duke University Press, 2001).

———. "What Is Sentimentality?" *American Literary History* 11 (Spring 1999): 63–81.

Howells, William Dean. "Criticism and Fiction," in *William Dean Howells Selected Literary Criticism*, vol. 2, *1886–1897*, ed. Donald Pizer (Bloomington: Indiana University Press, 1993), 295–352.

Hubbard, Elbert. *Little Journeys to the Homes of Great Teachers—Mary Baker Eddy* (East Aurora, N.Y.: Roycrofters, 1908).

Hudson, Winthrop S. "A Time of Religious Ferment," in *The Rise of Adventism: Religion and Society in Mid-Nineteenth-Century America*, ed. Edwin S. Gaustad (New York: Harper & Row, 1974), 1–17.

Hughes, Charles. *American Hymns Old and New: Notes on the Hymns and Biographies of the Authors and Composers* (New York: Columbia University Press, 1980).

Hughes, Richard T. "Christian Primitivism as Perfectionism: From Anabaptists to Pentecostals," in *Reaching Beyond: Chapters in the History of Perfectionism*, ed. Stanley M. Burgess (Peabody, Mass.: Hendrickson, 1986), 213–55.

In My True Light and Life: Mary Baker Eddy Collections (Boston: Mary Baker Eddy Library for the Betterment of Humanity, 2002).

James, Henry. "The Art of Fiction," in *The Art of Criticism: Henry James on the Theory and the Practice of Fiction*, ed. William Veeder and Susan M. Griffin (Chicago: University of Chicago Press, 1986), 165–96.

James, William. "The Varieties of Religious Experience," in *William James: Writings 1902–1910*, ed. Bruce Kuklick (New York: Library of America, 1987), 1–477.

Jay, Elisabeth. *The Religion of the Heart: Anglican Evangelicalism and the Nineteenth-Century Novel* (Oxford: Clarendon, 1979).

Johnson, Paul E. *A Shopkeeper's Millennium: Society and Revivals in Rochester, New York 1815–1837* (New York: Hill & Wang, 1978).

Johnson Paul E., and Sean Wilentz. *The Kingdom of Matthias* (New York: Oxford University Press, 1994).

Keller, Catherine. "Ms.Calculating the Apocalypse," in *Gender and Apocalyptic Desire*, ed. Brenda E. Brasher and Lee Quinby (London: Equinox, 2006), 1–13.

Kelley, Mary. *Private Woman, Public Stage: Literary Domesticity in Nineteenth-Century America* (New York: Oxford University Press, 1984).

Kermode, Frank. *The Sense of an Ending: Studies in the Theory of Fiction* (New York: Oxford University Press, 1967).

Kett, Joseph F. *Rites of Passage: Adolescence in America, 1790 to the Present* (New York: Basic, 1977).

Kim, Sharon. "Puritan Realism: *The Wide, Wide World* and *Robinson Crusoe*," *American Literature* 75 (December 2003): 783–812.

Kimball, Gayle. *The Religious Ideas of Harriet Beecher Stowe: Her Gospel of Womanhood* (New York: Edwin Mellen, 1982).

Kimball, President Spencer W. "The True Way of Life and Salvation," *Ensign* (May 1978). Found at Church of Jesus Christ of the Latter-Day Saints, http://www.lds.org/ensign/1978/05/the-true-way-of-life-and-salvation.

Kort, Wesley A. *"Take, Read": Scripture, Textuality, and Cultural Practice* (University Park: Pennsylvania State University Press, 1996).

Laderman, Gary. *The Sacred Remains: American Attitudes Toward Death, 1799–1883* (New Haven: Yale University Press, 1996).

Lang, Amy Schrager. *Prophetic Woman: Anne Hutchinson and the Problem of Dissent in the Literature of New England* (Berkeley: University of California Press, 1987).

Lawless, Elaine J. "Rescripting Their Lives and Narratives: Spiritual Life Stories of Pentecostal Women Preachers," *Journal of Feminist Studies in Religion* 7 (Spring 1991): 53–71.

Leslie, Madeline. *The Household Angel in Disguise* (1857; reprint, Boston: Shepard, Clark, 1860).

Lewis, A. J. *Zinzendorf, the Ecumenical Pioneer: A Study in the Moravian Contribution to Christian Mission and Unity* (Philadelphia: Westminster, 1962).

Life and Labors of Eliza R. Snow Smith, With a Full Account of Her Funeral Services (Salt Lake City: Juvenile Instructor Office, 1888).

Lindley, Susan Hill. "The Ambiguous Feminism of Mary Baker Eddy," *Journal of Religion* 64 (July 1984): 318–31.

Lingle, Walter L., and John W. Kuykendall. *Presbyterians: Their History and Beliefs* (Atlanta: John Knox, 1988).

Llewellyn-Jones, Lloyd. *Aphrodite's Tortoise: The Veiled Woman of Ancient Greece* (Swansea, U.K.: Classical Press of Wales, 2003), 98–107.

Lloyd, Gareth. *Charles Wesley and the Struggle for Methodist Identity* (New York: Oxford University Press, 2007).

Loetscher, Lefferts. *A Brief History of the Presbyterians*, 4th ed. (Philadelphia: Westminster, 1983).

Luciano, Dana. *Arranging Grief: Sacred Time and the Body in Nineteenth-Century America* (New York: New York University Press, 2007).

MacDonald, Ruth K. *Christian's Children: The Influence of John Bunyan's* The Pilgrim's Progress *on American Children's Literature* (New York: Peter Lang, 1989).

Maison, Margaret. "'Thine, only Thine!' Women Hymn Writers in Britain, 1760–1835," in *Religion in the Lives of English Women, 1760–1930*, ed. Gail Malmgreen (Bloomington: Indiana University Press, 1986), 11–40.

Mandelker, Ira L. *Religion, Society, and Utopia in Nineteenth-Century America* (Amherst: University of Massachusetts, 1984).

Mason, Lowell; Edwards Park; and Austin Phelps, eds. *The Sabbath Hymn and Tune Book, for the Service of Song in the House of the Lord*, (1859; reprint, New York: Mason Brothers, 1865).

Massa, Mark S., S.J. *Anti-Catholicism: The Last Acceptable Prejudice* (New York: Crossroad, 2003).

May, Henry F. "The Recovery of American Religious History," *American Historical Review* 70.1 (October 1964): 79–92.

McDannell, Colleen. *The Christian Home in Victorian America, 1840–1900* (Bloomington: Indiana University Press, 1986).

McDannell, Colleen, and Bernhard Lang. *Heaven: A History* (New Haven: Yale University Press, 1988).

McDonald, W.; Joshua Gill, et al. *Songs of Joy and Gladness* (Boston: McDonald, Gill, 1888).

McIntosh, Maria J. *Charms and Counter-Charms* (New York: D. Appleton, 1848).

———. *Woman in America: Her Work and Her Reward* (New York: Appleton, 1850).

McKeon, Michael. *The Origins of the English Novel, 1600–1740* (Baltimore: Johns Hopkins University Press, 1987).

McLoughlin, William G. *Modern Revivalism: Charles Grandison Finney to Billy Graham* (New York: Ronald, 1959).

———. *Revivals, Awakenings, and Reform: An Essay on Religion and Social Change in America, 1607–1977* (Chicago: University of Chicago Press, 1978).

Miller, Perry. *The Life of the Mind in America: From the Revolution to the Civil War* (New York: Harcourt, Brace, 1965).

Monk, Maria. *Awful Disclosures of the Hotel Dieu Nunnery*, ed. Ray Allen Billington (1836; reprint, Hamden, Conn.: Archon, 1962).

Moody, Joycelyn. *Sentimental Confessions: Spiritual Narratives of Nineteenth-Century African American Women* (Athens: University of Georgia Press, 2001).

Moorhead, James. *American Apocalypse: Yankee Protestants and the Civil War* (New Haven: Yale University Press, 1978).

Morgan, Robert J. *Then Sings My Soul: 150 of the World's Greatest Hymn Stories* (Nashville, Tenn.: Thomas Nelson, 2003).

Morrill, Susanna. *White Roses on the Floor of Heaven: Mormon Women's Popular Theology, 1880–1920* (New York: Routledge, 2006).

Nettleton, Asahel. *Village Hymns for Social Worship, Selected and Original*, 2nd ed. (New York: Goodwin, 1824).

Niebuhr, H. Richard. *The Kingdom of God in America* (Chicago: Willett, Clark, 1937).

Ninde, Edward S. *The Story of the American Hymn* (New York: Abingdon, 1921).

Noble, Marianne. *The Masochistic Pleasures of Sentimental Literature* (Princeton: Princeton University Press, 2000).

Noll, Mark A. *America's God: From Jonathan Edwards to Abraham Lincoln* (New York: Oxford University Press, 2002).

Nord, David Paul. *Faith in Reading: Religious Publishing and the Birth of Mass Media in America* (New York: Oxford University Press, 2004).

Numbers, Ronald L. *Prophetess of Health: Ellen G. White and the Origins of Seventh-Day Adventist Health Reform*, rev. ed. (Knoxville: University of Tennessee, 1992).

Orcutt, William Dana. *Mary Baker Eddy and Her Books* (Boston: Christian Science Publishing Society, 1950).

Papashvily, Helen Waite. *All the Happy Endings* (New York: Harper & Brothers, 1956).

Parker, Gail. "Mary Baker Eddy and Sentimental Womanhood," *New England Quarterly* 43 (March 1970): 3–18.

Pattee, Fred Louis. *The Feminine Fifties* (New York: Appleton, 1940).

Peel, Robert. *Mary Baker Eddy: The Years of Discovery*, vol. 1 of 2 (New York: Holt, Rinehart and Winston, 1966).

Pelletier, Kevin. "*Uncle Tom's Cabin* and Apocalyptic Sentimentalism," *Lit: Literature and Interpretation Theory* 20 (November 2009): 266–87.

"Pen Sketch of an Illustrious Woman," *Woman's Exponent* 9 (August 1, 1880), 33–34.

Phelps, Elizabeth Stuart. *The Gates Ajar* (1868; reprint, Cambridge: Belknap, 1964).

Pierce, Martha. "Personal Discourse on God the Mother," in *Women and Authority: Re-emerging Mormon Feminism*, ed. Maxine Hanks (Salt Lake City: Signature, 1992), 247–56.

Pippin, Tina. *Death and Desire: The Rhetoric of Gender in the Apocalypse of John* (Louisville, Ky.: Westminster, 1992).

———. "Eros and the End: Reading Gender in the Apocalypse of John," *Semeia* 59 (1992): 193–210.

Pittman, Emma R. *Lady Hymn Writers* (London: T. Nelson, 1892).

Porterfield, Amanda. *Feminine Spirituality in America: From Sarah Edwards to Martha Graham* (Philadelphia: Temple University Press, 1980).

Pratt, Orson, ed. *The Doctrine and Covenants, of the Church of Jesus Christ of Latter-Day Saints, Containing the Revelations Given to Joseph Smith, Jun., the Prophet, for the Building Up of the Kingdom of God in the Last Days* (1880; reprint, Westport, Conn.: Greenwood, 1971).

Prentiss, Elizabeth. *The Life and Letters of Elizabeth Prentiss*, ed. George Prentiss (New York: Anson D. F. Randolph, 1882).

Putney, Clifford. *Muscular Christianity: Manhood and Sports in Protestant America, 1880–1920* (Cambridge, Mass.: Harvard University Press, 2001).

Quinby, Lee. *Millennial Seduction: A Skeptic Confronts Apocalyptic Culture* (Ithaca, N.Y.: Cornell University Press, 1999).

Reed, Rebecca Theresa. *Six Months in a Convent* (1835; reprint, New York: Arno, 1977).

Remini, Robert V. *Andrew Jackson and the Course of American Democracy*, vol. 3 (New York: Harper & Row, 1984).

Reynolds, David S. *Faith in Fiction: The Emergence of Religious Literature in America* (Cambridge, Mass.: Harvard University Press, 1981).

Reynolds, William J. *A Survey of Christian Hymnody* (Carol Stream, Ill.: Hope, 1987).

Rogal, Samuel. *A General Introduction to Hymnody and Congregational Song* (Metuchen, N.J.: American Theological Library Association, 1991).

Romero, Lora. *Home Fronts: Domesticity and Its Critics in the Antebellum United States* (Durham, N.C.: Duke University Press, 1997).

Rubin, Joan Shelley. *The Making of Middle-Brow Culture* (Chapel Hill: University of North Carolina Press, 1992).

Ruether, Rosemary Radford. *Goddesses and the Divine Feminine* (Berkeley: University of California Press, 2005).

Russell, John. *The Mormoness; or, The Trials of Mary Maverick* (Alton, Ill.: Courier Steam Press Print, 1853).

Ryan, Mary P. *Cradle of the Middle Class: The Family in Oneida County, New York, 1790–1865* (Cambridge: Cambridge University Press, 1981).

Ryden, E. E. *The Story of Christian Hymnody* (Rock Island, Ill.: Augustana, 1961).

Samuels, Shirley. "Introduction," in *Culture of Sentiment: Race, Gender, and Sentimentality in Nineteenth-Century America* (New York: Oxford University Press, 1992), 3–8.

———. *Romance of the Republic: Women, the Family, and Violence in the Literature of the Early American Nation* (New York: Oxford University Press, 1996).

Sánchez-Eppler, Karen. *Touching Liberty: Abolition, Feminism, and the Politics of the Body* (Berkeley: University of California Press, 1993).

Sandeen, Ernest. "Millennialism," in *The Rise of Adventism: Religion and Society in Mid-Nineteenth-Century America*, ed. Edwin S. Gaustad (New York: Harper & Row, 1974), 104–18.

Satter, Beryl. *Each Mind a Kingdom: American Women, Sexual Purity, and the New Thought Movement, 1875–1920* (Berkeley, University of California Press, 1999).

Schilling, S. Paul. *The Faith We Sing* (Philadelphia: Westminster, 1983).

Schlesinger, Arthur M., Jr., *The Age of Jackson* (Boston: Little, Brown, 1950).

Schmidt, Jean Miller. *Grace Sufficient: A History of Women in American Methodism, 1760–1939* (Nashville, Tenn.: Abingdon, 1999).

Schneider, A. Gregory. *The Way of the Cross Leads Home: The Domestication of American Methodism* (Bloomington: Indiana University Press, 1993).

Scholten, Catherine M. *Childbearing in American Society: 1650–1850* (New York: New York University Press, 1985).

Schrager, Cynthia D. "Mark Twain and Mary Baker Eddy: Gendering the Transpersonal Subject," *American Literature* 70 (March 1998): 29–63.

Scott, Anne Firor. "Mormon Women, Other Women: Paradoxes and Challenges," in *The Mormon History Association's Tanner Lectures: The First Twenty Years*, ed. Dean L. May and Reid L. Neilson (Urbana: University of Illinois Press, 2006), 207–23.

Scott, Donald M. *From Office to Profession: The New England Ministry, 1750–1850* (Philadelphia: University of Pennsylvania Press, 1978).

Sedgwick, Catharine Maria. *Home* (1835; reprint, Boston: James Munroe, 1839).

———. *Hope Leslie; or, Early Times in the Massachusetts,* ed. Mary Kelley (1827; reprint, New Brunswick, N.J.: Rutgers University Press, 1995).

———. *A New-England Tale, and Miscellanies* (1822; reprint, New York: Putnam, 1852).

Seelye, John. *Jane Eyre's American Daughters from the Wide, Wide World to Anne of Green Gables: A Study of Marginalized Maids and What They Mean* (Newark: University of Delaware Press, 2005).

Shipps, Jan. "Dangerous History: Laurel Ulrich and Her Mormon Sisters," *Christian Century* 110 (10 October 1993): 1012–15.

———. *Mormonism: The Story of a New Religious Tradition* (Urbana: University of Illinois Press, 1985).

Sizer, Sandra S. *Gospel Hymns and Social Religion: The Rhetoric of Nineteenth-Century Religion* (Philadelphia: Temple University Press, 1978).

Smith, Eva Munson, ed. *Woman in Sacred Song: A Library of Hymns, Religious Poems, and Sacred Music by Woman* (Chicago: Standard Music, 1888).

Smith, Nicholas. *Songs from the Hearts of Women: One Hundred Famous Hymns and Their Writers* (Chicago: A. C. McClurg, 1903).

Smith-Rosenberg, Carroll. *Disorderly Conduct: Visions of Gender in Victorian America* (New York: Knopf, 1985).

Snow, Eliza R. *Eliza R. Snow: The Complete Poetry*, ed. Jill Mulvay Derr and Karen Lynn Davidson (Provo, Utah: Brigham Young University Press, 2009).

———. *Eliza R. Snow: An Immortal—Selected Writings of Eliza R. Snow* (Salt Lake City: Nicholas G. Morgan, Sr., Foundation, 1957).

———. *Poems: Religious, Historical, and Political* (Liverpool: F. D. Richards, 1856).

———. "Sketch of My Life," in *The Personal Writings of Eliza Roxcy Snow*, ed. Maureen Ursenbach Beecher (Salt Lake City: University of Utah Press, 1995).

Southworth, E. D. E. N. *The Hidden Hand or, Capitola the Madcap* (1859; reprint, New Brunswick, N.J.: Rutgers University Press, 1988).

Springer, Fleta Campbell. *According to the Flesh* (New York: Coward-McCann, 1930).

Sprinkle, Stephen V. *Disciples and Theology: Understanding the Faith of a People in Covenant* (St. Louis: Chalice, 1999).

Stanton, Elizabeth Cady, ed. *The Woman's Bible, Parts I and II* (1898; reprint, Hong Kong: Forgotten Books, 2007).

Stein, Stephen J. *The Shaker Experience in America: A History of the United Society of Believers* (New Haven: Yale University Press, 1992).

Stenhouse, Mrs. T. B. H. *"Tell It All": The Story of a Life's Experiences in Mormonism* (1872; reprint, Hartford, Conn.: A. D. Worthington, 1876).

Stern, Julia A. *The Plight of Feeling: Sympathy and Dissent in the Early American Novel* (Chicago: University of Chicago Press, 1997).

Stetson, Augusta E. *Reminiscences, Sermons, and Correspondence: Proving Adherence to the Principle of Christian Science as Taught by Mary Baker Eddy* (New York: Putnam, 1917).

Stokes, Claudia. "The Religious Novel," in *The Oxford History of the Novel in English: The American Novel: 1870–1940*, vol. 6, ed. Priscilla Wald and Michael A. Elliott (New York: Oxford University Press, 2014), 168–83.

Stokes, Olivia Egleston Phelps. *Letters and Memories of Susan and Anna Bartlett Warner* (New York: Putnam, 1925).

Stone, Jon R. *A Guide to the End of the World: Popular Eschatology in America* (New York: Garland, 1993).

Stouck, David. "Introduction," in Willa Cather and Georgine Milmine, *The Life of Mary Baker Eddy and the History of Christian Science* (Lincoln: University of Nebraska Press, 1993), xv–xxviii.

Stowe, Calvin E. *The Criticism and Interpretation of the Bible, Designed for the Use of Theological Students, Bible Classes, and High Schools*, vol. 1 of 2 (Cincinnati: Corey, Fairbank, and Webster, 1835).

———. *Origin and History of the Books of the Bible* (Hartford, Conn.: Hartford, 1867).

Stowe, Charles Edward, ed. *Life of Harriet Beecher Stowe, Compiled from the Letters and Journals* (Boston: Houghton, Mifflin, 1889).

Stowe, Harriet Beecher. *Agnes of Sorrento* (Boston: Ticknor and Fields, 1862).

———. *Dred; A Tale of the Great Dismal Swamp*, 2 vols. (1856; Grosse Point, Mich.: Scholarly, 1968).

———. "The First Christmas of New England," in *Betty's Bright Idea* (New York: J. B. Ford, 1876), 113–59.

———. *Footsteps of the Master* (New York: J. B. Ford, 1877).

———. "He's Coming Tomorrow," in *The Second Coming of Christ* (Chicago: Moody Press, 1976), 7–15.

———. *House and Home Papers* (1864; reprint, Bedford, Mass.: Applewood, nd).

———. *A Key to Uncle Tom's Cabin; Presenting the Original Facts and Documents upon Which the Story Is Founded. Together with Corroborative Statements Verifying the Truth of the Work.* (Boston: John P. Jewett, 1853).

———. *The Minister's Wooing* (1859; reprint, Ridgewood, N.J.: Gregg, 1968).

———. *My Wife and I: or, Harry Henderson's History* (New York: J. B. Ford, 1871).

———. *Oldtown Folks* (1869; reprint, New Brunswick, N.J.: Rutgers University Press, 1987).

———. *The Pearl of Orr's Island: A Story of the Coast of Maine* (1862; reprint, Ridgewood, N.J.: Gregg, 1967).

———. *Poganuc People: Their Loves and Lives* (New York: Ford, Howard, and Hulbert, 1878).

———. *Religious Studies: Sketches and Poems* (Boston: Houghton, Mifflin, 1896).

———. *Sam Lawson's Oldtown Fireside Stories* (London: Sampson Low, 1871).

———. *Uncle Tom's Cabin or, Life Among the Lowly*, ed. Ann Douglas (1852; reprint, New York: Penguin, 1981).

Strout, Cushing. "*Uncle Tom's Cabin* and the Portent of Millennium," *Yale Review* 57 (Spring 1968): 374–85.

Sweet, Leonard I. *The Minister's Wife: Her Role in Nineteenth-Century American Evangelism* (Philadelphia: Temple University Press, 1983).

Switzer, Jennie Bartlett. *Elder Northfield's Home; Or, Sacrificed on the Mormon Altar: The Story of the Blighting Curse of Polygamy* (1882; reprint, New York: Books for Libraries, 1971).

Taves, Ann. *Fits, Trances, and Visions: Experiencing Religion and Explaining Experience from Wesley to James* (Princeton: Princeton University Press, 1999).

Terry, Keith, and Ann Terry. *Eliza: A Poetess Comes to Zion* (Orem, Utah: Kenninghouse, 1995).

Tomlinson, Irving C. *Twelve Years with Mary Baker Eddy: Recollections and Experiences* (Boston: Christian Science Publishing Society, 1945).

Tompkins, Jane. *Sensational Designs: The Cultural Work of American Fiction, 1790–1860* (New York: Oxford University Press, 1985).

Toscano, Margaret Merrill. "Is There a Place for Heavenly Mother in Mormon Theology? An Investigation into Discourses of Power," *Sunstone* 133 (July 2004): 411–38.

Tullidge, Edward W. *The Women of Mormondom* (New York: Tullidge & Crandall, 1877).

Tuveson, Ernest Lee. *Millennium and Utopia: A Study in the Background of the Idea of Progress* (New York: Harper, 1964).

———. *Redeemer Nation: The Idea of America's Millennial Role* (Chicago: University of Chicago Press, 1968).

Twain, Mark. *Christian Science with Notes Containing Corrections to Date* (New York: Harper, 1907).

Ulrich, Laurel Thatcher. *Good Wives: Image and Reality in the Lives of Women in Northern New England, 1650–1750* (New York: Random House, 1982).

Van Engen, Abram. "Puritanism and the Power of Sympathy," *Early American Literature* 45.3 (Fall 2010): 533–64.

Wainwright, Arthur W. *Mysterious Apocalypse: Interpreting the Book of Revelation* (Eugene, Ore.: Wipf and Stock, 2001).

Ward, Austin N. *The Husband in Utah; or, Sights and Scenes Among the Mormons*, ed. Maria Ward (New York: J. C. Derby, 1857).

Ward, Maria. *Female Life Among the Mormons* (1855; reprint, New York: J. C. Derby, 1856).

Warenski, Marilyn. *Patriarchs and Politics: The Plight of Mormon Woman* (New York: McGraw-Hill, 1978).

Warner, Anna B. [pseudonymously as Amy Lathrop]. *Glen Luna; or, Dollars and Cents* (1852; reprint, London: James Nisbet, 1870).

———. *Hymns of the Church Militant* (1858; reprint, New York: Robert Carter, 1865).

———. *Susan Warner* (New York: Putnam, 1909).

Warner, Susan. *The Law and the Testimony* (New York: Robert Carter, 1853).

———. *Queechy* (1852; reprint, Philadelphia: J. B. Lippincott, 1907).

———. *The Wide, Wide World* (1850; reprint, New York: Feminist, 1987).

Warner, Susan, and Anna Warner [pseudonymously as Elizabeth Wetherell and Amy Lathrop]. *Say and Seal*, 2 vols. (Philadelphia: J. B. Lippincott, 1860).

Watts, Isaac. *Divine and Moral Songs for the Use of Children* (1715; reprint, New York: Hurd and Houghton, 1866).

———. *Hymns and Spiritual Songs* (1707; reprint, London: Strahan and Rivington, 1773).

Watson, Harry L. *Liberty and Power: The Politics of Jacksonian America* (New York: Hill and Wang, 2006).

We Knew Mary Baker Eddy (Boston: Christian Science Publishing Society, 1953).

Weber, Timothy P. *Living in the Shadow of the Second Coming: American Premillennialism, 1875–1925* (New York: Oxford University Press, 1979).

Welter, Barbara. "The Cult of True Womanhood: 1820–1869," *American Quarterly* 18 (Summer 1966): 151–74.

Wendté, Charles W., and H. S. Perkins. *The Sunny Side: A Book of Religious Songs for the Sunday School and the Home* (New York: William A. Pond, 1875).

Wesley, John. *A Collection of Hymns for the Use of the People Called Methodists*, vol. 7, *The Works of John Wesley*, ed. Franz Hildebrandt and Oliver A. Beckerlegge (Oxford: Clarendon, 1983).

———. *A Plain Account of Christian Perfection* (1872; reprint, Kansas City: Beacon Hill, 1966).

Wexler, Laura. "Seeing Sentiment: Photography, Race, and the Innocent Eye," in *American Literary Studies: A Methodological Reader*, ed. Michael A. Elliott and Claudia Stokes (New York: New York University Press, 2003), 63–94.

———. "Tender Violence: Literary Eavesdropping, Domestic Fiction, and Educational Reform," in *The Culture of Sentiment: Race, Gender, and Sentimentality in Nineteenth-Century America*, ed. Shirley Samuels (New York: Oxford University Press, 1992), 9–38.

Wheeler, Michael. *Death and the Future Life in Victorian Life, Literature and Theology* (Cambridge: Cambridge University Press, 1990).

White, Ellen G. *The Ministry of Healing* (1905; reprint, Mountain View, Calif.: Pacific, 1942).

White, O. Kendall Jr. "Ideology of the Family in Nineteenth-Century Mormonism," *Sociological Spectrum* 6 (1986): 289–306.

Whitley, Edward. *American Bards: Walt Whitman and Other Unlikely Candidates for National Poet* (Chapel Hill: University of North Carolina Press, 2010).

Whitney, Helen Mar. *Why We Practice Plural Marriage* (Salt Lake City: Juvenile Instructor Office, 1884).

Wigger, John H. *Taking Heaven by Storm: Methodism and the Rise of Popular Christianity in America* (New York: Oxford University Press, 1998).

Wilbur, Sibyl. *The Life of Mary Baker Eddy* (Boston: Christian Science Publishing Society, 1941).

Wilcox, Linda. "The Mormon Concept of a Mother in Heaven," *Sunstone,* 23 (September–October 1980): 9–15.

———. "Mormon Motherhood: Official Images," in *Sisters in Spirit: Mormon Women in Historical and Cultural Perspective*, ed. Maureen Ursenbach Beecher and Lavina Fielding Anderson (Urbana: University of Illinois Press, 1987), 208–26.

Wilenz, Sean. *Andrew Jackson* (New York: Times Books, 2005).

Woman's Exponent 1.12 (November 15, 1872): 96.

Young, Ann Eliza. *Wife No. 19, or That Story of a Life in Bondage, Being a Complete Expose of Mormonism, and Revealing the Sorrows, Sacrifices and Sufferings of Women in Polygamy* (1875; reprint, New York: Arno, 1972).

Young, Brigham. "I Hope the Brethren and Sisters Will Remember What Has Been Said," in *The Essential Brigham Young* (Salt Lake City: Signature, 1992), 213–17.

Zboray, Ronald J. *A Fictive People: Antebellum Economic Development and the American Reading Public* (New York: Oxford University Press, 1993).

———. "Reading Patterns in Antebellum America: Evidence in the Charge Records of the New York Society Library," *Libraries and Culture* 26 (Spring 1991): 301–33.

Zweig, Stefan. *Mental Healers: Franz Anton Mesmer, Mary Baker Eddy, Sigmund Freud*, trans. Eden and Cedar Paul (Garden City, N.J.: Garden City, 1932).

INDEX

Adoption, 165, 201–2

Afterlife, 18, 95, 165–68, 172, 173, 177, 241n74. *See also* Heaven

Alcott, Louisa May, 16, 159, 161; *Little Men*, 201; *Little Women*, 10, 14, 47, 51, 67, 195, 201, 207; "My Kingdom," 89–90, 98–99, 235n92; *Under the Lilacs*, 88–90, 98–99

American Bible Society, 4, 15, 55, 56

American Board of Missions, 112

American Home Missionary Society, 4, 26, 30, 103

American Revolution, 25, 110, 115

American Tract Society, 4, 15, 26, 30, 36–37

Anti-Catholicism, 4, 10–12, 15–16, 24–26, 30, 36, 51, 55–61, 110–12, 122, 144, 218n17. *See also* Catholicism

Anti-Catholic novels, 10, 51, 52, 56, 144, 146–47

Anti-clericalism, 7, 9, 10, 16, 23, 24, 40, 51, 53, 56–58, 65, 71, 147. *See also* Clergy

Apocalypse, 107, 117–25, 138–40, 210–12, 240n59

Arminianism, 26, 47–50, 53

Asbury, Francis, 43, 62

Atlantic Monthly, 127

Autonomy, religious, 6, 9, 10, 23–24, 47, 55, 62, 111; Methodism and, 26, 28

Barnes, Elizabeth, 40, 226n98, 253n52

Bay Psalm Book, 70–71

Baym, Nina, 2, 38, 107, 111, 223n40, 227n113, 228n115, 233n58, 241n79

Beecher, Catharine, 105, 126–27, 239n49

Beecher, Charles, 97

Beecher, Edward, 56, 218n17

Beecher, George, 55, 113

Beecher, Henry Ward, 73, 80, 91, 97, 101, 103

Beecher, Lyman, 27, 29, 34, 35, 39, 97, 111, 112–13, 233 n55

Belisle, Orvilla, 146, 147

Bell, Alfreda, 146, 147–48

Benevolence organizations, 28, 160, 163. *See also* Relief Society

Bennett, Paula, 173

Bentley, Nancy, 7, 65, 151

Berlant, Lauren, 40, 94, 139, 203, 234n76, 241n69

Bible, 1, 28, 35, 51, 65, 67, 75, 134–35, 197, 212–13, 241n77; Catholicism and, 16, 55–61, 124; King James Version, 55–57, 61; quoted, 29, 34, 60, 70, 109, 110, 112, 117, 122, 124–25, 133, 134, 136, 137, 182, 199; reading of, 10, 13, 15, 16, 49, 55–61; Revelation, 105, 107–9, 110, 114, 115, 120, 121–22, 123–25, 132–33, 135, 136, 138, 139, 186, 197, 211–12, 240n59; in sectarian conflict, 55–61; study of, 63–64; women and, 61, 123–25, 210, 211–12

Blackwell, Antoinette Brown, 31

Book of Mormon, 144–45

Brady, Jennifer L., 13

Brown, Candy Gunther, 13, 14

Brown, Gillian, 10, 107

Brown, Herbert Ross, 40, 104

Brown, Phoebe Hinsdale, 93, 97

Bryant, William Cullen, 93

Bunyan, John, 67; *The Pilgrim's Progress*, 13–14, 35, 51

Burgett, Bruce, 7

Burr, Aaron, 117, 129, 130

Bushnell, Horace, 103

Calvin, John, 70, 108
Calvinism, 1, 47, 71, 117, 189; criticisms
    of, 25, 30, 31, 36, 41–42, 52, 198, 199,
    225n81; decline of, 21–26; sentimentalism
    and, 21, 23. See also Predestination
Campbell, Alexander, 22, 103
Campbellism, 4, 17, 25
Cary, Alice, 39, 61, 92, 142, 159
Cary, Phoebe, 16, 92, 159, 234n68
Cather, Willa, 19, 184–85, 191–93, 203
Catholicism, 1, 15–16, 41, 110–12, 122, 130,
    210, 213–14, 220n13; Bible and, 16, 55–
    61, 124; criticisms of, 10, 11, 41, 55–56;
    immigration and, 4, 25–26; women and,
    30, 52, 124. See also Anti-Catholicism
Cherniavsky, Eve, 173, 224n63
Chesebro', Caroline, 38, 49
Child, Lydia Maria, 30, 124, 240n62
Christian Primitivism, 58–59, 112
Christian Science, 139, 181, 204–5; reading
    and, 213; tenets of, 181, 186, 191, 195–96,
    199, 200–201, 207, 210–13. See also Mary
    Baker Eddy
Church of Jesus Christ of Latter-Day Saints.
    See Mormonism
Clergy, 7, 8, 66, 70, 120, 122, 227n113;
    changes in, 22, 26–28, 32, 77; criticisms
    of, 10, 24, 28, 50–51; Methodism and,
    26–27, 77; women and, 7, 31–33
Coleman, Dawn, 2, 33, 44
Conduct literature, 13, 14
Congregationalism, 4, 71, 78, 79, 198,
    232n40; decline of, 25
Consolation verse, 143, 189–90, 202, 243n4
Conversion, 41, 43–49, 147, 150, 151, 156,
    157, 189–90, 226n96
Cott, Nancy, 38, 156, 223n48
Crosby, Fanny J., 16, 92, 96, 97
Cummins, Maria Susanna, 136, 161; The
    Lamplighter, 37, 47, 51–54, 121, 156, 163,
    189

Dalton, Lu, 143, 152, 162
Daynes, Kathryn, 155
De Jong, Mary, 95
Derr, Jill Mulvay, 175
Dillon, Elizabeth Maddock, 7, 9, 95, 222n34,
    234n74, 242n81
Dobson, Joanne, 40
Domesticity, 3–5, 9, 11, 23, 94–96, 101, 123,

242n81; Christian Science and, 192,
    195–96, 200–201, 210, 215, 252n29;
    Mormonism and, 144, 149–50, 161, 162,
    177, 194; religious nature of, 17, 107,
    126–36, 140, 175–76, 180, 194, 241n77
Douglas, Ann, 1, 21, 22, 28
Dow, Lorenzo, 43, 103

Ecumenism, 6, 9, 15, 199; hymns and, 72–75,
    78, 84, 90; in Second Great Awakening,
    59–62
Eddy, Mary Baker, 9, 19, 139, 140; biography
    of, 182, 184, 185, 187–89, 191–94, 196,
    198–99, 210, 203, 206, 251n19, 251n24;
    criticisms of, 181–85, 191, 193, 195, 198,
    201, 203, 206, 207, 213–15; defenses
    of, 192–94, 196; domesticity of, 192,
    195– 196, 200–201, 210, 215; leadership
    of, 19, 183, 184, 195, 196, 199, 205–6,
    209–16; as mother, 182–84, 187, 193–94,
    201–6, 208–11, 214–15; poetry of,
    185, 187–91, 200, 202–7, 214, 251n23,
    253n57, 254n64; reputation of, 181–85,
    187, 190–92, 195–96, 252n3; Science and
    Health with Key to the Scriptures, 181,
    185, 186, 195–97, 200, 201, 208, 210–13;
    sentimentalism and, 183–215, 250n8
Edwards, Jonathan, 13, 109, 130
Eggleston, Edward, 66
Election. See Predestination
Elizabeth I, 70
Emerson, Ralph Waldo, 34
Emotions, 23, 66, 83, 94–96; religious
    significance of, 15, 43–44, 72–73, 76–77;
    revivalism and, 40–41; in sentimentalism,
    39–40, 43–46. See also Sympathy
Evans, Augusta: Beulah, 45, 62, 201; St. Elmo,
    33, 37, 55, 134, 156

Fern, Fanny, 142, 156, 159, 161, 195, 201–2,
    241n69
Fessenden, Tracy, 2, 6, 224n66
Fiedler, Leslie, 186
Finley, Martha, Elsie Dinsmore, 14, 37, 39,
    201
Finney, Charles, 30, 34, 42, 48, 53, 79, 103
Fisher, Philip, 12, 40, 237n18, 242n90
Foster, Hannah Webster, 193
Franchot, Jenny, 111, 116, 124, 220n13
Fuller, Margaret, 92

Fuller, Metta, 18, 146, 148

Gill, Gillian, 183, 185, 252n31
Godey's Lady's Book, 154, 185, 188
Great Awakening (First), 25, 110
Grimké, Angelina, 30
Gustafson, Sandra, 46, 226n96

Hale, Sarah Josepha, 104, 135
Hatch, Nathan, 27
Hawthorne, Nathaniel, 20
Heaven, 18, 165–68, 172, 241n74
Heavenly Mother, 18, 173–76, 178, 180, 183, 210, 212, 249n89
Hendler, Glenn, 40, 226n97
Hinckley, Gordon B., 174
Holmes, Oliver Wendell, Sr., 93, 113
Hopkins, Samuel, 109–10, 117–19, 130–31
Howard, June, 40
Howe, Julia Ward, 16
Howells, William Dean, 184
Hutchinson, Anne, 9, 140
Hymnals and hymn books, 68, 71, 73, 79, 80, 90–92, 102, 170, 186
Hymns and hymnody, 7, 16, 170, 178, 204–7, 213, 245n24; criticisms of, 68, 70, 80, 82; ecumenism and, 72–75, 78, 84, 90; history of, 16, 68–80, 90–91, 232n40; Methodism and, 68, 75–78, 81, 84; Moravianism and, 74–75; populism and, 16, 68–69, 73, 76–79, 81, 82, 87–88, 90, 92–93; revival style of, 79, 80, 82, 88, 90–91, 97; in sentimentalism, 67–69, 80–92, 96–101, 230n2; in *Uncle Tom's Cabin*, 67, 84–88; in *The Wide, Wide World*, 67, 81–83, 91–92, 100; women and, 7, 16, 69, 80, 82–83, 88, 91–102, 183

Immigration, and Catholicism, 4, 25–26

Jacobs, Harriet, 124
James, Henry, 65
James, William, 44
John of Patmos, 107–8, 120, 121, 135–36
Judaism, 72, 107, 108, 110, 132, 135, 197, 207, 212,
Judgment Day, 14, 108, 109, 118, 137–38

Kermode, Frank, 132
Kete, Mary Louise, 40
Kim, Sharon, 2, 21, 226n86

Kimball, Spencer W., 170, 175
Know-Nothing Party, 4, 59

Lee, Mother Ann, 139, 140, 186–87
Leslie, Madeline, 45
Lincoln, Abraham, 103–4
Livermore, Harriet, 31
Longfellow, Henry Wadsworth, 143
Lowell, James Russell, 33
Luciano, Dana, 40, 243n4
Luther, Martin, 70, 108

Marriage plot, 117, 118, 132–36
May, Henry F., Jr., 19, 238n28
McIntosh, Maria, 49, 50, 55
McPherson, Aimee Semple, 215
Methodism, 220n13; clergy and, 26–27; characteristics of, 26–27, 46, 77–78; criticisms of, 3, 4, 7, 78; history of, 22, 26–27, 77; hymns and, 68, 75–79, 83–84; populism of, 3, 22, 26–27, 68, 77–78; tenets of, 48, 52, 77; women and, 26, 29–30, 62, 221n21
Millennialism, 17, 103–4, 210–12, 241n77; defined, 16, 106–9; history of, 103–4, 107–11; premillennialism, 108–9, 113, 115, 138; postmillennialism, 108–10, 113–23, 138; Harriet Beecher Stowe and, 17, 113–23, 126–41, 165
Miller, Perry, 48
Miller, William, 22, 27, 34, 103, 114, 136
Millerism, 4, 25, 106, 113, 140, 241n77
Milmine, Georgine, 182, 191–93, 203
Missionaries, 4, 11, 13, 39, 65, 79, 147, 151, 156–57, 166, 177
Moody, Dwight, 90, 103
Moody, Joycelyn, 45–46, 243n98
Monk, Maria; *Awful Disclosures of the Hotel Dieu Nunnery*, 10, 56, 146
Moravians, 74–75, 81, 83, 84
Mormon women, 142–44; public image of, 142–44, 146–59; social circumstances of, 142, 155–56, 161, 176–77, 179–80
Mormonism, 4, 11, 18; afterlife in, 165–68; criticisms of, 18, 23, 146–52; domesticity and, 149–50; history of, 25, 58, 150–51, 159, 161, 166, 177; polygamy and, 144–59; tenets of, 144–45, 153, 163, 166–67, 172–76, 179, 245n30, 247n64; uses of sentimentalism among, 144, 150, 152–67, 169–80, 184

Mother Church, 182, 186, 207, 208, 209
Motherhood, 11, 18, 19, 128–29, 148, 158,
    160, 173–76, 182–84, 186–87, 189–90,
    205–12. *See also* Eddy, Mary Baker, as
    mother and Heavenly Mother
Mother's Room, 182, 207–8, 213–15

Narrative form, 17, 106–7, 112, 114, 116–23,
    132–33, 138–39, 162, 165, 177, 237n18
Nation, Carry, 215
Nettleton, Asahel, 79–81, 93, 234n70
New Jerusalem, 112, 124–25, 127–28, 133,
    135–37, 139, 212
New Woman, 184
Newton, John, 81, 82, 85–87, 233n60
Noble, Marianne, 6, 21, 23, 40, 48, 52
Nord, David Paul, 14, 36
Noyes, John Humphrey, 22, 103

Oneida Perfectionism, 4, 23, 25, 159

Palmer, Phoebe, 184
Papashvily, Helen, 9, 40, 224n51
Paul, 29, 31, 70, 94, 183
Perfectionism, theology of, 7, 52–55
Phelps, Elizabeth Stuart; *The Gates Ajar*, 51,
    166, 241n74
Piatt, Sarah, 202
Pippin, Tina, 124, 139
Plymouth Collection, 80, 97
Polygamy, 161; defenses of, 152–59; as
    depicted in sentimental novels, 144–49;
    domesticity and, 145, 149–50; history of,
    144–46, 150–51, 168; slavery and, 145–49
Populism, 5, 16, 40–41; hymns and, 16, 68–
    69, 73, 76–79, 81, 82, 87–88, 90, 92–93;
    Methodism and, 3, 22, 26–27, 68, 77–78;
    Second Great Awakening and, 22, 26, 28,
    32, 68, 221n19; women and, 24, 64–65,
    92–93
Postmillennialism, 108–10, 113–23, 138. *See
    also* Millennialism
Prayer, 1, 27, 47, 49, 51, 94, 181, 186, 189,
    198, 202, 203, 205, 206, 212, 213
Preaching, 29–30, 34, 117; changes in, 32, 34,
    41, 77; sentimental literature as, 31–33
Predestination, 25, 26, 48–49, 77, 198
Premillennialism, 108–9, 113, 138. *See also*
    Millennialism
Prentiss, Elizabeth, 92, 96

Presbyterianism, 4, 48, 78, 162, 232n40;
    decline of, 27; New School of, 27, 42, 78
Privacy, 9, 23, 31, 82–83, 94–95, 101, 125,
    126, 129, 203, 207, 232n47, 234n74,
    235n84, 240n66, 242 n81
Prophecy, 27, 106, 112, 114, 115, 117–19,
    121–22, 133, 137, 138; women and, 8,
    17, 20, 123–24, 140, 153, 170, 174, 176,
    180–83, 197–98, 210–12
Psalms and psalmody, 27, 70–72, 75, 76,
    84–85, 235n80

Quakerism, 60

Reading, 83, 163, 224n61; of Bible, 10, 13,
    15, 16, 49, 55–61; Christian Science and,
    213; religious significance of, 10, 13–15,
    35–36, 40, 47, 55–57, 58
realism, 184–85
Reed, Rebecca Theresa, 56, 146
Reformation, 13, 70, 71
Relief Society, 160, 161, 163–64, 168
Religious press, 4, 13–15
Revivalism, 3, 5, 8, 14, 22, 26, 28, 34;
    criticisms of, 23, 39, 82; practices of, 40–
    41, 43–44, 46–47, 68, 69, 77, 78, 90–91
Revolution, political, 103, 104, 107, 110, 112,
    113. *See also* American Revolution
Reynolds, David S., 1
Roe, E. P., 66
Romero, Lora, 10, 130, 242n83, 252n29
Rowson, Susanna, 146, 193, 224n51
Russell, John, 150
Ryan, Mary P., 28, 222n29, 231n12, 232n47

Sabbath Hymn and Tune Book, 73, 80
Samuels, Shirley, 65, 230n2
Sánchez-Eppler, Karen, 40
Second Great Awakening, 15; characteristics
    of, 21–26; changes caused by, 22, 25–30,
    197; history of, 22, 25–26; Methodism
    and, 22; and sentimental literature, 22–
    24, 30–39; women and, 24, 28–32, 34–35,
    37–39, 43, 156, 163
Sectarian conflict, 2–4, 7, 9, 12, 17, 24, 41, 48,
    50, 55–61, 75, 109–12, 122
Sedgwick, Catharine, 136; *Home*, 31–32, 104,
    198; *Hope Leslie*, 59; *New-England Tale*,
    31, 36, 49, 59–60, 199, 227n108; religious
    beliefs of, 23, 31, 39, 48, 54–55

Seneca Falls convention, 19

Sentimentalism; Christian Science and, 204–7, 208–14; as clergy, 31–33, 44–47, 64–65; criticisms of, 1–2, 20, 21, 38, 40; as criticism of polygamy, 146–52; employed by Mary Baker Eddy, 183–91, 192–215; hymns and, 67–69, 80–92, 96–101, 230n2; literary characteristics of, 37–38, 67–68, 116, 133–35, 143, 146–47, 152, 154, 162–65, 171–72, 183, 187–88, 190–92, 195–97, 199, 207; Mormon uses of, 144, 150, 152–67, 169–80, 184; narrative form of, 17, 106–7, 112, 114, 116–23, 132–33, 138–39, 162, 165, 177, 237n18; religions contents of, 1–3, 5–7, 9–11, 23, 38–47, 49–52, 54–55, 57–64, 67–69, 80–90, 104–5, 114–24, 129–39, 146–50; religious contexts of, 3–4, 22–23, 33–42, 47–48, 52–53, 55–59, 80–81, 90–98, 101–2, 104–14, 123–25, 134–36, 138–41; religious influences of, 12, 15, 18, 141,163–80, 186, 204–11, 213–15; Second Great Awakening and, 22–24, 30–39. See also names of specific writers

Sermons, 15, 32, 41, 117, 213

Seventh-Day Adventism, 106, 140–41, 184, 241n77

Shakerism, 19, 23, 139, 159, 186–87, 251n19, 251n21

Sheldon, Charles, 66

Shipps, Jan, 162

Sigourney, Lydia, 16, 92, 143, 161, 202

Skinner, Thomas, 32–33, 42

Slavery, 2, 10, 49, 84–87, 104–6, 125–26, 194, 240n62; polygamy and, 145–49

Smith, Joseph, 27, 103, 145, 153, 160, 163, 168–70, 174, 177, 243n6

Smith, Joseph F., 174

Snow, Eliza R., 9, 18, 144, 153, 163, 167, 183, 210, 212, 247n69; biography of, 154–55, 160–61, 168–69, 174; "Invocation"/ "O My Father," 18, 170–80, 205

Social Gospel, 66

Southworth, E.D.E.N. The Hidden Hand, 38, 121, 156

Stanton, Elizabeth Cady, 17, 139

Stenhouse, Fanny, 149, 151–53

Stern, Julia, 7

Stone, Barton, 22

Stowe, Calvin, 114, 132

Stowe, Harriet Beecher, 9, 183; hymns and, 16, 68, 83–88, 92, 96–98, 204, 233 n.60, 234n80; millennialism of, 17, 104–41, 165, 210–11, 241n77; Mormonism and, 144–47, 149, 150, 159–60; religious beliefs of, 23, 48, 53, 111–14, 210, 239n38

—works: Agnes of Sorrento, 10, 51, 68, 83, 105, 112; American Woman's Home, 105, 126–27; Dred: A Tale of the Great Dismal Swamp, 39, 49, 87–88, 104–6, 129, 163; Footsteps of the Master, 105, 113, 128–29; "He's Coming Tomorrow," 105; House and Home Papers, 127–28; The Minister's Wooing, 17, 33, 49, 50, 105, 117–19, 122, 129–30, 132, 133, 136, 162–63, 207; My Wife and I, 33, 49, 65–66, 227n108; Oldtown Folks, 17, 84, 114–16, 119; The Pearl of Orr's Island, 17, 105, 118, 120–22, 134, 136–38, 197; Poganuc People, 37, 115, 134; Sam Lawson's Oldtown Fireside Stories, 50, 131–32, 195; Uncle Tom's Cabin, 1–2, 8, 17, 18, 20, 33, 43, 57, 192, 194, 195, 197; Uncle Tom's Cabin and hymns, 67, 84–88; Uncle Tom's Cabin and millennialism, 104–6, 110, 112, 118, 119, 125, 138; Uncle Tom's Cabin and Mormonism, 144–49, 152

Submission, 6, 7, 23

Swedenborg, Emanuel, 165

Switzer, Jenny, 148–49

Sympathy, 46–47, 51, 94, 194, 199

Tomlinson, Irving, 192, 196, 200, 209, 211

Tompkins, Jane, 1–2, 21, 36, 107, 236n96, 242n81

Towle, Nancy, 31

Tract literature, 15, 31, 35–37

Tullidge, Edward, 151–55

Twain, Mark, 19, 65; criticisms of Mary Baker Eddy, 181–82, 184–85, 192, 206, 213–14

Van Engen, Abram, 2, 21, 40

Waite, Catherine, 148

Ward, Austin, 149, 169

Ward, Maria, 153; Female Life Among the Mormons, 18, 146, 148, 156–57, 246n41

Warner, Anna, 32, 42, 50, 62, 63, 199; hymns and, 16, 68, 73–74, 92, 99–101

Warner, Susan, 37, 62, 159, 161; biography of,
    37, 42, 63, 199; hymns and, 16, 68, 700;
    religious beliefs of, 23, 39, 48, 62–63, 136,
    225n68; *The Law and the Testimony*, 64;
    The Old Helmet, 49, 82; *Queechy*, 43–44,
    49–40, 57, 61, 63, 197; *Say and Seal*, 50,
    92, 100; *The Wide, Wide World*, 14, 20,
    37, 45, 49, 51, 52, 57–58, 60–61, 64, 104,
    134, 150, 152, 156, 162, 165, 199; history
    of *Wide, Wide World*, 32–35; hymns in
    Wide, Wide World, 67, 81–83, 91–92, 100
Watts, Isaac, 71–73, 75, 76, 78, 79, 81, 84–87,
    90, 231n12
Wells, Emmeline B., 160, 173
Welter, Barbara, 52
Wesley, Charles, 76, 81, 82
Wesley, John, 48, 52, 53; hymns and, 60, 70,
    75–77, 81, 87, 90
Wexler, Laura, 2, 11, 52, 186, 254n70
White, Ellen Gould, 17, 140–41, 184
Whitefield, George, 78
Whitney, Helen Mar, 155–58
Whitney, Orson F., 157–58, 173
Wilbur, Sybil, 192–94, 252n33

Wilkinson, Jemima, 140
Witnessing, 46–47
Woman's Exponent, 18, 142–43, 157, 159–61
Women, religious authority of, 6, 19–20, 24,
    41, 43, 51–52, 61, 64–65, 69, 93–94, 102,
    123–41, 168–69, 174, 180, 213, 215–16;
    Second Great Awakening and, 24, 28–32,
    34–35, 38–39, 43. *See also* Eddy, Mary
    Baker; Heavenly Mother; Mormon
    women; Snow, Eliza R.; Stowe, Harriet
    Beecher; Warner, Anna; Warner, Susan
Wordsworth, William, 54

Unitarianism, 31

Violence, 4–6
Virgin Mary, 11, 95, 182, 210, 214, 250n6,
    254n70

Young, Ann Eliza, 157
Young, Brigham, 145, 159, 160, 168, 169

Zinzendorf, Count Nicolaus Ludwig von,
    74–76, 90

ACKNOWLEDGMENTS

THIS PROJECT has been immeasurably enriched by the contributions and support of many people. During the years I researched and wrote this book, I benefited from the significant support of Trinity University in San Antonio, Texas, an institution that genuinely sponsors faculty research. My incomparable department chair, Victoria Aarons, provided both financial resources for research travel as well as encouragement for this long-term project. Trinity University generously provided me with several semesters of research leave as well as financial support for two summers that proved indispensable to this project. In Trinity's Office of Academic Affairs, I thank Mark Brodl, Michael Fischer, and Diane Smith. With the help of Claudia Scholz, this project received a summer stipend from the National Endowment for the Humanities, for which I remain grateful.

Michael A. Elliott and Priscilla Wald have been long-standing mainstays in my professional and personal life, and it is a pleasure for me to able to thank them for their support, wisdom, and friendship. Augusta Rohrbach figures in the background of this book in more ways than I can count. She has been a longtime supporter of this project, supplying invaluable guidance on more than one occasion, and, as editor of *ESQ*, she helped me find the shape and central argument of several of this book's chapters. I owe Abram Van Engen particular thanks for his helpful, incisive comments upon reading— and rereading—this book's first chapter. Rubén Dupertuis has been a generous colleague and friend who permitted me to audit his superb class on the New Testament, fielded countless questions, and directed me to innumerable scholarly texts I would not have found otherwise. I also wish to thank Jill Mulvay Derr, the leading scholar of nineteenth-century Mormon women writers, who responded with extraordinary generosity to the e-mail queries of a stranger: she not only shared unpublished drafts of her research with me, but she also carefully scrutinized the fourth chapter, making invaluable suggestions and offering kind encouragement. James Ivy was a thoughtful reader of early drafts, and this book has benefited from his commentary. Mary De Jong, the premier literary scholar of American hymnody, was an early and important supporter of this project, and the book's second chapter, on sentimentalism and hymns, profited from Mary's invaluable remarks. Rev. Stephen Nickle, chaplain of Trinity University, kindly lent me texts, answered questions, and contributed to the warm climate of scholarship I have enjoyed at Trinity. Deborah Rhine helped me brush up on my musical skills in preparation for my research in American hymnody. Dwight Bigler and Carol Lynn Pearson were likewise generous with their time and commentary when I was in the early stages of working on the fourth chapter. Dawn Coleman organized a summer reading group that enabled me to read more widely in Stowe's corpus, and I am grateful to her as well as to Sarah Mesle and Kyla Wazana Tompkins for their stimulating conversation. Thanks are also due to Atilio Dupertuis, who graciously conducted painstaking research in the publications of Ellen G. White, tracking down references to Harriet Beecher Stowe. Maria Monteiro and Dr. Joseph Pierce generously contributed to my collection of hymn books. I also thank Sarai Santos for her help with administrative matters.

I am grateful to the Constitution Island Association for help researching the papers of Susan and Anna Warner. Faith Herbert has made extraordinary contributions to the Warner family archive, and I remain grateful for her generous assistance during and after my time there. Richard de Koster provided a tour of the Warner family home, and he likewise graciously granted me permission to quote materials in the Warner archive. Colonel Morris Herbert (retired) is a fount of wisdom about the United States Military Academy, and I thank him—and, of course, Faith Herbert—for a delightful afternoon touring West Point. Cathy Kelly generously volunteered her time so that I might continue my research in the Constitution Island Association research center, and Susan Lintelmann provided assistance while I conducted research in the library of the United States Military Academy.

Linda Smith Rhoads, editor of the *New England Quarterly*, provided indispensable editorial wisdom to this project at its earliest stages, as with her supervision of an article version of the book's last chapter, which was the initial germ from which this book grew. I am grateful to *ESQ* and *New England Quarterly* for permission to reprint the portions of this book that were originally published there. Thanks are also due to Brigham Young University

Press for permission to quote in full Eliza R. Snow's poem "Invocation, or The Eternal Father and Mother."

It is my pleasure to be able to thank publicly my editor at the University of Pennsylvania Press, Jerome Singerman, for his advocacy, encouragement, and wisdom. I likewise thank Caroline Hayes for her help. I am grateful to Patricia Wieland, who was an exacting, detailed copyeditor, and to Noreen O'Connor-Abel, the production editor who shepherded this book into print. This book was immeasurably improved by the sage recommendations of Nancy Bentley and Tracy Fessenden. I could not have asked for two more attentive, detailed, and generous readers, and I remain grateful for the significant contributions of both women to this project.

This book originally grew out of my upper-level course on sentimentalism at Trinity University, and it has been sharpened by the incisive comments and questions of the students who have taken that course with me over the years. I am grateful to Tracy Carlin, Kelly Merka Nelson, and Peggy Rensberger, who conducted research in support of the book's second chapter, on sentimental hymnody, and I am grateful for their contributions. Tres Johnson was an important interlocutor during the early stages of this project's development, and I am grateful to him for his candor and liberality during our many conversations. David McFarlane was also an important resource, and he generously shared with me his own thoughts on a number of the issues examined here.

Finally, I wish to thank my family. My husband, David Liss, has been my partner in all things, and this book has been enriched by his comments, enthusiasm, and encouragement. Our children, Eleanor and Simon, doubtless helped me to be more attentive to the workings of sentimental maternity. It is with love that I dedicate this book about nineteenth-century maternal authority to my own mother, Sophie Aron Stokes.